U.S.-MEXICO RELATIONS: ECONOMIC
AND SOCIAL ASPECTS

CONTRIBUTORS

Jorge A. Bustamante

Rolando Cordera

Jaime Corredor

Edwin A. Deagle, Jr.

Richard R. Fagen

Walter P. Falcon

E. V. K. FitzGerald

Manuel García y Griego

Bruce F. Johnston

Luis Maira

Donald A. Nichols

Mario Ojeda

Olga Pellicer de Brody

Clark W. Reynolds

Warren C. Sanderson

Tibor Scitovsky

Carlos Tello

Raymond Vernon

Arturo Warman

Sponsored by the
Project on United States–
Mexico Relations

U.S.-Mexico Relations

ECONOMIC
AND SOCIAL ASPECTS

Edited by
Clark W. Reynolds and Carlos Tello

STANFORD UNIVERSITY PRESS, STANFORD, CALIFORNIA

U.S.-Mexico Relations: Economic and Social Aspects was originally published in Spanish in 1981 under the title *Las relaciones México Estados Unidos,* © 1981 by the Fondo de Cultura Económica. The present edition has been revised, updated, and supplemented with new material.

6661
19 FEB 1990

Stanford University Press, Stanford, California
© 1983 by the Board of Trustees of the
Leland Stanford Junior University
Printed in the United States of America

Cloth ISBN 0-8047-1163-1   Paper ISBN 0-8047-1286-7
Original printing 1983

Last figure below indicates year of this printing:
94 93 92 91 90 89 88 87 86 85

Preface

THE Project on United States–Mexico Relations originated at a March 1979 luncheon meeting in Mexico City between the two editors of this volume. They agreed, in the aftermath of the discussions between Presidents Carter and López Portillo, on three major premises: (1) neither of the countries had yet developed a clear picture of likely social and economic trends over the next twenty years; (2) neither had a clear picture of the historical conditions, present structure, or reasonable range of policy prospects of its neighbor; and (3) both were, regardless of their respective preferences, certain to become increasingly interdependent economically and socially over the coming decades.

These three points of agreement suggested the need for some approach to the analysis of changing patterns of interdependence that would be fully binational, multidisciplinary, able to accommodate the range of ideologies and approaches of specialists in both countries, and useful for future policy formulation. Though recognizing that this would not be an easy task, given the history of differences in emphasis and perception between the two countries, the editors discussed the concept with associates, and were encouraged to proceed. Funding was provided by private foundations in the United States and by the government of Mexico. The Rockefeller Foundation supported a planning session at Stanford University in September 1979, attended by a number of specialists from both countries who were concerned about the implications of increasing interdependence between countries with different levels of income and very different values, institutions, and social structures.

This group decided to hold a working session at Chapultepec Castle in June 1980 and a conference later in the year to deal with a number of aspects of development of each country from the perspectives of both Mexican and U.S. scholars. This volume is the result of those meetings.

The full conference in November 1980 was successful in convincing interests in both Mexico and the United States to provide continuing support for a multi-year program, to be fully binational in membership, funding, and design. Subsequently the U.S. group has received assistance from the Andrew Mellon, Rockefeller, Ford, William and Flora Hewlett, and Arco (Ventures) foundations, with support anticipated from other foundations and members of the private sector. A binational Affiliates Program is being organized, to which institutions, individuals, and enterprises are invited to contribute both ideas and financial support.

Out of the 1980 conference and related discussions, working groups have been formed in the areas of Foreign Policy (with special attention to Central America), Agriculture and Rural Development, and the Management of Interdependence ("Integration/Disintegration"). Additional working groups and research activities are being planned in the areas of Finance, Trade, Industrial Policy, and the Social Agents of Development. Finally, the program is being expanded to bring its findings and ongoing discussions before the public in both countries.

We recognize that the binational analysis of interdependence is in its infancy. We hope that the knowledge developed in this program will be useful in looking at broader North/South and East/West questions in the coming years. The United States–Mexico relationship is of fundamental importance to the stability, growth, and prosperity of both countries, and the spirit of the Project is extremely constructive in respect to this relationship, despite wide differences in perception and approach. While the participants often disagree, there is a disposition to listen and respond pragmatically to the issues at hand, so that a basis can be established for policies that may serve the long-term interests of both countries. Recent political and economic problems have underscored the importance of such an approach, making this volume and the efforts that underlie it more relevant than ever.

The editors wish to acknowledge the exceptional support of representatives of the foundations mentioned above—especially that of Edwin Deagle, Jr., of the Rockefeller Foundation, who provided the initial impetus from the U.S. side, and of Jack Sawyer, President of the Mellon Foundation. On the Mexican side, President José López Portillo encouraged the group to proceed, and the National Sugar Bank of Mexico (FINASA) has been responsible for funding the Mexican participation to date. The project has received strong encouragement from representatives of the governments, private sectors, and academic communities in both countries.

The manuscript was ably prepared by Chuck Rodabaugh and Madeleine Rowse Gleason. Continued contributions to publications and related Project activities were made by the Associate Director of the Project on United States–Mexico Relations, Clint E. Smith. The research assistance of Robert McCleery of Stanford University is gratefully acknowledged. Administrative assistance was provided by Michael Gomez and Chuck Rodabaugh, both of whom helped in the preparations for the 1980 conference. Translations of the Spanish language papers were prepared by David Dye. The authors gratefully acknowledge the typing of the manuscript by Shirley Lambelet, Rebecca Reynolds, and Claudia Smith. Appreciation is also extended to Walter P. Falcon, Director of the Food Research Institute of Stanford University, for accommodating the Stanford component of the Project, and to Robert Ward, Director of Stanford's Center for Research in International Studies, and Ronald Herring, the Assistant Director, for their valuable support. In addition, the editors are grateful for the support given by Professor John Wirth, Director of Stanford's Center for Latin American Studies.

We wish to thank all authors of papers, formal discussants, volunteers, and participants at the conference and working group sessions, whose contributions have made the present revised and updated manuscript possible. It is their support, as well as that of individuals and institutions involved in a growing network of activities on United States–Mexico relations in both countries, that encourages the editors to proceed, as the scope of this project widens and deepens.

The editors are grateful for the assistance of Stanford University Press, in the persons of Leon Seltzer, Director, Jess Bell, Associate Director and Editor, and Norris Pope, Senior Editor. They are also grateful for the Press's willingness to consider this volume the first in a series of publications on U.S.-Mexico relations.

Clark Reynolds
Carlos Tello Macias

Contents

Contributors   xi

Introduction   1
Clark W. Reynolds and Carlos Tello

ECONOMIC AND SOCIAL PERSPECTIVES OF MEXICO

Mexican-U.S. Interdependence: Economic and Social Perspectives   21
Clark W. Reynolds

Prospects and Options for Mexican Society   47
Rolando Cordera and Carlos Tello

ECONOMIC AND SOCIAL PERSPECTIVES OF THE UNITED STATES

Prospects and Options for United States Society   83
Luis Maira

The Prospects for Economic Growth in the United States, 1980-2000   109
Donald A. Nichols

Comments on the Nichols Paper   133
Tibor Scitovsky

TRADE, INDUSTRIAL STRUCTURE, AND ENERGY

The Economic Significance of Mexican Petroleum from the Perspective of Mexico–United States Relations   137
Jaime Corredor

Trade and Investment in Mexico–United States Relations   167
Raymond Vernon

NATIONAL SECURITY

National Security in Mexico: Traditional Notions and New
Preoccupations   181
  Olga Pellicer de Brody

United States National Security Policy and Mexico   193
  Edwin A. Deagle, Jr.

FOOD, AGRICULTURE, AND RURAL DEVELOPMENT

The Future of a Crisis: Food and Agrarian Reform   205
  Arturo Warman

The Design and Redesign of Strategies for Agricultural Development:
Mexico's Experience Revisited   225
  Bruce F. Johnston

The World Food Economy: Recent Lessons for the United States
and Mexico   251
  Walter P. Falcon

EMPLOYMENT AND MIGRATION

Mexican Migration: The Political Dynamic of Perceptions   259
  Jorge A. Bustamante

The Problems of Planning for the Expected: Demographic Shocks
and Policy Paralysis   277
  Warren C. Sanderson

Comments on Bustamante and Sanderson Papers and on Research
Project ENEFNEU   299
  Manuel García y Griego

LONG-TERM RELATIONS BETWEEN THE
UNITED STATES AND MEXICO

The Future of Relations Between Mexico and the United States   315
  Mario Ojeda

The Politics of the United States–Mexico Relationship   331
  Richard R. Fagen

Mexico–United States Economic Relations and the World Cycle:
A European View   349
  E. V. K. FitzGerald

Index   369

Contributors

JORGE A. BUSTAMANTE is Professor of Sociology at El Colegio de México, in Mexico City, and Professor and Director of the Program of Mexico–United States Border Studies at the Centro de Estudios Fronterizos del Norte de México, in Tijuana. He is a widely published expert on U.S.-Mexican labor migration and border affairs.

ROLANDO CORDERA is a Deputy to the Mexican National Congress and also Professor of Economics at the Universidad Nacional Autónoma de México. He is co-author of the recent widely noticed book *La Disputa por la Nación* (1981).

JAIME CORREDOR ESNAOLA is Executive President of the Banco Cremi. He pursued graduate studies in economics at Stanford University, and has served as an adviser to the Mexican Secretary of the Treasury, National Energy Commission, and President. His publications include a number of articles on Mexican oil prospects.

EDWIN A. DEAGLE, JR., is Director of International Relations at the Rockefeller Foundation. He earned a Ph.D. in government from Harvard University, where he has also taught. He has served in a variety of capacities as a consultant and adviser to the American government, and has written widely on oil and energy.

RICHARD R. FAGEN is Gildred Professor of Latin American Studies at Stanford University. He earned his Ph.D. in political science at Stanford, and is widely known for his work on Cuba and Latin America and on U.S. foreign policy in this region. He is the author of *The Transformation of Political Culture in Cuba* (1969) and the co-editor of *The Future of Central America: Policy Choices for the U.S. and Mexico* (1983).

WALTER P. FALCON is Professor of Economics and Director of the Food Research Institute at Stanford University. He received his Ph.D. from Harvard University, where he subsequently taught. He has served as a consultant for the White House and, from 1978 to 1980, as Commissioner for the Presidential Commission on World Hunger. He is the co-author of *Food Policy Analysis for Practitioners* (1982) and of a forthcoming study of cassava policy in Java.

E. V. K. FITZGERALD is Professor of Development Economics at the Institute of Social Studies in The Hague. He received his Ph.D. from Cambridge University, and served subsequently as an economic consultant in England, Nicaragua, Peru, and Mexico. He has written extensively on Latin American economics and politics.

MANUEL GARCÍA Y GRIEGO is a Professor at the Center of International Studies at El Colegio de México, in Mexico City. He is co-editor of the recently published *Mexican-U.S. Relations: Conflict and Convergence.*

BRUCE F. JOHNSTON is Professor of Economics at the Food Research Institute at Stanford University. He earned his Ph.D. at Stanford, and has served subsequently in a number of advisory capacities. He is the co-editor of *Agricultural Development and Economic Growth* (1967) and co-author of *Redesigning Rural Development: A Strategic Perspective* (1982).

LUIS MAIRA is Director of the Institute for the Study of the United States at the Centro de Investigación y Docencia Económica, in Mexico City. He has published several articles on U.S.-Mexico relations and on Central America.

DONALD A. NICHOLS is Professor of Economics at the University of Wisconsin. He received his Ph.D. from Yale University, and has since served as Senior Economist for the Committee on the Budget of the U.S. Senate and as Deputy Assistant Secretary for Economic Policy and Research for the U.S. Department of Labor. His most recent work has been on problems of unemployment.

MARIO OJEDA GOMEZ is Professor of International Studies at El Colegio de México, in Mexico City. He earned his Ph.D. at Harvard University, and has since served in a number of advisory posts. His most recent publications have been on Mexican foreign policy and oil policy.

OLGA PELLICER DE BRODY is Director of the Department of International Politics at the Centro de Investigación y Docencia Económica, in Mexico City. She has published widely on U.S. and Mexican foreign policy, and is the co-editor of the next book in this series, *The Future of Central America: Policy Choices for the U.S. and Mexico* (1983).

CLARK W. REYNOLDS is Professor of Economics at the Food Research Institute at Stanford University, and U.S. Coordinator of the Project on United States–Mexico Relations. He earned his Ph.D. at the University of California at Berkeley, and he has since taught at Occidental College, Yale University, El Colegio de México, the Universidad Nacional Autónoma de México, and the Stockholm School of Economics. His publications include *The Mexican Economy: Twentieth-Century Structure and Growth* (1970).

WARREN C. SANDERSON is Associate Professor of Economics at the State University of New York at Stony Brook. He earned his Ph.D. from Stanford University and is a specialist in demographic economics.

TIBOR SCITOVSKY is Professor Emeritus of Economics at Stanford University. He is a specialist in international trade and welfare economics, and his recent publications include *The Joyless Economy* (1975).

CARLOS TELLO MACIAS is Professor of Political Economy at the Universidad Nacional Autónoma de México, and the Mexican Coordinator of the Project on United States–Mexico Relations. He is the author of *La Política Económica en México, 1970–1976* (1979) and the co-author of *La Disputa por la Nación* (1981).

RAYMOND VERNON is Professor of International Affairs at Harvard University. He has served as a consultant for a number of U.S. and international organizations, and his many publications include *The Dilemma of Mexico's Development* (1963), *The Myth and Reality of Our Urban Problems* (1966), *Sovereignty at Bay* (1971), *The Economic Environment of International Business* (1972), and *Storm over the Multinationals* (1977).

ARTURO WARMAN is with the Institute for Social Research at the Universidad Nacional Autónoma de México. His most recent major publication is *We Come to Object: The Peasants of Morelos and the National State* (1981).

U.S.-MEXICO RELATIONS: ECONOMIC AND SOCIAL ASPECTS

Introduction

Clark W. Reynolds and Carlos Tello

WHEN these essays were first conceived, the objective was to provide medium-term policy perspectives between the United States and Mexico, given the increased interdependence of the two systems. Since that time, both countries have seen changes of political administration and both are in the throes of severe economic crises that profoundly affect both domestic and foreign relations. In addition, the regimes have been tested by events in Central America, the Near East, and the South Atlantic, as well as by the apparent stalemate in North-South relations and stagflation in the international economy. All of these circumstances, in addition to measures being taken for a new regional approach to international policy, make the contents of this volume even more relevant than before.

The papers, originally commissioned by the editors for a conference in November 1980, have in most cases been revised and updated, and the editors have added notes, setting the studies in the perspective of mid-1982. Each essay contributes to a new binational approach to what might be called the political economy of organic interdependence. Despite sharp differences in philosophical and analytical perspectives, the authors are committed to the principle that history has linked the destinies of the United States and Mexico, that current events portend dramatically increasing interdependence, and that it remains to be seen just how much economic and social interaction is in the long-term interest of each partner. In addition, all participants view the process of organic interdependence as one that reaches to the very roots of both systems. Trade, investment, finance, technology, and tastes reach out and entwine both economies. Migration, the media, and demographic processes link their societies. No single dimension of analysis is sufficient to unravel these increasingly complex interrelationships. Hence the essays are an in-depth, multidisciplinary analysis from each specialty represented.

The discussions in this volume assess the extent to which different groups in each nation would benefit from more or less interdependence in trade, migration, agricultural and industrial production, finance and investment, foreign policy, and national security measures. Written by experts from both countries about both countries, the collection is unique in providing different perspectives on each major issue from each vantage point. Hence the United States is seen from both a domestic and a Mexican point of view, and Mexico is analyzed by its own specialists as well as by U.S. observers. The importance of such an undertaking cannot be overstated. It establishes the principle of binational policy analysis of two countries with very different systems at very different levels of income and productivity, joined by a common frontier and destined to be mutually involved in development.

Out of this first conference, working relationships have been forged that are unique in the experience of the editors. Workshops and conferences have been held, and future volumes are planned, in the areas of foreign policy (in press), agriculture and rural development (in press), and economic and social interdependence. Future areas of research include trade and financial relations, dynamic restructuring of the two economies in response to the changing international economic order, and demographic and labor market relations, as well as individual areas including energy, security, food policy, health and nutrition. Participation in these areas includes interested parties from business, labor, government, and academe, and members of the informed public. Close contact is maintained with related study programs throughout the United States and Mexico, and abroad, involving continual interaction in terms of research, program design, and outreach. It is hoped that this program will be a harbinger of binational and multinational approaches to policy relations by presenting alternative perspectives on common problems and encouraging practical efforts to deal with the issues, with the ultimate goal of mutually acceptable solutions to managed interdependence.

The first section, on "Economic and Social Perspectives of Mexico," presents two visions of the range of relationships facing the two countries over the next few decades. Reynolds' essay introduces the concept of full exchange (free trade, migration, investment, and technology transfer) to explore the consequences of degrees of openness between Mexico and the United States on Mexican growth and employment. Cordera and Tello see the options as a choice between two basically different political programs defined as neoliberal and nationalist. Both essays set their analyses in terms of conceptual extremes while recognizing that in practice policy choices must fall somewhere in the mid-range, owing to competing societal pressures and to constraints imposed by both the marketplace and existing institutions on the economic dimensions of policy space. The issues raised in these two essays, however, are fundamental to an understanding of the Mexican development dilemma. Both see the most significant debate to be not over *laissez faire* versus institutionally determined rules of exchange, or over the extent to which the state is to influence the process of exchange. Rather, the debate is over the social costs and benefits of alternative strategies expressed in terms of employment and labor income and in terms of broader economic, social, and political participation in the development process.

Reynolds postulates that if a main goal of Mexican policy is employment and income generation, then considerably more exchange betwen the two countries may be desirable in terms of both trade and migration. His essay also shows, however, that fuller exchange alone is not a sufficient condition for social and economic progress. Using the development of the Sunbelt in the United States as an example, Reynolds shows that the growth of productive, high-technology industries and high-yield agriculture resulted not from domestic exchange alone, but from collaboration among government, business, labor, and academe promoted by security considerations and a regional focus of national economic policy during and after World War II. The paper points out that, although these facts have tended to be forgotten in contemporary U.S. policy debates, they are part of history and have important implications for relations between the public and private sectors in the contemporary development of both countries or for relations between them.

Cordera and Tello set the framework for a debate between nationalism and internationalism, opting for the former as a means of controlling the degree of interdependence that they recognize must exist between the two countries so as to permit major economic and social reforms. In their terminology "nationalism" describes a position that calls for fundamental structural changes in the control of the production process and in the distribution of its benefits to favor labor. "Internationalism" of the neo-liberal program is associated with preservation of the status quo, which in their view would impede such reforms. The authors appeal to the principles of the Mexican Constitution of 1917 to support their concept of the nationalist program. Thus, there would be more, rather than less, regulation of the means of production and a greater role for the state, with increased constraints on the operation of international prices, investment, and other tools of economic power in Mexico in favor of the mass of the population. In referring to the 1979 Labor Congress' mandate for a "democratic, nationalist, and popular development project," the employment and income goals dealt with directly in the Reynolds paper are addressed indirectly in the Cordera-Tello paper in the context of a nationalist development program.

This program would favor food self-sufficiency in agriculture, regulation of petroleum and natural gas exports as a function of domestic economic goals, state promotion of industrialization including development of capital goods and popular consumer goods, and de-linking of prices, profits, and interest rates from the "international market." Support for such reforms, elements of which were reflected in the policies of the López Portillo administration, would be sought not only among the rural masses and the urban work force but also among groups of entrepreneurs prepared to link their fortunes with the reform program in the context of a "capitalist/mixed enterprise system" under the aegis of state planning.

In these two essays the fundamental nature of the Project on United States–Mexico Relations is apparent—namely, the interweaving of economics and politics through analysis of the impact of alternative economic programs on social relations. By placing the debate in a binational context, the discussions assume a relevance that transcends the concerns of each of the two neighbors and becomes an important step in the concretizing of the North/South dialogue in ways that permit issues to be examined in terms of the common interests of both parties.

The Reynolds and Cordera-Tello papers present two quite different perspectives on a common problem, namely, the increasing incorporation of the mass of Mexicans into the national economy and society with a fair share of the national product and an active voice in the political process. Reynolds sees this as being accomplished through a tightened labor market and growing labor power—brought about, in turn, by an economic policy favoring diversified trade, domestic job creation, and international production-sharing in which Mexico is permitted to supply components of value-added that better reflect its own comparative advantage. This would represent a sharp change from the essentially protectionist policies of recent administrations and would balance attempts to integrate Mexican industrial development vertically in order to include a larger share of wage-good production, labor-intensive exports of final goods, and components of production in North America that would be intensive in Mexican labor and resource inputs.

Such a process would be closely coordinated by the state and would not in any respect resemble a "North American Common Market" or a "neoliberal project" as characterized by one extreme in the Cordera-Tello paper, but it would definitely be a more open approach than their nationalist program as described. The inference is made in the Reynolds paper that, given the realities of Mexico's development potential, forced-draft rapid growth such as has been pursued in the past few years could not be expected over the medium run to tighten the Mexican labor market and raise real wages enough to satisfy its social and political goals.

The paper does not go into a detailed political analysis of its essentially economic arguments.

Cordera and Tello, on the other hand, focus on the political requirements for a mass movement in Mexico that would sharply alter the distribution of economic and political power in the direction of the majority of workers and away from the groups that currently dominate the policy process. They argue that such a change, to be successful, would have to be so fundamental that it would surely arouse the opposition of powerful segments of the property-owning class, the political elite, and officially favored labor unions. Little is said about the consequences of such changes for relations with the United States, but they may be surmised. In addition, despite the fact that both authors are economists, they view the likely economic opportunity cost for massive reforms in the entire system of wealth and power rather more in terms of eliciting opposition responses to the project than in terms of implications for the economy itself and the probable loss of economic degrees of freedom essential for its success. If the likely cost of adjustment were to be economic stagnation, decline, or dislocation, would it be possible to do more than man the barricades with such a project? This is more than an academic question, since a book developing the authors' themes became a best-selling element in the national policy debate prior to the 1982 Mexican election.

Clearly, in the case of Mexico, future policy must find itself somewhere between the extremes the writers suggest. Yet both papers argue that the economic dimensions of policy space must be taken into consideration whatever political-economic strategy is introduced, and that wages, employment, and increased participation in the national wealth for the mass of workers are fundamental to political stability and sustained economic growth. Popular participation in representative government is seen to be the only viable long-term solution for the country in the minds of all three authors, given Mexico's history, constitution, values, and commitment to increased popular education and social participation.

The fact that a democratic approach to political change conforms to the values and goals of Mexico's northern neighbors would favor such an outcome, even though the economic and social consequences of a truly popular regime in Mexico would challenge the understanding of the United States and its willingness to accommodate sharp changes in the policies, institutions, and attitudes south of the border for the sake of long-term stability and social justice. On the agenda for future research in this area is more explicit incorporation of economic analysis in the policy scenarios as well as more explicit attention to the international consequences of alternative national strategies.

The section on "Economic and Social Perspectives of the United States" treats the contemporary crisis of the U.S. economy as one that demands fundamental structural change. The essays by Maira and Nichols challenge the United States' ability to respond to its present national and international problems in terms of its highest values and goals. In the Nichols paper, contemporary economic policy is seen as inadequate for the task of restructuring the economy with price stability, full employment, and social justice. Such a reconciliation would seem to call for a political-economic approach more characteristic of the early days of the discipline of economics as an applied science than of its current condition. In the Maira paper, even more is asked of the United States. The presidencies of Jefferson, Lincoln, Theodore Roosevelt, and Franklin Roosevelt are recalled to illustrate watershed periods in American history when leaders arose, programs evolved, and institutions developed, capable of responding to the challenges of the times.

The Nichols paper reflects a fundamental optimism that, despite the challenges imposed on the economy in the 1970s by sharply rising energy prices, it was the failure of economic policy to respond properly, rather than any fundamental flaw in the nature of the economy or society themselves, that contributed to falling productivity growth, inflation, and unemployment. The author weighs the discipline of economics in the balance and finds it wanting. Its overreliance on what is termed "the neoclassical synthesis" of theory and policy analysis, which separates micro- from macroeconomic analysis and deals with questions of efficiency, equity, and stability in separate compartments, was considered viable in the 1950s and 1960s, when the economy faced few fundamental structural challenges. But the neoclassical synthesis proved inadequate when sharply rising energy prices (after 1973) required a more fundamental integration of micro- and macroeconomic approaches, so that the rise in the opportunity cost of energy could be met by falling real costs in other areas. It was not possible to contemplate true adjustment of relative prices dictated by efficiency considerations in a social and political vacuum, given the equity implications of falling money wages and real incomes of the majority of the population that would have been implicit under microeconomic efficiency criteria. As a result, money wages rose at the macro level with energy prices, as did the prices of other goods and services, resulting in adjustment through inflation, unemployment, and deficits in the balance of payments.

Nichols argues that today the neoclassical synthesis is still being applied or misapplied. Current record rates of unemployment, real interest rates, and persistent (though falling) inflation exacerbate the instability of relative prices and raise adverse expectations that plague investment plans and prevent the economy from recovering, despite tax and other "supply side" incentives. What is needed is a new approach that would coordinate structural, income, and demand policies. Determining the theoretical framework for such an integrated approach, and placing it in the framework of an open economy, is part of the author's current research. If a new approach, bringing together micro- and macroeconomic theory and policy analysis, is not found, he would qualify his rather optimistic projections about U.S. productivity growth.

The paper by Luis Maira sets the United States' economic crisis in a global historical framework and is considerably less optimistic about the ability of new economic policy alone to overcome the current malaise. The U.S. economy is seen to have exhibited a remarkable tendency to relate its essentially capitalist mode of production to its fundamental social goals by means of liberal democratic forms of political organization. In an age of increased technological complexity and global interdependence, this has been accomplished by the expansion of an "imperial presidency." The international system itself was accommodated by U.S. political economic development from FDR to Kennedy through the establishment of global alliances and institutions such as Bretton Woods and the United Nations in which, according to the author, the principle of U.S. global hegemony prevailed.

By the 1970s the predominant role of the United States in this system was under attack. The economic crisis of the 1970s is linked by Maira to the shifting pattern of international power and economic relationships in which the United States is no longer dominant. In view of the fundamental changes in the nature of international relations and related challenges to the domestic economy, the author calls for a new "historic program" that would be able to reconcile the basic values of the United States' social philosophy to the realities of our time. He claims that while no such project yet appears to be forthcoming, two approaches have been offered, each of which has its own limitations: the "neoconservative" project and the "transnational" project.

The transnational project is cited as one approach to national policy that arose out of the activities of the Trilateral Commission of the Carter administration and placed the United States in the role of principal actor in an ever-widening pattern of exchange of goods and services, capital, and technology, particularly among the developed countries. The neoconservative project is said to have arisen in the 1970s out of an odd coalition of libertarian ideologues, political conservatives, representatives of the affluent class seeking to preserve their wealth, disenchanted liberals, and those dissatisfied with perceived shortcomings of the imperial presidency from Nixon to Carter. Its most notable political success was the election of the Reagan administration partly as a result of the drastic shift in national perspectives that suddenly placed traditional liberalism on the defensive.

It should be noted that, while Nichols settles on the energy price rise of 1974 as a trigger for the contemporary decline in productivity growth, instability, and unemployment, Maira sees this initial attempt to radically alter relative prices between energy and non-energy products as a reflection of the underlying changes in the international system. By implication, policies to deal with the structural changes in the economy might well have to do with the changing structure of the world trading system and international power relations, as is dealt with later in the FitzGerald paper. For Maira the economy drastically needs restructuring, given changing international conditions, and the oil shock illustrates how much needs to be done. Unlike Nichols, who puts the blame on the failure of economic policy analysis to go beyond the neoclassical synthesis, Scitovsky in his remarks suggests that the United States' crisis is due to more fundamental problems, and Maira argues that it is the political program itself that has failed (suggesting implicitly that if the right new project were found it would include economic policies appropriate to the challenge).

While neither paper deals explicitly with the implications of the analysis for relations between the United States and Mexico, the implicit thesis appears to be that failure of the United States to resolve its domestic and international problems, owing to shortcomings of the neoclassical economic synthesis, the transnational project, or the neoconservative project, will almost certainly work against managed interdependence and harmonious bilateral relations. Stagflation in the United States has brought about crippling real interest rates that plague Mexico as well. Unemployment in the United States exacerbates the problems of limited export markets, migration barriers, and underemployment in Mexico. The political consequences of domestic economic instability and demographic interdependence of the two countries become even more difficult as resentment grows against Hispanics and other minorities and against undocumented immigrants (see the section on "Employment and Migration"). It might be said that a successful response by the United States to the present historical challenge is essential to economic and social progress in Mexico, just as such progress is an important condition for the future prosperity of the United States.

The section on "Trade, Industrial Structure, and Energy" deals primarily with United States–Mexico trade in global perspective (Vernon) and the implications for trade and industrial structure of Mexico's recent hydrocarbon bonanza (Corredor). Vernon presents the increasingly accepted view that the postwar period of progressive trade liberalization is coming to an end. In the future, preferential relationships associated with reciprocity are likely to eclipse movements toward increased multilaterality, with mixed implications for the United States–Mexico relationship. On the one hand, future trade agreements are likely to be confined to groups of countries at similar levels of development. Trade will be shared among developed countries and will be less subject to most favored nation treatment and more requiring of reciprocity, especially through special agreements on a country and commodity specific basis.

Given such a prospect, developing countries are likely to explore their own avenues for increased "South-South" trade, especially in view of increased barriers to their diversifying exports in the North. On the other hand, the very division of trade into multi-country blocs is seen by Vernon as likely to encourage both Mexico and the United States to pursue bilateral negotiations, since "preferences breed preferences."

Vernon's paper predicts that expansion of Mexico–United States trade will increase tensions, while expected increases in downstream investments by Mexico in the United States will reduce them. The treatment of tensions suggests that there will be a growing resistance to further integration of the two economies as the process evolves, though in neither paper is there any formal analysis of the social and economic costs and benefits of varying degrees of exchange. However, Corredor makes it quite plain that from the perspective of an economic advisor to President López Portillo the current trend toward rapidly increased "silent integration" is inconsistent with the "national project" and will be opposed by national policy.

If Vernon expects global protectionism to reassert itself in the North, including the United States, Corredor argues that Mexico's social and economic interests would not be served by pursuing a policy of openness along the lines of comparative advantage. In fact, he argues that Mexico's hydrocarbon bounty is capable of providing a surplus that could be used to promote import-substituting industrialization as well as incentives for non-petroleum exports through a two-tier oil and gas pricing system. Departing significantly from opportunity cost analysis, Corredor argues that domestic resource subsidies are in the national interest, though he recognizes that this may lead to wasteful utilization of nonrenewable resources and possible losses of foreign exchange and earnings. While this position elicited considerable discussion during the conference, it continued to reflect government policy to the end of the López Portillo administration.

The Corredor paper foresees increased utilization of the oil and gas surplus to promote additional exports and growth of the domestic economy, for which the author mentions that the Energy Program predicted a growth of 8 percent throughout the 1980s. Rapid import growth is cited as evidence that the economy has considerable absorptive capacity; and, at the time the paper was presented, increases in the real price of petroleum were expected to exceed real rates of interest on international borrowing, so the policy position of the government was one of maintaining a cap on energy exports while increasing foreign indebtedness.

Since then, real interest rates have risen significantly while the real price of energy exports has fallen, putting a severe squeeze on the balance of payments and the federal budget. In addition, the expanded liquidity effect of oil and gas exports, exacerbated by enormous increases in foreign debt in 1980/81, led to inflation plus lagged adjustment of the exchange rate. The overvaluation of the peso plus domestic price instability, credit stringency, and worsening balance of payments conditions led to a flight from pesos in early 1982, which was repeated in August as we go to press. The response was an abrupt devaluation that cut the value of the peso by 40 percent in February, and a second devaluation that reduced it by another 40 percent in August. Hence, conditions have altered significantly since the 1980 conference, and Corredor's arguments that non-oil exports must be encouraged (notwithstanding expected increases in protectionism) take on even greater significance today.

While the Vernon paper anticipates a falling relative share of the United States in Mexican trade, and vice versa, the Corredor references to increased "silent integration" indicate just the opposite, and especially for Mexican imports. Neither author is sanguine about the chances that the policy establishments in either country will favor more rather than less exchange, despite the important complementarities of the two regimes. In other words, the "international project" is implicitly rejected by Corredor (as it is, in a more extreme form, by Cordera and Tello). Vernon sees little chance that exchange between the two countries will be facilitated by reduced barriers except through possible binational trade negotiations that might be stimulated by the division of the global trading system into regional and national blocs elsewhere. Corredor sees Mexico's energy reserves as permitting more degrees of freedom for a trade-biased development strategy less oriented toward the United States, though neither paper deals with the employment problem in Mexico or the trade-offs between trade and migration.

The recent crisis in the Mexican economy and balance of payments provides evidence that high rates of growth of GNP cannot be sustained without severe inflation, fiscal deficits, and increased foreign debt or expanded exports of oil and gas under the capital-intensive plans of the López Portillo administration. Output growth appears to have an employment elasticity of only one-half, implying that an 8 percent growth rate results in a 4 percent increase in employment. Since the demand for jobs continues to expand at 3.5 to 4.0 percent per annum, the current slowdown in growth of GNP to a virtual halt raises problems of unemployment and underemployment that will become increasingly serious. This calls for a new look at alternative trade and investment strategies, especially in terms of their employment consequences. Such issues will receive increased attention in future activities of the United States–Mexico Project.

The section on "National Security" presents essays by Olga Pellicer de Brody and Edwin Deagle, which place the evolution of the security policies of their respective countries in historical perspective. Though from different vantage points, both authors see their nation's perception of national security as being at a watershed, and both see little apparent need for policy interdependence in security terms, at least at this time. Explicitly in the Pellicer de Brody paper, and implicitly in the Deagle, it is argued that attempts by the larger country to impose its security perspective on the smaller would be counterproductive. On the one hand, according to Pellicer de Brody, Mexico identifies national security with "social security." The threat from the outside is seen to be less from communism than from U.S. hegemony. Social security is expected to be achieved through gradual implementation of the principles of the Constitution of 1917, which implies far greater economic and social equality than is now the case. To accomplish this through reforms within the present system in Mexico, which the author feels is practicable, could be misinterpreted by those both inside and outside Mexico who have a different perspective.

Pellicer de Brody argues that the Mexican view of national security calls for a completely independent energy policy that employs energy resources to foster economic and social goals of the Mexican Revolution on which its national security depends. A foreign policy favoring "the Central American revolution" is seen to be a continuation of Mexican support for revolutionary change in the region, dating back to political (though not military) backing of the Arbenz government in Guatemala and of Castro in Cuba. Such measures are seen to fortify the objectives of Mexican internal stability.

The section on "Food, Agriculture, and Rural Development" views the relationship between the United States and Mexico in terms of (1) the crises of productivity growth in U.S. agriculture as it increasingly internationalizes (Falcon); (2) the policy challenges posed by the crisis of Mexican agricultural production and its consequences for productivity, inequality, and rural income (Warman); and (3) strategies for the development of small-holder rainfed agriculture in Mexico seen from an international perspective (Johnston). The perspectives from which these issues are joined, as well as the conclusions reached by the three contributors, illustrate the range of approaches that may be accommodated in an enterprise such as this, and the flexibility required of each country, given different points of view on contentious issues affecting the binational relationship.

It might not be too much to suggest that questions of efficiency, equity, and stability all take on different meanings, given the political, economic, and social perspective of the author, yet each contributes important insights and information essential to the eventual resolution of the issues on a binational basis. So crucial is this particular area of research and understanding to the future of both countries that the project elected to use the work of this session as the basis for a full working group dealing with issues of agriculture and rural development in the United States and Mexico. This working group, under the direction of Cassio Luiselli and Bruce Johnston, met in Cocoyoc, Mexico, in December 1981 and held a major conference in the same location in September 1982, the results of which will be published in this series.

The Warman paper places in historical perspective what he perceives to be the current crisis of Mexican agriculture, namely, its slow growth, increased dualism, and threatened dependence on primarily U.S. imports. Reflecting the widening Mexican national perspective at the beginning of the 1980s, Warman points to the fact that imports at that time accounted for one-quarter to one-third of national demand for basic grains and were directed toward the burgeoning modern market of its major cities.

At the same time, the need of the mass of the population for basic commodities was met by subsidizing imports, so that the cost of living was kept down artificially, particularly in urban areas, while farm-gate prices of the same commodities were not permitted to rise in step with the general price level. This process was exacerbated by the overvaluation of the peso (reversed in the 1976 devaluation, but continued again until February of 1982) that favored food imports over local farm production.

The author points to Mexico's history of agrarian reform, dating principally to the 1930s, and argues that land reform since that decade has virtually "stagnated." Thus the pressure on existing land has increased, and polarization has occurred between increasing numbers of minifundia and large holdings that account for a substantial share of marketed production. For small, rainfed subsistence farms, on which three-fourths of Mexico's rural population must depend, modern technology such as that employed in the irrigated regions of Mexico simply does not apply. The farms are too small, the marketed surplus too limited, capital availability too scarce and costly, and the orientation from which "peasants compete in the market to monetize their labor, not to realize a profit," too unsuitable for conventional productivity-enhancing policies to work.

If most of Mexico's rural poor are not in that part of agriculture which has contributed to most of the increase in output per capita, namely, the irrigated regions of the north and coastal plains, and if food-crop production by the end of the 1960s had shifted toward cash crops for export and feed grains for cattle, while land was increasingly used for livestock production, what policies might reasonably be pursued?

Warman points to two major programs. PIDER (Investment Program for Rural Development) began in 1973 and subsequently budgeted over one billion dollars, including substantial loans from the World Bank and Inter-American Development Bank that were joined to Mexican government contributions to facilitate the development of low-income agricultural communities. Warman argues that the program did not make a major impact on the production, productivity, and income of most small holders. He also feels that the more recent Mexican Food System (SAM), initiated during the López Portillo administration, did not address the principal questions of unequal access to land, capital, and other basic resources by the mass of the peasantry. Attempts to raise productivity through "modernization"—improved technology (implicitly that of the United States), higher farm-gate prices for basic food crops, government-shared risk programs, associations between private farmers and *ejidatarios*, cultivation of idle or pasture land, and mechanization, which are all part of the SAM program—and the Crop and Livestock Production Law are downplayed as solutions to the basic problem of rural poverty and inequality.

Since the time when the paper was submitted, crop production has increased significantly while grain imports fell off, so that in 1982 Mexican agricultural policy makers were giving considerable credit to the SAM program (as well as to nature—due to dramatically improved rainfall after the drought years of the late 1970s). The author comments on the renewed commitment of the government to improve food production, initially triggered by a declining agricultural trade balance, but sustained by peasant organization in the rural areas and by increasing pressures for improved conditions that are seen to weigh ever more heavily in national political calculations.

The Falcon presentation offers a view from the North that cannot be less than sobering for those advocating food self-sufficiency in Mexico. He is not sanguine about the ability of the United States to sustain its postwar growth in agricultural productivity, most of which depended not on increased inputs of land, capital, or labor, but on technological innovations. In his view this productivity trend is almost certain to be slower in the 1980s. The result, given expected rapid growth in world demand for food and feed grains as animal consumption grows in middle-income countries, will be a tendency toward rising real prices of agricultural products. Falcon stresses the implications to Mexico of the almost universal tendency among middle-income countries to have explosive increases in the demand for animal consumption with attendant pressures on feed grains. As the U.S. agricultural economy becomes increasingly international, it becomes ever more vulnerable to external shocks in the world food market, so that price fluctuations generated abroad are felt by the U.S. consumer and producer. This instability will almost certainly place pressures on the government for stabilization policies that could well become inexorable, however strongly resisted by economists.

The threat of upward trends and increased variability in international grain and related commodity prices is mentioned by Falcon as a reason for a new look at agricultural trade policy between Mexico and the United States that might be more feasible in the 1980s than in the 1970s. This position may be placed against the concern reflected in the Warman paper that "food policy" would become an instrument of foreign policy, to be used by exporting countries such as the United States to pressure Mexico in other areas. While neither of the authors states such viewpoints explicitly, the tradeoff is apparent in their respective presentations.

The paper by Johnston examines Mexico's agricultural sector in terms of the small-holder in semi-arid rainfed regions, whom Warman shows represents the majority of the peasant population. By drawing from comparative studies in South and East Asia and Africa, Johnston suggests that, although technologies may be available that are suitable to the small-holder, they are not likely to be imported from the United States, nor will they be similar to those employed on the large, irrigated farms of the North of Mexico. He presents a characterization of Mexican agriculture as "bimodal" (dualistic) compared to the relatively "unimodal" small-holder agriculture of Asia, where labor-intensive means of cultivation, new seed-fertilizer combinations, technical assistance, credit, and adequate pricing policies have significantly raised the productivity and incomes of small farmers. Like Warman, Johnston is skeptical that conventional programs of price incentives, input subsidies, crop guarantees, and the like will be sufficient to improve the lot of the small farmer who represents the majority of households receiving incomes below the minimum wage in Mexico today.

Johnston suggests that the prevailing attitudes in Mexico favor larger-scale units—the view even of those advocating reform of land tenure into large collective farms—and there is a tendency to demean the small holder and *ejidatario* as being incapable of operating in terms of technical or market-oriented efficiency. Countering this position, he believes that the Asian experience indicates that small holders can be relied upon to engage in significant improvements in productivity and market production, provided that the proper institutional and organizational factors are developed.

Given the magnitude of rural poverty in Mexico and the need for the agricultural sector to provide an ever-increasing surplus of crops to feed the burgeoning urban population, as well as the added burden implicit in the transition in demand from food to feed grains, none of the three writers is optimistic about the chances of resolving the problems. Warman favors a major restructuring of the access to rural resources so as to bring the mass of the peasantry to a higher standard of living. He does not address the implications of such a change for social and political stability or agricultural production and food self-sufficiency in the short and medium run. Mexico's agrarian history, however, provides countless examples of the cost involved in transforming the rural sector and of what can happen when conditions of the subsistence-level peasantry are allowed to deteriorate. Falcon focuses on the dynamics of demand in middle-income countries that are likely to cause an explosion in food and feed-grain requirements and that he believes would outstrip production gains of almost any Mexican rural development program, however successful. Johnston goes directly to the question of rural poverty and explores possible avenues for the development and implementation of alternative technologies for the mass of small-holders in rainfed agriculture more suitable to the Mexican case, and yet he does not examine the consequences for government expenditure on extension and other services, or on investment in the production and diffusion of new techniques.

In the past, the bimodal approach reflected in part the practical need of policy makers for rapid increases in output and a surplus for sale in the cities, and for increased foreign exchange earnings. That mandate, according to Falcon, will be even greater in the future. In the meantime there is a pressing need to attack the problem of the neglected small-farmer. This almost certainly implies a major diversion of resources from large holdings to rainfed agriculture, or an alteration of the economic, social, and political balance on which national security, according to Pellicer de Brody, rests. Would this be facilitated by more or less exchange between the United States and Mexico in terms of agricultural commodities, labor, other trade, or even technology and tastes? Whatever the decision, the papers in this section indicate that each country's problems in its rural sector will have an increasing impact on the fortunes of the other.

The section on "Employment and Migration" illustrates the increasingly important role that the labor flow between Mexico and the United

States plays in the destiny of both nations. Both the Bustamante and Sanderson papers indicate that, despite the growing links between their labor markets, the policies of neither country even begin to respond to the challenge of managed interdependence, nor do current proposals for changes in U.S. migration laws represent a significant step in the direction of a binational solution to what is clearly a transnational problem.

Bustamante argues that Mexico's impressive post–World War II growth performance, which permitted rapid gains in output per capita and concentration of wealth, owed much of its stability to the safety valve of migration of underemployed workers to the United States. Sanderson raises the specter of an explosive reaction by U.S. workers to perceived competition by foreigners for scarce jobs that could slam the doors to Mexican labor, precisely when external employment opportunities for Mexicans are most needed, that is, during a period of common economic recession. The political stability that migration provided to Mexico, from Bustamante's viewpoint, is seen by Sanderson to contain the seeds of instability, if and when migration laws become an instrument of beggar-thy-neighbor policies by the United States

The authors point to structural shifts in labor demand and supply in both countries over the past few decades. In the United States, employment opportunities have expanded employment in low-skill occupations while at the same time rapid demographic growth and agricultural stagnation expanded the number of job-seekers in Mexico. The gap between the two labor markets was increasingly filled by migrant labor to the benefit of both countries. The work of García y Griego, drawn from the labor ministry research unit (CENIET) studies on Mexican migration, indicates that gross flows of temporary migrants vastly outnumber the net increases in the stock of legal and undocumented migrant labor in the United States. Nevertheless, even the most conservative estimates suggest that by the end of the 1970s as much as one-fifth of Mexico's population derived some income directly or indirectly from labor in the United States.

Bustamante sees Mexican workers being unfairly used as historical scapegoats to explain unemployment, low wages, and unsatisfactory working conditions in the United States. Sanderson agrees that employers favor continuing the status quo as a minimum-cost solution to employment needs. In a position similar to that in the Reynolds paper he foresees growing employer pressures for low-wage foreign labor as the demographic profile shifts, reflecting a maturation of the labor force between now and the year 2000. This phenomenon will increase pressures for immigrant labor if the U.S. economy is not to face constraints on even a moderate (3%) rate of growth. In short, the stabilizing development of

Mexico, which Bustamante argues depended in the past on migration from Mexico, would, according to Sanderson, contribute to future stabilizing development in both countries by relieving Mexico of employment pressures and providing the United States with a steady flow of workers.

García y Griego suggests that in the light of recent research the amount of net and gross migration flows to the United States may well be exaggerated. It might be added that the recent oil boom is reported to have significantly tightened the market even for unskilled labor in Mexico (from the late 1970s to early 1980s), while recent INS interception figures indicate that at least through 1981 the gross flow from Mexico may well have decelerated. However, the economic crisis of 1982 calls into question Mexico's ability to sustain rapid rates of economic growth without severe inflation and balance of payments problems. Adjustments required to service the record foreign debt, which exceeded $70 billion in mid-1982, are certain to affect both private and public sector employment, increasing once again the importance of migration as a safety valve, at the very time when the U.S. recession is giving rise to protectionist pressures that, while more moderate than those hypothesized by Sanderson, will probably lead to unilateral restrictionist legislation (i.e., the Simpson-Mazzoli immigration bill presented to the U.S. Congress in July 1982).

Neither the history of immigration policy nor current approaches by either country begin to address fully the need for Mexico and the United States to recognize (1) the relationship between the essential interdependence of their labor markets and their respective economic development strategies, and (2) the effect on both countries of the fundamental gap between them in real wages and working conditions—a gap that provides the objective conditions for continued "silent integration" of their labor markets regardless of attempted restrictive policy measures. The papers indicate that the treatment of Mexican nationals by U.S. employers, government officials, and society at large is already an explosive issue that is bound to become more so in the future. U.S. and Mexican workers' interests are perceived to clash in the process. Neither government appears to favor a binational approach to migration policy, yet the authors argue that achievement of economic growth, political stability, and labor justice in both countries demands that the issue be placed high on the agenda for joint approaches to managed interdependence.

In the final section, on "Long-Term Relations Between the United States and Mexico," the prospects for joint policy formation are explored from the perspectives of the United States (Fagen), Mexico (Ojeda), and Europe (FitzGerald). The respective visions are perhaps more challenging than encouraging, given that conflicting interests, global perspectives, and debates over national policy must be accommodated before truly bi-national solutions to the problems and prospects of interdependence are forthcoming.

Fortunately, there is a glimmer of hope even in the most pessimistic predictions. The Fagen paper points to recent economic examples, including Mexican natural gas exports and the tomato trade with the United States, to show that even when historical difficulties have loomed large, the overlapping interests of consumers and marketing concerns in one country and suppliers in another may be sufficient to overcome the offsetting obstacles to mutually beneficial exchange. This is especially true when the political authorities recognize the need to view individual agreements in a broader framework of long-term alliances. Nevertheless, in both of these areas debates have been long and acrimonious over how much accommodation the United States should make to Mexican imports, and from the Mexican side over how much that nation's economy should be permitted to evolve in directions that make its own stability and development a function of U.S. market and policy conditions.

Ojeda points to the history of binational policy problems, dating back to the earliest days of independence of both countries, as a legacy dimming the prospects for future alliances. World War II is seen to have been a time when Mexico had no choice but to line up with the Allies, the quid pro quo being the opportunity to use the alliance to negotiate on issues of migration, indemnification for expropriated oil assets, and assistance for its own industrialization. Only in the event of a global conflagration does he perceive that Mexico would be forced to engage in another such alliance. Ojeda suggests that petroleum wealth will enhance his country's ability to deal as an increasingly independent state even with its assymetrically powerful neighbor, though he recognizes that oil power is a double-edged sword.

Fagen sees the declining imperial power of the United States as a problem that has already led to what he terms reactive nationalism in the 1980s and that will tend to work against future binational understanding. Here again, however, frustration in the United States with its increased global problems could have a favorable consequence by turning attention back to its own neighborhood and by increasing the disposition to a dialogue with Mexico on a more equal basis. Notwithstanding the many obstacles, both authors sense the need for a new relationship. Each country must see the other as a sovereign state, each increasingly impacted by the other's acts of commission and omission for stability, security, and equitable growth.

Both authors see that migration is an area of potential divisiveness in foreign policy despite the important economic complementarities it provides. Approaches to trade, finance, and investment will be affected by mutuality of interests between U.S. and Mexican businesses and consumer groups, as well as by the Mexican government. It is less clear how the explosive issue of migration, with its array of differing class and regional interest groups, can be resolved. Certainly, little progress has been made in binational approaches to migration policy in recent years. Only under the threat of World War II were Mexico and the United States able to reach agreements on the bracero program, and today powerful interest groups in both countries point to the abuses of that program to oppose guest-worker schemes for the 1980s.

The borderlands and the politics of race and ethnicity are pointed to by Fagen as areas that are only beginning to be understood, much less dealt with, as matters of mutual concern. The evolution of Mexican-American cultural exchange, economic activity, and political power north of the border is certain to play an increasing role in relations between the two countries. Neither author is clear as to how the balance of such relations might shift in the coming decades. To deal with such issues the U.S. steering group of the project has recently been augmented by a Chicano Advisory Board to assist in the identification of Chicano individuals, research, and policy perspectives for the future program.

FitzGerald, from a European perspective, cautions participants of both countries against an overly parochial view of binational problems that may stem from more fundamental changes in the international order. Mexico and the United States, as they approach the problem of organic interdependence, are harbingers of global structural change, whereby the pattern and location of production, the role of labor and capital, and the position of the state and private sector in the process, are all at an historic watershed. By the same token Europe has its own "North-South" adjustments to make, and it too is searching for a perspective from which to approach these issues. FitzGerald claims that the European perspective differs from the North American one in that it is broader, setting its own problems in relation to secular changes in the world economy and movements in the international trade cycle. He argues that the course taken by the world as a whole, as an increasingly interdependent system in which the development of "ex-colonies" and "southern states" impact the "northern" countries, will play a critical role in future United States–Mexico relations. Certainly in recent months these views have been prophetic, as world recession, declining energy prices, rising real interest rates, unemployment, military and security questions, and the Central American crisis have all been linked to global patterns of structural change, and yet all strongly influence United States–Mexico relations.

FitzGerald suggests that what is termed the European restructuring debate is not dissimilar from the kinds of issues that must be posed by economic policy makers in the United States and Mexico, even though the social, labor, and fiscal integration desired by each is much less than that envisioned by the EEC. From the first section of this volume it is clear that issues of dynamic restructuring must be part of the binational dialogue, inasmuch as they will be central to each country's perception and resolution of its own national goals. If "reindustrialization" occurs in the United States, how will this affect its own demand for labor, and what is the tradeoff between trade and increased mechanization of industry in the "North" and employment in the "South"?

The current international recession is a challenge to analysis from all political perspectives in terms of the fundamental secular issues of growth and accumulation versus full employment and static efficiency. The fact that recession is interdependent among countries at such different levels of development is crucial to the importance of an organic approach to interdependence of the kind taken here. The issues raise questions of the political economy of development that have long been dormant in the United States, except among students of developing countries and social historians. However, the "development approach," which perceives economic and social change to be part of an ongoing process of institutional evolution and political adaptation, is taking on new interest as the United States itself faces what are now being perceived as profound structural problems, related to its internal social and economic change under conditions of growing international interdependence. Hence, given the intrinsic interest of the problem and the need for new policies and institutions to fit a new era of increased internationalism, the United States–Mexico Project provides a basis for the revival and development of approaches to the analysis of economic evolution as a social process. From FitzGerald's transatlantic perspective, this begins at the border, but extends throughout the world.

Mexican-U.S. Interdependence: Economic and Social Perspectives

Clark W. Reynolds

BETWEEN Mexico and the United States there already exists a high degree of interdependence that may be termed "silent integration"— some of it operating outside of the law; and it is bound to increase over the next twenty years, during which time Mexican planners hope to see their country quadruple its economic product as its labor force doubles. While growth expectations for the United States are more modest, it too is experiencing an historically unprecedented economic internationalization in which Mexico has displaced Germany and the United Kingdom, to become its third largest trading partner. Given the desire of each country to preserve its national autonomy, the prospects for increased exchange pose a challenge to policy.

In assessing those prospects, numerous questions arise. What implications, for example, will changes in wages, profits, and rents have on the welfare of the two partners? Are wages in the two countries likely to converge as international interdependence grows? If so, how sensitive might the process of leveling be to alternative policies affecting that interdependence, involving trade, migration, investment, and technology transfer? Finally, how might governmental policies in each country be expected to deal with increasing interdependence? In this paper we undertake an examination of some implications of various degrees of exchange between Mexico and the United States in the light of their respective economic and political goals.[1]

---

[1] The material summarized here will appear in a forthcoming book by the author on economic relations between Mexico and the United States, sponsored by the Mexico–United States Border Research Program, under the direction of Stanley Ross, University of Texas, Austin, Texas, with support also from the Hogg and Kerr Foundations and Stanford University.

FROM ZERO TO FULL EXCHANGE:
A CONCEPTUAL FRAMEWORK

The method for analyzing the effect of trade and development on wages and profits in this study[2] employs at one extreme an approach introduced by the Swedish economists Heckscher and Ohlin.[3] In their view, trade occurs in response to differences in relative factor prices of the trading partners, while the prices reflect their respective endowments of labor, capital, land, technology, and tastes, and also provide gains from specialization along the lines of comparative advantage. Formalized versions of their approach were developed by Samuelson and Lerner to show that under certain highly restrictive assumptions trade alone might cause wages and profit rates to equalize between trading partners even in the absence of migration or capital-flows.[4]

While these formalizations of the "factor price equalization theorem" abstract considerably from reality, the original Heckscher and Ohlin approach was more dynamic, based in part at least on the economic history of Sweden. Over the past several hundred years Sweden has advanced from medieval agrarianism—through the export of copper, iron ore, tim-

[2] A number of colleagues in Mexico have pointed out that the use of the "full exchange" framework of analysis may be confused with advocacy of free trade, migration, investment, technology, and taste transfers between the United States and Mexico. Nothing could be further from the truth. This paper uses the "full exchange" paradigm as a way of placing limits on the extremes of economic regimes from zero exchange to full exchange (of which free trade is just one dimension), in order to explore some of the political-economic and social implications of approaching the other extreme. It will become clear that, although the analysis does not suppose the viability of anything resembling "full exchange" for either country, it does point to some of the economic and social costs of barriers to exchange, particularly in terms of both the employment of low-skilled labor and the rapid development of both countries with reasonable price stability.

[3] Eli F. Heckscher, *An Economic History of Sweden* (Cambridge, Mass., 1963), and Bertil Ohlin, *Interregional and International Trade* (Cambridge, Mass., 1933).

[4] See P. A. Samuelson, "International Trade and the Equalization of Factor Prices," *Economic Journal*, 58 (June 1948), 163–84; A. P. Lerner, "Factor Prices and International Trade," *Econca* (February 1952), reprinted in Lerner, *Essays in Economic Analysis* (London, 1953). See also M. O. Clement, R. L. Pfister, and K. J. Rothwell, *Theoretical Issues in International Economics* (Boston, Mass., 1967), ch. 1. Assumptions underlying the pure (Samuelson) factor price equalization theorem include two homogeneous consumption goods and two factors of production identical in both countries, incomplete specialization in production by either trading partner, perfect competition in both goods and factor markets, fixed supplies of factors in both countries including no net international migration or capital flows, identical tastes in both countries, different factor endowments but common technologies in the two countries, free and costless trade, and constant returns to scale.

However widely these simplifying assumptions may depart from prevailing conditions, the underlying principles serve as a useful point of departure for examining the effects of trade and other aspects of exchange. Relaxing the more rigid assumptions enables us to return to the broader historical perspective of Heckscher and Ohlin in which trade and welfare are related to the process of growth and structural change.

ber, and other primary products—to its present stage of highly advanced industrialization. This growth of production and trade in Sweden was accompanied by a demographic explosion in the nineteenth and early twentieth centuries as overwhelming in relative terms as that of Mexico today. In the last century, however, opportunities existed for Swedish labor to migrate to the United States, Canada, and other newly developing areas.

In addition to its increased trade and outmigration of "excess" labor, Sweden had developed an economic and social system capable of generating significant technological innovations. With these innovations came considerable local entrepreneurship and financial capital that could transform technology and ideas into profitable ventures. Resource rents and profits from innovations permitted an evolution from an initially raw-material and primary-product-based economy to one that specialized in the manufacture of intermediate and final goods. Much of the surplus generated by the process was accumulated and invested in further development of the economy as well as in productivity-enhancing economic and social infrastructure—highly advanced public education, for example. As a result, Sweden's initially low real wages and incomes rose to among the highest in the world in little more than a century. Heckscher and Ohlin attributed much of this progress to the gains from trade, but in fact migration, capital mobilization, and improved technology were essential complements to the exchange of goods and services.

For Sweden the process of exchange, while never *laissez faire*, was relatively free. The term *full exchange* is used here to designate the extreme case of complete freedom of movement of goods, services, labor, capital, and technology, as opposed to *zero exchange*, or complete autarchy. While there is no attempt here to advocate full exchange as a policy, the term is applied to the analysis of exchange between two economies such as those of the United States and Mexico, as a means of projecting gains and losses that might ensue if exchange were allowed to operate freely in all dimensions.

In practice every economy finds itself somewhere between the extremes of zero and full exchange—given its location, size, income, taste, and policies that affect trade, migration, and investment. Stated in its broadest form the Heckscher-Ohlin proposition might read as follows: For two markets approaching full exchange, the respective wage and profit rates will tend to converge until they are separated only by an amount reflecting transport and other relocation costs of goods and factors. Among other influences, the subjective preferences of workers to remain in the low-wage and low-income economy, rather than migrate, and the discounts placed by capital on national relocation, would merit consideration. Hence, for the wages of unskilled labor, migration may be said to be the ultimate equalizing factor. Labor will tend to migrate from a lower to a higher wage economy even after both have approached complete specialization of production if wages have not yet converged. The Heckscher-Ohlin proposition that exchange could lead to a gradual equalization of factor prices (reaching even to the wages of unskilled labor) was not static, but involved a long-term historical view of the process of exchange under conditions of major structural change. It is precisely such a dynamic perspective that we wish to apply to the analysis of relations between Mexico and the United States.

The concept of zero to full exchange in this study can accommodate the full range of possibilities of exchange between two economies through trade of goods and services, labor migration, finance, direct investment, and technology transfer. The expansion of the concept of free trade to full exchange recognizes that the latter is simply one extreme of a range of degrees of exchange in each of the major dimensions. This is not to advocate total *laissez faire*, but rather to provide a framework within which the interdependencies of the various types of exchange can be examined and the consequences of various degrees of openness tested. Indeed, one of the basic issues to be examined in the binational project that sponsored this volume is the degree of full exchange that would be socially and politically desirable for the two countries. While no consensus is either intended or expected, the object is to encourage a range of economic and socio-political analyses in order to clarify the options. Policy makers may then draw on these studies as they seek to harmonize the development of the two countries, at the same time minimizing the frictions that are bound to arise as forces of interdependence clash with those of autarchy.

THE DIMENSIONS OF ECONOMIC EXCHANGE

While the exchanges of values, tastes, and ideology may prove to be some of the most important elements in the evolving relationship between the United States and Mexico, we shall stress the four more basic economic dimensions of exchange: trade, migration, finance, and technology transfer. Though no more than an introduction of the problem is possible here, it is to be hoped that the issues raised will stimulate further research. The main focus here is upon the employment implications of the process of exchange, including the likely effect of tightness or slackness of the respective labor markets on the wages of unskilled workers in both countries. It is assumed that only if the labor market tightens at the lower end will the wage component of "factor price equalization" occur for unskilled labor both within Mexico and between Mexico and the United States. Hence development policies affecting labor demand in both countries are seen to be central to the goal of growth with equity that underlies both Mexican and U.S. development policy. As a result, policies affecting the four dimensions of exchange are viewed primarily in terms of their impact on the demand for unskilled labor.

Trade

A fundamental premise of the full exchange approach is that the process of trade and migration cannot be separated in the case of our two adjacent economies, where labor is relatively free to move. The formalized Samuelson-Heckscher-Ohlin model argues that, given common technologies, factor qualities, production of tradable goods, and incomplete specialization (plus a number of other strong assumptions), increased trade will lead to factor price convergence even without factor migration between the two economies. When one adds the possibilities of migration of labor to the capital-abundant economy and of capital to the labor-abundant economy, and in the absence of major differences in resource endowments, factor price convergence should accelerate. Why then have the wages of unskilled labor between Mexico and the United States differed by a factor of seven to one or more over so many generations?

First, at no point in history has there ever been completely free trade between the two countries—and this is especially true today. Barriers of distance, culture, transport costs, and language stood between the two economies even when legal barriers to migration or investment were minimal. Today both the United States and Mexico impose considerable obstacles to trade, with the degree of effective protection higher in the latter country. Both also have restricted labor migration, with Mexico protecting skilled labor and the United States attempting to limit the inflow of unskilled labor. In addition, a large and growing share of the output and employment of the two economies is in the production of nontradables such as services. As a result, the United States is becoming a high-wage service economy and Mexico a low-wage service economy. Without migration there is little tendency for either the prices of nontradables or the prices of factors employed in such markets to converge unless employment conditions tighten considerably within Mexico or slacken within the United States. Also, the technologies of the two countries are far from equal. Finally, natural resource endowments have in the past tended to favor the United States, especially in agriculture, though in the future Mexico's vast mineral and hydrocarbon reserves may shift the balance.

The existence of multiple factors of production—labor of varied skills, natural resources, capital of different vintages and qualities—greatly complicates the applicability of simple factor price equalization theories.

Different patterns of accumulation, investment, and research and development, which change the structure of each economy from period to period, provide additional complications. Mexico's current development plans, which call for a fourfold increase in GNP in twenty years, plus a demographically induced doubling of the work force, are sure to generate wage and employment effects that will eclipse those resulting from current trade policy or foreseeable alternatives. When the short-term employment effects of alternative trade policies are combined with their implications for growth and productivity in the long run, however, the resulting efficiency in use of the nation's resources will almost certainly have a substantial impact upon eventual employment, income distribution, and welfare. Strategies favoring a pattern of growth that overutilizes capital, under-utilizes abundant labor, and distorts the distribution of income away from the working class, will increase both pressures for emigration and demand for foreign investment; they will also defeat Mexico's goal of national autonomy and lessened external dependence.

Some rough estimates of the implications of recent trends in Mexico's foreign trade seem to indicate that, although exports remain relatively labor-intensive, the pattern of trade under import-substituting industrialization may have retarded the growth of employment as a whole. Table 1 provides data on man-years of labor required to produce one million pesos of final product by major production sector in 1970. In Table 2 those figures are applied to export data to estimate the amount of labor required to produce the observed level of exports, by production sector, expressed in constant 1970 pesos. Table 3 extends the estimated labor demand to 1979 and 1980, based upon trade data for those years, and also projects it to 1990, making use of two alternative projections of extractive and nonextractive shares of exports for that year.

Without taking into consideration likely productivity growth, labor embodied in Mexican imports is estimated to have grown on average by almost 1.7 percent per annum between 1960 and 1975. This compares unfavorably, in terms of labor absorption, with an approximately 2.8 percent average growth rate of employment in the economy as a whole, based on adjusted census figures for 1960 and 1970 and projections to 1975. In other words, in terms of labor utilization the export sector expanding at 60 percent of the rate of the economy as a whole remained relatively more labor-intensive while becoming less so. Note that in 1970 the national labor intensity of GDP was 17.5 workers per million pesos value added (Table 1), while the trade figure was 23.0 in that year, and 19.4 in 1975 (Table 2).

No productivity growth is assumed in the estimates in Table 2, since the 1970 labor coefficients are used for all three years. This almost cer-

TABLE I

Sectoral Definitions, Employment, and Labor Intensity, 1970

Activity	Workers (*thousands of man-years*)	Man-years of labor per million pesos of product
Agriculture, hunting, forestry, and fishing	4,466.8	43.0
Mining and quarrying (excluding petroleum extraction)	74.5	7.9
Extraction and refining of petroleum and natural gas	89.3	6.8
Food products, beverages, and tobacco	450.1	24.2
Textiles, articles of clothing, and other products	341.2	14.5
Wood-related industries and products	99.7	19.2
Fabrication of paper and paper products	92.9	12.7
Fabrication of chemicals, rubber, and plastics	174.5	8.7
Fabrication of non-metallic minerals except derivatives of petroleum and carbon	122.4	11.4
Basic metal industries	63.1	6.3
Fabrication of metallic products, machinery, and equipment	362.5	11.2
Nontradable goods	6,121.2	14.2
TOTAL	12,458.2	17.5 [a]

SOURCES: The labor force breakdown was obtained from Mexican government sources. The labor intensities in the final column are estimates obtained by completely inverting a 12-sector input-output table of the Mexican economy aggregated from Banco de México, *Matriz de insumo-producto de México año 1970*, table 1, p. 73.

[a] Weighted average of the above figures.

tainly overstates the growth of employment in the export sector between 1960 and 1975. For example, if productivity had grown by 1 percent per annum between 1960 and 1975, employment would have grown by only 0.7 percent annually, or from 345 to 382 thousand workers. The addition of productivity growth considerations would have contributed to a much faster decline in the ratio of labor to output from 27.0 in 1960 to only 18.5 in 1975. This strengthens the argument for loss of relative labor intensity in exportables. Part of the fall in the ratio of labor to output in the export sector is, of course, the result of changes in the composition of exports.

TABLE 2

Exports and Employment Generated, 1960–75

Activity	1960		1970		1975	
	Value of exports[a]	Estimated labor embodied[b]	Value of exports	Estimated labor embodied	Value of exports	Estimated labor embodied
Agriculture, hunting, forestry, and fishing	5,009	215.4	5,461	234.8	5,552	238.7
Mining and quarrying (excluding petroleum extraction)	1,370	10.9	914	7.3	1,397	11.1
Extraction and refining of petroleum and natural gas	343	2.4	480	3.3	3,472	23.8
Food products, beverages, and tobacco	690	16.7	2,274	55.0	1,777	43.0
Textiles, articles of clothing, and other products	3,523	50.9	609	8.8	1,104	16.0
Wood-related industries and products	72	1.0	96	1.8	137	2.6
Fabrication of paper and paper products	0	0.0	336	4.3	239	3.0
Fabrication of chemicals, rubber, and plastics	245	2.1	1,778	15.5	1,998	17.4
Fabrication of non-metallic minerals except derivatives of petroleum and carbon	108	1.2	224	2.5	285	3.2
Basic metal industries	988	6.3	1,618	10.3	2,084	13.2
Fabrication of metallic products, machinery, and equipment	436	4.9	2,242	25.0	2,605	29.1
TOTAL	12,784	311.8	16,032	368.6	20,650	401.1
Average man-years per million pesos of exports	24.4		23.0		19.4	

SOURCES: Total value of exports and their sectoral breakdown are from *United Nations Trade Statistics*, 1978, 1973, and 1963. Figures for 1960 and 1975 have been converted to 1970 pesos by means of a sectoral implicit price deflator series found in Banco de México, *Información económica-producto interno bruto y gasto*, 1979. Labor embodied is computed from export values by means of the sectoral labor ratios in Table 1. Estimates of labor embodied for 1960 and 1975 are computed assuming no growth in the productivity of labor.
[a]In millions of 1970 pesos.
[b]In thousands of man-years.

While much of the shift in recent years is toward trade in capital-intensive hydrocarbons due to the new oil and gas discoveries, as of 1975 this had little effect on the data in Table 2. Still, mining and quarrying exports were already rising at a compound rate of 7.2 percent per annum by 1975, much faster than total exports. The low average labor coefficient of 7.9 workers per million pesos of value in this sector contributed to the overall lag in export employment growth. Yet, even ignoring the minerals sector, labor-intensive exports grew more slowly than the average. For example, labor-intensive agricultural exports increased by only 0.7 percent per annum, relative to the 2.4 percent growth of all nonmining and quarrying, petroleum, and natural gas exports, while those from sectors with lower labor intensity—chemicals, basic metals, and machinery—grew by 14, 5, and 12 percent per annum respectively (Table 2) over the same fifteen-year period.

Table 3 shows actual exports and estimated export employment for 1979 and 1980, and projects both figures to 1990. Here again the data do not reflect the growth of labor productivity that Mexico has experienced and will almost certainly continue to enjoy. But it is clear that after a brief surge following the devaluation of 1976, both agricultural and manufacturing exports, which have traditionally employed the majority of export sector workers, declined in real value from 1979 to 1980. Some of the significant growth in estimated export employment in both sectors between 1975 and 1979 was subsequently lost, as the peso exchange rate lagged behind the rate of inflation during the oil boom. Meanwhile, employment in mining and petroleum showed such impressive gains that they more than offset declines in the nonextractive sectors, so that export employment as a whole, uncorrected for productivity growth, appears to have more than doubled between 1975 and 1980 (Tables 2 and 3).

Leaving aside the oil and gas bonanza, it is apparent that adjustment of the exchange rate in the mid-1970s, after such a long lag in devaluation (the previous one was in 1954), played a role in expanding both exports and export employment. Another factor was the slump in domestic demand that occurred during the period of presidential transition and devaluation, 1976–77. Just the reverse has happened since 1979, as the oil boom created a climate of expanded public sector expenditure and private investment, putting severe pressure on domestic capacity in both agriculture and industry. In the rural sector government policies shifted resources toward domestic food production, with a probable negative impact on exports, though this is debatable since supply conditions have also expanded.

The employment growth estimated in Table 3 has been much less than the phenomenal growth in export value might indicate, however, as trade

TABLE 3

Exports and Employment Generated, 1979–90

Sector	1979 Value of exports[a]	1979 Estimated labor embodied[b]	1980 Value of exports	1980 Estimated labor embodied	1990 Projected value of exports	1990 Estimated labor embodied
Agriculture (1)	10,284	442.2	7,207	309.9		
Mining (2)	1,835	14.6	2,347	18.6		
Petroleum (3)	21,767	149.1	46,104	315.8		
Manufacturing (4-11)	16,976	211.7	15,769	196.7		
TOTAL	50,862	817.6	71,427	841.0	175,000	(A) 2,046.2 (B) 1,537.7
Average man-years per mill. pesos of exports	16.07		11.77			(A) 11.69 (B) 8.79

SOURCES: Table 1, above; Banco de México, "Indicadores económicos" for the relevant years.

NOTE: Estimates A and B represent estimates of low (A) and high (B) shares of extractive exports in total exports for 1990. The (A) estimates are 113 billion pesos of extractive, and 62 billion of nonextractive, the (B) estimates 150 and 25 billion respectively. The total value of exports estimate is a slight reduction of an estimated 181.5 billion pesos for 1990 that appeared in Reynolds, "Labor Market Projections, for the United States and Mexico and Current Migration Controversies," in Food Research Institute Studies 17, no. 2 (1979), table A1.1; the estimate of 175 billion pesos reflects an adjustment downward to account for the 1979–81 decline in nonpetroleum exports. These estimates appear in C. Reynolds, R. Ramos, and R. McCleery, "The Impact of Foreign Trade and Export Strategies on the Distribution of Income for Low Income Households in Mexico," in Pedro Aspe and Paul Sigmund, The Political Economy of Income Distribution in Mexico (Princeton, N.J., 1983).

[a] In millions of 1970 pesos.
[b] In thousands of man-years.

has shifted toward more capital-intensive exports. Projections are made to 1990 on the basis of two alternative assumptions about the shares of oil and gas revenues in the total value of exports in 1990 (175 billion 1970 pesos). The "low petroleum platform" projections indicate that export employment in the absence of productivity growth would rise to over 2 million workers by 1990—a growth of almost 9 percent annually—while the high petroleum platform projections show a growth of 6 percent. In both cases the trends indicate that, even without allowing for productivity growth, man-years per million pesos of exports will have fallen from 23 in 1970 to between 9 and 12 in 1990.

We have also estimated the implications of a 2 percent annual growth in labor productivity between 1980 and 1990 in the export sector. This reduces the projected export employment to 1.4 million for estimate (A) and 1.0 million for estimate (B) in 1990. The study also indicates that in the presence of a more balanced pattern of effective protection, reducing the relative protection of less labor-intensive manufactures so as to favor agriculture, more than half a million additional jobs might be created in the rural sector by 1990, over and above those expected under the current regime.[5]

Since increasing reliance on oil-related exports exacerbates the shift away from labor-intensive exports, including agricultural commodities, the trend toward oil and gas should be reversed at least in relative terms. While the government ceiling (1.5 million barrels per day) was reached in February 1981, though actual exports were somewhat less, there is a continuing debate on whether the export platform should be increased. The slump in the second half of 1981 paralleled that of the world oil market and may be regarded as a temporary phenomenon, reflecting the current recession in major oil-consuming countries, that will disappear once those economies begin to recover by the mid-eighties. Until 1982, foreign exchange earnings generated by hydrocarbon exports plus associated borrowing permitted the peso exchange rate to be supported at a price which, given high and rising rates of domestic inflation, progressively overvalued its purchasing power relative to other international currencies. This grad-

---

[5] A separate study of the impact of alternative trade policies on employment and wages of unskilled labor has been prepared in cooperation with Raul Ramos and Robert McCleery at Stanford; some of its findings appear in Table 3. They indicate that, while Mexico's development plans, had they not met with severe foreign exchange constraints, might have had a significant impact on employment of unskilled labor through the sheer rapidity of output growth, trade policies tending to shift relative prices in favor of agricultural and food products by reducing the relative protection of final manufactures and intermediate goods would have had a much larger positive effect on the employment of unskilled labor than that envisioned in the plan. By tightening the labor market at the low end, especially in agriculture, this could raise the incomes of the poorest households and reduce pressures for both internal and external migration.

ual revaluation of the peso since 1976 worked against nonpetroleum exports and offset policies designed to protect import-competing activities. Though this too is debated, Mexican trade appears to be relatively price-elastic. Evidence for the 1976 devaluation showed sharply increased exports and reduced imports. Admittedly, though, the general deflationary effect of devaluation also had a major negative effect on import demand that is difficult to separate from the price effect of devaluation.

If trade is to have a significant impact on employment, oil exports cannot be allowed to distort the exchange rate or to permit a continuation of relative price bias against agriculture and other labor-intensive activities. At present oil is substituting for other more labor-intensive exports. It could be a useful source of foreign exchange, without sacrificing the goals of employment and improved income distribution, provided the peso exchange rate be allowed to move in relation to its relative purchasing power vis-à-vis other international currencies, and especially the dollar (since over 60 percent of Mexico's trade is with the United States). Some may argue that overvaluation of the peso could act as a brake on domestic price inflation by placing a ceiling price on tradables. This would occur, however, only in a pure state of free trade or under conditions of declining effective protection and reasonably competitive markets, and at the expense of domestic import-competing production that will lose markets—at least in the short and medium run—to imports. The sophisticated argument is based on the analysis of Blejer and others that domestic prices rise in an open economy in equilibrium in proportion to the rate of external inflation plus the rate of exchange devaluation.[6]

This approach is theoretically attractive because lower-priced imports substitute for inflationary-priced domestic goods, driving down the internal rate of inflation. In a fixed exchange rate regime, however, or in one with pre-announced devaluation, the adjustment occurs at the expense of a growing balance of trade deficit and unemployment in tradables production. In an economy such as Mexico's, with a large and growing nontrade sector (the tertiary sector now employs over 40 percent of the work force) and subject to legal minimum wages, certain prices regulated by government decree, a trade regime that relies heavily on nontariff barriers, and where petroleum export rents generate both liquidity and increased foreign exchange, the effectiveness of such an approach is severely restricted. Moreover, the political and social costs of unemployment of labor and capital in those sectors that would be obviously affected during the adjustment process cannot be ignored. For Mexico both industrial labor and management have significant political voices. While

[6] Mario Blejer, *Dinero, precios, y la balanza de pagos: La experiencia de México 1950–1973* (Mexico, 1977).

the Blejer theory has been applied with some success in strictly economic terms in Chile under an authoritarian regime, it has been much less successful in Argentina where both employment and output of import-substituting industries are of greater concern to policy makers.

In discussing the employment consequences of expanding exports of a given sector, our analysis assumes proportionality of labor inputs in exports and production for the domestic market. However, changes in the mix of products that comprise a sector, or differences in the labor intensity of domestic and export-oriented production of that sector could alter the results projected here. For example, some might argue that agricultural production for export takes place disproportionately in those regions of irrigation and greater capital-intensity where the labor/value-added ratio is lower than average for the rural sector, much of which involves primitive rainfed cultivation. Actually, however, a number of export cash crops from Mexico, including cotton, fruits, tomatoes, and other winter vegetables, are highly labor-intensive. Such exports have higher labor inputs than average in agriculture, especially when compared with wheat and corn production that are import-substituting activities. Recent trends in exports have worked against agriculture, while in the past few years food crop imports have accelerated.

Maquiladoras

The *maquiladora* program is one exception to the trend toward lower labor intensity of exports. At present these plants, processing intermediate imports for re-export, create well over 100,000 jobs annually, the majority of which are for young women. Most of the maquiladoras are located in the border region, although the program is being expanded to favor the interior of Mexico and especially the new industrial centers located near its "development ports." The major industrial centers—Mexico City, Monterrey, and Guadalajara—are specifically excluded, to avoid even greater concentration in those areas. Estimates of likely growth of employment under the program in the next five years suggest at least a doubling of the number of jobs, comparing favorably with the somewhat more than 800,000 jobs now generated directly by the export sector. While at present the multiplier effect of maquiladora value-added on Mexican production and employment may be relatively low, since a significant share of earnings is spent across the border, there is a potential for expanding linkages with the domestic Mexican economy. It is estimated that from one to three jobs are created in the United States for every Mexican job in the border plants through the demand for imports from supplies and purchases by Mexican employees who do much of their shopping north of the border. But as the program moves south and

as jobs become more skilled, this employment multiplier may be expected
to expand. In addition, the sponsors of the program argue that the training effect and possibilities for vertical mobility of the labor force are increasing over time in the poorer regions of the United States.

As real wages rise during the process of exchange, however, less competitive *maquiladoras* will be forced either to integrate into more complete production sharing activities or to move to cheaper areas if they are
not to be driven out of business. As of mid-1982, Mexican wages in these
firms were around $1.10 per hour. Though low by U.S. standards, such
wages are in the mid-to-high range for similar industries in the Third
World. (By comparison Haiti's labor cost is 50 cents U.S. per hour, or
less.)

The *maquiladoras* are criticized for adding little more than the un-
skilled-labor share of value-added to Mexico's economy, of employing
young women primarily rather than the severely underemployed male
work force, and of resisting unionization. In addition it is claimed that
they are enclaves with little integration into the national economy and are
"footloose," tending to move elsewhere when local employment conditions tighten. They are not regarded as a firm foundation for the integrated development of the national economy. Notwithstanding these criticisms, the benefits provided by *maquiladoras* in creating employment
tend to outweigh their other disadvantages, and for this reason the Mexican government strongly supports the program. It could be argued that
every effort should be made to further the integration of such activities
into the domestic economy. If this were possible, such highly efficient operations, which are heavily labor-intensive, could then begin to provide
Mexico's population with basic goods at a fraction of the cost of those
supplied by the highly protected inefficient "import competing industries" that now monopolize the national market. So far the interests of
import-competing industries and economic nationalists have bitterly opposed attempts to open the market to the *maquiladoras*.

Migration

Trade policy is closely linked also to migration pressures. Measures designed to protect the U.S. market from imports of labor-intensive goods
and services will exacerbate slack conditions in the Mexican labor market, leading to increased pressures for migration abroad as job opportunities become relatively more attractive in protected industries north of
the border. Offsetting the competition between jobs in the export sector
and jobs through migration, exchange policy designed to favor exports
may have a complementary effect on migration since devaluation of the
peso makes both peso exports and dollar earnings more attractive. Thus

in 1976 the sharp decline in the peso stimulated migration at the same time that it encouraged exports, although the accompanying domestic recession almost certainly added to migratory pressures. Between 1960 and 1975 the ratio of migrant jobs to export jobs rose steadily, in part probably because of the progressive overvaluation of the peso. This tended to discourage exports by working against the employment effect of comparative advantage in Mexico, thus depressing the domestic job market. With the 1976 devaluation both migrant and export jobs increased. The Mexican inflation rate of 30 percent in 1980, more than twice that of the United States, was only partially offset by peso devaluation. As a result one began to see the same downtrend in relative peso/dollar purchasing power that was so detrimental to the Mexican balance of trade in the 1960–75 period. This tended to reduce once again the trade share of employment creation.[7]

Estimates of Mexican migration indicate a steady increase in the number of Mexican workers who have joined the U.S. labor pool as temporary or permanent workers (Table 4). The figure now amounts to a significant percentage of the Mexican-born work force. Projections of the demand for labor in Mexico indicate that a 6.6 percent sustained growth of GNP by the year 2000 would be able to absorb the new workers coming into the job market up to that time but would not be sufficient to mop up underemployment including a number equal to those now employed abroad, which together amounts to around 10 million workers. In short, an optimistic 6.6 percent average rate of growth for the next twenty years will not tighten the labor market sufficiently for real wages of unskilled labor to begin to approach the U.S. level. And if GNP were to grow at only 6 percent annually (an impressive twenty-year average for any country), the labor surplus over and above underemployment and the number now employed in the United States would amount to from 3.3 to 4.3 million workers, or as high as 10 percent of the work force in the year 2000.

These projections assume that growth will continue to follow Mexico's Global Development Plan, which places heavy emphasis on capital-intensive manufacturing production. That strategy is also an important element of the Industrial Plan. The recent crisis makes it apparent that these plans were extremely overambitious. Without calling into question their objectives or the ability of forecasts such as this to project employment consequences accurately over two decades under conditions of major structural change, there is strong evidence that migratory pressures

[7]This section draws heavily on Reynolds, "Labor Market Projections," pp. 121–55. More recent estimates of temporary and permanent migration by Mexico's Labor Department research program CENIET do not significantly alter the basis of the calculations in Table 4. See also the paper by Manuel García y Griego in this volume.

TABLE 4

Mexican Contributions to the U.S. Labor Pool for Selected Years

(thousand workers)

Category of workers	1940	1950	1960	1970	1975
(1) Mexican labor force	5,858	8,345	10,213	12,955	15,400 est.
(2) Legal and undocumented temporary migrant workers (per year)	300	500	500	600	900
(3) Cumulative stock of permanent undocumented workers (beginning in 1940)		500	1,000	1,550	1,925
(4) Cumulative stock of legal immigrant workers (beginning in 1940)		30	210	470	650
(5) Total Mexican workers in U.S. labor pool[a]	300	1,030	1,710	2,620	3,475
(6) Mexicans working in U.S. as percentage of Mexican work force (5) ÷ (1) = (6)	5.1	12.3	16.7	20.2	22.6

SOURCES: Mexican labor force totals for 1940, 1950, and 1970 are from the census data on the economically active population age 12 and over (including unemployed). The 1960 census figure was adjusted to correct for overcounting of rural workers (for details, see Reynolds, "Labor Market Projections," p. 125n). For a detailed discussion of Mexican labor force and employment data, see Donald B. Keesing, "Employment and Lack of Employment in Mexico, 1900–70," in J. W. Wilkie and K. Ruddle, *Quantitative Latin American Studies* (UCLA Latin American Center, Los Angeles, 1977). His adjusted labor force total for 1950 is 8,272, and for 1960, 9,691. For 1940 and 1970 they are the same as the census figures. The estimates in row (2) are based on the number of legal temporary workers (including *braceros* from 1942 to 1964) plus an estimate of undocumented workers during the previous five-year period (double the number of illegals deported, reduced by one-fourth for nonparticipants in the work force). The figure is based on 20% more in 1975 to provide the most conservative possible estimate, in view of the speculative nature of the methodology used. Row (3) is based on the assumption that 10% of the seasonal migrants in row (2) elect to remain in the United States each year. Row (4) represents the net cumulative legal migration of workers, assuming that legal migrants from Mexico have a .65 labor force participation rate and a 5% attrition rate.

Figures on legal and undocumented migration and labor participation rates are from F. Ray Marshall, "Economic Factors Influencing the International Migration of Workers," in S. R. Ross, ed., *Views Across the Border: The United States and Mexico* (Albuquerque, 1978); Domestic Council on Illegal Aliens, *Preliminary Reports* (Washington, D.C., 1976);

Wayne Cornelius, *Mexican and Caribbean Migration to the United States: The State of Current Knowledge and Priorities for Future Research*, Monographs in United States–Mexican Studies, no. 1 (San Diego, Calif., 1982). The figures in the table represent estimated numbers of workers who will participate in the U.S. labor market at some time during the year cited, whether as temporary or permanent additions to the stock of manpower; they do not represent man-years of labor. Hence row (2) includes workers who might have been employed in Mexico as well as in the United States during that year, since the average period of employment of temporary workers in the United States is from three to six months. See Jorge Bustamante, "National Survey of Outmigration in Mexico: Description and Preliminary Findings" (paper presented at the Symposium on Structural Factors Contributing to Current Patterns of Migration in Mexico and the Caribbean Basin, Mexico City, 1978); Jorge Bustamante and Roberto Chande, "Análisis estadístico de las expulsiones de indocumentados Mexicanos" (Mexico City, 1979); and Cornelius, "Mexican Migration."

"When we speak of *Mexicans* in the United States, we refer to all legal and illegal immigrants from Mexico, and their progeny, who entered this country between 1940 and the present, regardless of place of birth. This is clearly not the same as "People of Mexican Origin," as detailed in a recent *Current Population Survey*. The magnitude of the difference (about 1.5 million people) can be explained as being all legal and illegal immigrants and their descendants who came before 1940. We are making the assumption—unrealistic, perhaps—that most of the illegals are counted in this survey. Otherwise, the gap would be greater.

will not diminish significantly during the next twenty years but will probably increase. This trend is due not only to domestic underemployment but also to a growing absolute gap in real wages between the two countries, a gap that is bound to increase still further unless Mexico's labor market tightens more than currently seems possible so that real wages soar south of the border, or unless real wages for unskilled labor in the United States fall significantly (something that would be socially and politically explosive).

The Mexican government's food and agricultural development program, Sistema Alimentario Mexicano (SAM), may help to absorb labor in the rural areas, slowing the rate of urbanization and raising real wages. But we have already seen that export crops tend to be very labor-intensive as opposed to domestic food crop production. A more detailed examination of the SAM program on employment is required before a final judgment can be made on this important issue. Whatever the outcome, it is certain that at least 7 million young job seekers will be emerging from the rural sector in the next twenty years. To absorb them in productive employment will require—at current levels of technology—$20,000 per additional job, or a total of $140 billion in new investment.[8] This would require three-quarters of the surplus from oil exports of 1.23 million barrels per day (estimated at $15 per barrel) throughout the period 1980–2000, and at the same time ignores the real problems of recycling foreign exchange earnings into expanded domestic employment on such a scale without severe inflation. It also ignores the additional need for investment in infrastructure, education, and social expenditures to complement direct investment in productive capacity. Finally, the estimate does not include the cost of expanded capacity needed to provide jobs for an additional 13 million young people entering the labor market from the nonagricultural sector, not to mention the need for a higher percentage of employment for the present unemployed and for those working abroad who may wish to return to Mexico.

It seems essential that a conscious emigration policy be formulated to complement Mexico's domestic employment and income distribution strategies, if real wages are to rise significantly at home and if labor-income convergence between Mexico and the United States is to occur gradually. Exports, however free to adjust along the lines of Mexico's comparative advantage, will not generate the same job-creating capacity as migration, at least not until well into the next century. Nevertheless, migration does represent a cost to Mexico in terms of the education, training, and skill formation of those workers who migrate abroad. They

[8]This estimate is based on the average incremental capital-labor ratio in Mexico in the 1970s, taken from official GDP statistics.

add to U.S. productivity by more than their wages, while detracting from the productive capacity of Mexico's domestic economy.

The remission of foreign earnings may be estimated at well over $500 million per year. This amounts to at least 0.5 percent of Mexico's 1980 GNP (in 1978 prices), and is one-eighth to one-sixth of the income of the poorest 10 percent of households. The opportunities that such employment provides for the income and wealth expectations of Mexican households are extremely important, together with the limited exposure to U.S. technology, work habits, and culture, some of which benefit Mexico productively. While on balance migration may favor the United States, though many debate this, both countries have benefited from Mexican migration. It has reduced factor scarcities in the United States and has relieved unemployment in Mexico while remitting foreign exchange to the poorer Mexican households.[9]

Finance, Foreign Direct Investment, and Technology Transfer

Interdependent with trade and migration are capital and technology flows to Mexico, and this is becoming increasingly the case over time, as investors make locational decisions in terms of access to labor as well as markets. As changes in Mexican law seek to increase the national benefits from imported technology, some U.S. firms prefer to import labor rather than shift to a foreign location. For others the *maquiladora* program and related trade policies offer encouragements to serve the U.S. market from plants located on Mexican soil. Finally, financial flows in both directions in response to relative yields on investment have become highly sensitive to the effect of trade and migration policy on the balance of payments, exchange rate, wage level, and degree of political stability. While it is not possible here to unravel all the threads of such interdependence, some of the main features should be identified.

U.S. direct investment represents 80 percent of Mexico's total direct foreign investment and has a long history in that country. In the early part of the century such investment tended to favor extractive industries, railroads, and infrastructure including telecommunications and electric power. Following expropriation of the petroleum industry in 1938 and the enforcement of restrictive policies on foreign ownership of mining, plus the nationalization of power, telecommunications, and transport industries, foreign direct investment has shifted toward those import-competing industries that have benefited from import protection to serve

---

[9] Elsewhere I estimated that the benefit of migration of Mexican workers to the U.S. economy in 1975 was at least $16 billion, or about $80 per capita on average for all U.S. citizens ("Analysis of the Impact of the U.S. Economy on the Economy of Mexico and its Border Region," revised, April 1980).

the domestic market. Demand for the products of such industries is still highly concentrated, primarily in the major urban areas and among the top 20 percent of households whose average incomes approximate those of the U.S. middle class (the top 5 percent of Mexican households today have an average family income of $27,000). The effective demand generated by this small minority of the population provides a market for a wide array of products that are virtually identical to those manufactured and marketed in the United States.

Today the pattern of foreign investment in Mexico is again changing. First with the border assembly plants (*maquiladoras*) and more recently through production sharing (in which Mexican subsidiary firms of a U.S. parent company produce part of the value-added of goods sold in both Mexican and U.S. markets) an open economy orientation is beginning to emerge for some of the more productive firms. Since they tend to utilize technology imported from the United States, they are relatively capital-intensive by Mexican standards, though not necessarily in terms of the U.S. capital-labor ratio. Over time foreign direct investment has increased the U.S. share of ownership in the leading manufacturing industries in Mexico, and such firms have tended to enjoy preferential access to external sources of financial capital, especially in times of domestic credit stringency. Since one of the policies of the Mexican government is to reduce rather than increase the relative power of foreign (and especially U.S.) firms, this raises a number of problems. Transnational enterprises have access to the widest range of technology. However, they also demand compensation for their patents, licenses, and know-how. Until recently such firms have tended to rely on sources of research and development in the home country, rather than to expend funds for this purpose in Mexico, in part to secure control over the returns to intellectual property.

The new phase of production sharing into which Mexico is entering means that transnational firms portion out different stages of production between countries in terms of relative factor costs. Thus they are able to increase their degree of Mexicanization, to strengthen Mexico's exports along lines of comparative advantage, and to increase employment. Here is an area in which trade and foreign investment are highly complementary and where migration may be reduced by production sharing. However, such a process requires considerable openness to trade, including access to intermediate products at a quality and price sufficient to make re-exports competitive on the world market. For maximum benefit such firms must also be permitted to compete with less efficient suppliers in the local market. In view of the relative market power and financial leverage of transnational firms with their greater scale economies relative to domestic firms, greater openness is likely to lead to more concentration, less domestic control of industry, and further inroads on national economic autonomy. This is the price that may have to be paid for rapid growth and employment, but it is certain to create internal social and political conflicts as well as increased friction with the United States.[10]

In terms of the profitability of enterprise, Mexico is clearly ahead of the United States, and any movement toward full exchange would probably favor the trend of U.S. savings supporting Mexican investment. Estimates of the quasi-rent share of GNP of the United States and Mexico from 1970 to 1977 over and above a normal return on plant, equipment, and other fixed capital indicates an astonishing gap between the two countries. Mexico had an estimated quasi-rent share of net national income (over and above wages and salaries and a normal return on fixed assets of 15 percent) of 21 percent in 1970, 25 percent in 1972, 18 percent in 1974, 9 percent in 1976 (a depressed year), and 12 percent in 1977. This share has almost certainly risen since the recent oil boom as profits for most firms have soared. The U.S. quasi-rent as a share of net national income (over and above wages and salaries and a normal return on fixed assets calculated at a rate of only 5 percent compared to an assumed rate of 15 percent for Mexico) was only 0.5 percent in 1970 and actually fell to minus 1.4 percent in 1977! The profit and rent situation in the United States since then has declined severely so that the current share may be expected to be even more negative than in 1977, increasing the contrast between the two countries.[11]

In short, Mexico offers a much higher return on capital and natural resources (and a proportionately higher return on equity) than does the United States, and the gap appears to be widening. Under such conditions, and assuming that risk differentials are covered by the 10 percentage-point differences in assumed normal returns on capital of 5

[10] Since the beginning of the 1970s Mexico has introduced a number of laws to restrict the operation of foreign enterprises, to increase the national share of returns from foreign technology, and to expand the degree of Mexicanization of important sectors of the economy. While at first, especially during the Echeverría administration, these policies appeared to discourage foreign direct investment, the oil bonanza and the policies of López Portillo have changed the picture. During the López Portillo administration there has been an increase of firms seeking access to the lucrative Mexican market and the product of its labor—which is still low-cost by U.S. standards. See Van R. Whiting, Jr., "The Politics of Technology Transfer in Mexico," mimeo (Department of Political Science, University of California, 1980), and *Programa Nacional de Ciencia y Tecnología, 1978–1982* (Mexico, October 1978).

[11] For these calculations, net national income equals GNP minus depreciation and indirect taxes. Calculations by the author and his assistant Robert McCleery based upon the approach used for international comparisons of profits, wages, and rents in "The New Terms of Trade Problem: Economic Rents in International Exchange," in C. P. Kindleberger and G. di Tella, *Economics in the Long View*, Vol. I, *Models and Methodology* (London, 1982).

and 15 percent respectively, financial and investment capital is likely to flow from the United States toward Mexico under conditions of relatively full exchange. The more open the financial and investment markets, the more this will occur, tending toward equalization of the marginal efficiency of investment between the two countries over the long run, just as wage equalization in labor markets may be expected to occur eventually under relatively free migration. However, the price of such adjustment is increased loss of Mexican control of its own internal economy. This has been opposed in the past and is likely to be even more politically unacceptable in the future. On the other hand, controls on foreign direct investment will almost certainly lead not only to increased pressures for outmigration but also to demands for greater stress on employment-generating policies within Mexico than the current global or industrial plans envision. Whatever the policy decision regarding foreign investment, the huge gap in profitability between Mexico and the United States, together with the expected growth of the Mexican market, will almost certainly increase pressures on both sides of the border for greater production sharing and foreign direct investment on terms that are likely to remain quite favorable to investors in the United States.

IS A GREATER DEGREE OF EXCHANGE NECESSARY OR SUFFICIENT FOR MEXICAN DEVELOPMENT?

From this examination of some key aspects of exchange between Mexico and the United States, it seems evident that properly designed strategies for trade, migration, investment, and technology transfer, while increasing absolute interdependence, may also permit an increase in the relative independence and power of Mexico. Indeed, they may be essential to the achievement of full employment and increased social participation in the economy, which are among the goals of government policy. Migration in particular may permit greater degrees of freedom for domestic development policy, which could ultimately eliminate the need for large-scale emigration of unskilled labor twenty years hence. On the other hand, short-sighted closed-door trade, migration, and investment policies could constrain the economy's potential for growth with distribution by worsening the slack in the labor market, pushing down real wages, and increasing the gap between rich and poor.

Eventual full exchange is, however, not feasible—economically, socially, or politically. It implies an extreme set of strategies that would carry with it a loss of autonomy and national control over each economy that would be unacceptable to either the United States or Mexico. Free migration would generate immense opposition in the United States from those groups that have struggled for so long to raise or at least maintain their real wages. This would include service workers, blue-collar workers, unskilled labor, and minorities. If allowed to operate fully, the iron law of factor price equalization could cut in two directions, lowering real wages in the United States even as it raised wages in Mexico.

The pattern of trade and comparative advantage derives from differing conditions of supply and demand between countries. Exchange everywhere is subject to a variety of tariff, migration, and foreign investment policies that "distort" the pattern of production away from that which would be dictated by conditions of full exchange. The case of the U.S. Sunbelt illustrates this point. California and the southwestern U.S. economy did not develop until enormous infusions of government-subsidized infrastructure in mining, railroads, irrigation, ports, and communications took place to "open up" the region to national and foreign markets. And only when the onset of World War II brought a need for regional diversification of U.S. industrial production did the federal government provide massive subsidies and investment in California heavy industry, and a guaranteed market for high technology manufacturing that provided the basis for what is now the backbone of the region's industrial economy.

Yet today the Sunbelt is on the cutting edge of the U.S. economy. Its industry and agriculture are the nation's leading sectors. Full exchange, in terms of interregional trade, financial flows, migration, and technology transfer within the United States was a necessary condition for California's development. But it was not sufficient. Full exchange simply complemented the government-supported development of leading sectors in the Southwest. And during World War II rationing and material-balance transfers of strategic resources by governmental and quasi-governmental agencies permitted many southwestern industries to expand despite the relatively high costs that would otherwise have prevented them from competing with firms in the East and Midwest. Government procurement still provides an important impetus for many electronics and aerospace industries.

The case of exchange between the two countries differs in many respects from this regional example. The United States is a political union of states determined to preserve its national autonomy. Mexico will never permit itself to merge economically so as to become a de facto region of the United States even though at one time its boundaries extended into what is now U.S. territory. The two social, cultural, and political systems are as divergent as any two trading partners can be. Hence the Sunbelt example does not apply except as an extreme paradigm. Yet this paradigm illustrates the essential prior role of government policy in regional development, reflecting in the case of the Sunbelt a strong public interest in national security, social welfare, and geopolitics, in particular. The California example illustrates something about the demands placed on economic planners and policy makers by Mexico's rapid growth strategy. If Mexico wishes to quadruple its economy in twenty years, its target GNP by the year 2000 would be between $300 and $400 billion (1978 dollars), or greater than the current level of California's gross regional product today (about $300 billion in 1980, and the seventh largest economy in the world). It took thirty years for California to achieve that level of production, from a gross regional product of $80 billion in 1950 (close to Mexico's 1978 GNP). What took thirty years to accomplish in California, with its initial advantages and a considerable degree of domestic full exchange with the rest of the United States, Mexico plans to accomplish in only twenty years.

The differences between the two cases far outweigh their similarities. While Mexico's work force is now many times that of California in 1950, the educational and training content is much smaller. The reserve of highly educated and skilled workers and managers available to California as of 1950 from its own resources as well as through migration from the other forty-seven states was well ahead of that of Mexico in 1980. On the other hand, Mexico's potential petroleum and gas reserves place it in a more advantageous position than did California's resource rents as of 1950, most of which still derived from the rich yet subsidized agriculture of its irrigated alluvial valleys. But the employment and resource transfer problems arising from the use of Mexico's petroleum economy to develop production and employment are much greater than those faced by California, which depended on rents from agricultural exports and capital inflows from the rest of the United States to bring about industrial expansion during and after World War II.

Mexico is almost certain to opt for a much lower degree of exchange with the United States than California experienced with the national economy, and for good reason. It is a proud and powerful nation that does not relish a future fused to the United States. Notwithstanding this, there is a strong momentum in the marketplace toward greatly increased interdependence. Fuller exchange than might be sought by nationalistic groups north and south of the border may prove essential to the achievement of income, employment, and growth goals in both countries. Since the integrity of language, culture, politics, and institutions is as much to be preserved as freedom from foreign hegemony, this places a great burden on policy makers north and south to devise approaches toward managed interdependence that will bring about the kind of growth with distribution, that will safeguard national autonomy.

A certain consequence is that, if social justice and political stability are to be secured in Mexico, wage, wealth distribution, and employment policies must be far more direct and drastic than ever they were in the United States, requiring measures that go well beyond the present plans of the Mexican government. And if the United States is to preserve its economic power and social progress in an increasingly interdependent world, it must be prepared to exchange goods and services, labor, capital, and technology with Mexico on a scale unprecedented outside its own borders.

Prospects and Options for Mexican Society

Rolando Cordera and Carlos Tello

For Mexico the last few years have been a time of search for development alternatives and for the elaboration of programs that could give rise to political equilibria and power alliances. Such socio-political reordering and confrontation about the future of the nation's development is born of national and international economic crisis, and, even more importantly, arises from a profound questioning of traditional political practices as well as major changes in life style, social behavior, and demographic structure.

Most significant is the fact that the best organized groups among the basic classes of present-day Mexican society are propounding explicit ideas of a global character about the problems the country faces, as well as about the solutions that must be found for them. As never before, the business of state must contend with the conscious intervention that these groups directed toward transcending partial and episodic involvement with affairs of state and establishing them as full participants in the long-term contest over the economic and political leadersip of the country.

What is at stake are alternative and even contradictory proposals that are the products of social distillation (perhaps even of a class nature) and of a discourse formerly presented almost exclusively as official state policy. The importance of these proposals within the ideological and institutional frameworks in which state decisions are made, as well as their specific forms, will in great measure determine Mexico's future profile as well as the orientation and content of its participation in world affairs.

THE STATE FACING CRISIS

The social and political differentiation underlying the awareness of change over the past ten years does not imply that the state, or the groups that have historically controlled its course, has either lost the political initiative or is simply a reflection of the renovating discourse of research that has permeated social affairs in Mexico in recent years.

First there was a mounting criticism of so-called stabilizing development, then the feverish search for an alternative model, finally baptized as shared development, and later—in the face of devaluation and the subsequent panic, rumors, and conspiratorial adventures among certain business groups—proposals for a social truce in preparation for a profound social and economic reform. A similar itinerary of dimensions can be traced in the field of political relations: a search for reconciliation of the state with intellectuals, and then, in the midst of a severe, though segmented, deepening of the social malaise, proposals for political opening and the revival of *agrarismo* from the top. Finally, starting in 1977, when the economy could no longer touch bottom and the country was living through the most pronounced recession in modern times, a revision of the electoral process was set in motion and the political reform was launched.

For many people among the dominant class and in certain high governing circles, however, the economic collapse of 1976 reinforced a conviction that the government would first have to modify its goals and reestablish the basic economic and financial parameters that had given rise to growth with stability in the 1960s. In this context change was identified essentially with restoring a kind of growth that would require only partial adjustments; it was taken for granted that this had been altered irrationally by economic myopia as well as by political ambition and desperation. With the help of oil, and after a period of wage and budget austerity, the economy would once again be ready to resume the path of growth and would then prudently come to grips with the country's principal social problems, especially the poverty of the majority.

This discourse, which achieved undisputed predominance in the wake of the calamity of the 1976 devaluation, was a powerful one and, with the recovery of the economy, might be expected to gain even greater force. However, many aspects of the recovery itself call into question the economic and political viability of a strategy based on the simple rehabilitation of the old model of development.

The Entrepreneurial Project

In the course of the economic crises in the past decade, business organizations moved from a defensive stance to an openly offensive one in which they abandoned plans for the defense of their prerogatives and assumed a dominating perspective on the present and future of Mexican society. The establishment of the Businessmen's Coordinating Council in

1975 served to bend the basic lines of force in a direction ever more favorable to the entrepreneurs, for the following reasons:

1. The deepening of the crisis and the lack of a government policy for both strengthening the state and attending to the interests of the popular classes limited the government's alternatives for action and led it to define a policy favoring, over any other objective, the recuperation of the "confidence" of the private sector.

2. As a result of devaluation, increasing unemployment, and declining real wages, the organizations of the working class turned in on themselves and centered their action around the defense of their own limited interests, abandoning those of the class as a whole. In addition, the independent unions that emerged during the decade experienced severe limitations on their actions.

3. Peasant organization weakened as the crisis advanced and the members passed from a struggle for land and rural justice over to inaction, and from land reform to security of tenure as their main goal.

4. As the crisis developed, public administration became permeated by the confrontation of interests occurring in society, the governing group lost cohesiveness, at the same time that capital gained it, through reducing the dispersion of its demands on the state.

A statement of principles of the Businessmen's Coordinating Council set forth some of the basic themes of its project: the concept of private enterprise ("the basic cell of the economy"); the role of the state in the economy ("economic activity is fundamentally an activity for private parties"); worker-management relations ("just and humane treatment of the worker"); the mass media ("it is considered indispensable that private property be preserved"); methods for controlling prices ("these are the cause of the stagnation in economic activity"); small property ("the backbone of the agricultural economy"); and education ("it would be fitting for the state to create a climate of liberty which would facilitate participation by the private sector").

This entrepreneurial outlook has been refined and reiterated in recent years in the midst of an economic recovery that has benefited business almost exclusively. With the aim of limiting state action as the guiding force in the economy, so that its intervention will serve the long- and short-term interests of capital, entrepreneurial spokesmen have expounded their traditional diagnosis: dishonesty in the public sector, its high level of expenditure, inefficiency in the administration of state enterprises, decay of the universities, excessive bureaucratic red tape, high taxes, and price controls are in their view some of the factors that limit the possibilities for a healthy, balanced, social and economic development. As a counterpoint they offer as solutions austere management of the budget, then lifting of price and wage controls, honesty on the part of the politicians, and greater political participation for businessmen. Just as in the past, business leaders play politics using supposedly technical arguments.

The Workers' Project

In 1979, the Congress of Labor, the representative of the organized Mexican labor movement, published a manifesto which pointed out that

the high concentration [of] wealth . . . and the ascendant power of foreign and domestic monopoly capital already pose threatening prospects for the nation, and in particular for the public authority which has for some time found itself subjected to the pressure of minority groups representing economic power. It is a vital necessity for the Mexican nation and people to bar the way against the offensive of such oligarchic forces . . . to put a popular, nationalist, and democratic project on the road to realization, one which will consolidate the undoubted advances achieved by the people and their revolutionary regime, respond to the present needs of the majority, and lend vigor to the struggle for the integral transformation of Mexican society.

Accordingly a program of action was proposed, based on the fundamental objectives of consummation of an agrarian reform of greater revolutionary content, the application of an economic reform supported by deep structural modifications, and the prosecution and deepening of the political reform.

This program finds its direct antecedents in the plans worked out by independent groups of workers who only a short time ago considered the organized labor movement irreconcilable enemies.

The declared aims of organized labor, then, are that the state exercise its right to impose on private property those requisites dictated by the public interest; that it rely on the active participation of workers in the direction of the economy; and that it reverse the tendency of capital accumulation so that it operates in favor of the state and the working class.

This discourse of the union bureaucracy is aimed not only at maintaining its relations with the state, but also at setting conditions for that process. Then one is dealing not with a merely transitory reaction, but with a revision both in terms of the significance of their alliances with the state and in certain of the concepts that have guided national development in the postwar era. In contradistinction to the past, economic demands (which are never given up) are now being framed within a wider set of proposals that seek to transform Mexican society by putting into effect a project responsive to the needs of the majority. This project represents a set of postulates that possess historical roots and express political and social relations still in force, and are therefore discussed simply as repetitive or demagogic.

Deterioration of the workers' conditions, insurgency among the rank-and-file and the development of independent unionism, the political and economic demands presented by workers, and the process of democratization in organizations affiliated to the Congress of Labor, have led the official union leadership to attempt this change of course, in the hope of retaining its structure and organization, and thereby its political position in the power structure.

The programmatic proposals and counterproposals that have been elaborated at the upper levels of union leadership undoubtedly might give the workers wider latitude for mobilization than has prevailed up to now, as well as a far-reaching program with which to orient their actions. Nevertheless, it seems clear that the organizations of the workers themselves, not the agreements between union heads and the governing groups, are the natural field for that politicization which alone will serve to implement the program and to renew the alliance between workers and government. In order to make the reform program a reality, then, the democratization of union organizations is seen not only as indispensable, but as a precondition for effective incorporation into national politics as a social force. Otherwise, the working-class project as advocated will remain a mere petition to whatever government happens to be in office.

Two Alternative Proposals

In large measure, the coordinates that will define Mexico's future profile correspond to a conceptual projection of the options now being presented to the country by important nuclei among its fundamental classes: the entrepreneurs—especially the groupings dominated by big capital—and the workers, in particular those organized around the CTM (Confederación de Trabajadores de México) and the Congress of Labor (Congreso del Trabajo).

These projections, moreover, match up coherently, if not in linear fashion, with the great alternative camps created by the present crisis in world capitalist society. The capitalists' plan possesses a close affinity with schemes for economic restructuring that are now being insistently promoted by economic and, in some cases, political elites in advanced capitalist countries and that have been given the label *neoliberal*. In turn, the proposals of the organized workers may legitimately be located within the framework of what we could call a *nationalist* project of development, which in the Mexican case would have as a necessary starting point a revitalization of both the discourse and the judicial institutional networks that originated with the Revolution and whose foundations were enshrined in the Constitution of 1917.

Save in exceptional circumstances, neither of these projects appears to have a certain prospect of being fully realized. The politico-economic combination that results—and the weight that each project assumes—in the social reality of tomorrow will be products of the struggle among classes, of the forms and propensities that state activity takes on, and of the degree of organization and persistence demonstrated by the social forces promoting them. Their concrete manifestations will be perceived in the economic and social policies that are implemented in the country day by day and in which, above all, the options in question will prove their currency and national political revelance.

THE NEOLIBERAL PROJECT

The neoliberal project is a metropolitan undertaking that has its origins in the industrialized countries and its principal promoters in the elites of big financial and transnational capital. It aspires to a fundamental restructuring of the world capitalist system in conformity with the diagnosis and perspectives of its promoters. In their view, only through a purging of the social and economic system forged amidst the fervor of Keynesian policy making after the war will it be possible for capitalism to go forward again and attain higher levels of economic progress and financial stability. According to transnational thinking, among the primary factors blocking accelerated development and therefore principally to blame for the current crisis are (1) an excess of democracy and the consequent deterioration of the legitimacy of governments and established institutions; (2) hypertrophy of the state as well as its disproportionate and inflationary deficit; (3) the growth of the unions and their interference in public policy; and (4) the rebirth of nationalism.

Thus, the key proposition posed by this project is that Mexico's long-run interests, as well as those of U.S. society, will best be satisfied if both economies are integrated into a global system of mutual complementarity. In that event the United States would furnish Mexico with a secure and growing market for its exports, with technology, abundant financial resources, capital goods, consumer goods at competitive prices, and, finally, with the possibility of absorbing its work force or, rather, that part of it that cannot be productively absorbed in Mexico itself. In exchange Mexico must be ready to furnish the raw materials and finished products that the U.S. economy requires, along with a growing market for its goods; to guarantee the foreign investment established there; to reach agreement on complementary industrial integration; and to strengthen the ties of friendship between the two countries through solidarity with, and international support for, the United States and its policies, especially with respect to the rest of Latin America. With the frontier thus widened and solidarity secured, Mexico would be converted into a paragon of liberalism and continental cooperation for other Latin American countries.

The neoliberal project is intended to be an integral response to the current crisis of capitalism, as expressed in lower rates of growth, loss of purchasing power of wages, and rampant unemployment and inflation. The crisis pertains also to the economic policy that has accompanied capitalism's postwar surge and must therefore be replaced with an alternative paradigm. Changing paradigms, which implies the displacement of Keynesian political economy by neoclassical economies, necessarily introduces changes of enormous importance in the conduct of economic policy. In particular, establishing full employment as the central objective of state intervention signifies, both in theory and in the practice of the capitalist state itself, incorporating the interests of the working class into policy. By contrast, conceiving the economy as a self-regulating system, as is proposed in neoclassical theory, implies viewing the working class as a mere "factor of production" that, only by behaving as such, can facilitate equilibrium in the market and a return proportionate to the effort it expends in production. Hence neoliberal theory insists on circumscribing union organization to the level of intra-enterprise relations and depriving the unions of all possibility of meddling in politics and the economy. Policy proposals made for the purpose of reestablishing conditions functional for the economic system's self-regulation advocate different routes: reducing to a minimum the participation of the state and its regulatory function; relying on monetary rather than fiscal policy instruments to allocate resources and channel the surplus; giving priority to monetary stability, even above economic growth and other objectives connected to the welfare of the popular classes; and, finally, freeing the interchange of goods and capital among all nations of protectionist fetters.

The inflation universally afflicting capitalism today constitutes the dominant axis of neoclassical theoretical reflections. In neoclassical diagnosis inflation can be combatted only through restoring basic equilibria between supply and demand. To its insistence on the importance of excess demand generated by deficit spending, the neoclassical argument thus adds another element—cost inflation—which, it maintains, inevitably reduces wages. After such a diagnosis the prescription emerges spontaneously: aggregate demand and costs must be reduced by attacking the causes of their rise, i.e., public expenditure and a work force that behaves in a monopolistic fashion, politically motivated. The recommendations are for policies of fiscal and wage austerity and productivity programs, with the goal of converting workers as individuals into production factors who will understand that their remuneration depends solely on their expending of effort. Thus inflation functions—at least ideologically—as a master element forging an iron cohesiveness between economies and politics.

Regardless of whether productive public enterprise is included, neoliberal discourse thus suggests that the state should limit its action to that which is necessary for establishing the general conditions for economic expansion—hence its emphasis on monetary as opposed to fiscal policy.

From the global perspective of neoliberal strategy, this assault against state gigantism is something more than a hypostatized, ideological recourse. On the one hand, the expansion of the state—and, within it, of public enterprise, independent of any functionality it may possess—is perceived by capitalists as a barrier to their opportunities for extracting surplus. On the other hand, the presence of state enterprises in dependent countries is seen as an obstacle, actual or potential, to the homogenization of the market and of production. The compromise equilibria reached on these matters, which depend on innumerable national and conjunctural factors, do not eliminate the central issue posed by neoliberal thought in regard to inflation and the state: the necessity to reexamine, as radically as possible, the conceptual framework guiding economic policy, the relations between the economy and politics, and, consequently, relations among classes and the mechanisms through which class power is perpetuated in capitalist society.

Together with public expenditures, the demands of the unions for higher incomes must, in this view, be moderated. Once a linear relationship between wage increases and variations in prices (wage-price spiral) is established, the conclusion is obvious: in order to contain inflation, one must contain the growth in its fundamental components, among them wages. In addition, wage discipline can achieve not only a reduction in prices but also full employment consistent with the rules of the economic system, i.e., one that enables the labor force to obtain its real price and not a politically determined one. If an equilibrium in the labor market is obtained by this means, greater unemployment may also be achieved, which will have the effect of diminishing the real income of workers as a whole. From the neoliberal viewpoint, however, this would be only a temporary disequilibrium.

Nevertheless, neither in rich nor in poor countries has neoliberalism's anti-inflationary policy achieved its desired objectives. The results of the application of the wage-containment strategy to the countries of the Southern Cone in particular have been dramatically revealing: fiscal and wage austerity, taken to the limit, have added to unemployment, the loss of purchasing power, the bankruptcy of small and medium-size firms, and a greater presence of foreign capital. Together with the continuing rise in prices, this has produced a superconcentration of economic power, but has failed to stimulate the kind of private accumulation that was perceived as a promise of better times ahead. Instead, there has been a growing diversion of the surplus to financial or real estate speculation, as well as massive imports of consumer goods destined especially for minority social strata.

In Mexico the potential support afforded by rapid economic growth to the anti-inflationary rationale is canceled by the country's basic economic and financial relationships.

The current arguments in favor of free interchange among nations, however refined in appearance, continue to be essentially the ones utilized by Ricardo at the beginning of the nineteenth century, and by the colonial powers as the basis for their unique international division of labor. If Mexico is better endowed for producing vegetables, fruits, and legumes, and the United States for producing grain; if Mexico can produce oil more easily, and the United States capital goods; then both countries would presumably benefit from greater specialization. As in Ricardo's citing of England and Portugal, neoliberalism's proposal ignores the fact that Mexico can produce grain as well as fruits and vegetables and can initiate the production of capital goods as well as of oil.

For those Latin American countries that began their industrialization in the 1930s, the argument for specialization in terms of comparative advantage is also supported by the defects and bottlenecks that, as accompaniments to industrial growth, have tended to widen and occupy the social and economic stage: the virtual incapacity of industry to make up, through exports, for the imports that its evolution requires, or to adapt technological innovations, or to forge significant, positive links with agriculture.

From this diagnosis, which with greater or lesser emphasis enjoys general acceptance, neoliberal doctrine concludes that the principal villains of the drama have been protectionism and state intervention. From such a conclusion, which at first sight offers an image of logical consistency and congruence with reality, it passes on to its policy recommendations: the necessity to eliminate protection and to reduce the state's economic presence to a minimum. From this perspective, therefore, industrialization ceases in fact to be the center of political preoccupation, and the nation's future comes to depend upon an incorporation into the world market in which national decisions remain completely subordinated to competitive signals. In theory at least, these signals, if qualified at all according to the unequal weights of the economic agents involved, never appear as such, for the free market paradigm always prevails in the argument.

Several explanations may be adduced for the fact that countries like Mexico have been the principal targets of the liberalizing crusade of the past few years. In the first place, industrialization itself, associated without further reflection with protectionism, appears to have little to offer socially. The industrialists form a weak stratum that is poorly articulated socially and is politically inclined toward conservative solutions offering at least a certainty of survival, even if only as importers and rentiers. Second, in the centers where neoliberal theory originated, there exist socioeconomic interests and coalitions capable of expressing themselves politically against liberalization projects that seek a rearrangement of world economic activity. Third—and of supreme importance—a small but efficacious bloc-in-power has emerged, which sees in the generalized internationalization of the market a relatively secure way of consolidating its dominance, of immediately increasing its share of the surplus and of social wealth, and of acceding to schemes of association with foreign capital that will permit it to evade or exit from the crisis not only as the dominant internal faction, but also as an actor at least partially recognized within the network of international domination that appears to be forming in the course of the crisis itself.

Seen in this light, the strategy of anti-inflation and of pruning industry through productive specialization appears as a means of buttressing a specific form of domination that corresponds to the interests of the most internationalized groups and the most powerful factions of financial capital. Proposals for economic liberalization, internal or external, thus always appear as fiats that, rather than liberalize, seek to regiment civic and political life in the immediate term.

The Concrete Manifestations of the Project

Mexico's development has increasingly been accompanied by the presence of foreign and national monopoly capital and by the influence that such capital exerts over social and economic policy. The neoliberal project would give it, as a new element, both a channel and a frame of reference. Moreover, it would imply significant changes in the future development of what will be a key determinant of activities in Mexico in the years to come.

The severe agricultural crises from which Mexico has been suffering for several years, for example—dramatically manifested today in an unprecedented level of grain imports from the United States—provide the defenders of the neoliberal project with a first-hand argument supporting changes in the land tenure system and agricultural strategy. The neoliberal project in the agricultural sector is defined by the consolidation of private property in land, the legalization of the renting of parcels, orientation of agricultural production toward export crops and industrial raw materials, and the use of policy instruments for agricultural promotion in conformity with these aims. Internal production of grain would have second priority, and the productive potential of the United States would be utilized for covering the deficit in domestic consumption. The division of labor thus established would permit the respective agricultural sectors of the two countries to be made complementary on the basis of indicators of efficiency and productivity.

Furthermore, the recommended process of agricultural development would promote the competition that now exists between the production of animal feed and of basic grains for human consumption. Relative prices, and agricultural-cum-livestock development policies more generally, would be adjusted so as to give priority to the production of feed-grains and meat, to the detriment of the production of basic foodstuffs. With crop and animal production left to the market forces, the production of livestock feed would proceed apace, and the dominant presence of transnational firms in the production of balanced feeds and processing of milk derivatives would be strengthened.

Mexico's oil wealth, the accelerated development of its capacity to exploit that wealth, and its consequent entry into the exclusive club of oil and gas exporters in a world context marked by the increasing scarcity of energy have given the country a new role in the international economic system and have lent a different content to its relations with the United States. The adoption by Mexico of a neoliberal strategy overall would obviously result in a policy of ever more accelerated petroleum exports around which, in turn, the web of relationships between Mexico and the United States would develop and become tighter and more complex. Mexico would not only be a commercial client of the first rank and a strategic supplier for the United States, but would come to form an integral element of U.S. national security preoccupations—something that in fact has already occurred. In addition, the adoption by Mexico of a neoliberal oil strategy would permit the rapid implantation of a nexus of economic and political interests, which would find in a process of frank integration with the United States many more benefits than disadvantages, and not only on the economic plane.

Furthermore, the magnitude of Mexico's petroleum wealth appears to be such that this strategy would not have reason to appear irrational, as a type of resource exploitation. With oil tied to the dynamics of international demand, in the absence of further strategic considerations, and facing the spectrum of necessities that presently determines Mexico's distribution of income, it is conceivable that such issues as tax reform, the financial structure of public enterprises, domestic manufacture of capital goods, and, of course, self-sufficiency in food—measures that are seen today as indispensable for the continuity, not to mention the acceleration, of economic growth—would be postponed.

Until recently these programs were presented as matters about which a long-range decision on the part of the state was urgent and inevitable. Today, however, the flux of petrodollars has opened up the possibility of evading such matters without putting global growth at risk, thus reinforcing the power of a social bloc that in any case would be in favor of an oil policy such as the one already described here. In addition, not undertaking the reforms would accentuate the "objective" necessity, determined by the requirement of overall economic growth, to deepen the above-mentioned strategy. The socio-economic inequalities and disequilibria that underlie the need for such reforms could therefore be permanently accelerated. In the case of Mexico, however, even in the context of a prolonged international crisis, thanks to petroleum it once again appears possible that a society that is becoming more and more fractured and polarized can achieve compatibility with a dependent economy in the process of rapid growth.

Division of labor in industry would also supposedly bring benefits for both countries, in the neoliberal project. The cheap and abundant manpower that exists in Mexico would be exploited through agreements on industrial complementarity. The United States would enjoy a secure and growing market for the export of its capital goods and equipment, including, of course, those of a second-hand variety. In the best of cases the expansion of industry in Mexico would take on an essentially horizontal character, leaving aside for later any aspiration toward reaching vertical industrial integration. Although this could be interpreted as keeping Mexican industry in a state of permanent backwardness, the neoliberal argument asserts that in the longer term an optimal industrial specialization would in fact take place, on the basis of which possibilities would be created for increasing employment of the work force. In this fashion a highly foreign-dependent industry would develop and would receive the benefit of infrastructure, goods, and basic services produced by the public sector, all of which would be oriented to its needs. Finally, within neoliberalism's integrationist scheme the entry of Mexico into the General Agreement on Tariffs and Trade (GATT) would become a logical step.

Other Implications of the Project

The neoliberal project would necessarily have repercussions on the policies put into practice in other areas. In the labor sphere, supported by the fact that the cost of the work in Mexico is, and will continue to be, lower than that which prevails in the United States, the project recommends an international division of labor based on activities using labor power intensively. In this scheme, union organization would be promoted at the firm level, but the tendency of workers to organize by branch of activity would be arrested, thus favoring corporate interests over those of class. The most probable outcome of this arrangement would be for wage differences to be maintained and for the distribution of income between capital and labor to retain its present structure. The fluid operation of such a labor policy would also imply, of course, that the unions would lose their organic links to the state and would find their sphere of action reduced to that of negotiation on the elementary and isolated terrain of the productive unit.

As far as peasant affairs are concerned, attending to and functionalizing the conditions in which the majority of the Mexican rural population lives would have high priority, on account of the explosive potential it represents. Any attempt to destabilize the countryside would naturally be prevented, and peasant organization and struggle repressed. Also, programs would be set up to attack the absolute poverty of the rural population directly, above all by way of subsidies to consumption. Such anti-poverty programs would run parallel with the employment possibilities offered by industrial complementarity agreements, and in general with the process of integrating the two economies. The labor power that could not be absorbed in the country would then be channeled to the United States through a program of controlled, long-term migration. Pockets of controlled poverty, relieved little by little through migration (both internal and to the United States), would thus appear to be the chief prospect for Mexico's peasant masses under the neoliberal project. Their productive function, and hence their participation in the market, would be essentially secondary.

Educational policy would also have to be reordered to conform with the neoliberal project. Resources, priorities, and the content of teaching itself would have to be made to respond to the needs of the productive framework resulting from the complementarity of the two economies. Article 3 of the constitution, with its egalitarian and nationalist aims, would thus give way to zeal in the preparation of middle-level technicians and highly specialized professionals, both of which would be given top priority. In addition, the participation of the private sector in education would increase, basically at the higher-education levels; graduates would then be recruited increasingly by private enterprise, and eventually by government, to fill its needs for middle-level cadres.

Other social welfare policies would be oriented by the criterion of favoring individual and/or group effort as against policies that give priority to class interests and work toward satisfying the neediest population groups within a program of social solidarity. Thus social security programs and guarantees, and the quality of the services associated with them, would respond to the income level and quota of the individuals covered, i.e., better service and larger payments for higher-income people. The benefits generally associated with collective bargaining between workers and employers would be determined at the level of the enterprise.

All of these measures would wrest power from the workers as a class, and their organizations, the unions, would also lose power in collective bargaining with capital. Differences among workers in regard to pay, benefits, and working conditions would, moreover, be fomented. Finally, struggle over wages would prevail over any other consideration, above all of a class or political nature.

The neoliberal project can count at present on a considerable base of social support. In the United States the large employers naturally battle for its establishment, inasmuch as the political, economic, and strategic benefits that the project would bring for the country and its ruling class are qualitatively and quantitatively greater than the costs associated with it. In particular, a good deal, if not the whole, of the payments made for Mexican oil and gas would find their way back to the United States through the many types of imports that Mexico would have to buy. Although a controlled, agreed-upon migration of semi-skilled Mexican workers to the United States would undoubtedly provoke social tensions of a certain magnitude, those tensions would be more than compensated by the benefits, both economic and social, that it would bring.

Within Mexican society there are also pressures working in the neoliberal project's favor. The possibility of lessening the social problems deriving from unemployment and underemployment through the migration of the excess work force to the United States is naturally highly attractive, especially for groups among the bourgeoisie who see in these phenomena, and in the poverty associated with them, a destabilizing potential that might negatively affect their interests as well as the position of privilege they presently enjoy. If to the foregoing one adds the resultant potential for importing durable consumer goods, a significant part of the Mexican middle class, hungry for the "American way of life," would have to be added to the bourgeois groups pressing for the project in question.

Along with Mexican executives and investors associated with foreign capital, other important groups of the bourgeoisie—bankers, large merchants, and landowners, for example—also have an interest in promoting the neoliberal project. It is in tune with the strategic vision they hold concerning the future of the country and is also, of course, in accordance with their traditional, ideological views.

Finally, small but powerful groups of industrialists—relatively diversified and efficient, and holding monopolistic positions within the national market—would also favor the neoliberal project in principle. Their reasons are varied: in the first place, their position of advantage in relation to the rest of industry in Mexico enables them to make forays into the U.S. market; second, many of them are already integrated into the international operations of the companies with which they are associated; and, third, they would gain power in their relations with the Mexican state, so that their proposals and positions would not have to be blended, as they now are, with those of other (especially small and medium) Mexican industrialists.

THE NATIONALIST PROJECT

The struggle to maintain and broaden national control over the general conditions in which production is developed—as well as the national management of resources, the strengthening of economic independence, and full exercise of national sovereignty in matters of social and economic policy—constitutes the nucleus of the principles defining and orienting the nationalist project of development. The project starts with a general hypothesis to the effect that, at present, the country's interests can best be satisfied if the postulates of the Political Constitution of the United Mexican States are fully developed and promptly applied. That constitution establishes the theses and programmatic principles of the project, creates the possibility of putting individual guarantees into effect, and defines the prerogatives of the state in regard to education, property, the exploitation of the nation's natural resources, its own participation in the economy, and the rights of workers. Here, too, are spelled out the scope and content of democracy, considered "not only [as] a juridical structure and political regime, but [as] a way of life founded upon the constant economic, social, and cultural betterment of the people."

On the basis of this constitutional mandate, the state, as the guiding force in the process of development, is charged with the responsibility for promoting the betterment of the conditions of life for the popular majority by acting upon relations of property—imposing on them modes of expression dictated by the public interest—and upon relations among social classes. In addition, the project presupposes that the principles and postulates of the Mexican Revolution, of the national state to which it gave rise, and of the social pact on the basis of which the country has evolved, still have prospects for development to offer to Mexican society. It can now look forward to progress in attending to the needs of the majority of the population, in tempering the extremes of wealth and poverty that currently exist, and in reaching a higher and more favorable level of economic and social evolution.

Although the nationalist project would unquestionably promote capitalist development in Mexico, such development—unlike the neoliberal program—would respond to a set of priorities centered on the principal objective of a broader and more vigorous internal integration of its economy and, in general, of all social and political relations. Taking the argument to an extreme, one might assert that in the nationalist project certain things appear viable and desirable that, from the neoliberal perspective, lack economic rationality in the strict sense of the term. Such would be the case, for example, with the production in Mexico of capital goods or the programmatic search for self-sufficiency in food. In both cases the social costs that will inevitably be incurred could have been avoided, in the short run, by means of a tight integration into the international market, and especially into the U.S. market. Nevertheless, from a nationalist point of view such costs compete disadvantageously with the longer-term benefits that would be brought about by a broader and more integrated productive base and by national self-sufficiency in goods that are considered strategic and whose internal production is feasible.

In the nationalist project, therefore, the political character of the economy is evident; even more, subordination of the latter to politics is not an *ultima ratio*, but rather a permanent, constitutive element in the process of development and in the decisions, both public and private, that make it possible.

In a general sense, the nationalist proposal finds support in all those theoretical developments that give priority to examining production. It is obvious that production and consumption are intimately and indissolubly linked; without production there can be no consumption, and without consumption the possibility of production does not exist. But this must not lead us to forget that it is the conditions in which production takes place that determine consumption, and not the reverse. What the nationalist project would add to the foregoing is that, in our era, these general conditions of production tend to take concrete form at the levels of the nation and the state; it is these entities, conceived as dynamic realities, that regulate and condition (actively rather than passively) the orientation and rhythm of the development of productive forces and relations and, consequently, the allocation of resources and even the criteria of rationality and optimality as well.

The general conditions in which production has developed in Mexico, the unequal character of the development of Mexican capitalism, and its subordination to and dependence on the United States, have all favored the emergence of a highly polarized economy oriented toward production of essentially superfluous goods and services. The economy has become dependent for its dynamism on a permanent concentration of the economic surplus that does nothing but reproduce social inequalities, as manifested in the widespread incidence of absolute poverty. There is nothing to indicate that this situation is going to change in any future economy that is liberalized and more closely integrated with those of foreign countries. Hence, the imperative of matching production more closely to the consumption needs of those who generate that production—namely, the workers; hence, the necessity to order the division of labor in conformity with the general interest; hence, the utility of the state intervention in the economic process, by erecting institutional barriers to the "general laws" of the economy to regulate their operation and impede the dissolution of the nation's social fabric. All are integral parts of the nationalist project.

In the nationalist project, which entails reviving intersectoral linkages as well as broadening and diversifying the productive base, it will be up to the state, from the outset, to provide new stimuli for commodity production and accumulation; i.e., its role as an exogenous agent in relation to the market must be recovered or reactivated, taking into account the interests of the popular classes. In essence this implies taking up, in the programmatic sense, the causes of full employment and better conditions of life for the workers of the countryside and the city.

Because of its negative impact on the living conditions of the popular classes, the fight against inflation also acquires a different dynamic in this context. In particular, such a fight cannot be based on wage containment or on reduction of public spending. On the contrary, it must be oriented toward reducing and even cancelling, as far as possible, the factors that provoke inflation: (a) a lag in the supply of necessary consumer goods relative to demand, which, in turn, is a result of investment lags; (b) a restrictive monetary policy shackled by the constraints of the international financial system; and (c) an increasing dependence of the national economy on the world system. It requires, in addition, greater reliance on fiscal policy than on monetary policy instruments—in fact subordinating the latter to the former for purposes of mobilizing resources and allocating the economic surplus generated in the process.

There are three problems that the state will unavoidably have to resolve before it can take up the tasks of social and economic reorientation inherent in this strategy. All are worth examining briefly.

In the first place, the state must deal with its own fiscal crisis, which will tend to grow worse as attempts are made to stimulate economic activity by means of public spending without at the same time introducing substantial corrections in its mode of financing. In addition, if it is to undertake a reactivating role within the framework of a kind of planning that looks beyond the short-term budgetary and financial horizon, the state must confront its own administrative and institutional decay. This will require defining the direction and magnitude of the process of diversification of the productive structure as well as the degree of control the state will have in new productive fields. Second, the unfolding of a type of state activity over and above the complementary and corrective actions that characterized such activity in the 1960s will necessarily run up against the interests of big oligopoly capital, whose dominance was established during the period of stable growth and has been consolidated in the course of the present crisis. Third, the fact that the state will effectively be reassuming its guiding and dynamizing role in the process of development implies that it will enter into contradiction with the objective trend toward the destructuring of national states—a trend that has been exacerbated by the current crisis.

It is worthy of mention at this point that expansion of the state is not a necessity of the nationalist project alone. From the perspective of big capital as well, what is sought is a remodeling of the state that would permit equipping it to fulfill its functions in the economic cycle, but that, on the other hand, would avoid any tendency for the state to grow on its own account or to depart from the developmental track on which capital wishes to keep it moving. *Grosso modo*, that track grants the state a predominantly regulative role, both in the economy and in politics, and seeks to make public enterprise a disciplined agent circumscribed essentially to the production of strategic inputs; this would not prevent it from continuing to operate as a surplus-channeling mechanism, but such channeling would be less generalized, more discriminating, and more in accord with the interests of big capital.

The state as a regulatory agent could produce different results—depending on the means of implementation—for its relations with the economy and the social classes. Consider, for example, the central question of foodstuffs. From the point of view of capital it might be more rational to seek an optimal combination of food imports and wage stability as a means of establishing a more or less stable relationship between wages and profits than for the state to commit itself to a policy of self-reliance based on programs of wide-scale support for the peasant economy. In the short run both options inevitably imply substantial imports of foodstuffs as well as relative wage containment. The second option also presupposes the strengthening, or restoration, of the state's political alliances with the peasantry and the labor movement, whereas the first option would lead to a situation in which state-peasant relations rested increasingly on repression and state-worker relations on an even more brutal wage stratification.

The latter alternative—not precisely the choice of the employers in general, but rather of large enterprises possessing a transnational vision and of certain groups within the state technocracy—is faced with the fact that the crisis has altered the framework of alliances between state power and the organized popular sectors that sustain it. In complex ways the political relationships within the public sector embody the very history of the Mexican state—a history of mass participation. The political bureaucracy is thus not merely an instrumental element in the pact of domination—the union bureaucracy even less so; both have interests as well as a notable, specific importance in the process of defining the future of the public sector, where in turn they find their material base. The latter is a dynamic element in the relation between state and economy whose potential, rightly speaking, has not yet been completely realized. While on the one hand this bureaucratic (but mass) presence places concrete, political limits on what we might call the pure neoliberal alternative, on the other hand it imposes from the outset a heavy corporative content on any development alternative that seeks to rely on a growing, productive public sector and on the state's active participation in social organization, i.e., any alternative that aims in effect to advance along the road of national capitalist development that emerged from the Mexican Revolution.

Given the fact that the Mexican state still presents itself as a social force of great potential in the material, productive, and labor spheres, the organization of a project of development around this social-material force cannot be dismissed through the reductionist method of politico-economic arithmetic (predominance of big capital = state as instrument of the dominant class = public enterprise ancillary to private accumulation). Furthermore, insofar as big capital advances in its search for hegemony, even when to all appearances this process culminates in the adoption of an economic policy of stabilization *à outrance*, the generation of new and sharper tensions in the rest of the pact of domination will begin to be manifested in various fields; without doubt, one of the principal arenas in which this conflict-situation will develop is the state apparatus itself, and hence its productive branches.

This dialectic is still in the process of formation. From the perspective of large monopoly enterprise the new oil surpluses undoubtedly heighten the need to define both the size and the orientation of the public sector. Objectively, however, they also expand the field of possibilities for putting into effect alternative strategies more in accord with national needs and directed explicitly toward satisfying, however minimally, the wants of the majority.

As has occurred in the past, the strengthening of the nation's productive base and the satisfaction of pressing popular needs find a point of support in the development of a strong state possessing a high degree of autonomy with respect to the dominant fractions of capital. Nevertheless, neither the expansion of the productive apparatus of the state alone, nor that of its other branches, can ensure that social production will evolve in the desired manner and to a significant degree. What is needed, in sum, is a new set of priorities for state action, along with a battery of stimuli for the private sector that are minimally coherent with those priorities. This presupposes internal, political changes that, to be effective, must be the result of larger alterations in the bloc in power and in the relations of force among classes.

The Concrete Manifestations of the Project

The nationalist project will also have implications for the future development of key activities in Mexico. In contradistinction to the liberal project, however, it does not exclude the participation of foreign capital, but seeks to subject it to its own program and to achieve a tighter integration of the national economy and under a different scheme of priorities. In terms of what they propose, both projects aim to make the country's capitalist development more rapid and more equitable. But there the similarities end, and the differences begin—above all in the definition of priorities as a function of the overall objective, the setting up of policies for achieving that objective, the political practice and social support on which those policies will be based, and the country's attitude toward imperialism.

The first of the priorities inheres in the actions to be undertaken in the rural milieu. It involves grounding agricultural and food self-sufficiency in the rehabilitation and strengthening of the traditional food producers, the peasants, by means of a coherent strategy based on state support and respect for peasant organization. The privileged subjects who would map out this strategy would be the peasants themselves, particularly those located in rainfed agricultural areas. Specific policies concerning the peasantry would then be defined around its particular needs, but always aiming at a more rapid development of its own potential. Above all, an attempt would be made to impose a substantial change of emphasis on agricultural development policy in order to effect a priority channeling of resources of all types to the most disfavored producers, in the belief that with sufficient support these strata of the rural population can also develop and produce surpluses.

Since the various policies composing this strategy would be made concrete through the organization of the producers themselves, peasant organization constitutes the central axis of the nationalist project with respect to the agricultural sector. Projects for peasant organization should of course take account of its innate heterogeneity and should consider, apart from regional differences, the substantial divergence that exists between peasant *ejidatarios* dedicated mostly to production for the market and those producing traditional items of consumption. The latter group comprises the majority and tends, moreover, to predominate in subsistence agriculture. In this context, too, permanent action on the part of the state is indispensable—to the end of preventing the free play of market forces from ruining *ejidal* organization and in effect robbing the project of substance by reducing it to a simple act of paternalism.

The current conflictual situations with respect to landholding in Mexico have their basis in the enormous mass of population formed by the rural underemployed for whom, up to now, there has been no political alternative to the indiscriminate invasion of lands. In the face of this problem, an in-depth revision of the system of land tenure would appear to be the first line of action. The needs of the rural population for better nutrition, employment, and overall welfare comprise yet another major problem to be resolved. As an essential point of reference in these areas it will be necessary to plan for the reorganization of *ejidatarios* and *minifundistas* as well as for the organization of day laborers, but without subjecting their democratic functioning to the interests of the state or to particular policies.

What we are proposing, in sum, is the establishment and consolidation of a system of operation for the traditional sector of the economy, on its own autonomous base, that would give rise to patterns of production and technological development congruent on the one hand with the global society's requirements for food and, on the other, with the expanded reproduction of the majority sectors within Mexican rural society.

Because of its strategic value and because of the historic struggle over its decolonization, oil symbolizes a crucial aspect of Mexican nationalism as perhaps no other element can. Therefore the defense of oil, in reality part of the defense of the nation, must not be limited to its economic or accounting dimensions; from a national perspective the question of oil is the question of the fate of all the natural resources necessary for the country's development.

As in the past, the nation will be living under the sign of oil in the decade now beginning. There are no clear prospects in the world for a lasting arrangement over the production, distribution, consumption, and prices of hydrocarbons; internally no minimally satisfactory economic evolution is conceivable without the export of a certain, even a considerable, quantity of petroleum. For this reason the debate—if it is to cease being fragmentary—must analyze the multiple dimensions inherent in the use of oil that, in the specific, current situation, reinforce its catalyzing role in regard to expectations and projects for national development generally.

The present discussion over the oil question, which points to an eventual broadening of the productive base, must therefore be situated within the higher compass of the political. In that context it would transcend both the merely technical domain and the field of economic-corporate interests. Reflection over oil policy, then, must be related to the overall direction of society and its strategic alternatives.

The nationalist project thus rejects the thesis that the production and export of petroleum will permit the country to attain a higher and more favorable level of development and that oil expansion should drive and determine the behavior of the economy as a whole. Instead, the project insists that the program of development for Mexican society as a whole must define the behavior of the petroleum sector. Even if oil permits the economy to take a breath and advance once again, the need for determining the pace and direction of its forward march is still urgent.

Achieving a more intensive and integrated process of industrial development—one that will advance in the mass production of selected capital goods, utilize the natural resources of the country more fully, be closely linked to the needs of state industry for inputs and equipment, and respond to established priorities in the fields of food production, education, health, and housing—constitutes the nucleus of the nationalist project's industrial policy.

From this objective derives the necessity to match production more closely to the needs, in this case, of mass consumption. Broadening demand will also lead to the exploitation and processing of the country's natural resources on location, which will contribute to a regionally more balanced growth. Broadened demand will lead toward utilizing the production of basic inputs to increase the country's supply capabilities and to promote the production of goods for popular consumption. Finally, by its very nature this set of industrial priorities will serve to speed up the production of capitalist goods within Mexico for the development of the agriculture, agroindustry, forestry, petroleum, steel, and other sectors.

Modernizing the country's industrial sector is now the unavoidable necessity. Leaving behind the false dilemma that identifies trade liberalization with modernization and efficiency, one must assume that the latter are products of society and history. Neither the class struggle nor constant action by the state toward eliminating private privileges—through fiscal policy and the systematic review of external protection, for example—is irrelevant to achieving a modern industrial sector. Making tax reform a reality, situating any review of protectionism within a framework of more refined industrial planning, and opening channels for dealing with workers' demands, are national paths toward the modernization of development, and can also be popular ones.

Other Implications of the Project

Without good diet, education, health, and housing it is difficult to exercise one's individual rights. In the nationalist project all these are social rights that determine basic priorities. To advance in the realization of these aims and to reduce, even eliminate, the accumulated lags, it is necessary to make development policy consistent with the effective exercise of these rights. An indispensable prerequisite is the generation of a greater amount of employment—not, however, as the ultimate objective of development policy, for employment does not constitute an end in itself. It is necessary to achieve a high and sustained rate of growth while the present structure of production is being altered.

In addition, industries such as energy, petrochemicals, steel, and fertilizers will have to continue to grow, using advanced technologies that are intensive in the use of capital per unit of production. The capital goods industry will also have to be promoted. To sustain the ensuing accelerated process of growth, the production of goods for popular consumption will have to be promoted more intensively; these are goods that, besides being basic, incorporate a greater quantity of labor and hence serve to help match production more closely to consumption. In some productive activities it will also be necessary to adapt imported technology to the situation of abundant manpower that prevails in the country and so to contribute to solving the problems of unemployment.

It is necessary to implement still other measures in support of the project: in particular, the form and depth for approaching the educational problem must be changed. Because of the importance that education assumes in the critical process of social and economic development, the state—and not private parties—must do everything in its power to attack the nation's educational problems with greater intensity. The definition of content by cycle, the design of new teaching methods, and the multiplication of aids to education are among the fundamental tasks to be carried out in order to eliminate the current shortcomings of the educational system.

If the right to health is to be translated into improvements in nutritional, sanitary, and hygienic conditions—and in general into an auspicious environment for the development of a dignified way of life—the solution of problems in these areas must also receive priority attention. The biggest governmental efforts in the health field must be oriented toward preventing sickness rather than toward medical treatment. In this regard it is essential to unify the various existing medical social security services and to establish common norms of operation for the state's actions. Their coverage must also be broadened to include the marginal groups and sectors, who require the most medical attention. Finally, it is necessary to pass from an individual and family concept of social security to a community one; in this process, systems of environmental hygiene, hygienic practices, and education for health must be considered matters of primary importance. Even if this implies conflicts of interest, it is necessary to reorient medical services and welfare services in general toward greater justice for the most populous and neediest groups.

The nationalist project seeks also to change the prevailing situation in regard to housing, giving priority to class solidarity and inverting the terms for benefiting from state programs in such a way that those most in need of housing will have quickest access to it. Indispensable preconditions are the unification of the housing services provided by the state and its agencies, and the solidarity of the labor movement. Likewise, in state schemes for constructing housing in the social interest it is necessary to go beyond the concept of individual property and to stimulate cooperative and municipal plans for housing, to be rented to the beneficiaries. In this way individual appropriation of the surplus value generated as the result of housing programs will be reduced, and even eliminated.

In Mexico all social reform and all significant modifications in the pattern of development have assumed that the state would set a mass politics in motion. This is abundantly demonstrated in the great moments in its history, in particular in the era of President Cardenas, when it became clear that the consolidation of the state and political system could take place only on the basis of an intense process of social and economic reform. There can be no socio-economic reform without a mass politics. There can be no mass politics without socio-economic reform. Nor can there be any consolidation or strengthening of the state without socio-economic reform, and hence a mass politics. The key for such a dialectic to render positive results to the nation lies in finding a way to translate it into state policy. Thus, if the popular classes are to be converted into the social base of the nationalist project, the state must be an active element in the reform process and must put a mass politics into practice. In Mexico such a politics has permanent, historic elements that define its basic profile. Nevertheless, in order to be effective it must incorporate all those elements that are producing the changes currently at work in the social structure.

The peasantry continues to be the major social contingent on which the nationalist project must rely. The differentiation that has taken place among agricultural producers over the last forty years requires the application of specific policies that take into account levels of development as well as access to land, types of crops, and regional peculiarities. Nevertheless, respect and support for the peasants' own organizations, as well as technical, economic, and financial backing, continue to be the main axes of a state policy that aims to be coherent with the project's overall objectives. In the countryside production, organization, and policy form an indivisible whole.

The presence of the working class is also fundamental. Because of the project's economic and political objective, and because of the need to equip the state to confront the external and internal pressures that its implementation will produce, the active participation of the labor movement in fact constitutes a keystone of the program. Nevertheless, that presence, as a mass presence, will be feasible only to the extent that labor organization increases, is restructured, and is democratized. At the same time, the workers' ties with the state will shake off their present, relative inertia and will assume the tutelary nature of labor law, with all its implications. The foundations of the nationalist project's labor policy are thus mass organization, internal restructuring, and effective labor justice.

The marginal population in the cities moves within a social and economic orbit very different from that of other classes. Moreover, it lacks an organization for conveying its problems to the authorities in systematic form, so that its communication with the institutional apparatus is sporadic, feeble, and dependent on official or meddlesome proxies. Whether this group participates in the project will of course depend on its degree of organization, and that in turn on the state's actions on collective consumption, supply of basic goods, the regulation of landholding, and so on.

It is also significant that the entrepreneurial camp, in spite of its apparent homogeneity, appears to be undergoing a process of redefinition and reshaping. Although the procedure creates difficulties for bargaining through the customary institutional channels, it does open up the possibility that the government carry out partial negotiations with important employer groups for creation of an employers' "pole" supporting government policy and participating actively, whether in association with the state or not, in major projects of economic diversification and access. The employers in question see their fate as linked to a broadening of the market and to the strengthening of the national economy. Locating these

groups, whether or not they form part of the new employer organizations, is thus a task of prime importance. Advances in negotiations with
them might even open the way for a more fluid and productive relationship with the whole propertied class, especially if the negotiations result
in putting joint projects into operation.

In the same vein, it should be mentioned that the bulk of the small and
medium industrialists and merchants have in fact been like putty in the
hands of the big economic groups who have taken the initiative in the
realm of employer policy. These sectors of the owning class constitute
the numerical majority and are undoubtedly of great importance in terms
of employment and even of investment. They are affected in a peculiar
way by the crisis, and lack mechanisms of institutional support. On account of their social importance, and because they represent a real possibility for the state to recover and augment its social base of support precisely in the area that now appears as the most conflictual, they deserve
emergency treatment on the part of the state.

The salaried middle classes today occupy a prominent place in Mexican society. Since they are composed essentially of the country's technical
and professional cadres, their political positions are usually of particular
importance, based on the extensive effects with which they shift and
make their views heard. Some segments of these classes—those, for example, whose activities are most closely linked to the development of education, culture, and in particular to public development projects—are in
principle more receptive to nationalist ideas than others. It can be asserted, for example, that professional technicians serving in areas where
labor is more highly socialized have a greater inclination to adopt political and ideological positions consistent with those of the project. This
may be seen most clearly in the state apparatus, and in particular in state
enterprises. It is here that organization will have to be strengthened and
the social and national import of the project propagated.

In recent years there has been insistent speculation about the prospects
for, and dangers of, a technocratization of the Mexican state and politics.
Such an argument, although it undoubtedly has a basis in reality, tends to
obscure differences of rank and background within the growing group of
technical experts and public administrators that the expansion of the
economy and state naturally produces.

Nevertheless, the acceptance and spread of technocratic roles within
the Mexican state is a reality that cannot be denied. This situation is demonstrated above all by groups of experts linked to the financial network,
for whom the economy and the society are to be subordinated to the at-
tainment of maximal values of the traditional, basically quantitative economic indicators. When such indicators are mechanically transferred

to the whole of society, their scale of measurement is completed by giving priority to stability at all costs, as well as by the acceptance, at the extreme, of an economic realism that has no room either for the calculation of social or political costs or for questions relating to national independence.

One variant of this position, which in practice may come to fuse with it to form an authentic technocratic coalition, is incarnated in certain groups of public administrators. These functionaries, who have reason to be preoccupied by the administrative crisis of the state, favor that position to the point of elevating it to the status of sole and exclusive key to the national "problematica" and would make politics a separate activity subordinated to the tasks of administration.

Without doubt, today more than ever before, good and efficient public administration forms part of any government program explicitly oriented toward confronting the problems of development. But politics, as the science of the state and as the art of resolving and channeling social conflicts, is the factor that must define the grand directions and mark out basic patterns for the administration to follow. As far as the nationalist project is concerned, this is an explicit and guiding principle.

Both for the specific goals of public administration imposed by the project and for the task of reorienting and restructuring the state agencies most closely connected to the popular sectors, the ideological education of administrative and technical cadres is also a pressing necessity. Adjusting the particular attitudes and ideologies of these groups to the terms of the nationalist project will not only assist in the formation of a bloc of socially and politically conscious experts on whom the project can rely. It may also, through discussion and open dialogue, broaden the ideological horizon and political behavior of many of those who presently form the technocratic groups' rank and file. This would imply not only equipping administration for greater efficiency, but above all forming technico-political cadres with a clear consciousness of the nation's problems, of the essentially conflictive nature of social reality, and of the social and political implications of the various strategic alternatives presented to them.

The possibilities for the success of what has been proposed up to this point will be considerably increased, to the extent that there is recognition on the government's part of the project's significance. Today, as never before, a nationalist project presupposes an alliance whose impact and effectiveness depend on the development of the forces that make it up, something that in principle works against all forms of paternalism and subordination. To be sure, the degree of political and ideological evolution of the forces mentioned here is very uneven; this poses at the outset serious challenges for the functioning of the alliance. However, if we are talking about translating the program into a set of lasting realizations, the predominant elements in any nationalist policy will have to be respect for plurality and congruence with the project's higher objectives: social justice and the strengthening of national development. For this reason the strategic role that democracy plays in this project must be paramount, above all when it is conceived as a long-range option.

ISSUES AND OPTIONS

The problem of reorientation of the state infrastructure to respond more effectively to the popular sector involves two larger issues that Mexico must address in the coming years. The far-reaching problems of inequality, in all its diverse manifestations, and the limits on autonomous control over the economic development process, are central historical issues that define the nature of Mexico's national development. Mexico's social course into the twenty-first century fundamentally depends on the steps taken to alter the future that these issues presently dictate.

Inequality

A great breach of inequality exists between Mexican rural and urban society. The tools of Mexican capitalism alone have been unable to alleviate this problem adequately. Although the neoliberals have proposed a solution based upon rapid industrial growth that would absorb rural and urban manpower and industrialize agricultural production, it is unrealistic to expect significant results.

To solve the problems resulting from this inequality, explicit decisions must be made by the state to set up massive and drastic programs for reallocating public resources, designed to lay a basis for continued revision of price relations between the urban and rural sectors and for raising rural income. The program must be long-term, not reducible to momentary and episodic actions, and must represent a permanent and integrated effort supported by the principal actors in the programs, through the organization of rural producers themselves.

Alleviating inequality between urban and rural areas and between regions will require new systems for the allocation of resources, thus raising the question of tax reforms in the broadest sense, i.e., a progressive revision of tax schedules and the implementation of an aggressive policy in regard to the prices and rates charged by public-sector firms.

Inequality also exists within the sphere of industrial production. Mexican workers today find themselves facing a very disarticulated and heterogeneous economic process that manifests itself in high rates of unemployment and underemployment. Both of these phenomena constitute a permanent threat to organized workers, both with respect to the stability of their jobs and to their effectiveness in achieving increases in real wages. This means that if workers are to obtain leverage vis-à-vis the producer, the organized labor movement cannot be indifferent to the orientation and content of the industrial policy. This policy is responsible not only for the growth rate of employment, but also for the average skill level of the employed work force and, to a great extent, for the conditions for its politicization. In the attempt to develop worker influence in the production sector, themes such as workers' control, co-management, and even self-management will demand increased attention in Mexico.

The National Character of Development

Thanks to Mexico's oil, the possibility of attaining higher levels of industrialization is at hand. Thanks also to oil, Mexico faces the enormous temptation to convert itself into a nation of *compradores*. Oil is only one of many factors that raise questions about Mexico's ability to determine its own course of development. Whether it will be able to pursue autonomous economic development or will be forced to bow under to the forces of economic global interdependence, remains to be seen.

The orientation that is impressed upon the evolution of the productive forces in terms of both pace and structure will determine the answer to this question. Without an expressed policy for the vertical integration of industry, designed to form a solid internal base for the accumulation of capital, neither greater national control over consumer goods industries, including intermediate goods, nor stricter regulations on investment from abroad will guarantee that development becomes more national and less dependent.

If Mexico is to retain national control over the evolution of the economy, it must make headway in determining the role and degree of participation of foreign capital; the level and intensity of natural resource exploitation; the development of long-range energy options; and the establishment of large industrial projects that will equip the country from within.

Matters relating to higher education, science, and technology must also receive greater attention. Scientists, technicians, and administrators of all types are strategic elements that must be fitted into Mexico's development framework; they cannot be isolated from the overall political battle that will be fought over the direction of the nation's economic development.

It is worth commenting on the problem of small and medium-sized productive and service enterprises. The fact that oligopolies have currently achieved a clear predominance in the Mexican economy has led people to ignore the social weight, and even the political potential, that these enterprises possess. In the context of a labor market so vexed by unemployment and marginality, small and medium enterprise has been a dynamic element in regard to jobs and in the supply of basic goods necessary for the subsistence of the popular sector. With a goal of a more nationally oriented development, it is impossible to disregard this potential although it is difficult to guide a strict development plan to incorporate these small enterprises.

The Popular Movement and National Options

Why is it that the near-term future will be defined by the issues just mentioned? It is, of course, because they sum up the great alternatives that are presently contending for dominance in the country. It is also because during the 1970s the popular movement in Mexico expanded, took on weight, generated programs, and in general entered the 1980s not declining but rather in the process of growth. It is this popular movement that will make the issue of inequality and national control of economic development central and defining ones in national life.

The popular movement to which we refer is a complex and heterogeneous social phenomenon composed of various classes, strata, and groups that possess different, even opposing, short-term interests. The hypothesis that the coming years in Mexico will revolve around questions of inequality and national independence is centered, above anything else, on the continued development of the popular movement.

Without any question, the complexity and heterogeneity that characterize this popular movement threaten solid and lasting progress. The movement must exercise solid leadership if it is to negotiate, through planning, the obstacles presently limiting the possibilities for implementing a project of development that will respond effectively to the needs and interests of the majority of the people.

The workers' movement has shown considerable signs of vitality and capacity to progress, and stands best prepared to take on the role of leader of the popular movement. Within Mexico's vast and complex popular camp the labor movement always appears as the most dynamic and coherent social force. It is true that depoliticization, repression, antidemocratic practices, corruption, and irregular and at times feeble growth have in good measure characterized the evolution of the country's labor organizations. Nevertheless, the international crisis, its effects on the Mexican economy, the wage policy combined with inflation, the distribution of the social product, and the uses to which the economic surplus have been put, all have given rise to the development of democratizing tendencies within the union milieu as well as to the revitalization of reformist plans within the union leadership.

The process of the union's internal renovation, which has democratization as its central axis, is furthermore a natural tendency as industry expands. The development of large enterprise, the growth, concentration, and greater education of the working population, promote a natural tendency toward democratization. The labor movement's effective conversion into a directing social force is, however, a process that is still in its early stages.

The direction and nature that national development should take, and the problems associated with a pressing set of social and economic inequalities, are intimately related. To the extent that it tempers inequality, development will be more national, and with a more just society the possibilities for defending the nation will be greater. Nevertheless, an economic growth combining defense of the nation with social justice will not occur automatically in the years ahead. On the contrary, the possibilities for an ever more dependent and denationalized kind of economic growth are real, and that kind of growth will not progress toward solving the popular classes' social, economic and political problems. The social forces, both internal and external, that are inclined toward a project of this type have gained ground over the last few years.

Large portions of the propertied class in fact, facing full economic crisis in recent years, have accentuated speculative and rentier inclinations, and today present a serious obstacle to any project of economic renewal that possesses a nationalist and popular orientation. Apart from this, however, and apart from market narrowing and the emergence of bottlenecks in agriculture and in some basic inputs and services—phenomena that are direct products of "stabilizing" development—there are other objective elements as well as elements of policy to be considered in evaluating the behavior of the capitalist class. Among the most important of these is the increasing weight of foreign capital in commerce and industry, in the face of which the bulk of national entrepreneurs see themselves as impotent and prefer the security of financial and real estate investments. Likewise, one must take into account the deleterious effect that inflation has had on investors' expectations. In the policy sphere in particular, it is well to keep in mind the effects of vacillation in global economic policy, and above all the great importance possessed by a monetary and credit policy oriented, under the pretext of achieving a stability that is today merely mythic, almost exclusively toward controlling credit supplies and money in circulation. These factors, together with the excessive industrial and financial concentration that typifies the Mexican econ-

omy, constitute the objective structural framework within which the behavior of entrepreneurs is presently situated.

For a propertied class formed in the hothouse of tariff, fiscal, and wage
policy protection, any change in development strategy, or even announce-
ment of change, introduces elements of uncertainty and confusion from
which the commanding heights of capital benefit, not only in terms of
their own expansion through absorption of other enterprises, but above
all in the shaping of an ideologically coherent capitalist bloc. Even when
observed objectively, the contradictions and fissures in the camp of the
propertied classes should be seen as the dominant elements.

It is necessary, in addition, to take into account that a sharp process of
ideological and even social differentiation has taken place inside the state
apparatus in the whole of its personnel and, what is more important, in
the groups that form the governmental coalition. The fact that many
members of those groups have been converted into property owners, and
even into prominent members of the employer community, constitutes a
differentiating element of the first order, both in regard to the daily business of government and with respect to putting into practice a set of measures of strategic and nationalist character. Furthermore, the exercise of
political power has taken place within, and has produced, a multitude of
institutions and norms. These in turn have caused a whole framework
of privileges, favors, and concessions tainted by corruption, to emerge directly, benefiting a good many of the groups referred to, and have also led
them to distance themselves further and further from popular interests
and sentiments. Many of the privileges that the bourgeoisie enjoy today,
and which to one degree or another would be seriously affected by a nationalist, not to mention a popular, reorientation of society, have been
translated into and are backed up by laws, regulations, and administrative agencies and practices. Modification of these legal-institutional crys-
tallizations will thus affect definite and powerful interests, and will require complex legal and bureaucratic proceedings in order to take place
within the frame work of a state of law.

Finally, the reorientation of Mexico's social and economic development in the sense described has been an obstacle and a danger to a state
that, in spite of advances and changes in recent years, still protects and
defends mass organization, particularly that of the labor movement. In
view of the boom promised by the advent of oil wealth, the leadership is
constantly faced with the temptation to seek out a new socio-political
accommodation. This would probably be discriminatory in content, but
would nevertheless benefit important nuclei of the working population.
In addition, the working population's capacity for mobilization, in a crucial and, on occasion, sharply conflictive situation in practice, is some-

thing that must still pass the test under not entirely favorable conditions, especially if one takes into account the lack of democracy and the history of persistent blockages to base-level participation that have attended its organizations. Under these circumstances, neither anyone nor anything can guarantee that even a partial turn in the direction of a nationalist project will not be translated into a strengthening of the corporatist-style domination that prevails today and that has been one of the most powerful social props for the so-called stabilizing government.

It is neither useful nor possible to sidestep obstacles or underestimate the dangers that have been referred to. That would be tantamount to ignoring present and social reality and wiping clean the slate of Mexico's more or less recent history. What we are attempting to set out here is the necessity of viewing these as obstacles to be overcome and dangers to be averted, not as definitive arguments against the viability of a national (and nationalist) path for the country.

Nonetheless, the inequalities and deficiencies of the popular movement, which have been noted; the complex, disarticulated, and deeply variegated panorama of the present socio-economic formation; and the masses' tradition of popular-national struggle, all allow us to affirm the fundamental relevance of what has been termed the constitutional project of development.

It remains to be seen whether the project contemplated in the 1917 Constitution will in and of itself permit that project to be turned into concrete political, economic, and institutional realizations. What does seem inevitable is that the Mexican people will have to journey—struggling all the way—along such a path toward qualitatively higher levels of social development. Otherwise, the most tangible prospects are for an even greater fracturing of Mexican society and its popular classes, a slow and tortuous growth of its laboring contingents, and a resulting permanent, organic weakness in the popular camp's possibilities for being converted into an active social bloc with transformative and hegemonic potential.

History's lessons show that nationalist options often involve negative implications for the majority and even for the development of the nation itself. Hence, the viability of the nationalist project depends upon the degree to which it is also able to be a popular project both in its content and in its predictable and concrete outcomes. Apart from this it is clear that there is no way for its promoters to aspire to mobilize, in the necessary degree, the social forces that the project requires in order to progress. At the same time, the very complexities of the social structure, the development registered by the totality of the working classes (with all its evident inequalities), and the growing difficulty and sophistication that affairs of state involve—especially in the face of the demands that the project imposes—make long-term social participation an element without whose aid the progress of the project seems uncertain or completely inconceivable. To put the matter succinctly, at the present time the implementation of a nationalist project such as the one sketched out here requires progressive doses of popular and democratic measures that cannot be looked on as mere temporary admixtures or concessions of a conjunctural kind, but rather must be seen as organic, constitutive elements of the project as a whole.

This must not, however, lead us to forget that the combination of these elements is problematic and at a given moment may come to be totally contradictory. Finding an optimal mix between them is an important challenge both to political imagination and to the tactical ability of the forces and groups promoting the project. It is also important to remember that once these difficulties have emerged they may give rise to premature and groundless frustrations. Also, promises are made today, openly or covertly, based on expectations from the oil boom. Social welfare, however, must respond to a productive logic of a wider scope if it is to avoid falling into an illusory improvement in incomes and consumption, supported basically by rents rather than evolved effectively out of the nation's economic capabilities. Welfare, if it is to merit the name, can only be viewed as a sustained and increasing stream of satisfactions whose enjoyment is generalized in an irreversible fashion. In a situation such as exists in Mexico, all this presupposes an enormous mobilization of internal resources that will restructure and augment supply. Anything else will stimulate a new scheme of disparities among and within classes—in particular among workers—that will give rise to a new incarnation of the corporative pact which has sustained the multiple exclusionary society presently existing in Mexico.

Without losing their ambivalence or departing from the general path imposed by the predominance of capitalism, both the social and economic reforms and the national tasks spoken of here present themselves as obligatory steps, as indispensable springboards for the construction of a new social regime capable of offering, as tangible possibilities, both general welfare and security as well as equality and democracy.

It can be argued that today the national and popular components of the project expounded here are in large measure inseparable from one another and that both find their concrete expression in a coherent program of social and economic reforms—a program inextricably linked, at its base, with the tradition, the great struggles, and the historic achievements of the Mexican Revolution.

Success in such a program depends not only on the existence of social forces objectively in need of it, or on the undoubted vitality of the traditions forged by the people in their struggles, or on the existence of material, human, and financial resources now considerably augmented by petroleum. It will also be necessary to put all these potentialities into effect, and above all to reach a situation where the social and material efforts inspired by this program are joined together in an authentic national project, giving them uniform shape or at least causing them to converge in a single mass. Such a project is an urgent necessity, especially if one takes into consideration that the other options at stake are also viable within the prevailing constitutional order and count on support from very powerful forces, forces which today fight on their behalf.

In this context, it is not idle to insist that the national and the popular movements require increasing mass participation, if they are to be expanded and converted into social realities. This participation can only aspire to become permanent by means of an ever-broadening democratization. For this reason, the question of democracy presents, from the outset, a problematic angle that cannot be resolved by means of a simple extension and broadening of parliamentary practice. To re-think democracy as an ascending process of social participation—one that overflows the traditional sphere of popular political affairs, transcends chambers, cuts across productive units, enthrones itself in rural communities and municipalities of every size, and that invades, conquers, or reconquers the corridors of executive power and the centers and redoubts of economic management and state administration—constitutes an indispensable exercise for the forces in Mexico that are struggling to implant a popular, national, and democratic form of development.

———◆———

Prospects and Options for United States Society

Luis Maira

IF ANY ONE characteristic distinguished the United States during the era of its constitution as a politically independent society, it was the close linkage that existed between the program and achievements of the founders of the nation and the coherence of the historic project that inspired their actions. From this viewpoint the United States appears not only as the first of the "new" nations that emerged as the result of the struggle against colonial domination, but also as the first country to define its political system and its productive structure in strict adherence to a precise political philosophy, in this case, liberalism.

As Karl Deutsch has commented in one of his works,

To be sure, the United States was not meant to commit errors but to be the world's first truly rational government. Its political system was shaped by the ideas of applied social scientists who were familiar with the social science of their time. Franklin, Jefferson, Hamilton, James Wilson, and especially Madison, all were men who had studied carefully what was then called "the science of government." These founders of the Republic were men who were deliberately trying to set up the United States as a piece of social engineering. They designed the American political system with several tasks in mind. It was designed for expansion across a continent, and in the minds of at least some, for further expansion across the oceans. It was also designed to attract capital from abroad and from within the country and to promote its investment in advanced technologies. And it was meant to give its inhabitants a better opportunity for spontaneity, freedom, and self-expression than could be found anywhere else.[1]

Several unusual factors undoubtedly helped with the realization of this new social project. Among them, experience with democracy and the mastery of administrative practice acquired within the political process during the colonial period, the relatively broad scale of an immigrant mass of

[1] Karl W. Deutsch, *Politics and Government: How People Decide their Fate* (New York, 1970), pp. 227–28.

diverse national origins, and the absence of ballast from a feudal structure and from long-standing aristocratic interests were certainly the most decisive. But all of these factors would probably not have resulted in such an original and vigorous country had they not lent dynamism by means of a vision of man, of economy, of government, of society, and of history that permitted their projection, in fruitful fashion, into the reality of that era.

The United States has managed to become, in this way, a country that has known only one mode of production, the capitalist, and only one form of political organization, liberal democracy, in the ever more marked variant of the presidential model that the constitutionalists at Philadelphia created. The fact that the same theory has dominated its development down to today, providing approaches and variants within a relatively restricted "ideological spectrum," has moreover been decisive in securing solidly the values and convictions inherent in its way of life, particularly in the spheres of property and individual liberty.

If we review the remarkable and prolonged negotiation that served to define the foundations of the state and nation between 1776 and 1791 (with the aim of determining the relevance of its ideas and conclusions), we will have occasion to reaffirm this notable link between political theory and plan of government, which constitutes at once its first great discovery and its contribution to applied political science. In that negotiation, in clear adherence to a common theoretical framework, the most complex contradictions of political organization were defined in exact balance and relationship: equilibrium between the prerogatives of the individual and those of authority, and between the jurisdictions of the states and the federal government. In like fashion, debate was initiated over strategies of development that led to exploring and deciding between the option of the United States as a modern agricultural nation or as a society that would embark upon the new alternative of urbanization and industrialization. The troubled debate that took place between Federalists and anti-Federalists during the initial years of the new republic, over its destiny and evolution, appears to have been equally fertile.

It is striking to note how, in the closing years of the eighteenth century, the strategic options that have organized political debate in the United States down to the present had already been clearly posed: whether, in regard to the tasks of the federal authorities, one should favor big government or limited government; protectionism versus free trade in the regulation of foreign commerce; isolationism versus imperial destiny in the conduct of international relations; and elitism (Hamilton's famous preoccupation with "the status of the rich, the wise, and the well-born") versus the humane and democratic spirit preached and defended by Thomas Jefferson.

The same constant of a clear inspiration in determinate politico-philosophical concepts has characterized the different readjustments and accommodations that the U.S. economic and political model has experienced over the course of its evolution.[2] On each occasion, particularly in periods of domestic or international crisis, in which the competencies and prerogatives of political actors have been redefined—usually with a tendency toward strengthening the federal government at the expense of the states' powers and simultaneously reinforcing the presidency at the expense of the power of Congress—the same inspiration has been recorded. So it was when Abraham Lincoln resolved to complete the process of the United States' democratization, when Theodore Roosevelt began to undertake the actions that would make the country a great imperialist power, when Woodrow Wilson decided to send U.S. armed forces to play a decisive role in the outcome of World War I, and when Franklin Delano Roosevelt signed programs for confronting and overcoming the Great Depression.

With the second Roosevelt, too, there began to be defined the bases of a great national project that would make the United States the world's foremost power after the Second World War and would for several decades assure its people levels of prosperity and expansion such as no country had previously known. Thus, if President Roosevelt became one of the principal figures of U.S. history in this century, it was above all because of his capacity to remodel the country's government and economy, again in conformity with precise political objectives and clearly established philosophic choices. This national project, the content of which was filled in during the Truman administration in the late 1940s, included a restructuring of political organization, of economic structures and the role of the state in their functioning, and likewise of the role of the United States in world politics.

The readjustment of the traditional political model that would lead finally to the "imperial presidency" began to be produced at the end of the 1930s.[3] Perfectly aware of the loss of capacity for leadership that presidents had been experiencing as a result of the growing complexity of state apparatus and functions, and of the risk of a progressive autonomization on the part of those bureaucratic interests that had begun to shape what later came to be called the "permanent government," Roosevelt set in motion the functioning of the commission that by 1939 had drawn up the Brownlow Report. Just as the chief of state had hoped, and

[2] See the analysis by André Tunc in his work *Les Etats Unis* (Paris, 1971).

[3] We concur with Schlesinger's analysis that the most decisive mechanism for redistributing powers between the Executive and Congress takes away the legislature's right to declare war, placing it de facto in the hands of the president, who exercised it in Korea and in Vietnam virtually without consultation or ratification.

in some measure induced, the conclusion of this group of experts was that the occupant of the White House needed a much broader and more flexible set of direct political advisors in order to guarantee effective direction of the different branches of government. Thus there emerged the Executive Office of the President, conceived as a kind of second government (a "personal" presidency capable of counterbalancing the "institutional" presidency constituted by the departments and central administration), with the aim of returning to the president control over the basic levers of political power and guaranteeing his capacity for leadership and mediation in the most complex matters. With the organic development of various bodies established in this office at the end of 1946, this presidential decision to recover the capacity for leadership in national affairs was realized with lasting effect. With the creation of the National Security Council, the existence of an instrument for coordinating all actions of the United States abroad, in the diplomatic, military, and intelligence fields, was also guaranteed (at least in theory).

With the setting up of the Council of Economic Advisors, the Executive was in addition endowed with a specialized body of consultants able to offer ideas on the future prospects of the economy, to assist him in elaborating principal economic plans and documents, and to offer him ways of securing better linkages among the different departments and public agencies that had to deal with the nation's ever more complex economic and financial activities. Moreover, by putting the Office of Management and Budget under his direct stewardship, the head of government was assured of control over the decisive factors in the balance of political power within each governmental organization: the ability to allocate public resources among different sectors and interest groups, and the right to restructure those sectors of government that exhibited low levels of political productivity or conflicted with the directions decided upon by the chief executive. The counterpart of this important readjustment in the political model was naturally a concentration of prerogatives that ended up destroying the last vestiges of equilibrium among the powers of state as intended by the classics of liberal thought and as envisioned by the nation's founders.

Recommendations extended, furthermore, to the functioning of the economy. From Roosevelt's New Deal to the application of the "New Economics" in the Kennedy administration, various developments manifested a process of constant expansion of the states' regulatory intervention both in the functioning of productive activity and in the achievement of specific social objectives. In the course of this expansion the United States took on the characteristics of a "welfare state," which for some time previously had been the European response to the progressive difficulties experienced in the capitalist state's functioning. Thus, between 1953 (the date of the creation of the Department of Health, Education and Welfare) and 1974 (a semi-symbolic moment in regard to the mature perceptions of its present problems), commitments for health, education, and social security programs, together with other income transfers, rose from 15 percent to 27 percent of total public spending. In the same period the expenditures of government increased from 28 percent to 33 percent of the value of GNP.

In this way, even though the negative attitude of U.S. political leaders with regard to expanding the scope of state property was not substantially modified, the economic functions undertaken by the public sector grew considerably, and government began to play a more active role in the resolution of periods of crisis.

Finally, we come to the redesign of the international system, which was effected as a basic complement to the government's efforts to deal with the principal threats then facing the United States; first, the expansion of Nazism and Fascism, and afterward that of the Communist world. In facing up to both perils, the U.S. political system was able to adopt, for the first time, a policy of alliances on a global scale, as well as to achieve a restructuring of the international order on terms favorable to its conceptions of how the world should operate. Once again Roosevelt's design in this area had a clear institutional projection, which went from the creation of the United Nations organization, in whose Security Council the political hegemony that the United States and its allies had begun to exercise in the new balance of forces was crystallized, to the Bretton Woods accords, which consecrated in unequivocal fashion the predominance of the dollar and of U.S. economic interests in the world's productive structure.

At the same time, in this ascendant phase, the government in Washington began to exhibit a great capacity to administer facets of its foreign policy with respect to regional and bilateral relations. A network of military alliances formalized in the years immediately succeeding the Second World War established a material and juridical bond for the military association linking capitalist countries, both developed and developing, with the United States. One also notes—in the creation of the North Atlantic, Central Asian, and Southeast Asian pacts, as well as in the Interamerican Reciprocal Assistance Agreement—precise forecasts of the most probable relations of forces in different regions and a well-measured selection of the countries that would fulfill the mission of being the United States' principal partners.

To assure maximum vitality for the new foreign policy framework, a basic accord between the two main parties concerning the nation's international objectives and activity was clinched at the end of 1946. This "bi-partisan approach," which would be ruptured only at the beginning of the 1970s in the wake of U.S. difficulties in the military conflict in Southeast Asia, was a decisive factor in permitting the successful management of U.S. interests in a Cold War context. Beginning with the formulation of the Truman Doctrine in 1947, the entirety of the state apparatus was thus able to act coherently and efficaciously in operations involving confrontation with the Soviet Union, which took place in various parts of the world. And in regard to the Truman Doctrine and the Cold War, it is significant that the formulation of the basic strategy of confrontation with the Communist camp, worked out in the State Department's Office of Policy Planning by George Kennan, served equally well to define a consensus for ensuring the cohesion of the diverse bureaus within the administration that participated in defining foreign policy, a fact that for thirty years provided the United States with the advantage of an apparatus.

Given all of the foregoing, one can assert that the results achieved by the United States from the end of the Second World War to the first half of the 1960s, besides being explainable on the basis of favorable factors of an economic kind, are to be comprehended above all in the ability of its political leadership to foresee and to manage the concurrent economic and political factors (both domestic and international) on the basis of programs and doctrines that shaped a global response. The overall design resolved in appropriate fashion the questions of how U.S. society should be organized and should function, and what its role as the principal force within the capitalist camp should be; it also made possible and guaranteed the prolonged prosperity of the postwar period.

Conversely, the inability to understand the limits of this project and the necessity to plan readjustments in it once its essential premises began to lose their relevance was a determining factor in the problems the United States has come to face in the last fifteen years. In other words, the phenomenon of capitalist crisis that emerged forcefully and persistently after 1966 made those limits evident and accelerated the exhaustion of the historic project formulated on the basis of Roosevelt's program. Thus, what has appeared objectively necessary for the United States for some years is to formulate an alternative just as global and complete as the project that has now lost its force, especially since under the new conditions the margins for correction and adjustment appear limited. In the absence of a response to this objective demand, the various elements of the crisis have naturally acquired greater speed and profundity and have become intertwined and complicated, to the point of provoking the difficult situation that currently conditions all efforts at future economic and political planning.

EXHAUSTION OF THE PROJECTS AND THE SHARPENING
OF THE CRISIS

It is virtually impossible to attempt to estimate the probable tendencies of United States society in the near term without estimating, in all their magnitudes, the elements of conflict and disorganization that have characterized the last few years and whose effects still persist.

Throughout the decade of the seventies the United States has seen the bases of its political and economic system shake and its leading role in the world change in a way that finds no precedent in history. Up to that time its political and economic evolution had always been characterized by an ascending trend, slowed only in the period stretching from the beginning of the great crisis in 1929 to the start of the Second World War. In that era, however, the nation's international position brought with it fewer linkages of interdependence with the rest of the world and imposed a direction function of lesser import.

The United States entered into crises following the last global attempt at rearticulating its aims and objectives through President Kennedy's "New Frontier" project, which was frustrated both by the brevity of its period of application and by the difficulties and opposition that some of its programs encountered. Coming immediately afterward, the "Great Society" program of President Johnson had narrower objectives but was compromised by the disorder and protest that marked almost the whole of his second term. From then on, both in the Republican administrations of Nixon and Ford and in the Democratic administration of President Carter, what has been attempted has been basically to search for correctives and partial solutions that might permit the crisis to be managed more or less effectively. In this context, the palliatives adopted have been less and less appropriate for setting things right again, to the point of displaying total insufficiency and incapacity in recent years.

In undertaking a reading of the crisis of the past fifteen years, the first thing that must be emphasized is its amplitude. This is expressed in all fundamental spheres of governmental activity in Washington: the operation of the political process, the behavior of the economy, and the nation's ability to affect, as well as to correct the functioning of, the international system. Today the dimensions and effective principal tendencies of that crisis form an inseparable part of the United States' future prospects.

The Political Crisis

One of the things that most surprises foreign observers of the U.S. political system is the almost absolute confidence, long maintained by political leaders, in the virtues and perfection of those forms in which the nation chose to organize its government. This has meant that neither leaders nor analysts have paid sufficient attention to the many disruptive factors inherent in its mechanism of political institutionalization, having lost sight of the precarious nature of the results of the negotiation that generated institutions and procedures, maintained up to now but hardly designed to confront the complexity of the contemporary political process.

A brief glance over these potential breaches of legitimacy, which date from the 1787 constitution itself or from various of its earlier normative complements, is appropriate. One might begin with the very mechanism for electing the system's principal actor, the president of the Republic, who by virtue of the functioning of the National Electoral College may reach the White House with only a minority of the popular vote, as effectively occurred three times in the nineteenth century. If modern liberal-democratic political systems seek to consecrate anything in a categorical fashion, it is precisely to assure the breadth of the support that those who aspire to govern must assemble in order to earn the right to exercise political power. Paradoxically, however, it has been impossible in the United States up to now to implement the principle of direct universal suffrage in the designation of the head of state, various proposals for amending the system having been either rejected or delayed, the most recent being that offered by President Carter in 1977, during the first months of his term. In the same vein, it is fitting to consider whether, in a situation where the president and the vice-president elected by a vote of the citizenry found it impossible to exercise their mandate, a legitimate procedure could be established by Congress for placing in the White House a candidate on whom the people had never had an opportunity to pronounce. Precisely this situation arose during President Nixon's second term, when the removal of Vice-President Agnew took place, followed very quickly by the resignation of the president himself when congressional approval for impeachment appeared imminent—the second such proceeding ever initiated against a head of state in the nation's entire history. It is astonishing, to say the least, that in a liberal-democratic regime, at a moment of maximum stress, it is accepted as legitimate to replace the holder of the highest political office with a potentially weak figure who may be unknown to the majority of the country and who lacks any direct political backing.

Several of the conditions under which Congress functions and the legislative process is carried out merit equal reflection. It is another virtually unanimous objective of political systems cast in the liberal-democratic mold to secure the maximum independence and separation between the legislators and the great organized interests that express themselves in society, whether these be employer groups, unions, professional organizations, or regional interests. In the United States, however, since the passage of the Lobbying Act in 1946, the right of all groups to try to influence the course of the process of rule-setting has been held sacred, so that the procedures by which professional organizations of lobbyists channel the views and resources of their constituents are required. In the last few years, with the extraordinary proliferation of lobbies,[4] a definite perception of the effects of this practice has begun to take shape. The most important thing to note, however, is that a direct link has tended to become established between bodies that function as pressure groups and specific firms, unions, or well-defined racial minorities whom they organize and control on a permanent basis. Hence, it is almost unnecessary to observe that, in the face of systematic assaults by organized forces who utilize intensively the most modern techniques and have set up national networks for laying siege to congressmen dealing with matters vital to their interests, it has become virtually impossible for congressmen, during the processing of any law, to make decisions with independence of judgment and consideration of the national interest. We are witnessing, therefore, a growing conditioning of the behavior of members of Congress that has been translated into an abandonment of the sharp political definitions (even without the liberal and conservative rubrics) that placed their seal on the work of the Congress up to the 1960s. In the past decade, as a result of the ever more organized and effective action of large pressure groups, we have indeed witnessed a virtual "psychological violation" of the true political will of members of Congress who, on many occasions, have been inhibited from interpreting the general interest of the nation and have had rather to act according to the dictates of the best-organized groups or of those with the greatest capacity to defend their specific interests.

To any inventory of the elements of the U.S. political regime that appear to foreign eyes as the determinants of increasing irrationality, one must also add the highly rigid character of the constitution itself in regard to reform. U.S. citizens are seldom surprised by the fact that the Philadelphia Charter has in practice undergone only fifteen amendments.[5] This is due fundamentally to the large number of requirements

---

[4]The estimate of offices that really operate, even though not registered with the secretaries of the House and Senate as the law requires, is approximately twelve to thirteen thousand.

[5]Specialists consider that the first ten of the present twenty-six amendments were part of the original constitutional process; amendment 21 (1933) had as its object the repeal of amendment 18 of 1919.

that accompany any attempt at constitutional reform, and not to the lack of a need to update or complement the basic law governing the fundamental principles of the country's political organization. The fact that three-quarters of the states of the Union must approve an amendment through express resolution of their legislatures, and that both branches of the federal legislative power must approve the text before it comes into effect, introduced a factor of uncertainty during the pre-ratification period and generated considerable difficulty in finding up-to-date and convenient rules for facilitating the restructuring of the political model and for aiding with its proper functioning.

Critical observations may also be extended to the functioning of the party system in the most recent period. Although a system of two great parties is supposed to guarantee security in the political process and to assure a constant flow of ideas regarding the framing of the nation's political and economic development (so that they contribute to its effective renewal), in practice the role of the parties has become less and less substantial and creative. Their lack of national dimensions has become accentuated to the point where one may well assert that in the United States there are a hundred political parties—two in each state—instead of the two that exist formally.[6] Both national committees have become simply coordinating bodies that lack the power to impose definite lines of action and organization throughout the Union. The plurality of points of focus and interest within the two great political forces is thus also accentuated, and in turn conspires against both their effective functioning and the coherence of their actions. If to this we add the recurrent, negative impact on the richness of political debate—the fruit of publicity campaigns launched through the mass media—we can see that a new level of mediation permits large groups and organized interests in search of support to appeal directly to the citizenry, bypassing that channeling function between global determinants and the demands of civil society that constitutes the essence of political parties' functions.

All of this has conditioned the gradual impoverishment of U.S. political life and also the ever-broadening chasm that divides the quality of its scientific production, the work of its principal universities, and the contributions of its most influential newspapers and magazines from the elementary level of political discussion as observed at election time. From a similar perspective, the passivity and skepticism of the electorate, which sees an abstention rate on the order of 50 percent of the registered voters as practically normal—making it very difficult for the new president to

---

[6]This was the judgment of the French political scientist Maurice Duverger, in *Instituciones Políticas y Derecho Constitucional* (Madrid, 1973).

reach the White House with the support of more than 30 percent of the electorate—seem almost natural.[7]

If a political system in which these negative factors are at play also registers the virtual absence of any capacity to "think" on a national scale and to define new political paths and strategies of development, it has met all the prerequisites for a situation of stagnation and lack of flexibility to pass over into a real crisis, as has in effect occurred.

Events in the United States at the end of the 1960s—the student rebellion in some universities, the protest movement against the war in Vietnam, the development of radical tendencies among various ethnic minorities, and the Watergate upheaval, which constituted a crystallization of diverse problems encountered in the functioning of government—were significant in revealing to new sectors of the population the problems of the capacity of the political system to assure an appropriate direction to affairs. As was clearly reflected in several of the Gallup organization's surveys to measure trust in certain U.S. institutions, this translated itself in some sense into a problem of legitimacy.[8]

This new opinion was clearly reflected both in the congressional elections of 1974, which brought to the Capitol one of the largest bodies of new Democratic legislators in memory, and in the 1976 presidential election. In the latter the determining factor, first in the political ascent of Carter and then in his victory, was his capacity to question the conduct of the whole of Washington's "political class" and to present as a contrast to its vices and weaknesses an image of rectitude, honesty, religiosity, and above all lack of connection with political affairs in Washington—something that in any other context would have been a point in his disfavor. At that moment, resolving the legitimacy problem of government had come to be more important than proposing substantive solutions to the country's economic and social problems. In this same vein the 1976 Democratic platform sought simply to mediate between the liberal and the conservative points of view, accentuating further the predominance of the former in regard to social issues but permitting the hegemony of the latter when the time came to define economic policy proposals.

Today the results of this choice appear fairly clear. A normal handling of the powers of the White House helped rapidly to return to the presidency its historic halo of trust and permitted the trauma of Watergate to

---

[7] In 1976 the president was elected by 29 percent of those eligible to vote, and in 1980 the winning candidate received less than 27 percent of the potential vote.

[8] An exception to the descending level of the grass-roots evaluation of political parties, unions, and the national press, prior to the early 1970s, was a relatively stable degree of confidence in the presidency and the Supreme Court. Between 1972 and 1973, however, a third of those who formerly trusted in the occupant of the White House ceased to do so.

be overcome. It was then possible to turn once again from the issue of legitimacy to the problem of administrative efficiency, which led to demands on the president to resolve the various conflicts being experienced by the nation, something that had not really been at the center of the Democrats' political designs in 1976.

In any case, what seems clear at this point is that the problems of the functioning of the U.S. political system lie not only in the question of "trust" in, or "credibility" of, the institutions, but also in an operational problem concerning the capacity of government to confront and resolve the principal problems that the country experiences; to assure minimum coherence in action to the distinct segments of the federal administration; to control and allocate financial resources; and to achieve concerted action between the public and the private sectors. From this point of view, a certain kind of conservative reasoning, such as that of Samuel Huntington in his well known work on the "Crisis of Democracy" for the Trilateral Commission, is quite correct in posing the problems of U.S. political organization in the realm of "governability."[9] This is in truth the most permanent aspect of the crisis, all the more so in particular situations such as that produced by the investigation into the behavior of President Nixon, when matters of political ethics acquired temporary preeminence.

Thus the continuing challenge consists of determining through what mechanisms and reforms rationality can be restored to the government of the United States; by what more effective means the functions of the state apparatus can be fulfilled, a projection beyond its proper sphere permitted, and its capacity to direct the whole of society reestablished—something that constitutes an inescapable task for any serious state.

The Economic Crisis

The discussion becomes even more complicated when we introduce a second dimension affecting U.S. society: the economic crisis. In the 1970s the United States saw itself affected in particular by two phenomena whose effects have been profound and prolonged. The monetary crisis, with the suspension of the convertibility of the dollar in 1971, had forced the dismantling of the entire scaffolding that had assured the United States a predominant position in the world economy for more than twenty-five years; and a recession occurred—the second deepest of the century—coinciding with an increase in the rate of inflation that led economists to consider that just as grave as the recessionary tendencies

[9] It is significant that the question of the U.S. system's political crisis has ceased to be a theme only for radical sectors and has come to constitute a preoccupation of some of the establishment's most lucid defenders.

was the ineffectiveness both of the theoretical instruments used to spark reactivation and of the economic theories then in vogue to offer any reasoned explanation of the new phenomena.

This economic crisis, whose erosive effects were magnified by the political climate in which it emerged, was much more prolonged than the previous crises in the postwar era (1953, 1955, 1960, and 1970); was accompanied by a fiscal deficit of enormous size, reaching a volume of approximately $100 billion by 1975; and coincided with high unemployment among the work force and under-utilization of installed capacity, which also reached impressive levels—so high, in fact, that the final estimate of the difference between the real GNP for 1974–75 and that which would have been achieved with full utilization of all resources was calculated to be close to $200 billion.

From that moment onward, the principal economic indicators have maintained a trend that has confirmed the most pessimistic projections of those who had spoken, at the beginning of the seventies, in terms of a long recessionary wave. In this context the position of the United States in the world economy has also suffered important reverses. The key question—the competitiveness of some of its industrial goods, goods that predominated in world markets for decades—is far from resolved; on the contrary, it is tending to become more complicated as the specialized productive development of intermediate countries and of those relying on export platforms increases the list of U.S. products that cannot meet the competition even in their own domestic markets.

In addition, the vulnerability of the economy has spread in recent years to two new and sensitive areas: energy and inflation. In 1979 the doubling of oil prices alone obliged the United States to pay out $45 billion of the $200 billion constituting the surcharge to the world's consuming countries. And this is one of the factors explaining the 13 percent increase in consumer prices that the nation recorded that year, thus entering the circle of countries with double-digit inflation, something that U.S. economists had often looked upon as a distant threat. The final report on the domestic economy that President Carter presented to Congress in January 1979, notwithstanding ritual phrases designed to promote a certain optimism about the future of the economy, failed to hide the somber panorama that emerges from the figures and projections.*

It is certain that the recent unfavorable results have been partly influenced by the erratic course of the previous administration's economic

---

*Editors' note: Subsequently the Reagan administration has seen the confirmation of those forebodings and by mid-1982 the economy faces record levels of unemployment, under-utilization of industrial capacity, and sustained fiscal deficits, the financing of which has produced the highest real interest rates in modern U.S. history.

policies, above all by the fact that in the middle of its term the Carter administration abandoned many of the targets originally set out as key objectives, such as the search for fiscal balance and the development of programs for reducing unemployment. But in this regard, too, the fundamental problem continues to be that it is no longer possible to simply try to administer the crisis; rather, it is necessary to undertake a whole series of changes at the structural level.

The Loss of International Hegemony

In many of the analyses designed to explain the United States' relative loss of position in world politics, the villain is perceived to be the impact of the passage from a bipolar to a multipolar world in which political bargaining has become more complex while the great powers' margins for hegemony shrink inexorably. This is a very complex factor if it is connected with its military implications, especially in view of the fact that the rise of both Japan and the German Federal Republic in the capitalist domain, and that of the People's Republic of China in the socialist world, have not been accompanied by a proportionate increase in their defense potential or by the assumption of greater responsibility in the security field. Therefore the combination of "political multipolarity" with "military bipolarity" continues to bring with it, for superpowers born in the previous bipolar era, practically the same responsibilities as before but no longer with a clear concession of leadership in international affairs.

This comment is especially valid for the United States, which has witnessed a sizable reduction in its relative global economic significance and power that, measured by the crudest indicator, translates into a drop in its share of the world's GNP from 50 percent in 1945 to 21 percent at the beginning of the present decade.

With respect to its political impact, the reduction of the United States' capacity to influence the international situation has been reflected in a number of ways, all of which are disquieting in terms of Washington's power. In the first place, the defeat in Southeast Asia led to a drastic reduction in its sphere of influence in that region, to a liquidation of important military alliances, and to a loss of global credibility in regard to attaining objectives that its leaders elevated to the status of being strategic. A second impact occurred by virtue of its setbacks in Africa, which began with the liquidation of the Haile Selassie regime in Ethiopia, with the implantation of numerous socialist experiments following the crumbling of the Portuguese colonial empire, and with the impossibility of sustaining the dominant position of white regimes in Southern Africa. All these phenomena gave rise to national struggles that in turn paved the way for radically oriented governments that, in general, look upon the United States as an adversary and have established alliances of varying degrees of intensity with the Soviet Union.

In Latin America, after the successful application of the containment strategy designed by Secretary of State Henry Kissinger—a strategy that in the early seventies succeeded in reversing the leading role of governments with nationalist or socialist projects, such as the military regime of Velasco Alvarado in Peru or the government of Salvador Allende in Chile—a new flowering of leftist experiments has occurred in Central America and the Caribbean, provoking convulsions and deep, generalized confrontations that have either liquidated or are causing to totter some of the oldest authoritarian regimes in the region, all of which define themselves as Washington's staunch allies.

Another determining element in the most recent international situation has been the active mapping out of a strategy contrary to U.S. interests on the part of countries from the so-called Third World, both through the creation of blocs grouping together countries producing strategic raw materials—of which OPEC and the International Association of Bauxite Producers are the most significant experiments—and through coordinating organs such as the Movement of Non-Aligned Countries or the Group of 77, in which the more radical countries have gained important influence in defining the platforms and programs of struggle.

As its own production percentage in relation to world energy consumption has declined, the United States has come to be directly involved in an energy crisis with respect to which, after the embargo and price rises that followed the Yom Kippur War in 1973, it had appeared initially to be in a much more advantageous position. In spite of the fact that the efforts undertaken by the Carter administration in this regard met with significant success, in the next few years—and until the long-range goals of the plan to conserve and re-equilibrate energy sources are achieved—this situation will continue to be an Achilles' heel as far as U.S. international hegemony is concerned.

Only in Europe, and there only in partial form, does one note in recent years important advances for U.S. interests. There the danger that governments of the extreme left might come to power in France and Italy, which around 1974 or 1975 appeared to open the possibility of putting into practice the ideas of Eurocommunism, has been somewhat abstracted, notwithstanding the recent more moderate socialist victory in France. A transition from authoritarian rule to moderate democratic regimes has been effected in Portugal, Greece, and Spain without the spectacular ascent of left forces in those countries. In addition, an effective *modus vivendi* has been attained with the rest of the governments in the area, a development favored by the consolidation in power of regimes clearly advocating an Atlantic perspective, such as those of Margaret Thatcher in Britain, the new coalition government in Sweden, and the current Portuguese government.

All in all, the picture in its entirety is far from offering easy prospects for a recomposition of U.S. power as we have known it up to the start of the present crisis. These problems are reflected particularly in the complex situation in the Middle East, with the loss of one of Washington's most strategic allies, Iran. The 1982 Israeli invasion of Lebanon raises new questions. How will it affect the rallying power that the Palestinian cause has provided for the radical Arab nations, almost all of which are grouped together in an active, anti-U.S. front because of Washington's support of Israel—a fact that has determined the U.S. government's virtual incapacity to resolve effectively the grave conflicts in the Persian Gulf? Probably nothing better reflects the United States' new and more difficult situation than the marginal role that U.S. diplomacy has been able to play in the Iran-Iraq conflict, its fruitless maneuvers for resolving the situation of the former employees of its embassy in Teheran, and the total inefficacy of the pressures it has exerted toward obtaining the withdrawal of Soviet troops from Afghanistan. Was any of these situations even imaginable in the immediate postwar years?

Naturally, this recounting should not lead us to conclude that the United States has ceased to be the principal guiding force in regard to the conditions for world order, or that we wish to ignore its primacy within the domain of the capitalist world. Our focus is directed to a more specific point; in the past few years profound and irreversible events have restricted its former margins of maneuver as well as the possibility of organizing the international system. The capacity to take decisions that will be adhered to by other nations, either developed or developing, has been altered. Beginning with the Teheran and Yalta conferences, the United States organized the postwar world and determined the rationales for all international affairs for nearly three decades. It is this capacity, not power in absolute terms, that it has lost in the context of the current crisis. Recovering its former role may be the project of some conservative sectors in the United States; nevertheless, realizing this task under the new conditions seems extremely difficult, even unimaginable.

OPTIONS FOR RESTRUCTURING U.S. SOCIETY

U.S. leaders project a very poor image, owing to the weakening of the parties, when it comes to defining the form in which the nation might overcome the crisis of the last few years and find new paths in which to orient its future. There is no doubt, however, that in influential circles of specialists interesting and far-reaching projects are being elaborated that may serve to frame the options the United States will face in the years to come.

The lack of capacity exhibited by the leaders of the two major parties in face of the evident necessity to provide global responses to their current problems became particularly apparent in the 1980 presidential election. While all the studies, analyses, and surveys were pointing out that the citizenry's real worries were directed to basic questions such as the preconditions for a new and dynamic push forward in the economy, the recovery of the United States' leading role in the world, and the reforms that are indispensable to any revitalization of government and political regime, the public debate consisted of nothing more than a succession of disputes over points of transitory importance or, in the best of cases, over isolated issues in regard to which reciprocal accusations ended up being more important than the proposals being made.

This situation obliges us, if we wish to explore the outlines that will guide the formation of a new national project—one that will reestablish the role that ideas have played in the design of the nation ever since the era of its birth—to direct our gaze not to the political parties but rather to those currents of thought and institutions that, because they are preoccupied with formulating policy proposals, have undertaken a global examination of and reflection upon the United States' future. Among these visions there are two that appear to us to be especially important. They bring together diverse elements that have permitted a national hearing and impact for their ideas, and they are linked in quite direct fashion to economic sectors that have had a dominant position in the country since the start of the Industrial Revolution just after the Civil War, when the nation's capitalist path was consolidated. We refer first to what may be called the neoconservative current of thought, one of the most active theoretical foci in the United States since the middle of the last decade, and secondly to the project elaborated by intellectuals and policy formulators who operate within the context of the transnationalization process that has its principal expression in the reports of the Trilateral Commission.

The importance of these two proposals resides, moreover, in the fact that the leaders advocating them maintain tight links to the two main parties, which (paradoxical as it may seem) permit their programs to be expressed through channels that, even though weakened, continue to be the only viable ones for lending a truly national dimension to new political projects.

The Neoconservative Project

In the contemporary history of the United States, there have existed numerous conservative and far-right organizations. Referring only to those that have played an important role in the period since the Great Depression, one could point to the Ku Klux Klan, with its racist views, the National Union for Social Justice of Father Charles Coughlin (probably the U.S. organization closest to Fascist thought), McCarthyism, the John Birch Society since 1958, and the "New Nativism" of Governor George Wallace in 1968. Many of these have had a national impact and significant numbers of adherents, reaching even into the millions. Nevertheless, as far as their influence is concerned, these have been movements of short duration that early took on a definitive character, almost all anti-Communist or racist, i.e., reactionary in the technical sense of the word, which caused them to lose steam almost as fast as they erupted upon the national scene. From an ideological point of view, they were movements that were unable to go beyond the narrow, ghetto-like visions characteristic of particular subcultures.

By contrast, the most significant factor in the emergence of the neoconservative current of thought in the 1970s was its national scope, its aspiration to offer a program for the whole of U.S. society, and the rapidity with which it has developed a capacity to confront the other currents and points of view that animate political debate in the United States. In its origins this current constitutes a response to several of the principal phenomena of the late 1960s, especially the appearance of the New Left, which welded together young intellectuals opposed to the Establishment, and the emergence of the liberal bloc that achieved a brief predominance within the Democratic Party, and in which the youth, women, and anti-war elements that pushed the candidacy of George McGovern at the end of the 1972 convention played an important role.

While these groups rapidly declined, the group of intellectuals who organized to oppose them from a radical right standpoint went on gaining influence. A cluster of intellectuals of national reputation, such as Irving Kristol, Daniel Bell, Seymour Martin Lipset, Nathan Glazer, Samuel P. Huntington, and Daniel P. Moynihan, they achieved an unheard-of feat: they permitted the neoconservative view to pass over to the offensive in an ideological confrontation of national scope.[10] The fact that this circle of intellectuals rapidly organized itself throughout the Union with the establishment of a series of study centers, and that they received support from the most representative groups of the business community, gave them the ability to broadcast their views from very well placed rostrums.

[10] See "Perspectiva de un viraje conservador en Estados Unidos y su impacto en América Latina" (presented to the seminar "América Latina en los 80," in Rio de Janeiro in September 1980 under the sponsorship of CLACSO and the International Relations Institute of the Catholic University of Rio de Janeiro, for my detailed recounting of the principal works of these neoconservative intellectuals and their critics.

An equally novel style, for right-wing sectors, began to stand out in their arguments. In place of the defensive posture characteristic of most conservatives, this new group exhibited a confidence and aggressiveness that led them to speak in terms of scientific objectivity and of correct approaches to social analysis, treating liberal or leftist intellectuals as people living in an illusory world dominated by ideologized visions that offered no hold on real life.

Another peculiar element of the new historical project elaborated by neoconservatives is that it has abandoned the empiricist tradition and organized itself around very basic propositions of political philosophy in regard to its vision of man, government, and society; it is on the basis of these theoretical constructs that neoconservatism seeks to build up an "alternative common sense" to that which has prevailed in dominant U.S. ideology in recent decades.

Although obviously aware of the necessity to face up to the need to restructure U.S. capitalism, neoconservatives conceive this task starting from a denial of the existence of any structural crisis in the country. They believe that the problems and conflicts that the United States is facing, in all spheres, cannot be explained on the basis of economic phenomena or by virtue of trends in the productive structure, but rather are the result of the erosive effects worked upon the nation's ideals by a counterculture ("adversary culture") that has caused the people to lose confidence and power, to the point of causing economic decline. This would not have been possible, however, if values and tendencies had not secured positions within the U.S. government that served to broaden the functions of the state, weaken the power of private initiative, and favor a virtual liquidation of the values and principles of authority.

A basic element of neoconservative discourse is thus a cutting rejection of all policies that have led to a broadening of governmental activity and an increase in public spending. In this fashion it recovers, in a new form, the classic preoccupation with avoiding Big Government and the Big State, asserting that after the New Deal state expansion was translated into an "overloading" of the activity of government that has ended up installing a "paternalistic state" in the United States. As Jude Wanniski has pointed out,

the only road open to the government to increase production is to make work more attractive than non-work. There are only two options consistent with this assertion. Either government increases the attractions of work or it decreases the attractions of non-work. Government can make productivity and work in the money economy more attractive than work and idleness in the domestic (or barter) economy by reducing the weight of regulation, taxation, or the level of tariffs. Likewise, the government is in a position to make non-work less attractive, whether by reducing subsidies for non-work (welfare system benefits) when they exist, or by increasing penalties for not working.[11]

As an alternative to state intervention, then, what is being brought to the fore is a revaluation of entrepreneurial initiative, at the same time that a decentralization of public functions is favored by proposals broadening the powers of states and local governments. This is congruent, moreover, with preoccupation over the restoration of traditional values and with the search for new social supports for the family and for religious values, inasmuch as the nation's solidity is seen to rest in large measure upon these foundations.

Finally, in this project there is a clear view of the world that has revitalized the notion of a "confrontation of civilizations" characteristic of the vision of the whole Cold War epoch. Neoconservatives thus recommend that we return to a global approach reemphasizing that the central competition in the contemporary world is between the United States and the Soviet Union as heads of the Western and Communist blocs respectively. Starting from this premise, they conclude that the positions of different countries in regard to this central conflict should determine the quality and intensity of the relations that the United States maintains with the other members of the international community. In a similar vein foreign policy comes to be fused with defense, and diplomatic activity is conceived primarily as an exercise to adjust the behavior of other governments to decisions adopted in Washington.

It is also important to point out that, although the neoconservative nucleus does not possess a precise party definition linking it officially with the Republicans, as is confirmed by the presence within it of an influential Democratic senator such as Moynihan* and one prominent collaborator in the Carter administration's National Security Council (Samuel P. Huntington), in practice its ideas are quite congruent with the new conservative hegemony that in the past few years has secured itself within the GOP around Ronald Reagan. This explains why a large number of the ideas, hypotheses, and proposals that its principal spokesmen have elaborated served as the basis both for the Republican platform in Detroit in 1980 and for the formulation of new policies prepared by teams of specialists in areas of economic, social, foreign, and security policy being implemented by the subsequent Reagan administration. In some fashion, therefore, this project has served as a reference point for the ideology of

[11] Cited in Roberto Bouzas, "La reorganización capitalista y el programa de Ronald Reagan," CIDE (Mexico, 1980), p. 7.

* Editors' note: As of 1982 Moynihan was said to be targeted for neoconservative opposition for his supposedly liberal views, illustrating the complexity of this issue.

the current administration, and some of its premises are being subjected to a decisive confrontation with reality as this volume goes to press. Nevertheless, this affinity should not lead one to conclude definitively or necessarily that the neoconservative project as such will constitute the Reagan administration's sole source of theoretical inspiration. That sort of prospect would have required, among other things, a coherent presentation of these ideas on the part of the Republican candidate during the presidential campaign, in such a way as to establish clearer linkage between such thinking and the will of the people, as well as a degree of homogeneity in the programs and team of the new administration that one cannot anticipate being realized and that has already been criticized by the more extreme spokesmen of the new right.

The Project of Transnational Reorganization

Whereas the program of neoconservative restructuring springs from reflection in the field of political philosophy and takes the U.S. national state as its spatial frame of reference, this second vision takes as its point of departure economic problems that are linked to international reorganization and seeks to define common criteria for the whole of the developed capitalist countries rather than solutions valid only for the United States. At the root of the original project, elaborated by the Trilateral Commission from 1973 onward, is the supposition that the national state tends to be bypassed as the organizing instance of political processes and that the crisis of capitalism, as it becomes more prolonged and its effects more complicated, imposes first of all the necessity to resolve certain problems of global management. A new actor, whose interests serve to redefine all processes, must be taken into account: the transnational enterprise. In this regard it suffices to recall some of the remarks of Zbigniew Brzezinski: "Multinationals are a creative way of adapting to the emergence of an interdependent world. Flexible and transnational instruments for the diffusion of technology, practical knowledge, capital, and production, . . . they prepare the way for real cooperation on a world scale; the final and logical culmination will be the end of the national entity and of national governments as we know them." [12]

It is interesting to recall that Brzezinski, in the prologue to *Communist Systems in Comparative Perspective* (1973), had already put forth the hypothesis of a progressive loss of competitiveness by the capitalist state and by liberal-democratic governments in the face of Communist political systems. In his judgment, in order to find in the Western world an

---

[12] Cited in *América Latina: los desafíos del tiempo fecundo*, ed. Sergio Spoerer (Mexico, 1980), p. 49.

equivalent to the centralization and effectiveness of political decisions in the East, the only possible reference point would be the leadership of the large corporations. Thus he commented, "My own view is that, either in 'degenerating' or in 'transforming' themselves, the several Communist systems will develop political processes and forms which will not duplicate the Western 'pluralist' or 'liberal' experience but which more likely will borrow from the administrative and technological experience of modern large-scale economic organization—and that their success or failure in so doing (i.e., transforming or degenerating) will be very much conditioned by the specific political settings of the several countries concerned." [13]

It is at this point in the argument that the hypothesis of a "crisis of democracy" emerging as a consequence of the loss of governability of liberal-democratic regimes in the form sketched out in the eighth report of the Trilateral Commission comes to play a functional role. This is also a point of consensus between transnational vision and the neoconservative, although it could well be argued that the same ideological construct plays a quite different role in each. In the case of the latter, the goal is to resolve the excessive "overloading" and distortion encountered in democratic regimes in order to create more favorable conditions for policy coordination in key capitalist countries. In this way the most crucial questions of global management may be broached and, with their resolution, favorable conditions created for the developed capitalist countries collectively to emerge from the crisis.

What are these central problems? Basically, they are those that engendered the policy recommendations set out in the early years of the Trilateral Commission reports: the establishment of a new international monetary system; the definition of new patterns of world trade, a redefinition of the forms of international cooperation, and the management of North-South relations; a legal framework for the oceans appropriate for exploiting the riches of the seabed; redefinition of the conditions for the functioning of world markets in raw materials; and the reform of international institutions and the creation of new mechanisms of consultation at the international level.

More than differences in approach, a point of capital importance that serves to demonstrate the basic antagonism between the two projects is the perception the second group possesses of the evolution of East-West relations. The supporters of the trilateral approach evaluate the partial agreements reached between the United States and the Soviet Union within the framework of a policy of détente. Naturally they believe that

[13] *Communist Systems in Comparative Perspective*, ed. Leonard J. Cohen and Jane P. Shapiro (New York, 1974), pref., p. 11.

there is a contradiction between the West and the Communist camp, but they are much more optimistic with regard to the possibility of avoiding nuclear conflict with the U.S.S.R. In the deepest sense, for them it is fundamental to create political conditions that will make the whole world (including the area controlled by the socialist countries) a market suitable for circulation of the products, technology, and financial flows of capitalism, of whose superiority they have no doubt. And in this view the socialist world is seen as a large potential field for new business and activity.

For this reason we find at the root of the recommendations made by this group, connected as it is to the most transnationalized sectors of the First World, acceptance of the challenge of peaceful coexistence in the form laid down by former Soviet Prime Minister Nikita Khrushchev at the twentieth congress of the Communist Party of the Soviet Union. They know that in détente there are risks, but they have faith that intelligent negotiation aimed at progressively broadening the open spaces for products and credits from the United States and its allies will in the end open the way for Western values and habits. By this slower and more oblique path they believe it is possible to consolidate the reign of their own way of life, particularly when one takes into account that the growing antagonism between the Soviet Union and China offers the countries of the West ever greater possibilities for diplomatic maneuvering.[14]

These, then, are the themes and the program of the second main approach pointing toward a global restructuring of the capitalist system, and one that we believe will exert a significant influence over the political debate in U.S. society in the next few years. Although the most frequently heard analyses (especially in Latin America) tend to associate this body of ideas strictly with the Carter administration, in our opinion this is a mistaken association based solely on the impact occasioned by the presence of numerous U.S. members of the Trilateral Commission in the initial governmental team of that administration, beginning with the president and vice-president themselves.

In fact, in some cases the proposals and programs of this transnational sector continue to represent pending projects (such as in the management of the international monetary situation), while in other cases such as détente initial adherence to its recommendations was subsequently aban-

---

[14] The views of the Trilateral Commission on this point are clearly manifested in the documents, "An Overview of East-West Relations" and "Collaboration with the Communist Countries in the Management of Global Problems," published in *The Triangle Papers* (New York, 1978). The most promising areas of collaboration, the relatively promising, and those that may only be effected over the long run are characterized in detail, and a whole strategy of approach and organization is set forth that contrasts dramatically with the Cold War international style of the neoconservative growth.

doned when the international situation altered (as occurred in matters relating to the Soviet Union and the socialist countries).

CONCLUSION

The views expressed in these two great visions are of themselves of little importance. Of interest is the prospect of their being converted into
national projects of historic dimensions for the purpose of resolving the
problems that U.S. society is facing—a prospect that is in turn related to
the significance accorded by the productive forces and the sectors that
support and favor them. If one were simply trying to compile an inventory of interesting propositions concerning the future of the United
States, one would include many other contributions from the academic
world, some of them probably more original and more rigorous.

On the other hand, the projects already enunciated possess a certain
viability of implementation in the event, which we consider likely, that
within a certain period of time a consensus develops among analysts and
U.S. policy formulators that a profound reorganization of the productive
structure and of the political system has come to be indispensable. Recent
debates such as those over industrial restructuring or the crisis of democracy, although limited in scope, appear to demonstrate that things can
move in this direction. If this is so, it is useful to begin to identify those
sectors that will form the base of support for one or another national
project, in order to break it down into its component parts and to estimate the forces that it can count on. By way of a preliminary hypothesis
one may assert that the neoconservative project basically expresses the
interests of three broad and influential sectors of U.S. capitalism: those
industrial and financial groups that produce for the domestic market
(principally small and medium producers); industrial sectors that, after
having occupied key positions in the economy and having been exporters, have also been confined basically to relying on the domestic market
on account of the deterioration of their ability to compete, and that,
moreover, wish to retain protectionist policies (e.g., automotive, steel,
and certain branches of the electronics industry); and, finally, large firms
connected to the weapons industry and to defense programs.

These economic sectors already act in a united fashion. In general
terms, in the 1980 presidential campaign they enthusiastically backed the
Republican platform and supported Ronald Reagan, on whose policy
planning staffs they have had an important say.

At the other extreme we find the large U.S. transnationals that operate
in what we might call the "civilian" domain and that wish, for that very
reason, to rely on international negotiations and the prosecution of
efforts at détente in order to create the basic conditions for trying out

their project more systematically at some future date. These groups have therefore stood closer to the Democratic party since 1976 and have particularly supported its plans for the nation's international conduct.

But both sectors will find their real options rather in the recuperation of the old tradition of U.S. politics, which established close ties between the social project and the handling of structural problems faced by the nation, than in transitory affiliations. For this reason we are convinced that, whether in the administration that took up its electoral mandate in 1981, or in the debate over the succession in 1984, the necessity for such a recovery will present itself with great force.

The Prospects for Economic Growth in the United States, 1980-2000

Donald A. Nichols

THE U.S. economy is now undergoing major structural changes. These changes are disturbing the normal historical relations that must be assessed in order to project the economy's path into the future. Analysts do not agree on their long-run consequences, and hence there no longer exists a consensus projection that can be used as a starting point for describing the likely path of any variable of interest. Accordingly, the economic projections postulated here must be treated with caution since they are subject to wide margins of error.

STRUCTURAL CHANGE IN THE UNITED STATES

The 1950s and 1960s were decades of remarkable stability in the economy of the United States, which emerged from the Korean War with unemployment below 3 percent and no inflation. Two decades of rapid, stable growth followed. This performance was due in large part to the wise decisions of economic policy makers; it was also partly fortuitous.

Policy makers were largely responsible for the absence of imbalances at the end of the Korean War. During the war the economy had been subject to strict wage and price controls and to central allocations of key resources such as steel.[1] The government had used credit controls to restrain auto demand when military tank and truck production was needed, and relaxed the controls just as military needs subsided. While the average level of capacity utilization was extremely high in 1953, it was distributed evenly enough within manufacturing so that bottlenecks were absent. Controls were dismantled piece by piece when policy makers judged that balance in a particular sector had been restored. The Wage

---

[1] For an excellent description of the wide-ranging economic policies of the Truman administration, see C. D. Goodwin and R. S. Herren, "The Truman Administration: Problems and Policies Unfold," in C. D. Goodwin, ed., *Exhortation and Controls* (Washington, D.C., 1978), pp. 9–13.

Stabilization Board had granted many exceptions during its tenure—and, indeed, had been widely criticized for its laxness—yet there was no wage explosion when controls were removed, signifying that a wage structure had evolved that was viewed as appropriate.[2]

Thus the economy began the postwar period in a position of balance. No sector needed an extraordinary expansion, no substantial movements in relative wages or prices were required for equilibrium. While this was due initially to the successful economic policies of the Truman administration, the remarkable balance displayed by the economy for the next two decades was due largely to a lack of structural challenges.[3] This period can be described as one of balanced growth—a phenomenon that attracted the concentration of the technical economic literature at the time.

Macroeconomic policy was not difficult in such an environment. The only problems faced were a succession of inventory cycles that could be smoothed with demand stabilization policies that became conventional by the end of the period.[4] Indeed, the only significant disturbance of balance, which came with the Vietnam War in the late sixties, could probably have been smoothed as well with a better use of demand stabilization policies.

Compared to these two decades, the 1970s were extremely turbulent. Major structural challenges, several of which had their roots in social imbalances that had surfaced in the 1960s, confronted policy makers, and economic performance suffered dramatically, partly as an inevitable consequence of the challenges and partly from the inadequate response of policy makers to them.

During the 1960s considerable social energy was devoted to the problems of racial inequality and the Vietnam War. These issues shattered the consensus over national goals that had existed in the two previous decades. Even before the huge baby-boom generation realized how their large numbers would restrict their personal economic and career achievements, they spent their energy on social causes rather than on personal advancement and learned how to use the political system to advantage. Public-interest law firms sprang up, financed by a large lobby of social

[2] John P. Lewis credits the Wage Stabilization Board of the Korean War with the subsequent low rates of inflation experienced in the United States ("The Lull That Came to Stay," *Journal of Political Economy*, 63 [1955], 1–19).

[3] In particular, James Tobin has argued that declining agricultural prices made this period an unusual one, and predicted a resurgence of inflation when real wages could no longer be increased by this means ("Labor and Economic Stabilization," in *The Employment Act, Past and Future*, ed. Gerhard Colm [Washington, D.C., 1956], pp. 115–19).

[4] See R. J. Gordon, "Postwar Macroeconomics: The Evolution of Events and Ideas," National Bureau of Economic Research Working Paper no. 459 (February 1980).

groups. The economic establishment organized to defend itself, and the battle between these groups fragmented the political process into small collections of mutually antagonistic special-interest groups. Their support in turn became important in congressional elections, and different lobbies gained power over different kinds of legislation. The legislation that emerged from this confusion in no way reflected consensus; rather, it reflected the most that the majority—temporary, perhaps—could force down the throats of the minority. Coalitions shifted from issue to issue so that no group won all its battles, but in several areas legislation of quite extreme form was passed. Its goals may have been subscribed to by the majority of the population, but the implementation as dictated by the technical requirements of the legislation was often extreme.

Industry, therefore, found itself at the outset of the 1970s having to satisfy legal requirements that it had opposed vigorously in Congress and lost. The general areas of concern are well known: production could no longer pollute the environment; special effort had to be made to recruit and promote female and minority employees; products and production methods had to meet new health and safety standards. The implementation of these standards often reversed the traditional burden of proof. Firms had to be prepared to prove that they were making an effort to change the demographic composition of their workers. Statements had to be filed in advance about the probable environmental effects of new facilities or production methods. Even in the universities, we can see the effect of this legislation on our own management; new layers of bureaucracy have been added to help see that we comply with these complex laws and—what is more difficult—to see that we can prove that we are complying. Industry has also become more bureaucratic and cautious as a result.

The more combative and contentious environment of the 1970s, in which these laws were first enforced, required a substantial increase in the resources devoted to conflict as well as to the genuine pursuit of the newly legislated goals. Fewer resources were left for continued economic growth. A crude indicator of the new resource needs of the 1970s is seen in the occupational changes made during the decade. While total employment had grown by 37 percent between 1950 and 1970, and the number of engineers by 130 percent, from 1970 to 1980 total employment increased by 26 percent, and the number of engineers by only 19 percent. At the same time, the growth in the number of lawyers was accelerating. After increasing by 48 percent between 1950 and 1970, it grew by 101 percent between 1970 and 1980. In other words, there were 4.9 engineers per lawyer in 1970 but only 2.6 in 1980. A few simple occupational statistics hardly prove that the nation's resources were increasingly devoted to conflict rather than to economic growth, but the data mentioned are in fact consistent with that view. One need not question the desirability of the new goals being pursued to recognize the substantial extra overhead which society now bears as a result of its more combative nature.[5]

Even with these substantial costs, we could perhaps have changed our productive machinery to accommodate these inner goals without a substantial disruption in economic growth, had we not been confronted in the mid-seventies with the energy problem. The dramatic increase in oil prices would have required a substantial restructuring of consumption and production habits even in the absence of changing social goals, but its consequences were especially severe because the environmental challenge being faced even before 1973 required a movement from coal, to nuclear energy, to petroleum and natural gas. To reverse this transformation that had just begun proved exceptionally difficult and expensive, and many fundamental questions connected with it and its reversal have not yet been answered. Indeed, the social consensus necessary for a clear energy policy has yet to emerge, and the resulting lack of direction in the U.S. economy today hinders its development.

ECONOMIC POLICY IN THE 1970S

The consequences of these challenges can be seen in the overall economic performance in the seventies, when unemployment and inflation were far higher than in the sixties, while productivity growth was lower. Much of the blame for this trend may rest with policy makers, though admittedly some decline in performance would have occurred even with optimal policy decisions.

Because the policy makers faced no major structural challenges in the 1950s and 1960s, they were able to use a simple strategy described by Samuelson as the "neoclassical synthesis." This strategy holds that macro-policy makers need only smooth out cycles in private demand; free-market price movements meanwhile would guarantee economic efficiency by directing resources to the industries where they are most needed. This strategy was the right one for the fifties and sixties, but hopelessly inadequate in the 1970s. The problem with it is the requirement that prices and wages be able to rise and fall freely. Some prices can and do rise and fall freely; some do not; and, in particular, wages will not fall without a substantial recession. In the 1950s and 1960s this posed no

---

[5] The occupational structure in 1980 compared to 1970 shows the following, additional changes: editors and reporters, up 32%; personnel and labor relations experts, up 55%; public relations experts, up 70%; social scientists, up 155%. Meanwhile, the number of private protective guards increased by 72%, to 548,000! United States Census of Population, 1960 and 1970; Bureau of Labor Statistics, *Employment and Earnings*, 28, no. 1 (Jan. 1981), 180.

problem, since the major price declines were centered in agriculture and high technology industries, neither of which required accompanying declines in wages.

In 1974, OPEC raised the price of oil from three dollars a barrel to thirteen dollars a barrel. If this increase were to be accepted without higher inflation and unemployment, as the neoclassical synthesis implied it could be, a transfer to oil producers of about 2 percent of national income would be required. That could be accomplished in the market only by wage declines of an equal amount, accompanied by proportional declines in other prices and in the receipts of other groups. Anyone who has studied wages knows that they don't decline except under extreme duress. Policy makers, therefore, were caught in an excruciating dilemma and, what is worse, they were not intellectually prepared to understand it, let alone to meet it. The choice they faced was to stabilize the price level—as the neoclassical synthesis suggested they should—which would cause a massive recession, since wages would not fall unless unemployment rose, or to stabilize employment, which would require a substantial increase in nominal demand to pay for the oil and would lead to higher inflation.

That this dilemma existed and was not understood is apparent from the proceedings of the summit of economists held at the White House in September 1974. Some warned of a growing recession, others insisted on reducing inflation. Conflicting advice was given for demand management. A literature has evolved since that meeting to describe the policy choice more clearly, but there were few who understood its implications at that time.[6] As a result, demand was first restrained, precipitating a major recession. The ensuing public reaction led to a re-expansion of demand long before inflation had subsided, and the economy emerged from the recession in the late 1970s with higher rates of inflation and unemployment than when it entered.

In 1979 and early 1980, the price of oil was again increased. The effect of those price increases was a further burst of inflation and another reces-

[6]Notable among the early exceptions are three papers that contain descriptions of the supply-shock mechanism and forecasts of the 1975 recession based upon it: Tobin, "Monetary Policy in 1974 and Beyond," *Brookings Papers on Economic Activity* (henceforth abbreviated as BPEA), 1974, no. 1, pp. 219–32; James L. Pierce and Jared Enzler, "The Effects of External Inflationary Shocks," BPEA, 1974, no. 1, pp. 13–62; and R. J. Gordon, "Alternative Responses of Policy to External Supply Shocks," BPEA, 1975, no. 1, pp. 183–206. An unpublished paper by the author also describes the mechanism: "Buffer Stocks as a Macroeconomic Policy Tool" (prepared for the Miami University Conference on Inflation, May 1975). Recent works by E. M. Gramlich: "Macro Policy Responses to Supply Shocks," BPEA, 1979, no. 1, pp. 125–66, and E. S. Phelps: "Commodity-Supply Shocks and Full Employment Monetary Policy," *Journal of Money, Credit and Banking*, 10 (May 1978), 206–21, describe the dilemma as an optimization problem.

sion. The version of this paper completed in May 1980 for the June conference in Mexico stated at this point, "While the consequences of this increase are now understood by many policy makers, there is no agreement over how to respond.[7] It appears that the same pattern of response that was adopted in 1974 will be followed. Money will first be tightened until a recession is caused. Then demand will be expanded to end the recession, but inflation will then be at a higher level than before the oil price increase." The predicted demand expansion has not yet transpired though a substantial tax cut was put in place in 1981. The recession is now widely recognized though there remains disagreement over how long it will last and how vigorous the recovery will be.

This is not the place to prescribe policies for responding to price increases like that in oil. It is clear, however, that some response is needed other than demand stabilization. The economy faces a major continuing challenge requiring a substantial structural transformation that, according to the neoclassical synthesis, could be accomplished only by a decline in money wages. But the fact is that oil-price increases do not cause money wages to decline. Indeed, through explicit escalator clauses and through historical behavioral responses, exogenous price increases have in the past caused nominal wages to accelerate.[8] Thus the policy prescriptions that follow from the neoclassical synthesis appear to be inadequate as a response to large oil-price increases. What is needed is an integration of structural policies with demand policies, which should themselves be combined with a strong incomes policy until the whole transformation is accomplished. At present there is no consensus among policy makers and academics about what strategy should be used, and one can only forecast bad economic performance until some consensus is reached.

GROWTH PROJECTIONS

For the reasons just described, economic performance was much weaker in the 1970s than in the 1950s and 1960s. A closer look at the performance of the economy in this period enables us to make a projection of economic growth to the year 2000. The selection of that year by the conference organizers does not represent in any technical sense a limit to the period of time over which projections can be made with confidence. In-

[7]The Council of Economic Advisers estimates that "gross oil drag" will increase by an amount equal to 3 percent of GNP in 1979 and 1980 (*Annual Report—1980* [Washington, D.C., 1980], p. 65). This is twice the size of the shock felt in 1974. The forecast of recession followed by expansionary policy also appeared in the first draft of this paper and was presented in Mexico in June.

[8]See George L. Perry, "Slowing the Wage-Price Spiral: The Macroeconomic View," BPEA, 1978, no. 2, pp. 259–91, and Gramlich, "Macro Policy Responses."

deed, the future is now much cloudier than it appeared to be a decade ago, and there is a great deal of uncertainty over the likely performance of the economy even in this decade. As a result, these projections should be treated as rough approximations with large standard errors.

While there are many areas where our assumptions about the future are shaky, they are weakest by far in the area of productivity growth. The growth of labor productivity has been stopped for almost a decade, and no one knows why. I project a return in the growth of labor productivity to 2.0 percent per year in the 1990s—not quite the level reached in the 1950s and 1960s. There can be little certainty about this projection, and one could well argue that productivity growth at a rate of only 1.0 percent per year would be consistent with the economy's recent performance. Because of the substantial size of this possible error, therefore, I have not tried to be precise about issues whose potential importance was on the order of a tenth of a percent per year, but have concentrated on the major issues that have been suggested as causes of the recent productivity decline.

The primary issues are capital accumulation and energy price increases, and their probable effect on productivity growth in the future, as compared with the past. Neither issue, in fact, can be shown to have been responsible for a major part of the productivity decline in the 1970s. The projections assume productivity growth returning to a level considered normal by historical standards and a slow recovery following the current recession. There are no separate projections for capital accumulation or energy usage, both of which are encompassed in the labor productivity figures.

The labor force projections to 1995 are those of the Bureau of Labor Statistics, as published in December 1980.[9] Traditionally, BLS has not projected a growth in illegal migration. In-migration and out-migration are assumed to offset each other in these projections, and I have used that assumption here. The major feature of the projections (Table 1) is the substantial decline in the growth of the labor force in the 1990s. It appears in all projections and can be expected with reasonable certainty, since the majority of the population who will comprise the labor force at that time are alive today. From a compound annual growth rate of 1.53 percent in the 1980s, growth declines to a rate of .92 percent in the 1990s. This phenomenon may well affect attitudes toward migration in that decade, and the need for labor will probably be higher than at any time since the 1960s.

[9] The projections are found in Howard N. Fullerton, Jr., "The 1995 Labor Force," *Monthly Labor Review*, 103, no. 12 (Dec. 1980), 11–21.

TABLE I

Projected Growth in the Labor Force, 1981–2000

(millions of workers)

Year	No. of workers	Year	No. of workers
1981	107.5	1991	123.5
1982	109.7	1992	124.5
1983	111.6	1993	125.4
1984	113.3	1994	126.4
1985	115.0	1995	127.5
1986	116.7	1996	128.8
1987	118.4	1997	130.0
1988	119.8	1998	131.3
1989	121.2	1999	132.7
1990	122.4	2000	134.2

SOURCE: For 1980–95, BLS figures in *Monthly Labor Review*, December 1980; for 1996–2000, unofficial figures were provided to the author.

NOTE: Compounded annual growth rates: 1980–90, 1.53%; 1990–2000, 0.92%; 1980–2000, 1.23%.

CAPITAL FORMATION

Capital formation and economic growth are linked in three important ways: (1) Capital is an important productive factor. (2) Output and employment must be increased in order to produce investment goods. (3) Firms try to acquire more capital when output is expected to grow. In the late 1970s both output growth and capital formation declined from the levels that had prevailed in the 1950s and 1960s. The press and the political campaigns emphasized the first linkage identified above as the reason for the decline. According to this view, tax incentives were needed to stimulate saving and investment, and more investment would bring with it a higher growth in productivity that would restore economic growth to former levels. I see little evidence to support this view and lean instead to the premise that the decline in output-growth removed the need or incentive to invest. Once economic growth is restored, capital formation will follow, which is the reverse of the view currently being publicized. Accordingly, in my projections I assume that capital will grow at the same rate as output, whatever that rate may be.

Table 2 reports the major components of saving and investment as percentages of nominal GNP for 1959, 1969, and 1979. Gross private investment for those three years was 15.93, 15.62, and 17.23 percent of their respective GNPs. The investment component most closely associated with productivity growth is probably gross nonresidential fixed investment. This figure is higher for 1979 (11.59%) than for 1969 (10.57%), and far higher than for 1959 (9.31%).

A slight decline is evident in the rate of personal saving. This decline has frequently been reported in the press, sometimes with the mistaken implication that household saving is the sole source of funds for business investment. In fact, the table shows that personal saving is small relative to business saving as a source of funds, and that the large percentage decline in personal saving from 1969 to 1979 was more than offset by a lesser percentage increase in business saving. Even if a further decline in personal saving were projected, the small size of this component indicates that such a projection would not be cause for alarm. Changes in other components could easily offset a decline in personal saving and permit investment to grow at a higher rate.

More than offsetting the decline in personal saving in the 1970s was the substantial growth of state and local government surpluses—not in the operating surplus, but in the increased pension reserves of civil ser-

TABLE 2

Capital Formation as a Percentage of GNP, 1959–79

Type of capital	1959	1969	1979
Nonresidential fixed investment	9.31%	10.57%	11.59%
Residential fixed investment	5.55	4.05	4.91
Inventory accumulation	1.07	1.00	0.72
Gross private domestic investment	15.93	15.62	17.23
Net foreign investment	−0.41	−0.21	−0.07
Gross private investment	15.52	15.41	17.16
Personal saving	3.86	3.75	3.57
Gross business saving	12.02	10.87	12.91
State and local government surplus	−0.08	0.22	1.11
Federal government surplus	−0.22	0.91	−0.61
Special drawing rights (IMF)	—	—	0.05
Gross saving	15.58	15.77	17.06
Statistical discrepancy	−0.04	−0.35	0.09
Saving plus statistical discrepancy	15.54	15.42	17.15

SOURCE: 1959 and 1969 data drawn from various tables in the *Economic Report of the President* (January 1980), data appendix. Data for 1979 are from the *Survey of Current Business*, special supplement, July 1981.

NOTE: Both numerator and denominator of the ratios above are measured in current dollars.

TABLE 3

Nonresidential Fixed Investment as a Percentage of GNP, 1950–79

(1972 dollars)

Year	Pct. of GNP	Year	Pct. of GNP	Year	Pct. of GNP	Adjusted pct. of GNP[a]
1950	9.37%	1960	8.96%	1970	10.23%	n.a.
1951	9.18	1961	8.69	1971	9.75	n.a.
1952	8.71	1962	8.87	1972	9.97	n.a.
1953	9.05	1963	8.85	1973	10.61	10.23%
1954	9.03	1964	9.26	1974	10.72	10.34
1955	9.35	1965	10.33	1975	9.45	9.02
1956	9.75	1966	10.82	1976	9.66	9.27
1957	9.69	1967	10.27	1977	10.25	9.90
1958	8.67	1968	10.27	1978	10.68	10.36
1959	8.73	1969	10.60	1979	11.01	10.69
Decade average	9.15%	Decade average	9.69%	Decade average	10.23%	9.97%

SOURCE: Economic Report of the President, January 1980.

NOTE: Investment and GNP have been deflated by their respective deflators.

[a]This column deducts from investment the outlays devoted solely to pollution abatement as shown in Table 4.

vants. New pension laws passed in the 1970s will require these reserves to grow further in the 1980s, making the state and local sector an even more important source of saving than it is today. Indeed, these pension laws will also require private pension reserves to grow. In 1979, saving in the form of additions to insurance and pension reserves (both public and private) was $77.9 billion—almost as large as the total $86.2 billion reported for personal saving. This contrasts with 1959, when pension and life insurance saving was $11.9 billion, a much smaller fraction of total personal saving of $18.8 billion.

The table also shows large swings in the federal deficit as a percentage of GNP. We have known, since Keynes, that the federal budget can be used to stabilize private fluctuations in saving and investment intentions. If private investment demand is strong, a surplus may be needed to keep GNP to noninflationary levels; if it is weak, a deficit can be used to keep unemployment to acceptable levels. This indicates that, by control of the level of government saving, the link between personal saving and investment can be broken, and that policies to stimulate private saving will not necessarily stimulate investment.

While Table 2 indicates no decline in the level of gross private domestic investment as a share of GNP in the 1970s, the data must be adjusted for several factors before a fair comparison can be made. In making these adjustments, I will consider only nonresidential fixed investment, which is presumably the kind of investment that brings with it productivity growth. Table 3, which shows real nonresidential fixed investment as a percentage of real GNP for the years 1950–79, differs from Table 2 in that the figures have been deflated by an index of investment goods prices while GNP is deflated by the overall deflator. As seen in Table 3, the modestly higher rate of capital goods inflation in the 1970s reduces somewhat the estimate of the share of GNP devoted to investment in 1979. Despite this, the investment ratio share remains higher in 1979 than in 1969, and the average for the decade of the 1970s still exceeds that for the 1950s or 1960s by a comfortable margin.

The last column in Table 3 reports the investment ratio after a deduction for pollution abatement investment, calculated from estimates provided by the Commerce Department and shown in Table 4.[10] The estimates are derived from surveys of businesses. One is tempted to place little faith in them because of the difficulty of separating out the share of a new investment process due to pollution abatement needs from the

[10] See Gary L. Rutledge and Betsy D. O'Connor, "Plant and Equipment Expenditures by Business for Pollution Abatement, 1973–80 and Planned 1981," *Survey of Current Business*, 61, no. 6 (June 1982), 19–25.

TABLE 4

Pollution Abatement Investment, 1973–80

(billions of dollars)

Year	Current dollars (*billions*)	1972 dollars
1973	4.9	4.7
1974	5.7	4.7
1975	7.0	5.2
1976	7.2	5.1
1977	7.3	4.8
1978	7.6	4.6
1979	8.4	4.7
1980	9.2	4.7

SOURCE: *Survey of Current Business*, June 1981, pp. 19–25.
NOTE: Expenditures by industry for 1980 were: electric utilities, 2.8 billion; petroleum manufacturing, 1.7; primary metals, 1.0; chemicals, 0.7; motor vehicles, 0.4; paper, 0.4; other, 2.2; total, 9.2 billion.

share needed for production. But the survey reports that, for 1980, 81 percent of anticipated pollution abatement investment was for "end-of-line" investment whose sole purpose was pollution abatement; only 19 percent was for equipment with a mixed purpose of adding to production and reducing pollution. The industrial composition of the pollution abatement investment completed in 1980 is also shown in the table.

It can be seen in Table 4 that the real value of pollution abatement investment decreased over the 1973–80 period. These estimates were subtracted from the deflated investment series in order to arrive at the investment data used to generate the last column of Table 3. In that table it is apparent that, on average, the level of investment over the 1973–80 period was a larger share of GNP, even after deducting pollution abatement investment, than in the 1950s and 1960s. Accordingly, it is assumed that, in the future, gross investment will not be kept below its historic ratio to GNP by pollution abatement needs.

The final issue addressed here concerns depreciation. Net investment grew more slowly than gross investment in the 1970s. In part, this was due to an increase in spending for equipment relative to physical plant, which increased the level of depreciation associated with a given level of gross investment. If Commerce Department estimates of depreciation are used, the size of this effect is larger than that for either the pollution abatement or the capital goods inflation adjustments. My conference discussant, Professor Tibor Scitovsky, points out that we should be more cautious about declines reported in net investment than in gross investment because of the inherent difficulties of estimating capital consumption allowances. He points out that depreciation allowances may overstate capital consumption, and if so the reported decline in net investment will be overstated as well. The declines reported here should be interpreted as upper bounds in this case.

Table 5 shows net private nonresidential investment in structures and equipment as a percentage of net private nonresidential product. This denominator is constructed by subtracting from GNP the production of government housing services, residential construction, and depreciation. The numerators are computed by the Commerce Department. The table documents a significant decline in the 1970s, to a level close to that experienced in the 1950s when productivity was much larger. Clearly, the bulk of the decline in investment was due to the 1975 recession and, by the end of the period, investment was above its average for the decade. Depreciation is not available for pollution abatement investment, so the gross data in Table 4 cannot be converted to a net basis to be subtracted from the data in Table 5. If the same ratio of net to gross investment holds for pollution abatement as for other investment, the average rate of investment in the 1970s would fall from 4.62 to 4.08 percent. Table 5 also shows rather large percentage swings in net investment as a share of output. There was a notable bulge in investment in the late 1960s when output growth was high, capacity utilization was high, and the investment tax credit had just been enacted. The year 1966, in particular, had very high levels of investment. There was a marked collapse in investment in 1975 when the unemployment rate reached a postwar peak, energy prices were high, growth forecasts low, and real profits negative.

In the projections that follow, I will assume that capital growth will not impose a constraint on future output. The increase in net investment required to restore it to its level of the 1960s is small as a share of GNP, certainly small compared to its past variation. There is no evidence that investment would remain low if growth were restored, bringing with it a higher level of profitability. If necessary, the investment tax credit could be expanded to cover structures, as was proposed by the Carter administration. A final check on the plausibility of my assumption is provided by a comparison of the saving rates and the growth rates for the past three decades. Growth theory tells us that the capital-output ratio will equal, in the long run, the ratio of the saving rate to the growth rate. Since the decline in the saving rate (investment divided by output) in the 1970s was smaller than the decline in economic growth, a continuation of economic performance of the kind exhibited in the 1970s would lead

TABLE 5

Net Private Nonresidential Investment as a Percentage
of Net Private Nonresidential Product, 1950–79

Year	Structures	Equipment	Total
1950	1.73%	2.83%	4.57%
1951	1.91	2.52	4.43
1952	1.78	1.88	3.66
1953	2.05	1.94	3.99
1954	2.26	1.19	3.45
1955	2.39	1.78	4.17
1956	2.84	1.72	4.56
1957	2.66	1.64	4.30
1958	2.22	0.33	2.55
1959	2.05	0.93	2.98
Average	2.19%	1.67%	3.87%
1960	2.30%	0.97%	3.27%
1961	2.25	0.61	2.86
1962	2.29	1.13	3.42
1963	2.10	1.38	3.48
1964	2.30	1.93	4.23
1965	3.02	2.85	5.87
1966	3.12	3.40	6.52
1967	2.72	2.75	5.47
1968	2.62	2.79	5.41
1969	2.72	2.91	5.63
Average	2.54%	2.07%	4.62%
1970	2.47%	2.08%	4.55%
1971	2.16	1.59	3.75
1972	2.05	2.20	4.25
1973	2.17	2.92	5.09
1974	1.74	2.90	4.64
1975	1.01	1.06	2.07
1976	1.06	1.87	2.93
1977	1.04	2.87	3.91
1978	1.34	3.32	4.66
1979	1.57	3.34	4.91
Average	1.66%	2.42%	4.08%

SOURCE: *The National Income and Product Accounts of the United States,*
1929–1974, and *Survey of Current Business,* July 1977, 1978, 1979, and 1981.

to a higher capital-output ratio than would have occurred in the 1960s. For each of the past three decades the ratio of the saving rate to the growth rate was 1.20, 1.10, and 1.18 respectively.

Longer-run studies of U.S. saving and investment confirm the view that the investment rate will not fall below its historic level for long. If consumer durable purchases are treated as an investment, and depreciation from the stock of durables treated as consumption, the rate of investment as a share of GNP has remained roughly constant in the United States for the past century. The level falls and rises with interest rates, the business cycle, and other factors, but it appears to vary around the same mean when long periods of data are examined.[11]

This long-run constancy indicates a limit to the likely effect that policy changes or economic events may have on capital formation. A saving rate that did not decline with the introduction of the personal and corporate income taxes is not likely to increase much if these taxes are reduced. While a major recession in the early eighties will temporarily reduce investment rates, and a business-oriented tax cut might raise them, a reasonable forecast for the next twenty years would be to keep the share of investment in GNP at its average level of the past century.

In this context I would like to point out two additional important issues that merit further research: first, the substantial decline in government investment in the 1970s, as reported in the GNP accounts (the decline is not evident in Tables 3 or 5, since they report only private investment); second, the substantially different behavior of household saving, if imputations for home ownership are subtracted from GNP and consumption (household saving net of imputations fluctuates substantially but is on average higher in the 1970s than in the 1960s). I am indebted to Professor Scitovsky for pointing out the latter issue.

RESOURCES AND TECHNOLOGY

Nineteenth-century classical economists concerned themselves with the issue of population growth in a world with finite natural resources. Their predictions of immiseration have not come true for the industrialized world. Theorists of growth of the 1950s and 1960s portrayed the process as a race between population and capital accumulation. Their explanation of constant or growing per capita incomes despite population growth is a useful description of the industrialized world as it has developed over the last two centuries. The modern growth theorists also

[11] See Paul A. David and John L. Scadding, "Private Savings: Ultra Rationality, Aggregation, and Denison's Law," *Journal of Political Economy*, 82, no. 2, pt. 1 (March/April 1974), 225–50, for a description of the long-run constancy of the saving rate.

considered technological progress, whose source was mysterious to them but which entered into the growth process in a fundamental way. Growth in per capita income depended on advances in technology according to this literature, though the determinants of those advances were unknown and remain so today.

The shocks of the 1970s have raised concerns that were ignored in the 1950s and 1960s and that echo the concerns of the classical economists. Advancing population with finite and depleting resources is again a problem being considered by students of industrialized economies. Opinions on the issue have not yet converged, and there is no consensus forecast of economic growth for the next century. It is probably too early to tell whether technology will progress at a rate sufficient to make economic growth a permanent prospect despite declines in the use of raw materials, or whether resource constraints and population growth will prove to be forces of immiseration too strong to be offset by technical progress. The answer to this question will only be revealed in time.

The effect of a declining resource base on economic growth would occur through its effect on labor productivity in the projections in Table 6. Labor productivity increases with improvements in technology and with increases in the levels of non-labor resources used in production. In the 1970s productivity growth collapsed, which some analysts attribute to the concurrent decline in the availability and use of energy. In my judgment the collapse was not due to a lack of physical productive power resulting from an energy shortage, and there seems to be little reason to project a continuation of low productivity growth based on energy availability, at least for the next twenty years.

While resource constraints may reduce our ability to grow indefinitely, the situation over the next twenty years promises little difference from that of the past thirty years. Technical progress will continue to provide increasing standards of living and to increase the output available from a given level of inputs. Resource use will decline somewhat, reducing the growth in labor productivity from past levels, but there is little evidence that the reduction will be as severe as that experienced in the 1970s.

Using different definitions of productivity, and different beginning and end points for the periods over which progress is to be measured, different estimates of the size of the collapse in productivity growth in the seventies can be obtained. Regardless of the criterion chosen, the reduction was substantial and was by any calculation the only reduction of its size in the twentieth century. Most analysts use the year 1973 as a point that marks the end of the period of rapid productivity growth. Since productivity varies substantially over the business cycle, its growth is usually measured from the peak of one cycle to the peak of the next. The year

1973 marks such a peak, following which the growth of productivity in the cycle was substantially below par. Some analysts find a lesser but significant deceleration in 1966 or 1968, and break the productivity experience into three periods with 1966 or 1968 and 1973 as the points of separation.

While there is considerable agreement on the existence of a decline, there is little agreement as to its causes. Even those who claim to be able to explain large parts of the decline leave much unexplained. A study by Christainsen, Gollop, and Haveman summarizes the estimates proposed in nine different studies and lists twenty-five different factors to which the several authors attribute the decline. They range from cyclical effects, to government regulation, to changes in the quantities of other inputs.[12] There exist, in addition, many separate studies of one aspect or another of the decline. One particular issue where further study is warranted is the effect of energy price increases on productivity growth.

It seems plausible that the increase in energy prices in 1973–74 was a major cause of the collapse in productivity growth. Of all the causes suggested, it is the one that changed suddenly and massively in 1973. Also supporting this view is the fact that other industrialized nations experienced a similar decline in productivity growth at the same time as the United States. Most of the other explanations that are offered consider causes that have taken place gradually or are specific to the United States economy.

While circumstantial evidence points the finger at energy prices, there is little agreement about the transmission mechanism that reveals how energy price increases reduce economic performance. There are many possible routes, some of which will be described here. The energy price increases of 1973–74 led to wage increases that permanently raised the level of the wage-price spiral; central banks then raised interest rates in an effort to reduce the inflation; meanwhile, higher prices reduced the real demand for output, leading to a decline in investment; as a result, unemployment rates moved up in all countries to levels not seen since World War II and remain today substantially above their 1973 levels.

On the product side, the higher real price of energy caused a redesign of products, capital goods, and production methods; compared to the stability of relative prices before 1973, the post-1973 experience must be bewildering to firms choosing production processes that will require them in the future to buy one group of products and to sell another; tal-

---

[12] The study was prepared by Gregory Christainsen, Frank Gollop, and Robert Haveman for the Joint Economic Committee of the U.S. Congress: *Environmental and Health/Safety Regulations, Productivity Growth, and Economic Performance: An Assessment* (Washington, D.C., August 1980). See especially p. 27 for a table of all the estimates in the studies cited.

ents that had presumably been devoted to implementing cost reduction were absorbed in the process of redesigning the capital stock. The interaction of all these factors left producers with the need to design new energy-efficient products; to produce them in new, energy-efficient ways; to accomplish all this in the midst of a massive recession accompanied by negative real profits, record real interest rates, and a substantial acceleration of wages; and to develop long-range plans using numbers based on untried inflationary accounting procedures.

It is not surprising that, in this environment, investment fell and other productivity-enhancing actions were inhibited. But there is little reason to expect future energy price increases to cause as much mischief and confusion as the 1974 increase did. Much of the problem of 1974–76 was avoidable, and only a small part of it was an inevitable accompaniment of the resource shortage of that period. How much was technological in the sense that a decline in energy usage inevitably reduced labor productivity, and how much was behavioral in the sense that a more intelligent use of economic policy could have averted it?

Denison provides an excellent discussion of the issue of energy usage and productivity from the technological perspective.[13] He cites a wide range of estimates and concludes that the energy price increase caused a reduction in usage that explains only 5 percent of the decline in productivity growth, or only 0.1 percentage points per year. His reasoning is quite neoclassical. Firms would substitute labor for energy if it saved them money. Energy usage per unit of output was about 4 percent lower in 1976 than would have been predicted on the basis of the trend from 1949 to 1973, and in 1975 was roughly 5 percent of total business costs. A reduction of 4 percent in an item that comprises 5 percent of total costs would reduce those costs by 0.2 percent. An increase in labor costs equivalent to 0.2 percent of total costs is the most that can be explained on the basis of rational substitution of labor for energy. Any larger substitution would cause total costs to rise, not fall. For this increase in labor usage over a three-year period, an 0.2 percent increase in total cost becomes 0.07 percent per year, which Denison approximates as an 0.1 percent per year increase in labor costs.

Other studies with much higher estimates of this effect are also cited by Denison, including Hudson and Jorgensen's, which attributes 35 percent of the decline in labor productivity growth (0.7 percentage points per year) to higher energy prices.[14] Jorgensen also uses a neoclassical ap-

[13] Edward Denison, "Explanations of Declining Productivity Growth," and "Pollution Abatement Programs: Estimates of Their Effect upon Output per Unit of Input, 1975–78," *Survey of Current Business*, 59, no. 8, pt. 1 (August 1979), 1–24 and 58–59, respectively.

[14] Edward A. Hudson and Dale W. Jorgensen, "Energy Prices and the U.S. Economy, 1972–76," *Data Resources U.S. Review* (September 1978), 1.24–1.37.

proach, as do others, who find the same large effect.[15] Their high estimates are derived from an estimation process that finds energy and capital to be complementary, with high energy prices causing a reduction in both energy and capital usage as well as an increase in labor usage. While this result is not implausible on *a priori* grounds, it remains an unconvincing explanation because the measure of capital services, as provided by Jorgensen, depends importantly on electricity usage. Variations here may provide a good measure of variations in the intensity of machinery use over short time-periods, especially if the price of electricity is relatively constant. If, however, the price of electricity changes drastically, one would expect firms to use less of it even without changing the usage of their capital stock. Electricity used for lighting can be reduced; motors can be shut off when not in use; air conditioning usage can be reduced; and existing energy-efficient capital can be used more extensively while less efficient capital is held in reserve. Berndt and Wood cite engineering results to indicate that substantial possibilities for energy-capital substitution exist, though they show how these results can be consistent with those of Hudson and Jorgensen.[16]

I believe that estimates of capital services dependent importantly on electricity usage should not be used in studies of energy-capital substitution unless it can be conclusively established that the amount of electricity used per unit of capital must remain constant. Failing that, the lower estimates of the effect of energy price increases on productivity are the best ones to use, and on technological grounds they indicate a very modest effect in the 1970s.

How can energy availability reduce productivity growth other than through the substitution of labor for energy inputs? A train of events described above showed energy price increases as a catalyst precipitating a series of private and governmental actions that raised inflation and unemployment, reduced growth and investment, and absorbed managerial resources that would normally be devoted to cost reduction in an environment of stable prices, stable production processes, and known future prospects. In particular, an inadequate government policy response must be blamed for the high rates of unemployment experienced during the decade, which can explain a substantial part of the decline in investment.

[15] Barry C. Field and Charles Grubenstein, "Capital-Energy Substitution in U.S. Manufacturing," *Review of Economics and Statistics*, 62, no. 2 (May 1980), 207–23, and Ernst R. Berndt and Mohammed S. Khaled, "Parametric Productivity Measurement and Choice Among Flexible Functional Forms," *Journal of Political Economy*, 87, no. 6 (December 1979), 1220–45.

[16] Ernst R. Berndt and David O. Wood, "Engineering and Econometric Interpretations of Energy—Capital Complementarity," *American Economic Review*, 69, no. 3 (June 1979), 342–54.

As much as a full percentage point of the productivity decline has been attributed to cyclical effects, low levels of investment, and a loss of economies of scale, all of which could have been avoided with a policy promoting full employment. Could such a policy have been designed without exacerbating inflation? I think so, but before outlining it I must first explain my productivity projection.

PRODUCTIVITY PROJECTION

I have projected productivity growth to recover in the next twenty years to a level of 2.0 percent per year—a figure still below the average of the 1948–73 period, and well below the best performance of that period. The expectation that productivity growth will be lower in the long run than in the 1950s and 1960s is based on the growing significance of resource scarcity. In the mid-seventies a decline in energy usage reduced productivity growth by 0.1 percentage points and will reduce it further in the future. Other resources may also pose limits, but I have not studied their possible effects.

My projection approaches, if it does not reach, the past level of productivity growth. It assumes a return to normal conditions, in the sense that structural challenges will eventually subside or, more accurately, will take place in predictable ways at predictable rates. The uncertainty over the future will diminish, as it has in the past seven years, and this will permit sensible planning decisions to be made. While technological breakthroughs will undoubtedly enhance the usefulness of alternative sources of energy, the uncertainty over their imminence and likely effects will diminish, making normal business procedures appropriate once again. Clean air and water, once attained, will take a constant or perhaps diminishing share of national product, not a growing share. And, finally, policy makers will become more efficient in attaining full employment without unacceptable levels of inflation. If these conditions are not all satisfied, my projection may be too high.

Except for cyclical effects, labor productivity is assumed to increase at the following compound rates: by 1.5 percent in the period 1980–85, 1.8 percent in 1985–90, and 2.0 percent in 1990–2000. Unemployment is expected to grow until 1981, then to diminish steadily until it reaches roughly 6 percent in 1984. After that, I assume further but slower progress in reducing unemployment to 5 percent by 1990 and to 4 percent by the year 2000 (Table 6, col. 2). An adjustment to the productivity projections is also provided, to account for the 1980–81 recession and the expected recovery from it.

Table 6 combines all the projections, in order to get an index of output

TABLE 6

Output, Labor, and Productivity Growth Projections, 1980–2000

Year	Labor force[a]	Employment rate[b]	Productivity trend	Cyclical productivity adjustment	Final productivity projections[c]	Output index[d]
1980	105,166	0.928	1.000	−.01	0.990	96,618
1981	107,471	0.918	1.015	−.01	1.014	100,040
1982	109,672	0.930	1.030	+.003	1.030	105,055
1983	111,552	0.938	1.046	.011	1.056	110,495
1984	113,301	0.941	1.061	.013	1.074	114,506
1985	114,985	0.944	1.077	.013	1.090	118,315
1986	116,690	0.946	1.097	.013	1.110	122,532
1987	118,376	0.947	1.116	.013	1.129	126,563
1988	119,876	0.948	1.137	.013	1.150	130,656
1989	121,201	0.949	1.157	.013	1.170	134,573
1990	122,375	0.951	1.178	.013	1.191	138,461
1991	123,532	0.951	1.201	.013	1.214	142,619
1992	124,483	0.952	1.225	.013	1.238	146,713
1993	125,387	0.953	1.250	.013	1.263	150,921
1994	126,423	0.954	1.275	.013	1.288	155,343
1995	127,542	0.955	1.300	.013	1.313	159,927
1996	128,834	0.956	1.326	.013	1.339	164,918
1997	130,031	0.957	1.353	.013	1.366	169,985
1998	131,345	0.958	1.380	.013	1.393	175,279
1999	132,741	0.959	1.408	.013	1.421	180,891
2000	134,155	0.960	1.436	.013	1.449	186,615

SOURCES: Labor force projections are by the Bureau of Labor Statistics. Other projections are the author's, as explained in the text.

[a]Average increment for 1980–2000, 1.23%; for 1980–90, 1.53%; for 1990–2000, 0.92%.

[b]Average increment for 1980–2000, 0.1%; for 1980–90, 0.24%; for 1990–2000, 0.11%.

[c]Average increment for 1980–2000, 1.92%; for 1980–90, 1.8%; for 1990–2000, 1.98%.

[d]The amounts are the products of the figures in cols. 1, 2, and 5. Average increment for 1980–2000, 3.35%; for 1980–90, 3.67%; for 1990–2000, 3.03%.

growth, which increases, as shown in the last column, by 3⅔ percent per year in the 1980s and by roughly 3 percent per year in the 1990s.

ECONOMIC POLICY IN THE 1980S

The structural challenges of the 1970s can be expected to continue in the 1980s. Energy and food prices will rise, and trend productivity growth will probably remain low in the early 1980s. If economic performance is to be satisfactory, the policy response to these challenges must be better than the responses of the 1970s. In particular, there is need for more coordination between structural policies, incomes policies, and demand policies. The neoclassical synthesis dominates policy analyses today. It suggests as a strategy that the role of structural policies is to remove market imperfections in order that microeconomic efficiency can be attained. The role of demand policies is to smooth the business cycle. For incomes policies there is no role, and between structural and demand policies no coordination is required.

The separation of demand from structural issues is reflected in academic circles in a split between microeconomics and macroeconomics. In the U.S. government, most agencies are assigned microeconomic or industry-specific structural issues, while the Federal Reserve, the Treasury, and the Council of Economic Advisers handle the macro issues. Professional economists who move between academia and government tend to carry with them expertise of one kind or the other and to view the world in terms of the neoclassical synthesis that justifies this separation.

In my view, the neoclassical synthesis failed a major test in the 1970s. When energy prices rose in 1973–74, no other prices fell. In particular, wage inflation did not fall. Because of this, the macroeconomic authorities had to choose between inflation and recession. Put differently, demand stabilization policies alone could not avoid the choice between inflation and recession, a choice the neoclassical synthesis implies is unnecessary.

A closer look at the energy policy dilemma indicates a major shortcoming in the intellectual foundations of economic policy. Following Musgrave's formulation, public finance issues have been classified into three boxes: stabilization, efficiency, and equity, and for much of the 1950s and 1960s this classification was adequate. In the 1970s, however, when energy policy was treated as an issue of economic efficiency, the inadequacy of the separation became evident.[17] As an efficiency issue, it is quite simple to demonstrate that domestic energy prices should be decontrolled so that they can seek world levels. As an equity issue, this policy is disastrous, since it redistributes enormous sums of money from poor energy consumers to rich producers. And as a stabilization issue, a high price is also disastrous, since it leads simultaneously to inflation and unemployment. Whether a high or a low price for energy is the best policy may be a moot point, but there can be little argument that the U.S. policy-making apparatus, supported by the very structure of academic economic theory, does not provide an arena where the issue can be properly addressed.

[17] See Alan S. Blinder, *Economic Policy and the Great Stagflation* (New York, 1980), for a discussion of economic policy during the 1974–75 recession.

My analysis of policy formation is still too undeveloped to permit me to recommend a proper way to air these issues. I will simply identify a few that will also have equity, efficiency, and demand consequences in the 1980s and whose proper resolution will require a more comprehensive policy apparatus than is in use today.

Variable interest mortgages will become common in the 1980s as bank deregulation frees up the interest rates payable to depositors. This will increase efficiency. With variable rate mortgages, however, macroeconomic fluctuations and monetary policy actions will have far different distributional implications that may of themselves constrain policy actions appreciably.

A continued growth in imports of manufactured goods will pose a variety of policy issues for the domestic industries whose sales are threatened by these inputs. The consistency of the chosen policies can be assured only by a comprehensive industrial policy based on employment and inflation objectives.

Food prices, which were relatively stable in the 1950s and 1960s, were extremely variable in the 1970s. Further instability can be expected in the 1980s. Food storage policies have macroeconomic and distributional implications that are too large to ignore. Energy policy in particular will continue to pose problems. Price increases large enough to cause a decline in real income for the average citizen will be resisted in a way that will cause both inflation and unemployment to rise unless policy integration is accomplished.

Issues of this kind made the decade of the 1970s miserable for the economy, and the intellectual foundation for policies to deal with them is still wanting. The policy makers were bewildered over the inadequacy of their policies to meet the new challenges; they had, after all, based them firmly on the neoclassical synthesis taught by the academics. The reaction of academics themselves to the bad performance of the 1970s was to withdraw from contact with the troublesome real world and to reject the policy makers as having learned their lessons badly. "We taught you to regulate markets with imperfections, but there are no markets with imperfections. We taught you to remove involuntary unemployment, but there is no involuntary unemployment," is increasingly the message of academics to policy makers.[18]

A new policy framework is needed. It must be comprehensive and pursue stabilization, efficiency, and equity objectives simultaneously. To this end, demand, structural, and incomes policies will probably have to be

[18] See James Tobin, *Asset Accumulation and Economic Activity* (Chicago, Ill., 1980), for an excellent discussion of the sorry state of macroeconomic theory today.

used in a consistent fashion. Because the problems we face can no longer be neatly categorized as micro or macro—as questions of distribution or of efficiency—a comprehensive policy is needed to restore to the economy the performance it exhibited in the 1950s and 1960s. Thus my projection of a recovery in the growth of productivity rests in a substantial way on my belief that a reformation of the economic policy process will be successfully completed. Without it, the miserable performance of the 1970s may continue.

Comments on the Nichols Paper

Tibor Scitovsky

THIS IS a beautifully written, sober, balanced, well-documented paper. The author has handled a difficult assignment extremely well, yet some criticism is warranted especially because of the great contrast between Nichols' optimism and Luis Maira's very pessimistic outlook in the paper that follows. Somehow I am impressed more by the latter's qualitative arguments than by the former's quantitative analysis, impressive as it is.

The main burden of the Nichols paper, as I see it, is to explain the drastic and rapid fall in U.S. labor productivity in the 1970s, and then to project from that experience into the future. The paper does an excellent job in sketching the cultural, social, and political background against which to view the economic debacle of the 1970s; it is careful and comprehensive in listing and examining each of the suspects that could be responsible for our present troubles; and the author does a good and, I think, fair job in exonerating the innocent. He is less good in finding the culprits, the factors responsible for the collapse of productivity and productivity growth; and because he cannot really explain the collapse, he does not quite believe in it either. Consequently, his projections for the future seem unduly optimistic—as if, not finding the causes of our problems, he had concluded that we had none.

Let me start with the exoneration of the innocent. I fully agree with his dismissing the much-quoted alleged fall in personal savings as a factor. He rightly points out that it is too small a source of saving to matter much; besides, that fall may well be a statistical illusion. After all, personal savings are calculated as a residual, not only of directly estimated quantities but of imputed quantities as well, which happen to be suspect.

He also stresses, quite correctly, that nonresidential investment has been keeping up to its customary ratio in GNP even after subtracting pollution abatement investment—probably because it depends mainly on business saving. I would not attach that much importance to the behavior of so-called net investment—the difference between gross investment and depreciation—because depreciation notoriously and grossly overstates replacement costs in a growing economy, while changes in depreciation fail to reflect changes in replacement investment. On the other hand, in light of the behavior of gross investment, as shown in Table 3, the figures do not really contradict the conclusion that capital formation has held up and is likely to hold up pretty well.

In short, I concur with the exoneration of saving and investment as non-guilty parties, but I am disturbed by the failure to find the guilty ones. Nichols deals with our loss of social consensus, the increase in conflict, the battle between different interest groups, the substitution of lawyers for engineers in industry, the tremendous increase in regulation, the shifting of the burden of proof from consumers to producers, from government to industry; and he describes graphically the tremendous problems of technologically adjusting to the great increase in oil prices in the midst of a recession. When it comes to quantifying the effects of all those factors on labor productivity, however, they somehow sink into insignificance. Why?

The reason, I think, is the author's exclusive reliance on the estimates made and assembled by economists trained in the national accounts approach, people like Denison. Denison undoubtedly is the person who did the most thorough and careful study of the causes of our declining productivity, but he himself admits that he can explain only the lesser part of the decline. The reason, I suspect, is that the aggregative approach in which he is immersed is ill suited to deal with the problem. An illustration is Denison's—and Nichols'—treatment of the effects of government regulation of business. Denison takes the cost of compliance and paperwork as a percentage of total production cost or investment cost, and—because such aggregative terms make that cost appear insignificant—he assumes the total impact of regulation to be insignificant.

That appears to me as just a first approximation, and certainly not the end of the story. In a second approximation one would look at the distribution of the burden of regulation. From a study by Robert Berney, it appears that the burden of regulation is indeed rather small in the case of large firms, but it is seven to ten times as great a burden per employee on small firms. Because they operate with a much smaller managerial staff than large firms, regulation diverts a much larger part of their scarce and valuable administrative resources. Statistics show a great decline in the relative contribution of small firms to GNP—a phenomenon alleged to be due mainly to the great increase in the burden of regulation. This is of great relevance, because it is the small firms in this country that are responsible for much of the innovation and adaptation of industry. Regulation, therefore, that weighs heavily on the small firm may have little impact on total output but a much larger impact on innovation, and so on growth. According to an NSF study, "half of the most significant new industrial products and processes of the post World War II period were developed by firms with less than 1,000 employees—a quarter of all important innovations were made by firms with less than 100 employees."

The Economic Significance of Mexican Petroleum from the Perspective of Mexico– United States Relations

Jaime Corredor

IN THE CONTEXT of a broad study of the future of trade and industrial relations between Mexico and the United States, one important aspect is the energy issue, and oil in particular. There is no doubt that new realities and perceptions concerning wider aspects of the economic, social, and political relationship between the two countries will develop around it. Broaching those wider aspects without first deepening one's understanding of the significance of the new petroleum situation in Mexico carries with it the risk that the special dimensions that Mexican-U.S. relations have begun to acquire will not be appreciated in all their magnitude.

It is a striking fact, for example, that owing to the recent discoveries of oil in Mexico a sudden and intense interest has been awakened in the United States with regard to its southern neighbor. Consequently, bilateral relations have become an important issue for discussion in that country's mass media and in its political, business, and academic circles. By contrast, just a few short years ago, if Mexico were mentioned at all in the U.S. press, it was only to report some spectacular incident or to cover the campaign of some politician in need of the Chicano vote. In U.S. governmental circles, relations betweeen the two countries had until recently constituted "a matter of secondary importance, studied superficially by lower-ranking officials in the State Department."[1]

It is evident that in view of Mexico's new oil potential the United States has begun to discern attractive situations of opportunity: to rely on a close and supposedly "more secure" source of energy supplies; to benefit from the economic growth that Mexico may undergo as a result of its petroleum

---

[1] Olga Pellicer de Brody, "La política de Estados Unidos hacía México: la nueva perspectiva," *Foro Internacional*, El Colegio de México, no. 74 (Oct.-Dec. 1978), p. 203.

push; to take advantage of a growing Mexican market; and to deepen investments in and industrial penetration of the country.

At the same time, the United States has discerned a number of uncertain and worrisome situations with regard to Mexico. In the economic sphere, for example, they are worried that Mexico, backed up by its oil, will try to diversify its foreign trade significantly or to obtain undue advantages in trade negotiations. This explains, among other things, their insistence that Mexico enter into the GATT.[2] In the political realm, there is worry about the importance Mexico might acquire in international forums, as well as the direction that its foreign policy might take, particularly in the Latin American region.

For Mexico's part, its relations with the United States have always been, for obvious reasons, of fundamental importance. Mexican interest in its northern neighbor is not a new phenomenon arising with the oil boom. Nevertheless, it may fairly be stated that as a result of the new oil potential the perceptions of Mexicans about the relationship have been sharpened. In a very special way the great majority of the Mexican people view their new petroleum wealth as a powerful instrument that the country must exploit in order both to accelerate its economic development and to pursue greater economic and political independence, particularly from the United States. The latter aspiration is profoundly rooted in Mexican national objectives that have been significantly reinforced in view of the potential expected from oil, which will consequently influence the course of relations between the two countries.

For this reason, in Mexico oil is viewed by many as an opportunity not to pursue a scheme of closer integration with the United States, but rather to reduce its dependence there. It sees opportunities to diversify foreign markets, to modify past trends in the relationship and eliminate conditioning influences that are incompatible with the country's aspirations and development strategy, to strengthen its position in financial and trade negotiations, to improve conditions for the transfer of technology, and to gain a wider margin of maneuver in foreign policy questions.

Simultaneously, oil generates perceptions of insecurity and risk in regard to Mexico's relationship with the United States—the risk that, through poor domestic management of the new energy potential and its far-reaching repercussions throughout the country, the inertia of Mexico's dependence, far from being broken, will be aggravated through a process

[2] After a long period of study and intense domestic political debate, President López Portillo announced on March 18, 1980, Mexico's decision, for the moment, not to enter the GATT (the General Agreement on Tariffs and Trade). Prior to that time, however, open insistence had been heard on the part of U.S. spokesmen, businessmen, academics, and even government officials to the effect that Mexico join the organization.

of "silent integration" that is automatic, out of control, and incompatible with the strategic objectives of the nation. Likewise, insecurity exists over the possibility that U.S. interests in Mexican oil may not coincide with, and consequently might be imposed upon, those of Mexico (see Table 1).

However, Mexico's new petroleum riches have had immediate effects not only in the realm of the perceptions and aspirations of each of the two countries in regard to the bilateral relationship. Changed events and trends have already been observed that are to be explained, on the one hand, on the basis of both the initial characteristics of Mexico's oil boom and the established inertial forces conditioning the relationship between the two countries, and on the other as the result of concrete political decisions taken by the Mexican government. For example, after the advent of the oil boom a greater direct penetration of U.S. firms in Mexico can be observed, a substantial number of new companies having been established, while existing ones have expanded their investments in spectacular fashion.[3] This has given rise, among other things, to a closer interrelationship of interests between private business groupings in the two countries. Similarly, processes of transnational integration have been accelerated in certain sectors such as the automotive industry and the *maquiladoras*, and border relations have intensified. The practice of establishing commissions, working groups, and bilateral cooperation agreements between border states on both sides has generalized.[4]

In the specific matter of hydrocarbons, one notes that as a result of the oil boom Mexican exports have tended to concentrate markedly on the United States, allowing that country to reduce its dependence on the Persian Gulf; between 1977 and 1979, 86 percent of Mexico's total exports of crude petroleum were directed to the United States.[5] In turn, whereas in 1976 Mexican oil represented only 1.6 percent of the total crude imports of the United States, by 1980 that proportion had risen to 10.8 percent, and in 1981 it may reach 15 percent.

Nevertheless, this phenomenon of concentration is beginning to be reduced as a result, first, of certain concrete policy decisions that the Mexican government has taken in regard to the diversification of foreign mar-

---

[3] According to data from the *Encuestas sobre actividad económica empresarial*, carried out by the Office of Advisors of the President of the Republic, foreign companies in Mexico have increased their investments in the period 1978–80 at an average annual rate greater than that registered by the economy as a whole over the same period: 16.1% in real terms. Likewise, the *Survey of Current Business* estimates that annual investment by U.S. enterprises in Mexico went from $347 million in 1978 to $1,003 million in 1980.

[4] The Commission on the Californias, for example.

[5] Various factors explain this initial concentration. A more attractive price, owing to geographic proximity; Mexico's slight experience as an oil exporter; and difficult conditions in the world market for oil up to 1978.

TABLE 1

Exports of Crude Petroleum from Mexico by Country of Destination, 1979–81

(thousand barrels per day)

Country	1979 Volume	1979 Percent	1980 Volume	1980 Percent	1981[a] Volume	1981[a] Percent
United States	442.3	83.0%	563.3	68.0%	743	49.7%
Spain	42.9	8.1	92.5	11.2	220	14.7
France	—	—	42.1	5.1	100	6.7
Japan	—	—	35.2	4.3	100	6.7
Sweden	—	—	—	—	70	4.7
Canada	—	—	4.2	0.5	50	3.3
Israel	40.9	7.7	56.6	6.8	45	3.0
Brazil	—	—	16.8	2.0	50	3.3
India	—	—	—	—	20	1.3
Jamaica	—	—	—	—	10	0.7
Costa Rica	0.3	0.1	4.9	0.6	7.5	0.5
Nicaragua	—	—	2.3	0.3	7.5	0.5
Yugoslavia	—	—	3.1	0.4	3.0	0.2
Other countries in Central America and the Caribbean	6.4	1.2	6.8	0.8	55	3.7
TOTAL	532.8	100.0%	827.8	100.0%	1,496	100.0%

SOURCE: PEMEX Gerencia de Comercio Exterior.

[a]According to contractual obligations announced by the Director General of PEMEX in August 1980.

kets, and, second, of fixing a ceiling on hydrocarbon exports. Thus, in 1980 the proportion of Mexico's total crude exports directed to the United States fell to approximately 68 percent, and by 1981, in accord with contractual commitments, this proportion may fall to slightly less than 50 percent of total exports, given the ceiling of 1.5 million barrels of crude exported daily.[6]

As far as the broader aspects of Mexican foreign trade are concerned, we may also observe how, with the oil boom, several trends in bilateral relations have been accentuated at the same time that policy decisions have emerged in Mexico to counter them:

1. Export statistics show a deepening of Mexico's dependence on the U.S. market precisely because of the concentration of oil sales: 56 percent of Mexico's total merchandise exports in 1976 to the United States, and more than 70 percent by 1979.[7]

2. Imports also increased—and with them Mexico's dependence on the U.S. market—as a result of the rapid growth of the Mexican economy: in 1976, 61 percent of Mexico's total merchandise imports came from the United States; by 1980 that proportion had risen to 65.4 percent. In turn, this signified that Mexico had taken on greater importance as a foreign market for the United States, having become its fourth most important client in 1980 with 6.2 percent of U.S. exports, compared to 3.3 percent in 1976.[8]

3. The decision not to enter the GATT, the intensification of its efforts to diversify its trade among other countries, and the establishment of the Mexican Food System (SAM) in order to achieve self-sufficiency in food have all served to counteract tendencies toward dependence and trade concentration.

It is evident from these considerations that the new oil potential is an important factor that impresses a whole new dimension on the context of Mexico–United States relations, emphasizing on the one hand the dif-

[6] The policy decisions formally established in the Energy Program presented to the nation in November 1980 stipulate, among other things, that (1) during the decade of the eighties, total exports of crude petroleum and natural gas will not exceed a maximum daily limit of 1.5 million barrels and 300 million cubic feet, respectively; (2) not more than 50% of total hydrocarbon exports will be concentrated in any one country; (3) Mexican exports will not come to represent more than 20% of the total imports of crude and refined petroleum products of any country (with the exception of the nations of Central America and the Caribbean, which will be supplied with up to 50% of their hydrocarbon needs).

[7] This is due also to the fact that hydrocarbons have taken on marked importance in the totality of Mexico's merchandise exports. Representing only 15.4% of the total in 1976, they increased to 68.1% of the total in 1980.

[8] Between 1977 and 1980 Mexico's total merchandise imports grew at an average annual rate of 46.9% in nominal terms, increasing from $5,889.8 million in 1977 to an estimated $18,572 million in 1980.

ferent interests and perceptions that have been generated in each of the countries, and, on the other, certain outstanding facts and trends that can already be observed in the bilateral relationship.

The manner in which oil will influence relations between the two countries in the future will depend on how strategic this resource continues to be at the international level, on its repercussions for Mexico's own development, on already established conditions and trends in the bilateral relationship, and on the diverse policy actions that are taken, on both sides of the border, as a result of oil and on the basis of the perceptions and interests that it generates, to sustain, accentuate, or reverse such trends. All this, in turn, will be conditioned by the way in which political and economic circumstances in each of the countries evolve.

Several analysts have tried to model U.S.-Mexican petroleum relations by hypothesizing unilateral actions taken by the United States and the resulting Mexican responses. Others have made simple extrapolations of present trends, finding that oil will deepen the integration between these two countries. What these analysts leave out of account is that Mexico, with or without oil, aspires to greater independence from the outside, which it considers an indispensable precondition for strengthening its integration as a nation and for advancing in a way congruent with its historical, political, and socio-economic characteristics. To fall, either by inertia or by express decision, into a scheme of economic integration with the United States would mean going against the very essence of the "national project," in part because—given the present conditions of inequality between the two countries—such a scheme cannot reflect a balanced process of integration and interdependence between two sovereign nations, but would instead intensify already existing conditions of dependence. In addition, the division of labor along the lines of comparative advantage that would result from such a scheme would be very detrimental to Mexico.

The present analysis proceeds from the assumption that the principal effects of oil on the future conduct of relations between the two countries will basically derive from the changes that in the first instance are produced in Mexico as a result of what the country wishes and is able to do with its petroleum wealth. Thus, it should be clear that this study will not be developed around unilateral initiatives that the United States might take or on the basis of the recognition of a process of integration—or, better said, of increasing dependence—that is predetermined by historical trends. Without ignoring the relevance of the other analytic options, we will explicitly assume two things here: first, that since petroleum is a factor that affects Mexico foremost and fundamentally, its most important implications for the future of the bilateral relationship will stem from what happens in this country; and, second, that Mexico's national objective of achieving greater independence from the exterior will remain in force.

The sections that follow will examine from this perspective the most important repercussions—above all, those of an economic sort—that petroleum may have on Mexico's future development in order to formulate, on that basis, various considerations having to do with possible trends in bilateral relations. Concretely, this will be done by analyzing the economic significance of oil as a factor that makes energy easily available domestically, and as both a real and financial factor in the development, delimiting at the same time the extent of its advantages and risks.

We conclude from this analysis that oil can play a very significant role in Mexico's economic development not only as a financial factor generating foreign exchange—the attribute most often emphasized in other studies—but also for other reasons that we try to emphasize here. Even so, its potential as an instrument of development—a potential that has been greatly exaggerated—is not exempt from certain limitations inherent in the very nature of the wealth it generates and the effects the latter produces. These limitations we will also attempt to delimit in some way.

Moreover, within the bilateral relationship we find that oil and its effects on the Mexican economy can be important elements supporting a reversal of the country's tendencies toward dependence and strengthening its international position if the government maintains a firm policy in this regard and if the benefits that this resource offers are taken advantage of. Otherwise, the oil phenomenon will provoke an accentuation of such tendencies. This does not necessarily mean that situations of conflict or friction are to be foreseen in future relations between the two countries, for although the relative importance of those relations will diminish—for example, in the commercial sphere, as a result of an effective policy of market diversification on the part of Mexico—it is probable that they will continue to be strengthened in absolute terms given the expected growth of the Mexican economy, and under the assumption that good neighborliness, respect, and mutual understanding will persist. We do not believe that the prospect of a Mexico which utilizes its oil in order to attempt to gain greater independence and to develop in accord with its own strategies and idiosyncracies is incompatible with the interests of the United States.

PETROLEUM AS A FACTOR IN DOMESTIC ENERGY SUPPLY

Mexico's abundant oil wealth provides the country, above all else, with the advantage of being self-sufficient in a resource of fundamental economic and strategic importance that can be exploited domestically. This takes on special relevance when one considers the prospects both for shortages and higher costs of hydrocarbons at the international level, and for the already high internal consumption of these resources that the size and energy structure of the Mexican economy dictate.[9]

For the purpose of evaluating the first attribute, we have identified five kinds of advantages that Mexico may obtain by utilizing its ample endowment internally. In the first place, Mexico will not have to divert important quantities of foreign exchange to the import of hydrocarbons, which means in turn being able to grow with fewer restrictions on the balance of payments and to attend more fully to the priorities of national development. To take one example, if Mexico had had to cover its total internal consumption with imported crude oil and natural gas in 1980, it would have had to make a foreign exchange expenditure of over $20 billion, which equals 1.4 times the value of all its non-oil exports in that year.[10]

Second, internal availability of hydrocarbons implies for Mexico the advantage of not having to confront the vicissitudes and risks of the international oil market, characterized as it is by instability and insecure supply. For this reason the country is protected against supply interruptions as well as against abrupt changes in prices, which might affect the functioning of the economy, make planning schedules more difficult to adhere to, and force the country to invest in costly inventories for contingency purposes.

In the third place, the ability to count on an abundance of oil riches offers Mexico the possibility of adjusting its economy to the higher cost levels of the "new energy era" in a gradual manner and therefore to benefit from the comparative advantage that this implies vis-à-vis countries that possess no oil. In effect, owing to the speed and intensity with which the new conditions of scarcity and higher costs of energy products have emerged at the world level, those countries that are deficient in oil have had to implement drastic and costly conservation measures, hastily restructuring their transportation systems and modifying, even eliminating, production processes that are highly energy-intensive. For the countries

[9] In 1980 a daily average of 1.1 million barrels of crude oil and 3.3 billion cubic feet of natural gas was consumed domestically. The total domestic consumption of primary energy has been growing at an average annual rate of almost 11% over the last five years, and the product elasticity of demand registered an average of 1.7 in the same period. Mexico figures among those countries with the highest intensity of energy consumed per unit of domestic production. Of total primary energy requirements, 90% are currently satisfied by crude oil and natural gas, 5% by hydroelectricity, 4% by coal, and less than 0.5% by geothermal energy.

[10] In Brazil and India, for example, the value of oil imports in 1980 amounted to nearly 60% of their respective export incomes, and in September 1980 Brazil's external debt reached $55 billion.

in question, all of this produces strong side-effects in terms of market re-duction, slower economic growth, inflation, and diversion of resources that might otherwise have been invested in projects and activities that are more profitable in terms of development.

Even if these repercussions are transitory in nature for the most ad-vanced countries and might eventually serve to impel technological ad-vance and development, for developing countries they tend to reduce the growth possibilities by necessitating an abrupt transition to new patterns of modernization before industrial stages have matured—or even, in some cases, been initiated—thus forcing the countries into situations of even more extreme dependence.

It is apparent, then, that countries that can count on abundant oil re-sources are not as interested in incurring the same costs of transition as the oil-importing, developing countries. Mexico in particular will pursue a policy of gradual adjustment of its domestic energy prices, which will permit it to reduce waste and expenditure of energy and also to avoid sudden and costly impacts on its economy, at the same time that energy is utilized as a means toward industrial development. In particular, the En-ergy Program stipulates that internal prices of hydrocarbons will grad-ually have to be adjusted over the next ten years until they reach 80 percent of the average international prices. "The policy of promoting in-dustry on the basis of energy supplied at prices below the international level must continue. This is an instrument which a developing country possessing an abundance of hydrocarbons may legitimately utilize in in-ternational competition. It is well to remember that the industrial growth of the presently developed economies was nurtured by an abundant sup-ply of energy products at low prices, at times at the expense of the producers."[11]

On the basis of a previous determination the National Industrial De-velopment Plan has established a structure of differential prices of hydro-carbons according to the geographic location of enterprises and the branch of activity to which they belong. This decision is aimed at utiliz-ing the country's energy resources as an instrument for the selective pro-motion of particular productive activities, as well as for the stimulation of exports and the geographic deconcentration of industry. Although this instrument of promotion is quite effective and its initial results may al-ready be discerned, one should not fail to note that its application is deli-cate, since in some cases it can involve distortions in the allocation of the country's resources.

From the Mexican point of view, the fact that the government keeps

[11] Secretaría de Patrimonio y Fomento Industrial, *Programa de energía (Resumen y con-clusiones)* (November 1980), p. 30.

the prices of certain energy items lower than the corresponding international prices in no way signifies the granting of a subsidy. Such prices reflect a situation of scarcity at the world level that of course does not exist in the Mexican case. What the country is really doing, then, is to exploit a comparative advantage in factor endowment based on the magnitude of its oil potential, on very low production costs,[12] and on the fact that, with its relatively large and diversified economy, Mexico contains strategic sectors that are high consumers of energy and are able to exploit that advantage in international competition.

Nevertheless, it must be recognized that, by attending to internal pressures, Mexico has already indulged in the luxury of maintaining very low prices for some energy products over a long period, a fact that has provoked the waste of a valuable and nonrenewable resource and has also shortened unnecessarily the era of the country's self-sufficiency. It is estimated that between 1974 and 1979 the real value of the income obtained by the domestic sale of the products extracted from one barrel of oil declined by more than 47 percent in constant 1970 prices. At the same time, the differential between the domestic price and the international prices has grown noticeably; in September of 1980, the value of one barrel's worth of products sold domestically was calculated at $7.80 compared to a value of $32.70 if the same barrel had been exported.

Fortunately, cognizance has now been taken of the necessity to adjust domestic prices upward, albeit gradually and selectively, in order to avoid abrupt impacts or the elimination of the comparative advantage. What is especially worrisome is the high level of wastage that is presently being recorded, as well as the risk of falling into an excessive technological delay vis-à-vis the world advance toward new productive structures that are more efficient in the use of energy. In this area the Energy Program contemplates a conservation target for 1990 equivalent to a million barrels of oil daily, to be achieved through price adjustments and direct regulatory measures.

Fourth, the availability of an ample hydrocarbon potential means that Mexico will not be forced, like many other countries, to implement a policy of hastened transition to new sources of energy supply. In other words, oil relieves the country of the urgent necessity to make very large investments in the development of alternative sources, and this permits it to schedule its financial resources for use in activities and projects that are of higher priority for its economic and social development.

[12] On September 1, 1980, proven reserves of hydrocarbons (crude oil, gaseous fluids, and natural gas) reached a total of 60.126 billion barrels of crude petroleum equivalent. In addition, 30.042 billion barrels of probable reserves and, including both of these categories, 250 billion of potential reserves were estimated. The average cost of extraction per barrel in Mexico is estimated to be less than 14% of its international price.

Such investments will of course have to be made eventually, but at a more gradual pace and perhaps at lower relative cost and greater efficiency, to the extent that international technological development advances and the country is able to count on a greater internal ability to discriminate among the options available. Furthermore, at a gradual rate of investment the country will have greater opportunity to incorporate its domestic industry into the process of developing substitutes and to assimilate foreign technology.

In Mexico's case—taking into account its pressing necessities to invest in sectors like education, health, social security, crop and livestock production, fishing, transportation, and capital goods, among others—it is undoubtedly advisable not to divert scarce resources unnecessarily in order to embark on an accelerated process of substituting energy sources. There is no point in incurring the kinds of costs and pressures faced by countries deficient in petroleum. Neither is it advisable for Mexico to incur delays, which in this area can end up being costly for the country later on. The important thing, therefore, is to determine an appropriate rhythm of investment in alternative sources that will permit the country to do two things: to take full advantage of its petroleum potential and to guarantee a future in which the country will continue to enjoy energy self-sufficiency.

Fifth, and finally, the ample availability of hydrocarbons at present, and their secure supply in the future, give Mexico the opportunity to further the development of certain industrial sectors, be they those linked to the processing of oil and natural gas themselves (refining and petrochemicals) or those characterized by high intensity in energy use (e.g., the cement and glass industries, fertilizers, steel, etc.). This is feasible because (1) the country now possesses a relatively large industrial plant, along with human resources trained and experienced in its operation and a broad domestic market that assures growing volume of demand, and (2) these are basic industries that strengthen and support the country's whole industrial apparatus, generate their own technological advances, and permit oil to be exported with a higher value added.

Despite all the advantages, the development of these kinds of industries beyond what is required to cover domestic consumption needs, i.e., for export purposes, presents a number of inconveniences that must also be evaluated. These industries are highly capital-intensive, generate relatively little employment, and compete for scarce domestic resources with other activities of high priority for the country's development. On the other hand, because of the excess installed capacity in several of these industries at the world level, particularly refining and petrochemicals, their products currently confront strong competition in international markets—a situation that can be expected to persist in the medium and long term as oil-surplus countries, with few options for channeling their enormous surpluses internally (e.g., Saudi Arabia, Libya, and Kuwait), continue to intensify investments in these areas.

In any case, it is foreseeable that in Mexico these industries will maintain a rate of growth higher than the national average and that, in spite of the inconveniences, an additional capacity will be generated in them toward the end of diversifying and making the country's export structure more flexible. At the same time, it is both feasible and in the country's interest for this type of industry to begin to internationalize its activities through the export of engineering services and technological patents, or even by participating directly on contract in the construction of plants in other countries. This would, moreover, bring with it intersectorial linkages that would aid both the internal and the external development of other branches of industry—for example, that of capital goods.

In conclusion, in analyzing the economic significance of oil as a factor contributing an ample domestic supply of energy, we have identified in this part of our study a series of important benefits that Mexico can take advantage of to propel its economic growth, to devote greater resources to the country's main priorities, to increase its non-oil exports, to achieve a better geographic distribution of its productive system, and to strengthen certain strategic branches of its industrial sector. Among other things, this signifies that Mexico, in contrast to other net oil exporters, may obtain, on account of the degree of diversification and relatively large size of its economy, enormous benefit from its petroleum resources not only, or even principally, by way of export, as many suppose, but rather through the domestic exploitation of these productive resources in general use. Furthermore, these factors impose a limit on the level of oil exports that the country ought not to exceed in the future, despite its copious reserves.

It is evident that the advantages accruing to Mexico from domestic utilization of its new petroleum wealth would decline significantly within a framework of formal integration with the United States, inasmuch as the rate of exploitation would have to be accelerated, and the era of self-sufficiency, from which the potential for generating such advantages is derived, would consequently be shortened.

PETROLEUM AS A REAL FACTOR IN
NATIONAL DEVELOPMENT

Another advantage that Mexico can exploit as an oil producer derives from the material or "real" impact of the oil industry on the whole economy: the markets for goods, services, and labor. Its size, dynamism, and linkages with other sectors of the economy permit it to generate significant multiplier effects—at both the national and the regional levels—on employment, technological advance, human capital formation, and the development of other productive activities. Inasmuch as the oil industry in Mexico began to develop many years ago, it benefits from the accumulation of experience in the field, as also from the fact that proprietorship and management are totally in the hands of the state.[13] The relatively large and diversified economy of which oil is but one sector can likewise benefit from its domestic stimulus.

Since 1973, when the first important discoveries of hydrocarbons in the Mesozoic region of the states of Tabasco and Chiapas were made, oil activity in Mexico has experienced a great and sustained dynamism. Because this dynamism has been much greater than that of the rest of the country's productive sectors, the industry has taken on increasing relative importance in the overall development of the economy. There are a number of indications that exhibit, in one way or another, and quantify this phenomenon:

1. The total production of crude oil, condensates, gaseous liquids, and natural gas, measured in terms of volume, has grown at an annual average rate of 16.8 percent over the last seven years: from an average daily level of 525,000 barrels of crude oil and liquids and 1,854 million cubic feet of natural gas in 1973 to 1.9 million barrels of crude and liquids and 3,548 million cubic feet of gas in 1980 (see Table 2).

2. In value-added terms, the Gross Domestic Product (GDP) of the petroleum sector, including basic petrochemicals, has grown from 1974 to 1980 at an annual average rate of 13.7 percent in constant prices of 1960—a rate significantly higher than the 7.3 percent registered by the industrial sector or the 5.4 percent registered by the economy as a whole.

3. Whereas in the period from 1960 to 1973 the oil sector's share of industrial GDP and of total GDP of the economy measured in constant 1960 prices was never greater than 12.5 percent and 4.3 percent respectively, in 1980 that share reached 17.9 percent of industrial sector GDP and 7.0 percent of the whole economy. In 1982 it is expected that the latter proportion will rise to not more than 10.0 percent, assuming a maximum level of crude oil production of 2.75 million barrels daily (see Table 3).

[13] Constitutionally speaking, hydrocarbons in Mexico are the property of the nation, and all activities connected with them—exploration, production, refining, transport, distribution, marketing, and basic petrochemicals—take place under the exclusive responsibility of a single entity, Petroleos Mexicanos (PEMEX), created in 1938 after the expropriation of the foreign companies as a decentralized agency of the federal government. As such, PEMEX today is the country's largest enterprise, standing out even among the principal petroleum companies in the world.

TABLE 2

Mexico: Production and Trade of (a) Crude Oil, (b) Natural Gas, (c) Refined Products, and (d) Basic Petrochemicals, 1970–80

Year	Production				Imports				Exports			
	a	b	c	d	a	b	c	d	a	b	c	d
1970	486.6	1,822.5	167.9	1,931.4	—	48.8	17.3	189.0	—	106.3	22.4	66.0
1971	485.8	1,762.7	169.0	2,097.0	1.9	53.2	24.9	203.6	—	55.9	17.3	67.6
1972	505.5	1,803.8	184.9	2,323.0	31.4	43.2	25.5	270.3	—	27.0	9.4	46.8
1973	524.7	1,854.0	197.2	2,650.0	64.7	42.4	33.2	228.9	—	5.5	8.7	44.2
1974	652.9	2,040.3	223.4	2,978.0	17.0	34.2	23.6	253.8	—	1.1	6.7	21.2
1975	806.3	2,154.5	233.2	3,634.9	—	15.9	25.0	251.5	15.9	—	2.6	13.9
1976	894.3	2,108.7	258.8	3,947.0	—	17.2	15.7	355.1	94.2	—	1.2	1.7
1977	1,085.5	2,046.0	288.4	4,196.3	—	9.6	8.9	552.4	94.3	6.6	1.6	30.2
1978	1,329.6	2,561.4	307.9	5,785.4	—	8.5	13.5	541.1	201.9	—	0.7	700.8
1979	1,618.1	2,916.7	335.4	6,346.0	—	11.0	10.0	651.7	364.9	—	3.7	750.0
1980	1,935.8	3,548.1	401.4	7,224.0	—	—	5.4	762.1	532.9	280.9	17.0	755.2

SOURCES: 1970–79: PEMEX, La industria petrolera en México; Secretaria de Programación y Presupuesto. 1980: PEMEX, Memoria de labores.

NOTES: Figures in (a) are thousands of barrels per day and include crude oil, condensates, and gaseous liquids; in (b) millions of cubic feet per day; in (c) millions of barrels per year of fuel oil equivalent and include liquefied gas, gasolines, fuel oil, diesel, kerosenes, lubricants, paraffins, asphalt, and naphtha; in (d) thousands of metric tons per year.

TABLE 3

Mexico: Total, Industrial Sector, and Petroleum Sector GDP Real Growth

(percent)

Year	Total GDP growth	Growth of industrial GDP	Growth of petroleum GDP	Share of petroleum GDP in Industrial GDP	Share of petroleum GDP in Total GDP
1970	6.9%	8.2%	10.0%	12.4%	4.3%
1971	3.4	2.5	3.4	12.5	4.3
1972	7.3	9.3	8.9	12.5	4.3
1973	7.6	9.2	2.7	11.7	4.1
1974	5.9	7.2	14.8	12.6	4.5
1975	4.1	4.3	7.9	13.0	4.7
1976	2.1	3.9	10.6	13.8	5.0
1977	3.3	4.8	15.8	15.3	5.7
1978	7.3	10.2	14.7	15.9	6.0
1979	8.0	10.3	15.4	16.6	6.5
1980	7.4	10.2	16.9	17.9	7.0

SOURCE: 1970–78: PEMEX, *La industria petrolera en México*, and Secretaría de Programación y Presupuesto. 1979–80: PEMEX, *Coordinación y estudios técnicos*.

4. With regard to oil exploration activity, proven reserves of hydrocarbons—which include crude, liquids, and natural gas—have gone from a level of 5.432 billion barrels in 1973 to 60.126 billion in 1980. During the 1974–80 period, spending on exploration undertaken by PEMEX grew at an annual average rate of 18.7 percent in constant 1960 prices.

5. During the 1974–80 period, gross fixed investment in the petroleum sector grew at an annual average rate of 27.4 percent in real terms, which compares with 13.6 percent for the public sector and an estimated 9.0 percent for the whole economy. Whereas in 1973 investment in the oil sector represented 10.9 percent of public sector investment and 4.3 percent of total investment, by 1980 these percentages had grown to 27.2 percent and 12.1 percent, respectively (see Table 4).

6. As far as employment is concerned, the number of personnel hired directly by PEMEX has grown from 1978 to 1980 at an average annual rate of 8.9 percent, which compares with an estimated 6.3 percent for the country's manufacturing sector. If the personnel hired by PEMEX contractors were taken into account, a more rapid growth of direct employment in the sector would undoubtedly be registered.

If to the foregoing we were to add the stimulative effects on other sectors linked to oil, as well as its repercussions at the regional level and its impact on technological advances and the training of personnel, we would have a more complete picture of the important role that oil has played as a "real" factor in the country's economic development.

TABLE 4

Mexico: Total, Public Sector, and Petroleum Sector Investment Growth

(percent)

Year	Total investment growth	Growth of public investment	Growth of petroleum investment	Share of petroleum investment	
				Public investment	Total investment
1970	8.3%	n.a.	n.a.	7.8%	2.8%
1971	−3.7	−25.8%	13.9%	12.0	3.3
1972	13.4	40.7	21.6	10.4	3.5
1973	16.0	34.3	41.8	10.9	4.3
1974	8.7	2.9	7.5	11.4	4.3
1975	6.9	23.7	29.4	11.9	5.2
1976	−2.9	−8.7	51.3	19.8	8.0
1977	−8.4	−6.7	19.8	25.4	10.5
1978	15.8	27.9	45.2	28.8	13.2
1979	20.4	18.7	17.4	29.1	13.1
1980	15.8	17.0	6.7	27.2	12.1

SOURCE: Banco de México, *Informe anual, 1980*; the PEMEX data are taken from the preliminary budget and were deflated with Bank of Mexico indices.

It must, however, be recognized that this phenomenon is exceptional in character. Even if it was necessary, given the dire circumstances in which the country found itself, to multiply PEMEX's productive capacity several fold in just a few years in order to exploit the new oil wealth rapidly, it is difficult to suppose that such activity will continue to grow indefinitely at such a pace. Alongside the positive effects of the current oil dynamism, there have also been serious repercussions that will undoubtedly take on greater relevance if the growth of oil activity is not moderated.

In the first place, the concentration of domestic resources in an industry intensive in the use of capital occurs to the relative detriment of other sectors that, though perhaps less profitable in the microeconomic sense, may be of greater importance and priority for the country in terms of employment generation, productive strategy, or social benefit. A pace of petroleum activity as intense as that observed up to now necessarily diverts scarce domestic factors from other areas at a faster rate than they can be resupplied using the oil surplus. To persist in behavior of this kind would undoubtedly lead to the "petrolization" of the economy or to tacit recognition of the country's integration with its northern neighbor.[14]

[14] Among the domestically scarce factors of production are skilled manpower, public and private management capability, electricity, communications, etc., whose supply cannot automatically be increased with the excess resources generated by oil. Within a framework of

Secondly, taking into account the present and future conditions of the Mexican economy, if PEMEX's expenditures and investments were to continue to increase at the same high levels already observed, serious implications for the management of budgetary policy would result. If, for example, the government decided to increase total public spending at the same rate as that of PEMEX in order to maintain equilibrium in the structure of the budget, demand pressures in the economy would undoubtedly provoke a higher rate of inflation; if, on the other hand, it decided to avoid this greater inflation, compensating for PEMEX increases by reducing spending in other areas, a number of priority items would probably be affected and public expenditure would become even more concentrated in the oil sector.[15]

Third, the wide gap in growth rates between the oil sector and the rest of the economy has generated bottlenecks in strategic areas such as transportation and port services. It has likewise occasioned a large and rapid increase in imports of machinery, equipment, and raw materials by PEMEX, minimizing—even eliminating—the multiplier effects that petroleum activity has on other sectors of the economy.[16] For the country to be able to take full advantage of these stimulative effects it is necessary, among other things, that the rhythm of petroleum activity be accommodated in some way to the possibilities for expansion of the sectors linked directly or indirectly to it. Otherwise, imports will increase beyond a point that is desirable, which is equivalent to exporting the country's prosperity.

Finally, it is obvious that oil activity has had strong side-effects on the development of the geographic regions in which it has been concentrated by introducing into them copious resources that impel local growth and modernization and contribute to decentralizing the country's productive system, but at the same time provoke all too sudden changes in the social and economic condition of the areas.[17] It is enough to visit the oil zones of the Southeast to observe an inflationary process that is considerably stronger than the national average, along with a constant shortage of housing and of urban and social services that the government, faced with a rapid growth of population and economic activity in general, cannot

---

wider integration with the United States, pressures derived from these kinds of limiting factors would diminish.

[15] In 1973 PEMEX spending represented only 13.0% of the total spending of the public sector; by 1977 this proportion had risen to 19.0%, and by 1980 reached 28.9%.

[16] It is estimated that the import content of the investment realized by PEMEX reached 65% in 1978.

[17] Of the 25.8 billion pesos that PEMEX spent on exploration and drilling in 1979, almost 70% was devoted to the Southern Zone.

succeed in resolving. We also find in these areas congestion in the transportation and communication systems and drastic changes in their productive structures, all of which work to the detriment of traditional economic activities.

For all these reasons, it is desirable to moderate the pace of hydrocarbon activity and make it more compatible with the rest of the country's economic growth. The danger is that the internal rationality and inertia of the oil industry might push it toward undesired levels of production and export, and also that a postponed slowdown would have to be more severe, thus affecting not only the economic and political position of PEMEX itself but also the sectors and regions of the country whose dependence on PEMEX actions is most marked.

To what point is it desirable to moderate the dynamism of the oil sector? Even if it is neither suitable nor justifiable for this sector to continue to grow at such high rates, it is still necessary to recognize that we are dealing with a key activity, of fundamental importance for the country's development strategy. The industry must maintain strong growth in the future, even at a rate above the national average, and yet—while allowing for multiplier effects on the rest of the economy to be generated—not so excessive as to intensify the negative side-effects.[18]

However, this rate of growth of petroleum activity might conceivably prove to be incompatible with the hydrocarbon production and export ceilings that it is desirable for the country to maintain. In order to avoid this risk, it would be advisable for Mexico's oil industry to begin to expand its activities abroad, collaborating with other countries in their efforts to explore for or develop hydrocarbon deposits, or participating by means of construction of refineries and petrochemical plants. The industry could then sustain a rapid rhythm of activity without having to increase the exploitation of hydrocarbons domestically, and the expansion would at the same time promote exports in sectors connected to it—capital goods, for example—and also generate a greater export capacity in the economy as a whole.[19] This would appear to be a very beneficial choice for Mexico, and less risky than the proposal that the country channel the dynamism of its oil industry, not so much to increase produc-

---

[18] The Global Development Plan drawn up by the Secretariat of Programming and Budget at the end of 1979 envisioned a slowdown in the growth of PEMEX investments for the 3-year period 1980–82, setting it at an annual average rate of 21.5% in real terms, in contrast to the 27.1% observed from 1977 to 1979.

[19] These kinds of options have already been contemplated at an official level with Spain, China, Costa Rica, and Cuba, and are also contained in the agreement that Mexico signed with Venezuela to guarantee oil supplies to Central American and Caribbean area countries on August 3, 1980.

tion and exports as to generate excess capacity for contingency purposes that would offer the United States greater security in its energy supplies.[20]

PETROLEUM AS A FINANCIAL FACTOR

Under present world conditions of scarcity and increasing costs of conventional forms of energy, oil also signifies for Mexico the possibility of generating large financial surpluses that it can use to expand its efforts at social and economic development. Basically, these surpluses derive from a worldwide redistribution of resources from consuming countries to net oil producers that accrues as a result of the broad differential existing between the international prices of hydrocarbons and their current costs of production.[21] Their importance for Mexico is twofold: they are surplus resources that increase the country's capacity for payments abroad, and they augment the government's capacity for action in managing the economy.

One means of quantifying the magnitude of the surplus resources that Mexico has been generating through the exploitation of its oil is an examination of the figures on current pre-tax savings of PEMEX. Some rough calculations will serve to demonstrate the increasing importance of these resources.

1. In 1974–80, after the initial discoveries in the Tabasco-Chiapas Mesozoic region, PEMEX generated an accumulated total of 445.7 billion pesos in current savings before taxes, due principally to the increase in prices and volumes of exports as well as, in some measure, to a decline in average production costs on account of the higher productivity of the deposits exploited in the Southeast (up to 40,000 barrels a day).

2. Of the 445.7 billion pesos generated by PEMEX as total current savings during this period, the federal government absorbed almost 63 percent in taxes, the rest being left over to finance investment in the oil sector itself.[22]

3. Current savings accumulated by PEMEX from 1974 to 1979 covered almost the entire current-account deficit accumulated by the non-oil public sector during the same period.

4. It is estimated that PEMEX current pre-tax savings in 1980 reached

---

[20] This proposal, which has been discussed in the U.S. Congress, was formulated originally in a Rand Corporation study by David Ronfeldt, Richard Nehring, and Arturo Gandara, *Mexico's Petroleum and US Policy: Implications for the 1980s*, R-2510-DOE (June 1980).

[21] This broad differential between price and cost of production is due less to a monopoly power exercised by the net oil-exporting countries than to the fact that what is sold is a nonrenewable natural resource.

[22] This remainder that is left over for PEMEX investment covers only a part of that investment, the rest being financed with domestic and foreign credits.

220.9 billion pesos (5.9 percent of GDP and 22.9 percent of total investment in the country's economy). If from this current saving we take away the amount invested by the enterprise itself, we find that the remainder was sufficient to pay for 35.2 percent of non-oil investment by the public sector and 11.8 percent of non-oil investment in the economy as a whole during the same year.

These surpluses are important also because they are produced and therefore controlled by the public sector, and can be assigned in a direct and effective manner to meet the country's priority social and economic needs. Moreover, the fact that the greater part of these resources is generated in foreign currency—through net direct and indirect exports of hydrocarbons—signifies a greater payment capacity for the country abroad, and consequently fewer balance of payments restrictions on its development. This is especially important for Mexico when we take into account the country's level of development, the strong dependence on imports that results from the nature of its productive structure, and the particular problem of external disequilibrium that it faces on account of a very weak non-oil export capacity.[23]

Precisely because surplus oil resources come mainly in the form of foreign exchange, however, their utilization encounters certain restrictions. Foreign currencies are means of payment that, from an economic point of view, serve only to acquire goods or services of physical and financial assets abroad, or to cover the servicing of the accumulated foreign debt. That being so, when foreign currencies are utilized in the country's development process, their contribution is subject to the availability of complementary national resources. To try to apply additional quantities of foreign exchange above and beyond the limits of the domestic shortage would adversely affect the functioning of the economy.

What, then, is the most appropriate level and rate of expansion of the foreign exchange earned by oil that would permit Mexico to grow economically not only at a strong and sustained pace, but also in a balanced fashion congruent with its national objectives? Apart from considerations of energy self-sufficiency and of the nature of the productive system that place limits on hydrocarbon exports, the answer depends, in the financial sense, on three principal factors: (1) the "physical" capacity of the economy to absorb foreign exchange through the importation of goods and services; (2) the type of development strategy the country adopts; and (3) the convenience and possibility of utilizing alternative sources of foreign exchange.

[23] Whereas before 1977 the petroleum sector registered a deficit on its external current account and thereby increased the nation's total foreign debt, thereafter it began to register surpluses, which by 1979 came to cover almost 30% of the deficit of the non-oil sector.

With respect to the first point, there is no doubt that the Mexican economy has demonstrated a capacity to absorb foreign exchange, something that is reflected in the high growth rate of imports of goods and services observed in the years 1978–80.[24] This is due, among other things, to the economy's relatively large size, to its high degree of diversification, to an industrial structure quite dependent on imports—especially in the capital goods lines—and with a large participation by foreign interests, to a geographical location bordering on the U.S. market, and to the existence of well-developed and fast-acting financial, information, and communications systems that facilitate the importation process.

Mexico's capacity to absorb foreign currency, however ample, is not infinite; it is fundamentally conditioned by the size of the economy and by the availability of factors and resources that are difficult or impossible to import or that lack close substitutes (as is the case in transportation and communications, skilled labor, private and public managerial capabilities, and banking and public services). To the extent of the scarcity of resources, "physical" limitations are at once encountered that make the application of larger amounts of oil-derived foreign currency earnings futile, whether used for consumption or for investment, productively or unproductively.[25] For this reason, generating foreign exchange—through increased exports of hydrocarbons—greater than the economy could absorb, would be equivalent to feeding inflationary pressures and wasting the nation's oil resources.[26]

Second, the level and rate of growth of oil-derived foreign exchange receipts most suitable for the country depend on the type of development strategy adopted, and particularly on what that strategy stipulates by way of limits on the participation of foreign investment, the degree of self-sufficiency and openness of the economy to foreign trade, and relative emphasis on domestic consumption or investment.

[24] For the years 1978, 1979, 1980, imports of goods and services grew at an average rate of 50.1% annually. Their share of the Gross Domestic Product, measured in real terms, went from 3.9% in 1977 to 7.2% in 1980. The elasticity of demand for imports in relation to GDP, which had traditionally been about 1.5%, increased to nearly 4.7% in 1980. It must be emphasized that the bulk of the increase in imports took place in the categories of capital and intermediate goods, and on a lesser scale in consumer goods. In 1980, when the largest grain imports in the country's history were made, the consumption goods category represented only 13% of total merchandise imports.

[25] In a scheme of broadscale integration with the United States, "physical" absorption capacity would of course be greater. However, this would imply that financial surpluses would be invested not so much in Mexico as on the other side of the border.

[26] Mexico currently faces a difficult situation in regard to bottlenecks, principally in the areas of transportation, warehousing, electricity, and skilled Mexican power, which will take time to resolve and which impose, in and of themselves, a clear limitation on the econ-

It is clear that a strategy which emphasizes the majority participation of national capital in Mexican enterprises and promotes import substitution by protecting certain economic sectors will require a lower level and rate of growth of foreign currency earnings than would an open-economy strategy that is more liberal in its provisions concerning foreign trade and external investment. Similarly, a strategy that gives preference to the investment process might result in a lower level and rate of application of utilizable foreign exchange than one that assigned priority to the population's standard of living through the importation of consumer goods.

In Mexico's case, the development strategy as adopted places special emphasis on the industrial, agricultural, and livestock sectors, applying generalized mechanisms of import protection and substitution and establishing food self-sufficiency as a basic objective.[27] At the same time, the strategy assumes that the financial surplus earned from oil will be utilized principally for productive investment, within the prevailing restrictions on foreign participation. On the basis of such strategic considerations, it is estimated in the Energy Program that the country can sustain an annual rate of growth in real product of 8 percent throughout the decade of the eighties—encouraging autonomous development in industry and in the agricultural and livestock sectors—without the need to export more than 1.5 million barrels of crude daily and 300 million cubic feet of natural gas.

Also for reasons of strategy, the desired amount and pace of generating petroleum exchange earnings could be altered, depending on one's expectations about the future international price of oil, and—once anticipated inflation is discounted—on interest rates. For example, if estimates foretell a growth in the international price of oil lower than the expected rate of interest in real terms, for reasons of economic rationality it would be desirable for the country to accelerate oil production in the present rather than leave the resource in the ground for future exploitation. In that case, the surplus foreign exchange earnings that could not be applied internally in a productive manner compatible with the country's overall strategy would be used either to acquire physical and financial assets abroad or to redeem the foreign debt ahead of schedule, with no negative repercussions on the behavior of the domestic economy.

The policy of the Mexican government up to this point—expressly opposed to increasing the volume of oil exports in order to accumulate in-

omy's capacity to absorb foreign currency. In turn, the rate of inflation in 1980 reached a level of approximately 30%.

[27] This strategy does not aim at a situation of total autarchy. For example, the objective of food self-sufficiency includes only basic food items, and the special policies for strengthening the domestic industrial sector do not include all of its branches.

ternational assets, or to amortize the nation's foreign debt ahead of time—includes an implicit assumption that the world price of oil in real terms will continue to rise at a rate above the real yield of international assets.[28] It might be argued, however, that, to the extent that world market conditions for energy supplies change and the international price of oil tends to stabilize in the longer term, Mexico's authorities would consider it convenient to begin to generate a certain oil surplus to be invested abroad or to pay off the foreign debt.[29] For strategic reasons it might also be convenient to undertake some industrial investments abroad, thus allowing the country to assure itself of foreign markets and to achieve a fuller transfer of technology, or else to engage in financial operations that would reduce the risk implicit in keeping oil in the ground while waiting for its price to rise.[30] In the final instance, a balance between risks and yields ought to be pursued through an appropriate combination of industrial and financial assets and petroleum kept in the ground.

Another type of strategic consideration that might influence the level and rate of generation of petroleum surpluses derives from the fact that hydrocarbons can be a handy instrument of international negotiation. In this connection, oil export volumes have to reach a certain magnitude in order to be attractive to the importing countries and in order to incline them to offer in exchange advantages of commercial interchange or better terms in matters of industrial and technological cooperation. The policy espoused by the Mexican authorities up to now has been that the country must take advantage of the strategic importance of its hydrocarbon exports, seeking in exchange not only a conventional monetary recompense but also a broader scheme of commercial interchange and economic cooperation with its clients that would bring the country additional benefits and would contribute to greater diversification of its foreign relations. In return, Mexico offers those clients security in supply and seriousness in negotiations. It is estimated that the volume of current Mexican exports is already sufficient, by and large, to permit it to main-

[28] Objective reasons of a political nature have also influenced this policy, e.g., how does one explain to a population in which large numbers of people can barely satisfy their most elemental needs that the country is accumulating billions of dollars abroad, which cannot, however, be utilized immediately to raise their standard of living.

[29] Of course, exactly the opposite might happen: if the international price of oil were to increase beyond what was expected initially, it would be desirable for Mexico instead to reduce its export volume and keep the oil in the ground.

[30] Consider, in the first case, the purchase by Mexico of a Spanish firm and, in the second one, the sales of "petrobonds" in the international market, which are a form of financing that permits sharing with buyers the risk that the export price of Mexican oil may not turn out to be as high as expected. The petrobonds are long-term financial assets with a guaranteed rate of interest but, being denominated in barrels of oil for export, have an ultimate yield indexed to the international price of this resource.

TABLE 5

Mexico: Exports of the Petroleum, Primary, and Manufacturing Sectors as
Percentages of Total and Merchandise Exports, 1975–80

Type of export	1975	1976	1977	1978	1979	1980[a]
Petroleum sector exports[b]						
Percent of total exports	6.7%	6.8%	11.3%	16.0%	24.6%	42.0%
Percent of merchandise exports	15.7	15.4	22.3	30.7	45.2	68.1
Primary sector exports[c]						
Percent of total exports	12.5	14.2	14.3	12.9	11.0	6.2
Percent of merchandise exports	29.1	32.1	28.2	24.8	20.2	10.1
Exports of manufactures[d]						
Percent of total exports	20.8	20.6	22.7	21.3	16.9	11.4
Percent of merchandise exports	48.4	46.7	44.8	41.0	31.0	18.5

SOURCES: 1975–78: Banco de México, Balanza de pagos. 1979–80: Banco de México, Informe anual.
[a]Preliminary.
[b]Includes crude oil, natural gas, refined products, and petrochemicals.
[c]Includes agriculture, livestock raising, forestry, hunting, and fishing.
[d]Includes food, textiles, chemical and nonmetallic mineral products, metal products, machinery and equipment, and wood
and paper products.

tain a long list of clients, the principal of whom have petroleum allocations of substantial magnitude.

Finally—on the subject of the possibility and convenience of utilizing other sources for generating foreign exchange—the alternatives are the export of non-oil goods and services, and increased foreign indebtedness. The country could substitute income from either of these sources for petroleum earnings and thus slow down the exhaustion of its reserves. For reasons of trade and production strategy, it is important for Mexico to develop non-oil exports, since with them the country is able to stimulate a number of its key economic sectors, employ its particular factor endowments more efficiently (i.e., export more labor-intensive products), and reduce the risks implicit in excessive dependence on exports of hydrocarbons. It would be a grave error if, on account of its petroleum riches or the magnitude and dynamism of domestic demand, Mexico were to neglect or renounce its potential as a non-oil exporter (which has not been taken proper advantage of). In our opinion Mexico ought to make better use of its surplus petroleum resources to strengthen the other supporting sectors of its economy, thereby establishing a source of foreign exchange that would substitute eventually for oil (see Table 5).

The option of foreign indebtedness must be evaluated in terms of both strategy and economic rationality. On the one hand it is important to compare the advantages of oil-derived foreign exchange receipts with the disadvantages of foreign credits. The latter can represent a greater dependence for the exporting country in the sense that their availability is subject to possible interruptions and to implicit or explicit restrictions on their allocation—something that does not occur with foreign exchange generated by oil. On the other hand, depending on what expectations one has about the future behavior of the world price of oil and real interest rates, it is important to determine what will be more profitable: producing and selling the oil *today*, or contracting more debt and leaving the oil underground.[31]

The strong growth of foreign indebtedness recorded in Mexico in recent years suggests that the country has understood the convenience of making use of this expedient as a complement to foreign exchange earnings. In financial terms, it is considered to be more advantageous than increasing volumes of hydrocarbon exports.[32] Unless conditions in the

[31] In the last few years, in spite of increases in nominal interest rates, the profitable course has been to increase indebtedness, as the international price of oil has grown substantially. In 1980, for example, it was possible to pay off debts contracted in 1977, plus interest, with fewer barrels of oil than it would have been necessary to pump out of the ground and sell in that year if the debt had not been contracted.

[32] The country's annual external indebtedness, measured in terms of the current account

world oil market are substantially modified, or the management of the country's economy becomes seriously complicated, it is more than likely that Mexico will continue with the policy of preferring increases in the foreign debt to exceeding the stipulated ceilings on petroleum exports.

THE FUTURE BEHAVIOR OF THE BILATERAL RELATIONSHIP

On the basis of foreseeable effects and changes that will occur in Mexico as a result of petroleum, it is possible to hypothesize a number of implications for the course of Mexico–United States relations.

With regard to Mexican exports of crude oil and natural gas:

1. For diverse reasons of a strategic, economic, and energy nature, it appears that Mexico, notwithstanding its copious reserves, will continue to adhere to a policy of containing the export of crude oil and natural gas within the maximum limits contemplated in the Energy Program, unless conditions in the international oil market are significantly altered or the management of the country's economy requires a change in that policy.

2. It may also be assumed that Mexico will continue with its efforts to diversify export markets for its hydrocarbons, attempting to take advantage of the strategic importance of these exports within the broader schemes of trade negotiations and economic cooperation, and consequently granting preference to direct government-to-government arrangements.

3. In this perspective, it is not foreseeable that the volume of hydrocarbons that Mexico exports to the United States will rise; on the contrary, it is even probable that it will diminish, along with its importance as a direct supplier of oil and gas.* This does not imply, however, that cooperation between the two countries in the oil area will cease to be important. Today Mexico makes slightly more than 50 percent of its total foreign sales of hydrocarbons to the United States, and the great majority of its imports of machinery, equipment, and raw materials undertaken by PEMEX come from that country. If the efforts on Mexico's part to diversify markets bear fruit, they will result in the creation of a more flexible and independent trading structure in the petroleum sphere; however, its relationship with the United States will continue to be the most important of all of its foreign relations, and the United States will continue to be able to count on a significant and close provider of hydrocarbons.

---

deficit, has gone from 1.8 billion U.S. dollars in 1977 to 6.6 billion U.S. dollars in 1980, and the total foreign debt of the public sector from 15.9 billion U.S. dollars in 1976 to approximately 32.3 billion U.S. dollars in 1980.

*Editors' note: This position notwithstanding, Mexico and the United States in 1981 signed an agreement to supply the United States's strategic petroleum reserves with Mexican oil. Also, it is beginning to be recognized by experts in both countries that material benefits might accrue from modest increases in natural gas sales.

In regard to Mexican exports and imports of refined products and petrochemicals:

1. It is probable that Mexico will go on gradually increasing the value added of its oil exports, replacing crude oil by refined products and petrochemicals. In this way the composition of the exchange of petroleum products between Mexico and the United States will tend to be modified; insofar as the process affects the interests of some United States enterprises, this will perhaps provoke certain tensions and conflicts.[33]

2. The Mexican government will continue to promote policies that seek national self-sufficiency in these products. Therefore, whatever imports of them occur in the future will be of no particular significance.

In regard to industrial cooperation between the two countries in the petroleum sphere:

1. In light of the dynamism predicted for Mexico's oil industry, it may be expected that a broad field of cooperation with companies from the United States and other areas will continue to exist in the specialized areas of engineering, installation, and operation of platforms, etc. Of course, the constitutional restriction of not permitting the direct participation of foreign capital in the activities of exploration, production, and refining of oil, as well as in basic petrochemicals, will continue in effect.

2. To the end of being able to sustain a certain rate of growth without pressing on the desired volume of domestic production, it may be expected that the Mexican petroleum industry, together with various collateral sectors, will tend to go abroad to cooperate with other countries in the exploration and exploitation of hydrocarbons, or to participate on contract in the construction of petrochemical plants and refineries. This may open the door for a new type of cooperation between Mexico and some foreign companies—even U.S. companies—to operate in third countries (through joint ventures), although it may also signify a new field of competition with the United States.

In regard to the proposal to generate a surplus hydrocarbon capacity in Mexico for situations of contingency or crisis in the United States:

1. Apart from the political inconvenience and risks that such a proposal implies for Mexico, one would also have to take into account the economic costs that the country would incur in increasing the concentration of its scarce domestic resources in a sector that, by its very nature,

---

[33] This change in the composition of oil exports could imply for Mexico the necessity to assure itself of its own channels of distribution for refined products and petrochemicals in the United States. Moreover, for reasons of technological interchange, and in order to give greater flexibility to the production and sales apparatus of its oil industry, Mexico might in the future come to be interested in acquiring a share of the capital of some U.S. refinery.

will already have to grow at quite high rates in order to cover increasing internal demand, to keep up a considerable volume of exports, and to be able to operate in other countries. As a consequence, it is unlikely that this proposal will be of interest to Mexico.

2. The proposal also prompts a number of queries: What degree of excess capacity would be necessary? Who would pay for it? Who would decide when to use it and when to stop using it? Would it not be simpler, in the case at hand, for the United States and other consuming countries to invest in contingency reserves within their own borders?

In regard to Mexican imports of non-oil products:

1. The prospect of a high and sustained rate of growth that has emerged on the basis of oil has converted the Mexican economy into an ever more attractive and important market for U.S. exports; in addition, few countries of Mexico's size present similar possibilities for future import growth. This implication holds true even if the country's efforts to diversify its import sources and to reduce the import content of its growth continue.

2. Nevertheless, the strengthening of protective measures that is foreseen in Mexico, in an effort to stimulate the development of certain key sectors of its economy, makes it possible that future reactions on the part of U.S. groups will arise.

In regard to Mexican exports of non-oil products:

1. Given the policy of gradually adjusting domestic prices of hydrocarbons, it may be assumed that among Mexico's non-oil exports those with a high energy content, such as the sectors of secondary petrochemicals, the synthetic-fiber textile industry, the plastics, glass, and cement industries, etc., will take on greater importance. This may provoke reactions on the part of those in the United States who interpret the policy of low energy prices in Mexico as a subsidy (and not as the country's exploitation of a comparative advantage on the basis of factor endowments).

2. In order to avoid excessive dependence on exports of hydrocarbons and to generate other sources of foreign currency, it is to be expected that Mexico will actively push the growth of its non-petroleum exports, which can also provoke frictions to the extent that the United States tries to counteract the Mexican incentives with compensatory measures.

3. As a consequence, a change in the structure and dimensions of Mexico's non-oil exports to the United States is foreseeable, and in this process Mexico will attempt to utilize its oil as an instrument of negotiation and market diversification.

In regard to the investments of U.S. companies in Mexico:

1. Direct investments will surely continue to grow, attracted by the rapid and sustained growth of the Mexican economy as well as by se-

curity in the domestic supply of hydrocarbons and their low domestic prices (this will be especially attractive for companies with high levels of utilization of these resources).

2. For its part, Mexico will certainly continue to strengthen its legislation with regard to transnational enterprises and transfer of technology, a trend that will condition the process mentioned above.

In conclusion, then, it may be affirmed that relations between the United States and Mexico have acquired a new dimension as a result of Mexico's oil. As the Mexican economy takes on ever greater importance as a counterpart of the U.S. economy, and as trade, investment, and technological cooperation between the two countries broadens, these bilateral relations will grow progressively more intense and frictions may arise, above all in regard to specific policies of industrial and trade promotion that Mexico will implement on the basis of oil. If the spirit of understanding and mutual respect in handling the negotiations persists, however, the frictions will be overcome, for there is no fundamental conflict of interests between the two countries. Not only will the United States continue to be very important for Mexico, but it will benefit in the future to the extent that Mexico succeeds in furthering its own process of social and economic development.

Trade and Investment in Mexico–United States Relations

Raymond Vernon

THE PRINCIPAL economic and political factors likely to affect trade and investment between the United States and Mexico during the next decade or two fall into three categories: changes in the international trade regime; changes in the structure of international industry; and changes in energy prospects.

THE INTERNATIONAL TRADE REGIME

The trade relationships that have existed between Mexico and the United States have been shaped by one overriding fact, namely, the commitment of the United States to a global trading system that it had been largely instrumental in creating and sustaining. The United States had come out of World War II as the undisputed leader of the non-communist world. Its perceptions as to how that world should be organized for international trade inevitably reflected its own national interests. Although the U.S. blueprint was not intended to be inimical to the interests of others—indeed, quite the contrary—it was bound to be compatible with the values and perspectives of the country that created it. The General Agreement on Tariffs and Trade (GATT), which evolved from the original U.S. proposals, incorporated substantial modifications that the U.S. government felt it could accede to in the interest of gaining acceptance for its general principles.

From the time when the GATT was negotiated in 1948, those principles came to represent the norms of the international trading regime. Inasmuch as all the major industrialized countries and many of the developing countries were members of the GATT, the influence of these norms pervaded practically all trade outside the communist area. Although Mexico steadfastly refused to join the GATT, its trade relations with the United States and other countries were as much affected by the GATT regime as if it had been a member.

The norms of the GATT were expressed in two propositions: that the import tariffs on industrial products were to be reduced gradually, while import licenses and quantitative import restrictions on such products were to be eliminated, and that the restrictions that remained on imports and exports were to be administered in a nondiscriminatory pattern.[1]

From the very first, both provisions were breached in various ways—in most instances by resorting to some well-recognized exceptions specified within the agreement itself, and hence formally consistent with the GATT. Among these exceptions was a special regime applied to agricultural products—originally at the insistence of the United States, but later with the wholehearted support of the Europeans.[2] In addition, countries in balance-of-payment difficulties were given almost a free hand in fashioning their own import and export restrictions. At the same time, custom union arrangements and free trade area arrangements were given a blessing as exceptions under the GATT.[3]

There were also some exceptions, never recognized in the GATT, that assumed considerable importance. The international oil trade, for instance, was always conducted without reference to GATT rules. In trade between members of the GATT and socialist countries, no serious attempts were made to apply the rules of nondiscrimination. In addition, various countries successfully evaded the GATT by negotiating so-called voluntary export agreements, pursuant to which exporters undertook to curb their exports under threat of even more restrictive action on the part of the importing countries.

One of the most important areas excepted from the GATT's general principles, however, has been the practices of developing countries with respect to their imports, not only from the advanced industrialized countries but also from other developing countries. This exception has been based partly on the basis of balance-of-payments, partly on economic development grounds, and justified both by specific reference to the GATT's provisions and by a general understanding that the developing countries would not be expected to conform to the GATT's basic rules. The implicit bargain under the GATT, therefore, was essentially this: developing countries were to be entitled to such benefits as they might incidentally get, largely by virtue of the principle of nondiscrimination in the GATT as the advanced industrialized countries lowered trade barriers. No reciprocal obligations were to be enforced upon the developing countries with respect to their behavior either toward the advanced countries or toward

[1] UN, *General Agreement on Tariffs and Trade*, I, *Final Act* (Lake Success, N.Y., 1947), Article 1.
[2] GATT, Articles 11, 16.
[3] GATT, Articles 12, 24.

one another. And they were to leave the governance of the GATT and its related activities in the hands of the advanced industrialized countries, these being the countries that were expected to conform to its provisions.

In general, these spoken and unspoken rules prevailed until the late 1960s or early 1970s. During that time, tariff rates imposed on imports by the United States and Europe dropped to perhaps one-third or one-quarter of their starting levels, while the European nations dismantled the elaborate systems of import-licensing restrictions that they had imposed in the immediate postwar period. The size and scope of these reductions were determined by agreements among the advanced industrialized countries. At the same time it was the developing countries—Mexico included—who, although they had little if any say in the decisions, benefited from the reductions that resulted from the unconditional most-favored-nation policies of the importing countries.

Indeed, the advanced industrialized countries went even further in their different treatment of imports emanating from the developing countries. For instance, by 1968 the United Nations Conference on Trade and Development (UNCTAD) succeeded in persuading the advanced countries to extend a variety of tariff preferences to products originating in the developing countries.[4] Although the measures were carefully tailored to avoid injuring the advanced countries' own sensitive industries, they were nevertheless of value to many developing countries, including Mexico.[5] Meanwhile, the European Economic Community (EEC) developed a series of agreements that granted duty-free access to its markets for the products of a large group of developing countries in Africa, the Caribbean, and the Pacific.[6]

By the early 1970s, however, the signs of a new phase began to appear. An ambitious group of trade negotiations, the so-called MTN, conducted under the aegis of the GATT, was completed in Geneva in 1979. These produced yet another round of tariff reductions on the part of the advanced developed countries, to be applied to the products exported from all GATT countries, as well as from Mexico.[7] Other results of the MTN negotiations were portentous.

[4] See Tracy Murray, *Trade Preferences for Developing Countries* (New York, 1977), esp. pp. 5–17.

[5] Gustavo del Castillo V., "The Generalized System of Preferences and Mexican–United States Relations" (presented at 1980 meeting of Latin American Studies Association), xerox.

[6] Cf., for instance, S. Friedberg, "The Lomé Agreement: Co-operation Rather than Confrontation," *Journal of World Trade Law* (hereafter cited as *JWTL*), 9, no. 6 (Nov./Dec. 1975), 691–701; G. K. Helleiner, "Lomé: Market Access and Industrial Cooperation," *JWTL*, 13, no. 2 (Mar./Apr. 1979), 181–86; and C. H. Kirkpatrick, "Lomé II," *JWTL*, 14, no. 4 (July/Aug. 1980), 325–59.

[7] For a full report on all aspects of the negotiations, see GATT, *The Tokyo Round of Mul-*

By the 1970s some of the countries in the "developing" category (the so-called newly industrializing countries or NICs) had achieved a fairly high degree of industrialization; in several, indeed, per capita incomes were higher than in some of the nations that were expected to adhere to the GATT obligations. In the course of the negotiations during the 1970s, therefore, it became apparent that the advanced countries were no longer prepared indefinitely to grant nondiscriminatory treatment to all developing countries; some, it was made clear, would eventually be expected to reciprocate in one form or another. That signal was communicated in a number of different ways—not only in the tariff negotiations themselves, but also in the provisions of several new codes formulated for dealing with various non-tariff trade barriers. One such code, for example, was aimed at reducing discrimination in the buying practices of governmental agencies, while another was directed to the use of export subsidies. In each case, the advanced industrialized countries insisted that the privileges extended would be available only to those countries that were signatories to the codes, hence only those that had undertaken reciprocal obligations.

The decision to apply the benefits of these codes only to their signatories was symptomatic of the fact that international trade relations had reached a watershed, comparable in significance to the abandonment of the fixed exchange rate regime in the early 1970s.[8] It appears likely that the advanced countries will no longer move on a global basis to reduce existing import and export restrictions. The general principle of unconditional most-favored-nation treatment, from which the developing countries have heretofore benefited, has lost most of its force as a norm in world trade relationships. In the future, deviations from that principle by the AICs, including the United States, will tend to be more overt and more explicit. If that prognosis proves sound, nations unprepared to make trade commitments that are regarded as "reciprocal" will find themselves excluded from the benefits that other nations are receiving. For the United States–Mexico relationship this will present an especially difficult problem. If Mexican leaders feel that any reciprocal trade agreement with the United States would be politically unacceptable at home, a painful impasse in U.S.-Mexican trade relations could develop.

Will the AICs maintain open markets among themselves? Their extraordinary performance in reducing tariffs and other import restrictions over the past thirty-five years suggests that powerful economic forces

---

tilateral Trade Negotiations (Geneva, 1979), and *The Tokyo Round of Multilateral Trade Negotiations: Supplementary Report* (Geneva, 1980).

[8] Cf. Thomas D. Willett, *Floating Exchange Rates and International Monetary Reform* (Washington, D.C., 1977), p. 22.

must have been served by such a policy. Yet the trade liberalization record of these countries during the same period has not been quite so simple. Even as they managed to find the political will to demolish their import restrictions in a series of major negotiating sessions, each of them also put in place a series of lesser restrictions with narrower application to individual countries and individual products. Most of these restrictions affected developing countries; many were applied also to the manufactured products of Japan.

The seeming contradiction between adopting a general policy of trade liberalization and imposing tight restrictions for selected products from designated areas has been especially marked for the United States. On a little closer examination, however, the causes of the apparent contradiction are evident enough. Since World War II domestic industries have been learning that the U.S. political process, when presented with a simple choice between the principle of open markets and that of protection, is likely to elect for open markets. Domestic interests have therefore learned to avoid frontal attacks on the principle and to present their cases as exceptional situations—situations entailing "unfair" competition, or demanding temporary relief, or requiring the collection of obscure facts. As a result, after numerous amendments of the applicable statutes, these interests are now in a position to harass and hamper importers, simply by their ability to institute an endless succession of legal proceedings, and to demand unlimited quantities of information, thereby threatening the growth and continuity of any given stream of imports.[9]

Similar developments have been occurring in Europe, through actions of the EEC and also through less transparent devices applied by individual countries. Europe's systems of jurisprudence have always left governments with a considerable amount of administrative discretion in matters of trade restrictions, and governments have been using those restrictions selectively, with increasing disregard for the principles of the GATT.[10]

The increase in such cases raises the possibility that the general trend toward trade liberalization among the AICs may be swamped by the cumulative force of individual cases. The risk clearly exists, but a large-

[9] Cf. M. J. Marks, "Recent Changes in American Law on Regulatory Trade Measures," *The World Economy*, 2, no. 4 (February 1980), 427–40; T. R. Gordon, "Revolution in Trade Politics," *Foreign Policy*, no. 36 (Fall 1979), pp. 49–62. In addition, an excellent summary appears in C. J. Green, "Legal Protectionism in the United States and Its Impact on United States–Japan Economic Relations" (prepared for the Advisory Group on United States–Japan Economic Relations, July 1980), unpublished.

[10] For an account of such measures as they affect Japanese exports, see Kazuo Nukazawa, "The United States–Japanese Collision Course," in Diane Tasca, ed., *United States–Japanese Economic Relations* (New York, 1980), pp. 39–49, and Masamichi Hanabusa, *Trade Problems Between Japan and Western Europe* (New York, 1979), pp. 7–11.

scale movement to choke off the trade among advanced countries is likely to require a more frontal attack, entailing questions of principle. In that case, I anticipate that the U.S. preference for the principle of open markets, at least as it applies to other advanced industrialized countries, will reassert itself.

The main reason for this expectation is that the political forces in the AICs that have a stake in supporting the principle of open markets appear to be growing rather than declining. The enormous importance that the avoidance of inflation has acquired in the political processes is a case in point.[11] Coupled with the growth in the political strength of consumer-oriented groups, this factor represents a rather new force in the shaping of national trade policy. Increased concerns related to the consumer, however, would probably not be sufficient to block a protectionist wave. A more important fact is that every industrialized country now has a major stake in exporting to the others. The size of that stake, when related to their respective domestic economies, is unprecedented, commonly running at one-quarter or more of their gross national product. Even the United States now exports 7 or 8 percent of its nonagricultural output, most of it to other industrialized countries.

The possibility that interests in the AICs will mobilize to resist a strong protectionist threat is fortified by other factors. In the United States more than half of the industrial output is accounted for by firms that own and operate substantial facilities abroad, and in other countries the proportion is almost as high. To be sure, the stake of these multinational firms in open markets is no guarantee against a protectionist policy; the case of the automobile industry is evidence enough. But even there, the overseas stake of U.S. firms has generated a certain schizophrenia on the part of the industry and its labor union allies, accompanied by a willingness to explore the possibilities of negotiation with exporters in preference to unilateral acts of import restriction.[12]

The responses of the labor unions in the United States and elsewhere are likely to be more protectionist than the responses of businessmen. But even among the leadership of U.S. labor organizations there is a recognition that the United States cannot cut itself off from other markets without reducing exports and adding to inflation.

[11] See "Carter Trade Plan Falling into Place," *New York Times*, June 13, 1977, p. 1, and *Economic Report of the President 1980* (Washington, 1981), p. 183.

[12] For example, while the United Automobile Workers initiated an anti-dumping case against car manufacturers in West Germany, Britain, Japan, Belgium, Canada, France, Italy, and Sweden in 1975, in 1980 it called for Japan to adopt voluntary export restraints until the U.S. automobile industry could retool. See "Pact Sought in 'Dumping' of Foreign Autos in U.S.," *New York Times*, May 5, 1976, p. 1, and UAW advertisement, *New York Times*, October 28, 1980, p. A23.

In Europe the political balance between open borders and protectionism is complicated by the operations of the European Economic Community. Its existence has brought liberalization in some aspects of international trade and restriction in others. History suggests, however, that each addition of a country into its web of preferential relationships has led countries outside the web to place additional pressure on the Community to admit them inside or to reduce its remaining import restrictions.

Another factor that suggests the possibility of continued liberalization on the part of the advanced industrialized countries concerns the strategies of national officials responsible for trade policy. Officials everywhere are aware that their best strategy for preventing an increase in trade barriers in response to the pressures of domestic interest groups is to have negotiations in process for further trade barrier *reductions*. Accordingly, officials fearing domestic restrictionist pressures may well begin to make new proposals for trade negotiations. If negotiations for further trade liberalizations resume in the 1980s, it is unlikely that the advanced countries will extend the resultant benefits to the NICs unless, of course, the NICs are prepared to make reciprocal commitments. In a formal sense, to be sure, any GATT negotiations of the 1980s will continue to be global in scope. As long as the GATT exists as an institution, the NICs and other developing countries will probably continue to receive invitations to negotiate on trade matters. But if advanced countries demand that the NICs offer reciprocal concessions in order to gain the benefits of any resulting agreement, the chances are strong that many of the NICs will reject the offer. Indeed, this is one way of interpreting the decision of Mexico in 1979 not to join the GATT.

Will the LDCs engage in trade negotiations among themselves? Their record on this score has been quite abysmal so far.[13] In Latin America, after some initial successes in the Asociacion latino-americano de libre comercio (ALALC), the trade liberalization movement ground to a halt, and the Central American Common Market has suffered a similar fate. The Andean Pact, after making considerable progress, now seems under a cloud. The many African movements come and go, so far with little durable effect, and in Southeast Asia ASEAN (Association of Southeast Asian Nations) has made litte progress on trade matters.

[13] Cf. Business International Corp., *Operating in Latin America's Integrating Markets: ANCOM/CACM/CARICOM/LAFTA* (New York, 1977); Arthur Hazlewood, "The End of the East African Community: What Are the Lessons for Regional Integration Schemes?," *Journal of Common Market Studies*, 18, no. 1 (September 1979), 40–58; George C. Abangwu, "Systems Approach to Regional Integration in West Africa," *Journal of Common Market Studies*, 13, no. 1 (1975), 116–33; and Ramesh Ramsaran, "CARICOM: The Integration Process in Crisis," *JWTL*, 12, no. 3 (May/June 1978), 208–17.

It is not farfetched, however, to contemplate the possibility that negotiations for lower trade barriers among the LDC may be effectively resumed. In the past few years an increasing number of such countries have become export-oriented. As long as these countries were successfully penetrating the markets of the advanced industrialized countries on an increasing scale, they felt little need to try to open up borders among themselves. But the threat that would be posed by the ending of the GATT-inspired most-favored-nations era could turn the developing countries back to looking to one another for their opportunities. Much depends on whether the lesser Latin American countries can overcome their reservations over the future economic role there of Brazil and Mexico, and on whether those two countries can surmount their wariness of each other. Much depends also on whether those two countries, as incipient hegemonies, will be prepared to offer some concessions in order to make an open trading system work—whether, for instance, they will be prepared, as in the Andean Pact, to offer trade liberalization measures to the lesser nations without demanding a full *quid pro quo*. This possibility needs considerably more exploring before a solid projection can be made; on present impression, the prospects seem slight.

The possibility of a preferential trade arrangement between the United States and Mexico should not be ruled out. In the event of U.S. participation in a preferential arrangement with other advanced countries and Mexican participation in a similar Latin American plan, both countries would probably seek some means for developing mutual, supplementary preferential schemes. The EEC experience is instructive in this context. As noted earlier, each new preferential arrangement has created the basis for yet another agreement; preferences beget preferences. The EEC trade structure has also provided legitimizing precedents such as the Lomé convention, for example, and various preferential bilateral trade agreements. It remains a close judgment, however, whether such trends will eventually draw Mexico into the process of negotiating preferential arrangements with the United States.

The question, whether exchanges between Mexico and the United States will increase, is too complex for casual analysis. The visible factors are hauling and pulling in different directions. The oil trade, for instance, demands its own special analysis, and the non-oil trade is itself being affected by a number of powerful factors. Whether or not Mexico and the United States find it expedient to enter into some sort of bilateral trade agreement, the flow of non-oil trade between them is likely to continue to be of the utmost importance to Mexico. That importance may, however, be on the decline, in part because of the changing technology of transportation and communication. Distance has become less significant as an impediment to trade; the cost of creating trading links is less sensitive to distance than was once the case, as witness Mexico's ability to establish new ties with Japan. As the cost of communication continues to decline, the acquisition of knowledge and experience by Mexicans with regard to trading opportunities abroad will grow rapidly. These factors are already reflected in an increasing geographical diversification in the patterns of imports and exports of most countries, which will probably continue. Yet, despite this trend, the propinquity of Mexico to the United States will be a dominating factor for some time to come.

The possibility that Mexico and the United States may each have a diminished position in the trade of the other is enhanced by the changing character of their comparative advantage. The nature of the United States' shift in competitiveness is already clear in industrial trade; she must share her once dominant position with Europe, Japan, and others. Mexico's familiarity with alternative sources of capital goods, already well advanced, will presumably advance further. The Mexican subsidiaries of U.S.-based multinational enterprises, too, will contribute to the trend, as their original U.S.-sourcing bias weakens over the course of time.

The bigger change, however, may well come from the Mexican side, a consequence of the strong shifts in internal structure. In this context it is possible to detect a number of different strands of some importance. One possibility is the appearance of the Venezuelan syndrome—an overvalued currency created by high government expenditures and high wage rates without a commensurate increase in productivity; such a pattern could price labor-intensive Mexican products, both industrial and agricultural, out of the U.S. market. If the demand for Mexico's oil remains strong in the 1980s, some movement in that direction seems almost unavoidable. On this complex subject I defer to the agricultural specialists.

The developments in agriculture on both sides of the border could likewise alter substantially the patterns of international trade. A potential factor for increasing trade between the United States and Mexico is the export from Mexico of energy-intensive, intermediate products, from crude oil and petrochemicals to aluminum ingots. Although such a possibility is quite real, the uncertainties it faces are considerable. Accordingly, that possibility may not prove strong enough to offset the factors tending to reduce the trade links between the two countries.

The propinquity of the U.S. market to Mexico suggests that such trade, even if its relative importance for Mexico declines somewhat, will still be essential there. On the U.S. side, trade with Mexico will be less vital because of the giant size of U.S. markets. For both sides, however, changes in relative levels may still occur, and the question is whether such changes will bring in their wake more friction, or less.

My own estimate is for more friction—for two reasons. On the Mexican side, more trade generates an increased sense of dependence. On the U.S. side, it provokes the responses of a series of narrowly focused interest groups, pointedly aiming their restrictive efforts at Mexico. The anticipation that Mexico may find itself less dependent on trade with the United States, therefore, offers the hope of slightly reduced tensions between the two countries over trade issues. On the other hand, there is the danger that, if the reduction in trade is achieved at the expense of reduced growth rates in Mexico, the friction could arise in other forms.

THE INTERNATIONAL STRUCTURE OF INDUSTRY

Several trends in industrial structure have a bearing on Mexican-U.S. economic relationships. One such trend—exceedingly powerful and little remarked—is the continuous deconcentration on world markets of industries in which multinational enterprises have predominated in the past. In the world markets for many products, the number of participating enterprises has grown rapidly,[14] and it is this factor, perhaps more than any other, that lies behind the increased bargaining strength of the LDCs. As that trend continues, individual multinational enterprises will probably exhibit diminishing strength in their negotiations with the LDC governments.

It is not at all clear, however, that the *aggregate* place of multinational enterprises in the economies of the developing countries will diminish. The very success of the LDCs has had the paradoxical effect of their generating a series of new and difficult technological needs. Each new need has opened up a new opportunity for multinationals, even as their position in the established lines has declined. The net effect of these two opposing tendencies is indeterminate for any country, depending on its rate and patterns of growth, with the result that tensions here may well continue.

The expectation that multinational enterprises in the aggregate may expand in numbers and that their aggregate offerings in individual product lines may grow in world markets has a disturbing corollary for Mexico, where future exports may be adversely affected. The number of competitors offering energy-intensive products in world markets in steel, nonferrous metals, and chemicals, for instance, is likely to increase. This

---

[14] That trend is strikingly shown in the oil industry as well as in copper, aluminum, and various other industries. See my *Storm over the Multinationals* (Cambridge, Mass., 1977), p. 81.

prospect is especially strong with respect to other oil-exporting LDCs who will be putting new processing facilities on line in the mid-1980s.[15] It is characteristic of these entities that their downstream links to markets are relatively weak; they will, accordingly, have some transitional problems in establishing a market position. With extremely high fixed costs and low variable costs, firms in such a situation can be counted on to cut their margins between raw material costs and final selling prices. A reduction in profit margins will be all the more likely in view of the fact that many of the prospective exporting countries, including Mexico, are in a position to subsidize both capital costs and energy costs.

Just how difficult the markets in such products may be for sellers depends in part, of course, on the degree of overall shortage that exists for crude oil. If it is very scarce, exporters could try to impose a system linking their sales of crude oil to sales of industrial products, which are thereby forced on the importing countries. This process could produce the requisite exports, albeit accompanied by high levels of tension. If Mexican firms such as PEMEX were to adopt the practice, the reaction on the U.S. side would probably be quite bitter.

The United States–Mexico relationship, however, could easily develop a special twist of its own. For various reasons that have been thoroughly developed in the literature, crude oil producers and metal fabricators see considerable advantage in integrating downstream toward their markets.[16] That, in fact, has been a principal factor in the creation of many multinational enterprises in these industries. So strong is this tendency that even state-owned enterprises are sometimes found investing overseas in downstream facilities. Press reports to the effect that PEMEX has acquired an interest in distribution facilities in Spain, for instance, suggest that Mexican firms are not immune from such pressures.

The obvious question arises: will PEMEX and other Mexican producers of energy-intensive products be moved by the same factors that have induced others to establish direct institutional links into downstream markets? And will these links appear in considerable number in the United States? The answer could affect expectations regarding United States–Mexico relations in various ways.

On the whole, it seems probable that the development of Mexican-owned subsidiaries in the United States will tend to reduce the risk of tensions between the two countries. In this respect it has the opposite

[15] See Economist Intelligence Unit, *Quarterly Economic Review of Oil in the Middle East*, Annual Supplement (1980).

[16] See M. A. Adelman, *The World Petroleum Market* (Baltimore, Md., 1972), pp. 89–100, and Edith Penrose, *The Large International Firm in Developing Countries: The International Petroleum Industry* (London, 1968), esp. pp. 46–50.

effect from that of increased trade; as Mexican industry develops its own foreign subsidiaries in the United States, the Mexican government's disposition to subject foreign-owned subsidiaries in Mexico to special new restrictions will be subject to further inhibitions. It is not clear that added inhibitions would be desirable in all respects from the Mexican point of view. But if they should develop, they would tend to reduce one minor source of potential friction between the two countries.

If PEMEX or other state-owned enterprises establish subsidiaries in the United States, their very presence may deter friction. Various signs point to the possibility that the U.S. government, in an effort to screen out subsidized items, will subject the exports of state-owned enterprises to increasing scrutiny. If that should occur, enterprises that have a network of U.S. subsidiaries will have more options than those that are simply exporters. To avoid the dumping accusation, for instance, Mexican parent firms could demand full cost for their products from such subsidiaries, without fear that the subsidiaries would take their business elsewhere.

ENERGY PROSPECTS

Lurking behind most of these observations is the assumption that Mexico's possession of oil will increase its bargaining power measurably, but still not overwhelmingly. Such an assumption is easily prone to major error. The innumerable projections that have been made of the future supply-demand situations for oil and gas vary tremendously, but for the most part they suggest fairly tight supplies over the long term.[17] Projections of this sort are frequently built up from two groups of assumptions. One group is narrowly economic, dealing with standard supply-demand variables. If an open competitive market were operating, that group of assumptions might provide a sufficient basis for a long-term projection. Because that is not the case, a second set of assumptions, of a political character, is applied—assumptions about the behavior both of the various OPEC countries and of the consuming countries.

The reason it is important to make the distinction between economic and political factors is that the narrow economic variables, considered on their own, do not foretell a certain shortage. Their results, on the whole, seem to suggest an indeterminate outcome; surplus seems no less plausible than shortage during the next ten years. The projections appear particularly sensitive to three critical assumptions: the degree of improved fuel efficiency to be expected from new generations of space-heating, transportation, and processing equipment; the role of the command economies, the USSR and the PRC, in future markets; and the capacity of

[17] See, for example, Carroll Wilson, ed., *Energy: Global Prospects 1985–2000: Report of the Workshop on Alternative Energy Strategies* (New York, 1977), pp. 127–96.

the "lower 48" in the United States to maintain their oil production through secondary recovery techniques. Because of the speculative nature of these assumptions, any projections based on them are unavoidably soft for the medium term and practically worthless for the longer term.

When political projections are introduced, however, sporadic shortages appear to be almost inevitable. Individual political projections, to be sure, are even more chancy than economic ones, but in this context almost any unforeseen political change is likely to increase shortage, not reduce it. What we confront, therefore, is the prospect of a shortage induced by political factors of an unspecified nature—a truly uncertain prospect in which to project Mexican and U.S. energy policy.

As a result of these forces, one can easily picture a situation in which there are several years of glut, punctuated by sudden, drastic curtailments of supply. The results of such an occurrence would be detrimental to United States–Mexico relations. During the glut, PEMEX might find itself pushed to market more of its output in the United States than it felt wise, simply because more distant markets were unprofitable. And during the sudden shortage, PEMEX might find itself the object of greater demands from the United States than Mexico was prepared to fulfill. The proposition that a high level of trade between the United States and Mexico represents a potent source of tension seems reaffirmed in this instance.

CONCLUSION

From the political viewpoint, the overall pattern of trade and investment relations between Mexico and the United States is not reassuring. From years of habit, Mexico and the United States have grown accustomed to their asymmetrical trade relations. On both sides of the border, import restrictions by Mexico have been seen as normal, an indisputable prerogative of a developing country. At the same time, import restrictions by the United States have been seen as exceptional, providing a basis for protest and objection on the part of Mexico. Mexico is bound to regard a change in those norms, such as a movement toward bilateral bargaining, as threatening.

One development that could ease the tensions is the possibility that Mexico may reduce its dependence on the U.S. market in non-oil trade. In energy-intensive products, however, the medium-term prospect is one of frustration on the part of exporters due to transitional problems of excessive competition. And in the international trade in oil and gas itself, the possibility of sharp irregularities in world supplies suggests the threat of a roller-coaster quality in U.S. demands, which would inevitably generate tensions at every stage in the process.

National Security in Mexico: Traditional Notions and New Preoccupations

Olga Pellicer de Brody

T HE ISSUE of national security does not occupy a privileged place in reflections about Mexican political life. Since the end of the Second World War, with the advance of the civilian faction of the revolutionary family assured and with the mass organizations and their mode of articulation with the state consolidated, this theme has lost prominence in the political discourse of Mexico's dominant groups. It has been thought that since Mexico is neighbor to the greatest military power of the contemporary era, it made little sense to invest resources in either armaments or plans with which to defend against external aggression. It has also been thought that the high degree of control achieved by the state over the demands and conflicts of various social groups made it unnecessary to convert national security into a central element in the legitimation of the governing group.

It has only been quite recently that events of a different nature and direction have arisen that have invited new reflections upon the national security theme. The first of these was Mexico's emergence as a petroleum exporter and possessor of the most important and gigantic deposits discovered in recent times. The second factor has been the situation in Central America and the opinions expressed in the United States about the possible effects of the advance of revolutionary movements on Mexico's internal situation.

It would be premature to come to any conclusions about the degree to which either of these phenomena, Mexican oil and the crisis in Central America, will affect traditional notions about national security matters. Nevertheless, it is not too early to ask: why have they lent new relevance to the problem of national security in Mexico? To what extent do they facilitate the participation of new actors in the definition of that security and in projects for defending it?

PETROLEUM AND NATIONAL SECURITY

Mexico's petroleum riches surfaced precisely at a time when the energy issue had been converted into a central preoccupation of all the industrialized countries in the capitalist world, particularly the United States. It has been pointed out repeatedly that no other developments in the recent past have put the political elites mapping U.S. foreign policy in such a vulnerable position as have the Arab oil embargo of 1973, the oil price rises that took place under the aegis of OPEC, and the loss of control over the Persian Gulf area that followed the Islamic Revolution in Iran.[1] Uncertainty regarding both prices and the very possibility of obtaining supplies of crude also coincided with several circumstances that served to widen the dimensions of the U.S. energy crisis: strong dependence on imported oil, which represented more than 40 percent of the total consumed in the United States; pessimistic projections about the possibility of moving, in the medium run, toward a new epoch characterized by the widespread use of alternative energy sources; and, finally, the U.S. government's difficulties in putting into practice effective programs of energy conservation or coal utilization (proof of this may be found in the vicissitudes and failures of Carter's first energy plan).

It is not surprising, therefore, that Mexico's oil has been seen as one of the most efficient means for alleviating the U.S. energy problems. In effect, to the extent that increasing supplies on the world market would contribute to stabilizing prices, for Mexico to export in significant quantities would provide a more comfortable margin of maneuver in organizing the transition to other energy sources, and could become a secure source of supply in case any aggravation of the Middle Eastern situation were to paralyze (to cite only the most alarming prospect) shipments from the principal U.S. supplier, Saudi Arabia.

In its capacity as an oil producer, Mexico has acquired vital importance for the United States. It would be wrong to rejoice in this fact, however, if one considers only the probable increase in Mexico's bargaining power that will result. For what is certain is that, because of the strategic value of its natural resources, Mexico has been placed in the category of those countries that merit a "special policy" on the part of the United States. Reflection about the general lines of such a policy and about its implications for Mexico's national security has thus become a necessary task.

During the decade of the seventies, a special policy toward petroleum

[1] See Richard R. Fagen, "El petroleo mexicano y la seguridad nacional de los Estados Unidos," in *Las perspectivas del petroleo méxicano* [El Colegio de México] (Mexico, 1979), pp. 327–42.

producers was clearly defined by the United States in the case of the Middle Eastern countries. After the events of 1973, the former made an effort to perfect the methods it was employing there to attain its priority objective: to maintain a level of production that would permit it to import oil in reasonable quantities and at reasonable prices. Several strategies were followed toward this end. Alliances with leaders of the key countries in the area, such as Iran and Saudi Arabia, were strengthened through the setting up of massive programs of military and economic assistance— programs designed to consolidate the positions of dominant groups who showed themselves most favorable to U.S. interests and who were, moreover, in favor of a type of economic development that, by creating greater "interdependence" with the United States, would make another embargo like that of 1973 improbable. At the same time, financial investments by those countries in the U.S. economy were facilitated, thereby providing an argument to justify intensive exploitation of oil resources. Of course, if peaceful means turned out to be insufficient for assuring the petroleum flow, military intervention was conceived as an "ever present alternative for a consumer who is deprived of essential supplies." Such intervention has been widely discussed, and is considered by diverse groups in the United States as a risky prospect—but at certain moments inescapable.[2]

In the case of countries in the Western Hemisphere, the policy toward oil producers, who up to now have occupied a secondary place within the spectrum of U.S. suppliers, has not been defined so as to include such aggressive features. Not only was Canada able to resist proposals for a common energy policy with its neighbor to the south, but Venezuela also succeeded in reducing its production levels without giving rise to a situation of open conflict with the United States. The question then is what U.S. policy toward Mexico would be, given various scenarios in which Mexico (1) either increased its production up to 5 million barrels a day or failed to reach that figure, and (2) either converted itself into a key country supplying the United States in case of international emergency or resisted a closer energy relationship between the two nations.

It would be wrong to make forecasts for Mexican policies like those formulated some years ago for Iran. For one thing, the resounding failure of the U.S. "extra special" relationship with that country made evident the necessity to be more cautious in policy toward countries that are capable, as is Mexico, of strong nationalist reactions. For another, Mexico's internal contradictions, its geopolitical situation, and the established tra-

[2] For good discussions of problems of the U.S. energy situation and the relationships with oil-producing countries, see the Congress' publication, *Project Interdependence: U.S. and World Energy Outlook Through 1990* (Washington, June 1977). See in particular John Collins and Clyde Mark, "Military Solutions to U.S. Petroleum Problems," in ibid., pp. 726–50.

dition of United States–Mexico relations are very different. The economic development of Mexico in the last thirty years, coupled with its geographic proximity to the United States, has resulted in a complex web of linkages between the two countries in which it is difficult to act only with an eye to the oil problem. Intervening here are the multiple interests of U.S. businessmen and financiers in the Mexican economy, the movement of Mexican workers to the United States, the value of "good neighborliness" for the whole complex of inter-American relations, and the repercussions that Mexico's internal problems may have on daily life in the United States. Because of all these factors, it would be difficult even in case of a serious worsening of the energy crisis to view Mexico only in terms of its role as a supplier of energy products. This has already been made plain in the caution with which policy toward Mexican oil has evolved and in the fact that pressures in favor of a rapid increase in Mexican production have weakened, attention being directed instead toward the overall organization of commerce between the two countries and toward the delineation of plans for relying on Mexican crude in case of emergency.

Nevertheless, it is highly probable that elements of a special policy toward oil-producing countries will be evident in U.S. policy toward Mexico in the next few years. These may include approaches toward groups within Mexico who are favorable to a close energy relationship with the United States, the offer of opportunities to invest financial surpluses there, and pledges to promote interdependence between the two countries, thus supporting a type of economic development that will ultimately make Mexican and U.S. interests coincide in energy matters. Finally, one foresees proposals for greater vigilance over the course of Mexico's political life.

As in other world regions, overt military intervention would be unlikely in view of the complexity of the relations between the two countries. Certainly, the greater sensitivity in the face of political events in Mexico is one of the circumstances, though not the only one, that lies behind U.S. preoccupations with the situation of Central America and with Mexico's national security.

THE REVOLUTION IN CENTRAL AMERICA AND THE NATIONAL SECURITY OF MEXICO

No one doubts that the Sandinista Revolution, like the Cuban, represents a decisive juncture for the U.S. presence in Central America and the Caribbean. One cannot yet predict the direction the revolution in Nicaragua will follow or the degree to which a politico-economic project of frankly socialist inclination will be implanted there. But it is evident that

U.S. influence has vanished from the command posts of Nicaragua's political leadership, and that the Sandinista example has given a push—perhaps a decisive one—to the revolutionary struggles of other countries in the region.

Such a situation is presently giving rise to great concern in the United States. It is believed that the current situation in Central America is only a prologue to a stage of history in which the United States will see its capacity for control over the area visibly diminished while the influence of Cuba increases in proportion. It is in light of these fears that U.S. interest in Mexico's role in the Central American region, and its preoccupation with the trends of Mexico's foreign policy, must be viewed.

It is well to remember that sympathy for revolutions in Latin America is an outstanding feature of Mexican foreign policy. Several examples serve to demonstrate this point. Mexico was the only country to object to the imposition of sanctions against Cuba, and maintained diplomatic and economic relations with the island at moments when the aim of inter-American policy was to isolate the regime headed by Fidel Castro. Somewhat later, it was one of the most enthusiastic supporters of the government of Salvador Allende, and upon his fall opened its doors to receive exiles, both Chilean and of other nationalities, who were fleeing the military regimes of the Southern Cone. Mexico currently gives unconditional support to Nicaragua in the form of both technical and financial assistance and in sales of oil. At a critical state of the Cuban Revolution—because of a conjunction of domestic and international situations favoring the recrudescence of old interventionist desires to weaken the revolutionary regime—the president of Mexico also made a gesture of support and sympathy by visiting the island. Finally, Mexican leaders have expressed their respect for the attempts of revolutionary groups to change the anachronistic political structures of countries such as El Salvador.

This solidarity with revolutionary movements in Latin America responds, among other things, to the importance allotted to revolutionary values in the political discourse of the Mexican leadership and to the necessity for maintaining their effectiveness in a political system that insists on presenting itself as emanating from the revolutionary movement of 1919. This does not mean that the Mexican government has given signs of any interest in committing itself more directly to the efforts to transform Central America's outmoded political structures. Adhering firmly to nonintervention, it has refrained from furnishing arms or military assistance to rebel groups. Aside from this, there are no indications of any strategy on the part of Mexico—or of other countries of this hemisphere—that, taking advantage of moments of change, would extend its influence below its southern border, thus laying the bases either for a larger economic penetration or for urging the Mexican political model as the best choice for social change in the region.

Regardless of whether or not the Mexican government's project for Central America is aggressive—and there are reasons to argue that it has only limited interests and commitments there—the fact remains that its foreign policy has become an obstacle to the advance of projects sponsored by other countries in the hemisphere. In the name of avoiding violence, Venezuela—and to a lesser degree Costa Rica—have attempted to push support for regimes that include Christian Democratic participation, such as the present junta in El Salvador. During the Carter years, the United States also explored the possibility of securing allies for a policy designed at canceling the revolutionary option and afterward seeking forms of "peaceful transition" toward regimes with greater political stability. By the very weight of its traditions Mexico makes difficult—and even impossible—any concerted action in the international arena in favor of such projects.

There are various reasons why the United States looks upon Mexico's policy toward Central America with apprehension. On the one hand, it is an indication of the persistence of nationalist and revolutionary values that not only are dysfunctional for any international action taken to stem the advance of the Central American revolution, but also presage difficult negotiations when the United States tries to secure a deeper commitment in the hydrocarbons field. Thus its interest in popularizing ideas to the effect that, in accord with the so-called domino theory, Communist subversion might spread from Nicaragua right up to Mexico's oil zones is easily understood. In a television appearance, no less respected a figure than Henry Kissinger referred to the dangers of this "process . . . which has not yet reached its culmination, which has already spread from Nicaragua to El Salvador, which is aimed at having an effect on Guatemala and surely will have an impact on Mexico. And it is in this last case that it will be a very grave matter for us."[3]

With the same alarmism, coupled with unfounded judgments about the presence of revolutionary groups in Mexico, Constantine Menges, a Reagan advisor on foreign policy matters who has taken charge of interpreting the effects of Mexican policy in Central America, has pointed out that "the extreme left believes, surely, that Mexican foreign policy has become, objectively, one of its most valuable supports during the transition to power and its consolidation in the countries of Central America and the Caribbean. There is no doubt that if the left takes power in El

[3] Program on NBC, September 3, 1980, 9:30 p.m. EST.

Salvador or Guatemala in the near future, all the clandestine groups based in Mexico which now send support to the revolutionaries will be used by Cuba and the new extremist governments to send assistance to Mexico and produce there a second and 'more authentic' Mexican revolution."[4]

Up to now such statements have come almost exclusively from commentators and members of the U.S. political elite. In the event of a determined upsurge in the revolution in El Salvador and Guatemala they may well find an echo in the most conservative sectors of Mexican society as well. The Central American problem will then be converted into a problem for the internal life of Mexico, although for reasons quite different from those in the alarmist visions of Constantine Menges. It will be a danger to the extent that it becomes a pretext for unleashing an offensive similar to that contemplated in Mexico in the years following the triumph of the Cuban Revolution. It is well to remember, for example, the events of 1961, when business groups and the most reactionary sectors of the clergy, inspired by a desire to counteract the Cuban Revolution's effects on Mexico, carried out a widespread mobilization in order to advance their own positions and cut the ground out from under the best-known figures of the "left wing of the revolutionary family" headed by General Cárdenas.[5]

As the decade of the eighties began, Mexico faced the dual prospects of pressures coming from the United States to influence decisions on oil matters, and a possible campaign that, to the end of altering the alignments of its foreign policy, would manipulate in alarmist fashion the fear of the spread of revolutionary activity in Central America to the national territory of Mexico itself. What effects will all this have on the traditional notions of national security that have reigned, with slight variations, since the late 1940s? Answering this question obliges us to make a brief review of the chief characteristics of those notions.

NATIONAL SECURITY IN MEXICO

One outstanding feature of the national security issue in Mexico is the slight participation of the military sector both in the definition of the concept of national security itself and in the decision as to the most appropriate means of confronting the dangers that threaten it. In response to a reporter who asked him about the meaning of national security, Secretary of Defense Felix Galvan confirmed the peripheral role played by

[4]"Current Mexican Foreign Policy and United States Interest," mimeo (Washington, D.C., June 1980).
[5]On the reactions of the right in Mexico to government policy toward Cuba, see Olga Pellicer de Brody, *México y la revolución cubana* (Mexico, 1972).

the armed forces in efforts to lend content to this term when he replied: "This is my definition, and please excuse me if it is not the most appropriate one. I understand by national security the maintenance of social, economic, and political equilibrium, guaranteed by the armed forces."[6]

In his straightforward response, the army high commander left implicit one of the most interesting phenomena of the contemporary Mexican state: the fact that the particular features of the social, economic, and political equilibrium that constitutes the very essence of national security—the ideology that inspires it, the relations among classes that it facilitates, and the respective share of power it grants to each—are not matters for the army to decide. Since the end of the 1940s the army has been kept in the hands of the civilian apparatuses of the state, i.e., the mass organizations affiliated with the dominant party, and the elite who have generally denominated the "revolutionary family." As defined by actors such as these, national security in Mexico acquires connotations different from those frequently encountered in other Latin American countries and from those that prevail in U.S. political thinking. It is defined not in terms of the "danger of aggression" but rather in terms of the fulfillment or non-fulfillment of the great objectives fixed in the Constitution of 1917. Some of those objectives have already been achieved and constitute the firmest support for national security in the ideology of the dominant group. For proof of this it suffices to cite the 1938 oil expropriation and consequent recovery of national resources for the benefit of the nation, as well as the state's dominion over key economic sectors such as communications, electricity, petroleum, and basic petrochemicals. Other objectives have not been attained, those relating to the agrarian problem being the most obvious, but they continue to be effective as instruments of mobilization and as values around which important political forces rally at certain moments. And this still allows one to claim legitimately, as the paper *Uno más Uno* did, that

for Mexicans, national security begins with, and is grounded in, social security in its widest sense. Security is the fulfillment of the basic constitutional mandates emerging from the revolutionary pact of 1917, it is the resolute defense of natural resources, the generation of wealth, the equitable division of income. . . . It is the certainty that, even if inequalities have not been suppressed, the possibility of opening a space for real action permitting progress in that direction has not been closed off. Insecurity comes about with the jettisoning of the concepts of sovereignty and social interest.[7]

The peculiarities of the Mexican notion of national security are incomprehensible unless one pays attention to several circumstances. The

[6] *Proceso*, September 22, 1980, p. 6.
[7] *Uno más Uno* editorial, September 13, 1980.

first of these is the process that led in the 1940s to the so-called depoliticization of the army—in other words, the retreat of the military sector in the face of the civilian apparatuses of the state. From that point onward the government started up a policy that, among other things, reduced weapons expenditures to a minimal level. Thereafter the idea of aggression or the threat of aggression, either internal or external, began to lose its relevance for the political discourse of the dominant groups.

The second circumstance that may be cited is the fact that, although the military's participation in the maintenance of political stability has not totally disappeared, it occurs only in exceptional cases or in a purely residual manner. Such participation was undoubtedly decisive in putting down the railroad strikes of 1959 and the student movement of 1968, but it can be argued that these were unusual events in Mexican political life. The presence of military men is also constant (but likewise secondary as a factor of stability) in the surveillance and maintenance of communication in rural zones, and in the crises that crop up over state governorships. Such cases cannot, however, be considered decisive for the stability of the reigning political system.

This stability has been achieved, thanks to the solidity of civil institutions and to the constant efforts of the directing group to refine and modernize its mechanism of control. Among such mechanisms are a number infrequently encountered in other political regimes, such as the mobilization of support for the government on the part of diverse class sectors by means of the manipulation of revolutionary ideology and of promises and hopes—for example, those accompanying the change of presidents at six-year intervals; the systematic mobilization of the organizations incorporated into the party in support of governmental actions; "controlled" negotiations with the labor movement that on the one hand consolidate the positions of the official leadership and, on the other, give privileged sectors of the working class sufficient incentives to neutralize their demands; the imposition of an iron discipline among leaders of the political apparatus, who must accept the supreme authority of the president in office. Within a political system of this kind, there is no room (or there has not been up to now) for situations in which Manichean visions of "international Communist aggression" could flourish.

An awareness of the character of the groups that define national security in Mexico, and of the efficient functioning of civilian institutions in controlling political activity, are the necessary antecedents for understanding the resistance of the Mexican government to accepting concepts and mechanisms formulated within the inter-American system during the Cold War. In that arena, in addition to propagating a critical vision of the schematic use of the idea of international Communist aggression, Mexico has also developed its own concept of sovereignty and has opposed militarization of the system.

It was at the 1954 meeting in Caracas, as a result of the discussions and proposals made concerning the Guatemalan issue, that the Mexican government first made clear its rejection of erroneous interpretations of the notion of Communist aggression. For example, after insisting that Communist intervention could not be defined in the abstract, one of the Mexican representatives pointed out the possibility that a Communist regime might arise in the Americas as the result of the freely expressed will of the people, i.e., without being "instigated by foreign agents." Were such a thing to occur, from the Mexican point of view any reaction that violated the principle of nonintervention would come under reproach.

In regard to the idea of sovereignty, Mario Ojeda, who has studied Mexico's policy toward the problem of security of the American continent most thoroughly, has pointed out that "Mexico has been characterized as having followed its own interpretation of sovereignty. It might be said that it has adhered to a posture very close to that of full sovereignty."[8] At first glance it would appear that the rest of the Latin American nations have defended that principle with equal determination. In fact, they have not done so, for the reason that the advent of the Cold War, and the fear of internal subversion aided from without, brought several governments in the hemisphere face to face with the necessity to revise existing interpretations. They were obliged to accept the thesis of "limited sovereignty" and, as a consequence, to justify acts of unilateral and collective intervention.

In order to carry out those interventions, attempts have been made to advance the militarization of the inter-American system, an idea that Mexico has consistently opposed. In 1948, at the Bogota meeting, Mexico was the principal obstacle to the creation of the Interamerican Defense Council. It did indeed permit the Interamerican Defense Board, which had been created during the war, to go on functioning, but this was an organ with consultative functions only, remote from those of the hemispheric general staff as contemplated in proposals for the council's creation.

From then on, in addition to rejecting the bilateral accords with the United States concerning defense against external aggression or the struggle against internal "subversion," Mexico has voted against collective actions of a military kind decided upon during consultative meetings. The best-known case was its opposition to the inter-American peace force operating in the Dominican Republic in 1965. In accord with this policy,

[8] Mario Ojeda, *Alcances y límites de la política exterior de México* (Mexico, 1976), pp. 35–87.

Mexico has been the Latin American country with the least participation in U.S. programs of military assistance. The only program in which it has participated has been the training of officers, who have been sent in relatively small numbers when compared with those from other Latin American countries.

These features of Mexican government policy vis-à-vis the inter-American system, coupled with its interest in sustaining revolutionary-style values and positions for ideological ends, serve to situate the general sympathy toward the revolutions in Central America to which we have referred. Despite the alarmist calls of U.S. analysts, it is not easy for Mexican leaders to distance themselves from this generalized sympathy.

CONCLUSION

In responding to the question of how the oil situation or the problems of Central America might affect the notion of national security or the role of the military sector, it would be hasty to dismiss the impact on the traditional position of the military in the Mexican political system. Like any other interest group in Mexico, the military will seek ways of participating in the benefits derived from petroleum exports, which, while necessitating a firmer defense of the oil riches, will at the same time favor an increase in the resources destined for the military sector. In fact, recent years have already witnessed a growth of military industry in Mexico, of the appropriations destined for the Ministry of Defense, and in general of the idea that, in accordance with the country's strategic and international importance, it will be necessary to support and "modernize" those sectors charged with "guaranteeing" order and security.[9]

This does not mean that openings for greater military participation in defining the nature of the country's social, economic, and political equilibrium, or in the resolution of situations that threaten national security, can be perceived. Up to now, everything suggests that support will grow for the tendencies in the direction of assimilating national security into a policy on petroleum in accord with the postulates of the 1917 Constitution—a policy not in conflict with the idea that hydrocarbons should be utilized fundamentally for the internal benefit of the nation and that their production cannot be decided upon as a function of external needs. The evolution of oil nationalism in the past few years, the dialogue with the United States in this regard, and the decisions of March 1980 concerning production ceilings, all point in this direction.

With respect to the Central American situation, the brief review of Mexico's traditional position in the inter-American system throws into

---

[9] See the chapter concerning national security in the Global Plan of Development drawn up by the López Portillo government.

relief the degree to which sympathy for social change in that region is deeply rooted in the traditions of Mexican diplomacy. This is not the first time that Mexico has expressed support for Central American revolution (it is enough to cite the example of the Arbenz government in Guatemala). Neither is it the first time that certain voices in the United States have tried to exert pressure in order to derail this policy. The fact is that, as long as the organizations that shape the Mexican political system remain capable of guaranteeing the country's political stability, there will be few prospects that alarmist fears about the spread of subversion to Mexican territory will be realized. This will not, of course, prevent situations of conflict similar to those that shook the country at the start of the 1960s, in large measure as a result of the impact of the Cuban Revolution, but these will be momentary mobilizations that can be neutralized or absorbed by the state apparatus.

The possibility that the Mexican notion of national security itself will change depends on the capacity of the present system to go on projecting its legitimacy as grounded in "the certainty that, even if inequalities have not been suppressed, the possibility for opening space for real action permitting progress in that direction has not been closed off." [10]

[10] *Uno más Uno* (as in n. 7 above).

United States National Security Policy and Mexico

Edwin A. Deagle, Jr.

UNITED STATES national security policy has had a profound effect on Mexico and Latin America over the past two hundred years. In the main, the reverse has not been true, despite episodes throughout this period of war, territorial acquisition, and armed intervention by the United States in the internal affairs of Latin American countries. Almost from the beginning, U.S. national security policy has been concerned for the most part with balance of power politics outside the Western Hemisphere, mainly in Europe. The legacy of this history remains to this day the key determinant—and constraint—to U.S. policies toward Latin America.

For the purpose of this analysis, U.S. policy can be usefully categorized over time into four periods. The first, from roughly the beginning of the nineteenth century until its end, was marked by the search for basic security of the U.S. territory itself and by territorial acquisition—a time, paradoxically, of military weakness. The second period, from the turn of the century until 1942, was characterized by hemispheric military dominance but relative weakness in a global context. The third period, from 1942 to about 1971, was the era of American strategic superiority and a global balance of power alliance system. The fourth, from 1971 to the present, can perhaps be described as a period of transition away from U.S. military (and economic and political) global dominance to a more pluralistic system not yet in equilibrium.

Developments in each of these periods profoundly altered American attitudes toward national security. Yet, with regard to Latin America, U.S. national security policy has changed relatively little, and for the most part only in tactical modalities of action—not in strategic concept. Indeed, the basic theme of U.S. security in terms of Latin America has been a remarkably consistent and stable policy of regional hegemony—mainly political and economic but, when thought necessary, military. Though subject quite literally to several profound conceptual revolutions, U.S. strategic concerns have always been preoccupied with the world outside the Western Hemisphere.

1800−1898: THE SEARCH FOR TERRITORIAL SECURITY

The War of 1812, though a victory for the United States, was a sharp reminder of its vulnerability to military action by one or more of the European powers with colonial bases in the New World. American independence had been won and preserved by a combination of balance of power politics in Europe abroad and, when needed, the occasional provision of local military superiority at home. But the existence of European colonial empires in the Western Hemisphere was both a threat to the territorial security of the United States and an impediment to its territorial expansion.

The French Revolution and subsequent Napoleonic wars in Europe set in motion forces that greatly altered the face of the New World, and with it the context of U.S. national security. The dissolution of the Spanish and Portuguese empires in Latin America permanently diluted European power in the Western Hemisphere—a development of which the United States quickly took advantage.

The Monroe Doctrine, promulgated by the United States in 1823, is widely thought to be an expression of both the growing local military power of the United States and its isolationist desire to avoid entanglements with the continually warring powers of Europe. In fact, the Monroe Doctrine was an expression of neither and was instead an instrument of U.S. balance-of-power politics in Europe. Following the formation of the Holy Alliance in 1815 by the monarchical governments in continental Europe, Russia in 1821 claimed the northwest coast of North America. This claim threatened U.S. and British interests in the region and, more importantly, signaled a resurgence of European colonialism as counter-revolution swept continental Europe.

Originally proposed by the British as a joint U.S.-British declaration to offset the plans of the Holy Alliance to recover the Spanish Empire, the Monroe Doctrine was instead issued unilaterally by the United States. Under the ingenious premise that British sea power would be used to enforce the alliance against continental Europe as a matter of British self-interest, the Monroe Doctrine excluded Britain as well, as a safeguard against possible British designs in the Western Hemisphere.[1]

In the main this strategy worked throughout most of the nineteenth

[1] Federico G. Gil, *Latin American−United States Relations* (New York, 1971), pp. 58−63.

century. The continental powers in Europe were denied access to North America by British sea power, and the United States was free to use its meager military forces (and rapidly growing wealth) to consolidate its territorial acquisitions. In fact, it made virtually no effort during most of the nineteenth century to enforce the Monroe Doctrine, despite interventions in Latin America by Britain, France, and Spain. Instead, the United States sought to use balance of power diplomacy in Europe to make the doctrine self-enforcing. Thus, in 1848, for example, President Polk added new political meaning to the doctrine by interpreting it to mean that the United States would not permit transfer of a colonial possession from one European power to another, thereby inhibiting imperial consolidation in the Western Hemisphere via victory on the battlefields in Europe.[2] Meanwhile the United States annexed Texas and California and invaded Mexico.

Throughout the remainder of the nineteenth century (except for the Civil War) the United States relied little on military power for its security, flourishing instead under the global seapower reach of Britain, whose imperial interests lay mainly elsewhere. Within the Western Hemisphere the United States employed balance of power tactics as well, using its growing political and economic resources to keep the Latin American republics weak, divided, and increasingly dependent on their northern neighbor. Indeed, U.S. policy during this century was based on a surprisingly deft understanding of political and economic counterpoints to military power—a sophistication seriously eroded in the next century.

1898−1942: FLIRTING WITH MILITARY POWER

The American Civil War taught a generation of political and military leaders how to employ large-scale conscripted military forces—a lesson learned sixty years earlier in continental Europe. Yet this institutionalization of a new experience rubbed against a deep-seated fear of militarism and governmental authority that had been one of the key hallmarks of constitutional theory in the United States since 1775, and thereby set in motion a conflict in philosophical concepts of military governance not clearly resolved until after World War II.

It is well known that American attitudes toward military power—from a global point of view—have always been ambivalent, even up to the present. Fluid, conflicting attitudes within the United States have yielded remarkable oscillation in the global scene but, until very recently, a paradoxical bias toward the use of military force in Latin America.

The key figure in America's politics when it began to flirt with military

[2]Ibid., pp. 65−66.

power at the turn of the century was undoubtedly Theodore Roosevelt. A quintessential power politician, he became a forceful spokesman of the latent but deep and widespread sensings in the United States of its potential influence in the world. In 1897–98, as Assistant Secretary of the Navy, Roosevelt managed virtually by himself to increase the size of the U.S. Navy, to increase its combat readiness and deploy it to wartime stations, and to shift the balance of sentiment in the United States government toward war with Spain.[3] The subsequent defeat of Spain in Cuba and the Philippines marked a new era in U.S. concepts of national security. For the first time there existed in the United States the notion that it could be a global rather than a regional power. For reasons other than territorial security, the United States had engaged and defeated a major European country. From this point onward Americans would be both fascinated and repelled by the existence of global power. In global terms U.S. public opinion oscillated between the seductive taste of military power and the tradition of anti-militarism; in Latin America the result was almost uniformly in favor of militarism as a powerful new addition to the economic and political tools of regional hegemony. Ironically for Latin Americans, the new regional expression of U.S. military might in the Western Hemisphere took place in a context in which hemispheric threats to U.S. territorial security had all but disappeared.

From 1850 to about 1930, U.S. policy toward Mexico and Latin America had little to claim for it. The 1902 Platt Admendment to the Monroe Doctrine, the forceful creation of the Republic of Panama and the Panama Canal, the Pershing expedition into Mexico, the occupation of Vera Cruz and the seemingly endless episodes of "big stick" diplomacy in the Caribbean and Central America—all point to the effect in Latin America of U.S. mindless flexing of growing muscle. Indeed, the contrapuntal force of isolationism and disdain for global politics abroad in the United States in the period before and after World War I found virtually no expression in Latin America. Instead, Latin American countries were buffeted continuously not only by the overwhelming political and economic power of the United States, but also by relentless episodes of military intervention, which bore no relationship to the famous U.S. ambivalence toward its capacity for global leadership. Small wonder that Mexicans and Latin Americans wondered about this alleged ambivalence.

One reason for the American military preoccupation with its southern neighbors was the Panama Canal. Originally envisioned as a boon to commerce, the canal took on more and more strategic significance as events unfolded during the first years of the twentieth century. The Hay-

[3] Edmund Morris, *The Rise of Theodore Roosevelt* (New York, 1979), pp. 565–612.

Paunceforte Treaty of 1901 guaranteed the neutrality of the canal in peace and war, and implicitly charged Britain with its strategic security (through naval power), leaving the United States to provide military police in the Canal Zone.[4] The Japanese defeat of Russia at sea in 1905, the naval race between Germany and Britain before 1914, and the Japanese seizure of Shantung province in China in 1914 outlined the new importance of U.S. naval forces and the contribution of the Panama Canal to their strategic mobility. The canal opened as World War I began, leaving Americans with the firm conclusion that it was essential to the security of the United States. By 1917, the Hay-Paunceforte Treaty was being interpreted as permitting the United States to assure its strategic defense.[5]

Beginning about the middle of the Hoover administration (1929–33), the United States began to develop political and economic concepts about its relations with Latin America that for the next three decades counterbalanced its continuing immoderation in the regional use of military power. This was the beginning of the Good Neighbor policy, which marked the first stage of U.S. maturity in design and execution of its regional and global foreign policies. But the strategic impulse toward global rather than regional military conceptions of national security occurred definitively during the period 1939–42: the time when British global seapower—the guarantor of U.S. independence for 150 years—began to disintegrate.

In the late 1930s, as the Axis governments' power and intentions became clear, U.S. attitudes polarized radically. On one side, those who interpreted U.S. global policies as isolationist (as distinct from the traditional balance of power strategy) urged neutrality. On the other hand, the dominant force was a coalition of those who believed in balance of power diplomacy (and who therefore advocated helping Britain retain its capacity for global seapower dominance) and those who felt, as had Theodore Roosevelt, the latent power and therefore global responsibilities of the United States.

Early developments in World War II propelled this ambivalence in U.S. policies toward a strategy of hemispheric defense. Japanese naval expansionism in the late 1930s led to a concentration of U.S. naval forces in the Pacific. By early 1941, however, the Nazi battle for naval supremacy over Britain in the Atlantic rekindled concern about the strategic importance to the United States of the Panama Canal. At the same time Axis political influence in Latin America, the naval threat to Brazil of potential Nazi use of naval facilities in Dakar, West Africa, and the belated recognition

[4] Norman J. Padelford, *The Panama Canal in Peace and War* (New York, 1942), pp. 125–31.

[5] Ibid., pp. 29–30, 124, 139–40.

of potential Axis strategic air power based in Latin America and the Caribbean, all combined to push U.S. strategic planners in the direction of vigorous defense of the Western Hemisphere.[6] The United States expanded the dimensions of its Good Neighbor policy of the 1930s and moved toward a policy of hemispheric collaboration in defense.

By early 1942 formal war with both Japan and Germany, the loss of U.S. naval forces at Pearl Harbor, and the imminent defeat of Britain sharpened U.S. concerns about hemispheric vulnerability. Indeed, had Hitler carried out his initial plan for the invasion of Britain, the United States would probably have adopted the strategic defensive, based on hemispheric defense against an Axis attack launched against Latin America from West Africa.[7]

Events in World War II took a different course, however. Hitler abandoned plans for the invasion of Britain and instead invaded Russia. General Montgomery, after the defense of El Alamein, put Rommel on the defensive in East Africa and was powerfully aided by the U.S. invasion of West Africa, thus ending the Axis threat from Dakar. The Japanese suffered strategic defeats at Midway and the Solomon Islands. By the end of 1942, the threat to U.S. security in the Western Hemisphere had receded, and the United States had assumed the strategic offensive in Europe and the Far East. From that point onward, Latin America became virtually a permanent backwater in the strategic calculus of U.S. national security.

1942–1971: UNCHALLENGED STRATEGIC SUPERIORITY

For the remainder of the war, U.S. strategic military policy largely ignored Latin America, particularly Mexico. The settlement of disputes resulting from Mexico's nationalization of U.S. oil concessions in 1938, economic cooperation in the provision of strategic materials, half-hearted cooperation in radar monitoring of Lower California, and Mexican participation in air operations in the Philippines—all contributed to a new U.S. strategic sense of "benign neglect" of Mexico lasting with only occasional interruptions to the present.

Globally, the war had drained Britain of its economic power, its empire, and thereby its strategic naval superiority. For the first time in nearly 150 years the United States could no longer rely on the European balance of power strategy to guarantee its national security. Within five years after World War II, the United States assumed—albeit reluctantly—the mantle of global leadership. As it did so, the strategic importance of Latin America, and of Mexico in particular, declined to its lowest point in this cen-

---

[6] Stetson Conn and Byron Fairchild, *The Framework of Hemispheric Defense* (Washington, D.C., 1960), pp. 4–7, 25–29.

[7] Ibid., pp. 110–21.

tury. Remarkably, U.S. strategic policy had undergone a profound revolution, from traditional security to global hegemony based on military superiority; yet the consequences for Mexico and Latin America changed much less.

During this period, however, one new theme began to take shape in U.S. strategic thinking, a result of the later stages of the Cold War: insurgency. Castro's revolution in Cuba and his subsequent flirtation with Moscow struck two resonant chords in the American psyche.

The first was a direct inflammation of U.S. nervousness about global communist imperialism. Soviet bombers and missiles in Cuba, like the threat of Nazi air power in Latin America twenty years earlier, posed a new territorial threat to the United States based on new military technology. The Cuban missile crisis in 1962 echoed a powerful U.S. response to these new fears.

The second response sprang from an ancient concern about internal discord in Latin American governments, founded a century ago in U.S. strategic weakness and in fear of European manipulation and disruption of Latin American internal politics. The Bay of Pigs episode and, to some extent, the intervention in the Dominican Republic (and Chile) are manifestations of this deep-seated, traditional fear, within the context of a new global preoccupation with communism.

The period from 1942 to 1971 was a time of enormous U.S. political and economic global domination—a culmination of more than a century of uninterrupted economic growth. It was also a period of unprecedented U.S. military superiority. This heady wine quickly caught the fancy of many Americans who had tasted the exercise of that power in World War II. For the first time, the United States had large peacetime military forces, with global power and responsibilities. The economic and political roots of power, relatively speaking, receded in the face of this new national preoccupation with military force—with important and contradictory implications for Latin America.

President John Kennedy launched his administration with, among other things, a new sensitivity to the effects of past U.S. neglect and hegemonial arrogance in Latin America. He also opened a new offensive against the machinations of the communist bloc, refurbishing U.S. military forces and revitalizing U.S. competition for influence in the emerging Third World. These contradictory themes collided in Cuba in 1961 and 1962, and in the Dominican Republic in 1965, setting the stage for a new wave of contradictory U.S. actions toward Latin America.

Three themes emerge from U.S. policy toward Latin America during this period—all forged out of the curious amalgam of historical U.S. strategic weakness, new leadership responsibilities, new obsessions with military power, and the phenomenon of international communism. One theme was the arrogant tradition of intervention in Latin American affairs—politically, economically, and, if necessary, militarily, to maintain regional hegemony. A second theme was world leadership, which tended to breed in American attitudes a strategic neglect of hemispheric security as well as a benign resurrection of the Good Neighbor policies. The third theme was an almost rabid fear of communism, especially in its new and threatening strategy of insurgency in the emerging states of the Third World.

At any given time one of these themes might predominate, resulting in an Alliance for Progress one moment and a Bay of Pigs the next. Oddly, the instability of U.S. national security policy as it affected Latin America during this period had little to do with the global strategy equation, which clearly favored the United States. Rather, it resulted from an uncertain and immature understanding of the relative balances among political, economic, and military roots of global power and, as a consequence, a growing obsession with the newest of those instruments: large military forces. Indeed, this obsession was to prove costly as the United States lost, in sequence, its military and then its economic, global hegemony.

1971–1982: AN UNCERTAIN TRANSITION

Five events mark this period of transition. Characteristically, they all affect U.S. interests outside the Western Hemisphere. Chronologically (but not necessarily in rank of importance) they are: (1) Soviet achievement of strategic nuclear parity and global military power; (2) the withdrawal of Britain from the Middle East and the rise of OPEC as a powerful political and economic force in global affairs; (3) the United States defeat in Vietnam; (4) the growth of economic power in Europe and Japan; and (5) the visible emergence of revolution and insurgency in Central America. None of these developments signaled an absolute decline in U.S. power; the first four point to a change in relative power, particularly in military and economic terms. The last, like Castro in 1961, touches sensitive nerves in the United States, mobilizing the contradictory American attitudes toward the region all at once. The result is an emerging national requirement for preeminent diplomacy—an element of national competence not really demanded of the United States since the early nineteenth century, when its economic and military powers were at their weakest. Whether the United States will navigate this transition successfully remains uncertain; indeed, new challenges, especially in Mexico and the Caribbean, will both sharply test the American people and profoundly affect the future of Latin America.

In addition to the five transitional forces affecting U.S. national security policy, a new element has begun to emerge over the past decade—the growing political and economic power of the Third World. More than one hundred new nations have emerged from the wreckage of colonial empires, seeking independence, political stability, and economic well-being. This fact is starkly elemental in its impact on international politics and therefore on U.S. strategic concepts of national security and foreign policy. For the moment, it seems clear that the uncertain transition in American strategic thinking since 1971 has yet to digest this development. Mexico—as a rapidly developing country (with all that entails in its economic relations with the United States), unique in its proximity to the United States (with powerful migratory consequences), blessed with oil (a new and important determinant in U.S. national security calculations), and strategically engaged in Central America—finds itself uncomfortably close to the center of conflict and controversy within the United States about national security and foreign policy.

On the one hand, migration to the United States and the growing power of the Mexican economy weaken historical shibboleths in the United States about its unchallenged regional hegemony and foster a Good Neighbor policy. Further, Mexico's political and economic emergence as a leader in the global context of North-South relations creates pressures on the United States to deal with Mexico sensitively and respectfully.

On the other hand, Mexico has vast reserves of oil, and the fact that it is close to the United States and outside OPEC is a matter of enormous strategic significance to both the United States and its allies. One reason for this is that proximity makes the United States a "natural market," particularly for natural gas. Perhaps the more important reason is that, in the event of war in Europe, the United States could protect an oil lifeline from Mexico much more readily than the one from the Persian Gulf to Europe. Seen from this perspective Mexico has a new stature in U.S. strategic planning, compounding its importance as a bordering state.

As the 1970s drew to a close these contradictory concerns manifested themselves as a kind of national schizophrenia toward Mexico, especially in the policies and actions of the Carter administration. The problem has been exacerbated by the flow of undocumented workers from Mexico to the United States, opening new domestic disputes there and further complicating relations between the two countries.

In theory these problems are the offspring of the transition outlined earlier, and one might expect that, all things being equal, relations between the United States and Mexico would improve over time. Indeed, initial actions of the Reagan administration moved this way. But all other things are not equal. Decades of repression and misery have produced

strong left-wing revolutionary movements in Central America, tangling
the strategic interests of Mexico and the United States in unprecedented
and difficult ways. Increasingly, the Reagan administration has found itself constrained by a power array of political forces from the right that
push national security policy toward an assertive, confrontational posture toward the Soviet Union. In Latin America this could very well be
seen as a return to a heavy-handed "friends or enemies" approach to
dealing with local Marxist movements and obsession with the military
elements of the U.S.-U.S.S.R. competition for influence in the region.

Economic xenophobia within the United States could reinforce these
pressures from the right, especially with regard to Mexico. Impatience
with perceived economic damage—real or imagined—flowing from
Mexico's trade and labor relations with the United States could easily fuel
confrontations over national security policy. One can easily envision a disastrous mix of Washington initiatives toward Mexico: more oil and gas
production, for economic and security reasons; concessions on agriculture, trade, and labor migration, for economic protection of American
markets; and a tougher Mexican stance toward Marxism in the Caribbean and Central America, both as a support for U.S. policy in the region
and for Mexico's own "protection." Some of these recidivist elements are
apparent in the Reagan administration's efforts thus far to define its policies, but the outcome of those efforts is still far from clear. President Reagan's foreign policy team is in the main pragmatic and experienced, and
there is no obvious reason why its policies won't avoid a confrontation
with Mexico over what is at stake in Central America.

Mexico has begun to play an important role in defining strategic alternatives for managing the explosive events in Central America. There may
emerge a bargain to be struck, reflecting an essential compatibility of
long-range strategic interests of both the United States and Mexico. The
United States has an enormous stake in the economic and political vitality of its southern neighbor, of far greater strategic interest than undocumented workers, oil, cheap tomatoes, or access to marine resources.
It is also in the interest of the United States to promote and support regional solutions to problems in the Caribbean and Central America.
Mexico is in a far better position for regional leadership than is the
United States. It has the right colonial legacy—not the wrong one.

Mexico has a political tradition born of feudalism and revolution
much broader than that of the United States—broad enough to encom-
pass the full range of political diversity in the region. Mexico—thanks to
its oil and its extraordinary economic development achievements—may
have the resources to play an important role not only in the region, but in
the world at large.

It is in the interest of the United States to recognize these matters and to proceed accordingly. The Caribbean Basin Initiative is a step in the right direction, as are the recent discussions between Mexico City and Washington over solutions in El Salvador. But for the United States, as for Mexico, two centuries of lopsided and discordant relations die hard. Moreover, the legacy of the past is reinforced in the United States by its continuing confusion about its global obligations, especially regarding the Third World, at a time of Soviet assertiveness. The danger is that the Reagan administration may have gotten itself so powerfully committed to a "winning" solution to the military manifestations of upheaval in Central America that it has deprived not only the United States of options, but Mexico as well.

On the other hand, strong Mexican leadership is probably the last clear chance to be seen in the summer of 1982 for widening the options available to the United States—if they are not already foreclosed. Placing events in Central America in the global context of U.S.-Soviet competition for influence and security not only raises the stakes for the United States far out of regional proportion but also increases the chances that militarization of the problem will fail. Patient, assertive Mexican leadership, however, can reduce the strategic temperature in Central America and allow the United States to escape the consequences of its hegemonial past as well—a bargain for everyone.

The Future of a Crisis: Food and Agrarian Reform

Arturo Warman

A T THE BEGINNING of the 1970s the existence of a severe crisis in
Mexican agricultural production was becoming clearly evident.
Nevertheless, in spite of various governmental efforts a decade has gone by
without production attaining constant and satisfactory rates of growth.
Although a firm consensus has not been reached about its nature or about
its causes, the gravity and duration of the crisis have prompted the general recognition that this is not a cyclical or temporary phenomenon but
rather a structural problem of the agricultural sector and of the Mexican
economy.

The crisis makes prediction about the future, and even middle-run analysis, difficult. In the immediate term, the prolongation of current tendencies will be affected by a number of powerful forces. One variable of great
importance—the behavior of the Mexican state—that in the past has contributed to the emergence and deepening of the tendencies manifested in
the crisis, seems to offer prospects for re-orientation.[1] This flexibility is not
the result of a decision taken voluntarily by the state apparatus but instead
constitutes a response to forces and pressures exerted upon it. Those
forces, in turn, will either adjust to or contradict both one another and the
state's decisions, depending on their orientation, direction, and purposes.
Given the action and reaction of diverse social groups, the possibilities for
changes of importance in the agricultural sector appear to be very high.
Continuity does not appear to be either a probable or an acceptable alternative. The situation seems fluid.

---

[1]The adoption of the Mexican Food System as a public sector strategy for confronting
the agricultural crisis was made public on March 18, 1980. The Office of Advisors to the
President of the Republic has made public, to a limited degree, the documents and studies
on which the adoption of the SAM was based.

THE PROBLEMS

Under these conditions, the best way to predict the near-term future would seem to be through an effort to identify some of the central problems as well as the limits to and possibilities for their resolution.

Foodstuffs

Maintaining a sufficient supply of basic foodstuffs, grains in particular, appears to be the central problem of Mexican agriculture and the severest expression of the current crisis. From about the middle 1950s until 1970, the country had been basically self-sufficient in grain. Even in the first half of the 1960s wheat surpluses of a certain size had been produced, and corn surpluses also, to a lesser degree and with less regularity. In the seventies, however, domestic supply began to depend increasingly on imports, to the point where they represented on average between a fourth and one third of national consumption toward the end of the period; this works out to four or five million tons of grain annually.

It is worth noting that the volume of imports corresponds, in rough terms, to the demand of the "modern" sector. In this context I refer to direct consumption in the large, industrial cities—Mexico City in particular, Guadalajara, and Monterrey, and in exceptional cases other cities of more than one hundred thousand inhabitants—as well as to industrial demand from plants producing flours, oils and other derivatives, and balanced feed for animal consumption. A dual market has apparently been formed in which modern Mexico supplies itself with imports while the traditional market—provincial cities and the rural areas—continues to rely on national production.

Official declarations aside, which always mention self-sufficiency as a national objective, it seems clear that actions taken by the state have facilitated and favored the shaping of the situation. As a partial analysis of government policies has appeared elsewhere, I will mention only a few of their effects here.[2] The policy of guaranteed prices has not favored the production of basic foodstuffs over other agricultural products. The price of corn remained fixed in absolute terms for a decade (1963–72), and subsequent increases have been both late in coming and smaller than the accumulated inflationary lag, so that the relative price levels of the early 1960s have not been recovered. The same phenomenon occurred also

[2]Bibliography concerning the effects of state policies on agricultural production is ample, if uneven. Among the most recent studies are Gustavo Esteva et al., *La batalla en el méxico rural* (Mexico, 1980); Cynthia Hewett de Alcantara, *Modernizing Mexican Agriculture* (United Nations Research Institute for Social Development, 1976); and Roberto Melville, "Intervención del estado en el campo mexicano" (manuscript from the Centro de Investigaciones Superiores del INAH, 1979).

with wheat, cultivated by commercial farmers, in contrast to corn, which is cultivated mostly by peasants.[3]

The deterioration in prices discouraged increases in commercial production and provoked the abandonment of these crops by entrepreneurially oriented production units, inasmuch as it was impossible to make a reasonable profit commensurate with that from other possible productive activities. This translated into a modification of the whole crop pattern, above all on the irrigated lands with the greatest production potential. The result was a decline in the production of foodstuffs and an increase in other crops, among them several also protected by guaranteed prices but destined for industrial consumption or forage, in those products where deterioration either did not take place or did so to only a lesser degree. It is worth mentioning that for corn and wheat the guaranteed price functions as a maximum price and not as a support minimum, because any tendency toward price increases is slowed down by imports at subsidized prices.

The official price policy, moreover, does not operate to regulate peasant or other non-commercial units of production, although it undoubtedly affects them severely. Peasants have not abandoned the production of foodstuffs, mainly corn and perhaps beans, to the same degree as have commercial farmers. An important part of peasant production is dedicated to supplying the producers themselves in order to satisfy an important share of direct food consumption. This production for self-supply has been maintained in spite of the "negative profitability" of corn cultivation, since for peasants dependence on the market has always been more risky and economically burdensome than independent cultivation. In addition, the lands in the hands of peasants, which are of the poorest quality and pose the greatest risks, frequently do not facilitate the technical substitution of one crop for another. To this must be added the difficulty, or even the impossibility, of obtaining paid work during the seasonal farming cycle, the low levels of average rural wages, and the high seasonal variations in the prices of beans and corn in rural markets. A final consideration is that the objectives and organization of the peasant unit of production itself make independent cultivation for self-consumption rational and advantageous despite the fact that, from a cost-benefit point of view, the profit is negative.[4]

[3] The best synthesis in terms of a theoretical characterization of the peasant is that by Alejandro Schejtman in "Economía campesina y agricultura empresarial: tipología de productores del agro mexicano" in draft for the Economic Commission for Latin America (July 1980). I am utilizing the concept as specified in "Las clases rurales en México," in Arturo Warman, *Ensayos sobre el campesinado mexicano* (Mexico, 1980).

[4] The crisis in the production of basic goods (corn) has been analyzed by, among others, Luis Gómez Oliver in "Crisis agricola, crisis de los campesinos," in *Comercio Exterior*, 28,

For various reasons, production by peasants for self-consumption generally requires external credit support, almost always contributed by usurers or local monopsonists and not by national credit institutions. These private loans, for which the peasant pays 100 percent interest, are guaranteed and paid off out of the harvest the producer obtains. Such usurious credit contributes to regulating the autonomous production activity of peasants, who will strive, often without attaining it, for a harvest sufficient to cover both the debt and their family consumption. The volume of produce delivered as payment for the peasants' debts serves first of all to supply the traditional markets, where the monopsonist can obtain higher than the national prices, while only the surpluses are destined for the modern market. Paradoxically, linking institutional credit to technological input packages does not change this situation for the peasant and probably aggravates it by channeling all production toward the modern market.

Under these circumstances, peasants attempt to regulate their production of basic foodstuffs so as to approximate the requirements defined by direct consumption and the payment of debt obligations or exaction of surpluses from their autonomous production. At the same time, however, they try to avoid the creation of a surplus free of obligations for the purpose of obtaining income in the market, since this underlines the negative profitability of the crop or, more strictly defined, the slight recompense that they receive for the work invested in producing basic foods.

Although peasant production of corn has stopped increasing, there is no evidence that, once stabilized, it has declined to any significant degree. Apparently the peasants' best lands are already dedicated to the more intensive types of crops or have passed into the hands of entrepreneurs and have then been taken out of corn cultivation. The poorest lands, where negative profitability or low remuneration for labor in each cycle has been most severe, seem to have been abandoned by the peasants themselves. To offset this, the use of chemical fertilizers among peasants has spread, probably with the intention of cultivating medium quality lands more intensively by eliminating periods of fallow or rest, but without obtaining any increase in the annual yield per unit of surface area. Technical innovations and other conditions of dependence have also raised the monetary costs of crops, forcing the peasants to go more deeply into debt and, as a consequence, to deliver increasing proportions of their harvest to the market through moneylenders and monopsonists, even as they limit the production of unencumbered surpluses for the market.

---

no. 6 (June 1978), 714–37. Carlos Montañez and Horacio Aburto, *Maíz, política institucional y crisis agrícola* (Mexico, 1980); and Arturo Warman et al., *El cultivo del maíz en México: diversidad, limitaciones y alternativas* (Mexico, 1980).

The relative stability in the peasants' production and supply of corn, which is relatively unaffected by the market process and which in one fashion or another satisfies the direct consumption demands of three-quarters of the rural population, has permitted the state to force down the prices of basic foodstuffs and to focus its attention on supplying the modern market, thus separating it from the traditional market. Supply for the modern market economy has rested on a subsidy system that provides for the delivery of basic grains to the consumer at low and constant prices, well below selling prices plus the cost of handling and storage. Insofar as this directly affects the fixing of the minimum wages which are applicable to the majority of employed workers and to which the salary scale in the modern sector is set, this food subsidy to the urban centers has been a cornerstone of the economic policy of industrialization.

From the state's point of view, supplying the urban centers and the modern sector has had a higher priority than the needs of farmers, especially of peasant producers. Accordingly, policies have been adopted, successively and in combination, that were aimed at depressing domestic prices of basic foodstuffs while the supply of the modern market is covered by imports.[5] The limitations and contradictions of price policy when different types of producers compete in the market may be illustrated in the case of beans, of which there was a severe shortage in 1974. A significant portion of the supply of this legume derives from the fact that it is cultivated together with corn. Stagnation in corn production thus implied stagnation in the supply of beans. In addition, in spite of, or perhaps because of, the incorporation of fertilizers, continuous use of the peasants' lands severely affected the yields obtained from beans planted alongside corn. Furthermore, bean prices were permitted to decline even more than corn prices under the support program, a fact that also contributed to the reduction in supply. Since there is no international market in beans, increased imports of this essential element in the Mexican popular diet were not an option. Hence the poorest people, for whom the consumption of beans is critical because it constitutes their most important source of protein, could no longer afford them, in the face of illegal price increases, speculation, and hoarding that accompanied the shortfall in supply.

The state decided to meet the crisis by utilizing its handiest and most flexible instrument, and the one thought to be the most powerful: pricing policy. By 1975, the guaranteed price for beans had risen from 2,000 to 6,000 pesos per ton, or 300 percent at one stroke. The new price made the cultivation of beans attractive for those commercial producers en-

---

[5] The analysis sums up the basic point made in Warman et al., *El cultivo*.

dowed with the best land and the greatest capital resources. Peasant producers, with severe physical limitations on the land available to them, reacted more slowly and hesitantly to the price increase. In the course of a single agricultural cycle, commercial producers were able to saturate the market and, thanks to guaranteed prices, to obtain excellent profits. The poorest segments of the population, on the other hand, deeply resented the new higher prices and further reduced their consumption of this essential nutrient. The state then found itself with surpluses that could not be sold abroad owing to the lack of any significant international market for the commodity. The increase in prices had become simply a speculative windfall for large producers. Demand, rather than being satisfied, was artificially restricted by the price mechanism. The "surplus" stored up by the state did not contribute to the people's diet.

This episode of the beans might have demonstrated the relative ineffectiveness and risks of pricing policy as a regulator of production in cases where different kinds of producers, with different scales of production, compete on the market and respond in unequal manner and at different speeds to the same stimulus. The same episode might also have illustrated another very grave phenomenon: the deterioration in nutritional levels of the majority of the population—and particularly those in the rural areas—resulting from economic policies that ignored its needs and productive capacity. However, the warnings were ignored and the country's dependence on food imports grew steadily.

Land Distribution

The option of importing basic foodstuffs has been linked, if not integrally connected, with a degree of continuity in other state policies toward the rural areas. All have contributed to an increasing polarization among social classes in the countryside through the concentration and accumulation of resources and power in the hands of an ever smaller proportion of the population whose interests are directly linked to those of large-scale transnational enterprises.

After 1938 Mexico's agrarian policy of land redistribution stagnated. Between 1964 and 1970 enormous stretches of land of no economic value were divided up, and from 1970 to 1975 the state purchased marginal lands from large proprietors for distribution in collective fashion among insignificant numbers of peasants. In spite of such political measures, peasants have not received new endowments of land with any potential for agricultural production. Nor did the expropriation episode of 1976 alter this trend, although it had and continues to have political consequences of the highest importance.

Stagnation in official redistribution has not, however, implied any freezing of the real agrarian structure. For one thing, a significant number of new *campesinos* have been incorporated within the lands that the above-mentioned group controls, leading to a severe increase in pressures on the land. Moreover, by means of invasion, renting, or other illegal procedures, large owners have expropriated peasant lands. This process is essentially connected to the spread of cattle raising, under the control of large proprietors, which has grown relatively faster than other crop or livestock sectors. This de facto appropriation of peasant land is selective and is concentrated in areas with the greatest productivity potential, so that its effect is greater than may be supposed. While a larger number of *campesinos* must produce on fewer and poorer lands, large properties have consolidated and strengthened themselves vis-à-vis a growing number of *minifundios*. Paralysis in land distribution has also implied greater inequality in the relative and absolute distances separating different types of producers in the Mexican countryside. From 1950 to the present, the dominant feature of the agrarian scene has thus been concentration, which has reached levels similar to or even higher than those of Latin American countries that have never experienced land reform, let alone social revolution.[6]

From about the mid-1940s up to 1965, agricultural production in Mexico grew at a perceptibly greater rate than the increase in population, and buttressed the so-called Mexican miracle. The most important single factor in this process was the sustained growth of the surface area cultivated, i.e., the expansion of the agricultural frontier. This phenomenon had two principal components: (1) the opening of new lands, as a result of public investment in irrigation, dedicated entirely to commercial agriculture and the incorporation into production by peasants of the lands bestowed by the radical reform of Cárdenas; (2) increased use of land in rainfed zones for the production of basic food crops for consumption by farm households and for sale in the market (which because of the increased land use was adequately supplied). While the first process required large investments of capital, the second occurred on the basis of the peasants' own labor. Moreover, during the same period the peasant population almost doubled in absolute numbers.

The territorial reserve that had been given to the peasants during the years of agrarian reform became exhausted by the 1960s and has not been substantially enlarged by new endowments since then. Hence strat-

---

[6] For this classification of agrarian concentration, see Sergio Reyes Osorio et al., *Estructura agraria y desarrollo agrícola en México* (Mexico, 1974), which is here updated in accord with the 1970 census. For the comparison with other Latin American countries, see Solon Barraclough, *The Latin American Agrarian Problem* (Santiago de Chile, ICIRA, n.d. [ca. 1972]), and Andrew Pearse, *Agrarian Change Trends in Latin America* (Santiago de Chile, n.d. [ca. 1972]).

egies for absorbing the larger population, which continued to grow in absolute terms, had to be modified. Soil use and peasant cropping patterns were adjusted to accommodate the increasing supply of labor. As peasants turned to marketable and even speculative crops, sometimes at enormous risks, the cultivation of basic food crops, which offered the lowest remuneration to labor, stabilized.

The conditions under which the peasants exhausted the agriculture frontier in their areas, based on the incorporation of labor power at the lowest possible recompense, produced complex and paradoxical effects. Large private owners in the seasonal farming zones oriented their operations toward cattle raising in the extensive mode of open pasturage. The profits of these *latifundios* per unit of surface area remain higher than those obtainable in the crop raising sector.* On large spreads, cattle raising remains safe from the limitations that affect commercial agriculture in rainfed zones—i.e., state control over prices of the product; peasant competition, which is more evident for basic agriculture products than for livestock; and pressures for land redistribution, from which the livestock holdings are protected by "certificates of inaffectability" (state guarantees against appropriation). Lands dedicated to cattle raising embrace a large share of the agricultural frontier, equal in size in some regions to the area under cultivation, which the owners are hesitant to open up to crop production.

Resources for Production

The closing of the agricultural frontier is thus not a technical problem, but rather a socio-economic one, the result of the phenomenon of concentration of property deriving from the suspension of the agrarian reform coincident with the increase in peasant population.

The concentration that characterized landholding in Mexico manifests itself even more sharply in other resources for production. The distribution of both fixed and operating capital is extremely unequal. Actions taken by the state have played an important role in shaping this concentration. Fixed capital formation in the crop-and-livestock sector has depended mostly on public investment, which has contributed more than one-half of the total. This proportion, which implies a very low rate of private investment in the countryside, is accounted for by the construction of large-scale irrigation works, which up to 1975 absorbed three-quarters of all public investment in the rural sector.[7]

The pace and intensity of construction has not slackened, although

---

* Editors' note: SAM policies and related government programs introduced more recently are designed to raise the return for crop production and insure against risk to the farmer.

[7] Appendices to Mexican presidential reports; for the historical development, see Clark

after 1975, with the setting up of PIDER (Program of Public Investment for Rural Development), an attempt was made to bring the benefits of public investment to zones that had not previously received it. The results of this program, given its relatively reduced nature and magnitude, have not affected the general trend in any significant way.[8] The benefits of large-scale irrigation have been achieved through various mechanisms, legal or illegal (but tolerated and even abetted by the state), by a small number of large agricultural or stock-raising units, many of which act as production agents for transnational companies. The appropriation has been free and continuous, as the state has systematically and generously subsidized the operating deficits of the large national irrigation districts that had originally been delivered at no cost to their beneficiaries.

Large rural enterprises have also appropriated the bulk of other types of public investment, such as credit, price subsidies for fertilizers, the profits from agricultural research and its propagation and extension. These resources have supplied or complemented the working capital of rural entrepreneurs and have contributed to increasing their profits and diminishing their risks. Such enormous advantages and subsidies, which amount to billions of pesos, have not been oriented so as to direct those entrepreneurs' operations toward supplying the food needs of the country. On the contrary, state policies have favored the concentration of commercial activity in the most profitable lines of production as well as the transfer of profits to other sectors of the economy. This transfer of capital from rural enterprises to other economic sectors has demanded a constant subsidy by means of public investments, which replace whatever is lacking to assure the continuity of business activity.

Two examples will serve to illustrate how state action facilitates and permits the concentration of commercial production in the most profitable branches of agriculture or livestock raising. The first is water management in the large national irrigation districts. The cropping plan that serves to regulate the distribution of water is formulated by a directing committee on which federal-level functionaries have a predominant position, followed in number by the large commercial farmers, represented through their producer associations; in last place are the *ejidatarios*, represented by the official peasant confederation. Individual *minifundistas*, assimilated to the private sector, are not represented at all.

Because the availability of water is generally limited, in part due to the

W. Reynolds, *The Mexican Economy: Twentieth Century Structure and Growth* (New Haven, Conn., 1970).

[8] For results of PIDER, see the publications of the World Bank, Washington, and the studies by the Centro de Investigaciones del Desarrollo Rural (CIDER) within the Secretariat for Programming and Budget of Mexico.

inefficient use of this precious resource for commercial farming, the crop plan spells out which producers will receive water, in what quantities, and for what specific purposes. Official credit institutions adhere to this plan and, once it has been sanctioned by higher federal authorities, open up credit lines only for specified crops and areas. In the largest and most important irrigation districts, situated in desert regions, areas and crops not specified in the plan may not be seeded. Corn has occupied last place among the priorities established for these irrigation districts. An official attempt was even made to eradicate the cultivation of corn from the national districts—a decision justified by the crop's low profitability, which in turn stems from its low guaranteed prices. The preference that directing committees have granted to the more remunerative crops has been instrumental in the loss of land by *campesinos* with rights to its use in the large water districts. They lack the capital and political connections necessary to apply the means of production supplied by the public sector and frequently find themselves forced to rent their lands to large entrepreneurs at a price equivalent to the earnings traditionally made from corn growing. Hence the cultivation of corn as of 1980 had practically disappeared from the large national water districts, which themselves generate almost half of all agricultural production.[9]

In the case of wheat, those who abandoned its cultivation in the face of the stagnation in price guarantees were the commercial producers. As long as such prices were favorable and permitted high rates of profit, producers in the irrigation districts not only saturated the national market but also produced a surplus equivalent to one-half of domestic consumption. Owing to the difference between the higher internal price and the low international price, this surplus had to be exported at a substantial loss, which was, however, totally covered by the state and had no effect on producers' profits. Because the capacity and volume of commercial production in the water districts provoked many wheat producers in rainfed areas—many of them peasants who had never received support comparable to that given the larger producers—the rainfed cultivation of wheat in Mexico has practically disappeared. Subsequently the state attempted to make up its losses by allowing the real official price for wheat to decline. As a result, commercial farmers ceased cultivating it and went over to the planting of oilseeds, which were subsidized by more attractive price guarantees. The country then had no alternative but to resort once again to importation. In this case, the direction committees did not exert any pressure to maintain cultivation, but rather deprived it of priority,

[9] Secretariat for Programming and Budget of Mexico, *Manual de Estadísticas Basicas: Sector Agropecuario y Forestal* (Mexico, 1979).

alleging low profitability. Water-use policy, governed by strict criteria of profitability, has thus always worked to the benefit of large entrepreneurs, despite the fact that irrigation constitutes the single most important item of public investment in the countryside.[10]

The orientation and management of official credit have also favored commercial producers and have contributed in an important way to the country's inability to satisfy its demand for food. Importation of corn had been going on since 1973.[11] Three years later a national survey undertaken among producers of grains showed that, while only one out of every five producers of corn was supported by official credit, more than half of sorghum producers enjoyed such support.

The growing of sorghum in Mexico must be attributed to the active promotion undertaken by the official bank on its behalf. On account of its ecological adaptability, sorghum is a crop capable of competing with corn and beans in combination, but unlike them it is a totally commercial crop, none of which is consumed by the producers. (In Mexico, it is not used for human consumption.) The commercial nature of the crop has been interpreted as an advantage by the official bank for agricultural credit. For one thing, centralization of the market and the fact that nothing is retained by the producers for self-consumption have facilitated bank control over the recovery of loans, as has the fact that cultivation is totally mechanized. Sorghum growing requires purchased inputs and, because it is totally market-oriented, generates greater cash flows than traditional corn cultivation—something that has also been interpreted as an obvious benefit in terms of national economic development. Moreover, it has been argued that sorghum is a higher-yielding crop than corn and one whose price is less subject to fluctuations, although the incorporation of modern inputs into a different crop system makes comparisons between physical yields immaterial in terms of costs and benefits when prices result from economic policy decisions. On the basis of these criteria, since about the mid-1960s the cultivation of sorghum has had a higher priority than the cultivation of corn in the official credit programs of the Mexican government. To all appearances, this situation continues unaltered.

However, what has been perceived as an advantage from the point of view of credit, and of economic development understood simply as growth, has clearly clashed with peasants' needs. For peasant producers

---

[10] This process is clearly illustrated in the magnificent book by Cynthia Hewett cited in note 2, above.

[11] The survey was carried out by the Secretariat for Agriculture and Livestock of Mexico. For partial results from it, see *Econotecnica*, 2, no. 2; for a more complete analysis: Carlos Montañez y Horacio Aburto, *Maíz*.

sorghum has generated neither employment nor satisfaction. In the best of cases its cultivation has brought with it a modest income that does not compensate producers for the effective separation between land and labor that the planting of the crop entails. In aggregate terms as well, the expansion of sorghum growing, which now covers more than 1.5 million hectares and occupies second place behind corn, has brought about a significant deficit in the production of basic foodstuffs and has wrested enormous amounts of land away from the peasants' control.

State policies, which implicitly control the greater part of the resources dedicated to Mexican agriculture, have both permitted and facilitated concentration of this resource as well as its transfer as capital to sectors privileged by the official policy of industrialization. Consequently, they have led to an accentuation of social and economic polarization in the countryside and a severe worsening of the peasants' already limited capacities to produce and subsist.

Imports

When the contradictions in the structure of agricultural production had manifested themselves in a supply insufficient to cover national demand for basic foodstuffs, imports were resorted to. As is demonstrated by the significant and growing volumes of grain imported since 1972, purchases abroad were no longer used as an emergency short-term measure but became a permanent practice. Several circumstances favored this option. With the elimination of restrictions on farm production in the United States in 1973, international supplies appeared to be abundant and to have good prospects for further growth.[12] The prices of basic grains appeared to be similar to or slightly lower than domestic prices. Mexican exports of crops and livestock had risen at an accelerated pace, and the agricultural trade balance registered positive figures that gave grounds for believing in the value of comparative advantage. Imports, centralized and on a large scale, also seemed easier to manage than efforts to increase scattered internal purchases, and as a result it was believed that the volume of subsidies to urban and industrial consumption would be reduced. But, above all, imports would permit sidestepping decisions about the rural sector that would affect the precarious political equilibrium in the countryside; time had been bought to allow policies of traditional agricultural development to change the situation there.

At the end of a decade of food imports, the advantages of importation

[12] National Academy of Sciences, *Agricultural Production Efficiency* (Washington, D.C., 1975); Lester R. Brown, *By Bread Alone* (New York, Praeger, 1974); *Scientific American*, 235, no. 3, dedicated to agriculture and nutrition. See also the paper by Walter P. Falcon in this volume.

have vanished. The volume of the international supply has not been sufficient to protect Mexico against mounting difficulties in guaranteeing that its domestic needs would be met. In the case of beans there was no international market, and the irregularity of external supply was translated into shortages and higher prices internally, but even in products for which an international market was well established, as in the case of corn, significant problems were encountered in obtaining the large volumes the country required. In 1979, when a severe drought and early frosts affected production, Mexico with its large purchase requirements found no suppliers on the international market; only the "fortunate" cancellation of U.S. sales contracts to the Soviet Union permitted the problem to be resolved. Resorting to international supplies in the future does not appear to make sense either, inasmuch as the need to have recourse to imports presents itself not only in Mexico but also in many other dependent countries—at times as the reflection of a new form of international division of labor resulting from the transnationalization of production. In the face of a multiplying demand, moreover, the capacity to export grain is concentrated in a few countries—all highly developed, with the exception of Argentina, and with very unequal contributions to supply—two-thirds of which originates in the United States. Mexico's dependence on U.S. supplies is accentuated not only by long-standing political and economic ties but also by her limited port capacity, which forces a significant portion of the imports to be routed overland.

The favorable prices have also changed and will do so more sharply in the foreseeable future. From 1972 onward, the average prices of purchases abroad have been higher than domestic prices in Mexico. In the exporting countries—highly mechanized, intensive in the use of fertilizers and other petrochemicals, and capable of massive shipments over great distances—agriculture depends to a high degree on hydrocarbons, and its prices have risen in proportion to the price of oil. Although some people believe that it will slow down, the spiral in the price of oil does not appear to be reversible. It is ironic that Mexico has to sell crude oil in order to buy wheat and corn, products grown using precisely this raw material.

For another thing, U.S. agriculture is experiencing a process of intense concentration into a reduced number of productive units of larger size. Several studies assert and demonstrate that the result will be an increase in the prices of U.S. agricultural goods.[13] Moreover, the inflationary trends that affect grain-exporting countries, the United States in particu-

---

[13] For tendencies toward concentration, cf. Dan Morgan, *Merchants of Grain* (Penguin Books, 1980).

lar, do not permit optimism about the behavior of agricultural export prices. In addition, what looks like an interactive relationship appears to exist between international prices and domestic prices in Mexico. International prices seem lower than national prices when the currency is overvalued. When this situation is corrected, however, they turn out to be higher than domestic and present no advantage from the point of view of the subsidy to urban and industrial consumption.

The increases in the prices of imported grains must also be analyzed, taking into account a new condition, namely that Mexico's agricultural trade balance has ceased to be positive, or is so only to an insignificant degree, when averages are calculated over prolonged periods of time.[14] In some years the balance has been negative, and if the tendency toward the growth of imports continues, deficits will be a regular and constant problem. Crucial in this new situation are not only the increase in imports but also the relative deterioration in the prices of traditional agricultural exports in relation to the prices of grain, a deterioration that once again reflects a new division of labor in the world market. Imports of food in the future will thus weigh heavily upon other sectors of the economy, i.e., upon oil. If the trends toward increasing international food prices continue on their present course, the forecast enunciated in the National Plan for Industrial Development, to the effect that the petroleum surplus will be eaten up by agricultural imports before the end of the century, will have to be taken seriously.[15]

In the immediate term, other problems connected with importation present themselves with greater urgency. The most severe of these are the insufficiencies of port infrastructure, rail transport, storage, and internal distribution for handling large volumes of food imports. From 1975 onward, with import volumes at less than four million tons, severe congestion was experienced in the ports and on the railroads. The direct and indirect costs for the rest of the economy resulting from this congestion are not known, but appear to be sufficiently high to increase substantially the final cost of imported grains. In order to avoid congestion, truck transport is being used systematically, which makes the initial cost of grain almost insignificant relative to its delivered cost. These grave problems present themselves when imports are destined only for the modern urban market, where available infrastructure is concentrated. By 1980 it has become necessary to allocate some of these supplies to rural areas as well, and for this purpose neither infrastructure nor mechanisms of distribution exist. The economic, political, and social costs of this process of market-widening are not yet clear but will obviously be high.

[14] See *Manual de Estadísticas Basicas*, as in note 9, above.
[15] See *Plan Nacional de Desarrollo Industrial 1979–82*, I (Mexico, 1979).

Plans have been elaborated to rebuild the needed infrastructure, which will entail making gigantic investments. If food imports could be eliminated—in view of the fact that the movement of petroleum is accomplished through an independent network—with only a few modest improvements effected, the available infrastructure would be adequate for commerce in all other products. This consideration, which is hardly ever taken into account, is essential for evaluating the costs of dependence on import food supplies. The profit and loss estimates at the level of a peasant's plot, and the microeconomics of the farm unit that has served as the basis for the analysis of comparative advantage, cannot give an adequate account of the complex economic consequences that such dependence produces on either the national or the international level. Even less can they give an account of the social effects produced in a situation where the majority of productive units in the agricultural sector are not businesses that engage in investment for profit but rather are social units seeking their own preservation and reproduction under improved conditions.

Dependence on food imports has other costs that cannot be quantified, in the area of political sovereignty and the defining of a national development model. "Food power" in the international arena is not a fiction but a force that is currently being applied and will become even more important in the future. The new international division of labor implies that the majority of the world's population will depend increasingly on a few powerful countries for their biological subsistence. The new relations of power deriving from this situation are very complex and should not be oversimplified, much less ignored. Although a decision in favor of self-sufficiency—not to be confused with autarchy—has been declared by the Mexican government, its implementation accommodates alternative strategies.

SOLUTIONS

The adoption of the Mexican Food System (*Sistema Alimentario Mexicano* or SAM) in March of 1980 as the state's global strategy for confronting the crisis gave priority to the achievement of self-sufficiency in a few basic crops.[16] The strategy has important implications, at various levels, that are worth analyzing briefly in order to evaluate its impact on the factors causing the present crisis and on their future evolution.

The first effect is that the SAM, taken as a whole, elevates the importance of agriculture in the area of government programs, especially for the production of basic food crops. This translates into an increase in the public investment dedicated to agriculture. In the decade of the 1960s

[16] See Cassio Luiselli Fernández, "Porque el SAM?" in *Nexos*, no. 32 (Mexico, August 1980).

less than 10 percent of such investment was allocated to the crop-and-livestock production sector; in the 1970s this proportion was increased to 20 percent. It would seem that, with the oil discoveries, the earlier tendency for a transfer of capital from agriculture to other sectors declined in importance as a state strategy, and an attempt was even made to reverse the flow. This perception may, however, be misleading. In the past, by virtue of being concentrated in certain branches of activity and with certain types of producers as its beneficiary, public investment was one of the most effective mechanisms for generating a transfer of capital from agriculture and stock raising to other parts of the economy. It has consequently been one of the most powerful factors in the process of resource concentration of wealth and extreme polarization among rural producers. The specific mechanisms adopted by the SAM do not yet appear to be of either the magnitude or the orientation necessary to reverse the historical process that has facilitated this transfer of capital.

Moreover, under the name of the SAM, the most divergent and at times contradictory public actions have been carried out. Most of the time they have amounted to prolonging and modernizing traditional forms of intervention in the Mexican countryside, which—unchanged—are clothed in the guise of a new strategy. These nominal alterations, this veritable loading of terminology should not be confused with the actions proposed by the SAM. Nor should one ignore the fact that not only does the SAM's strategy not suspend the previous pattern of state activity but even assimilates it. For many *campesinos* SAM thus looks like a new name for the same policies that have either excluded them or, as a condition for including them, have separated them from the direct working of their own land. It can justly be asserted that this is not what the strategy intends, even though it is in fact what frequently occurs. Up to now the system has not acquired the momentum, the force, or the clarity to reorient public sector action in its entirety, and is instead an add-on to a process with its own inertia.

The specific supplement added by the SAM to public sector activities aimed at orienting production toward basic grains may be characterized, up to the present, by two types of actions. The first consists of subsidizing the purchase of inputs used in the production of corn and beans, fertilizers, improved seeds, and agricultural insurance. In appearance, such subsidies are of a general nature and may benefit any producer of basic grains. In fact, they are regressive in character and favor the large commercial producers. According to the most recently available data (1976),[17] only half of the area seeded in corn received fertilizer, while a quarter

[17] See above, note 11.

received improved seeds, and another quarter received credit and associated insurance. These areas are in general under the control of the largest producers, whose commercial orientation is also clearest. Even though in the last few years credit and obligatory technological packages associated with it have reached other producers, there is no evidence that the tendency to support those occupying the highest rungs of the social structure in the rural areas has been modified.

The second kind of specific action deriving from the SAM refers to the raising of guaranteed prices, not only in absolute terms but also relative to those of other competitive products like sorghum. Up to now this change has been introduced cautiously, and the real price of corn is far from having attained its level of the early seventies. Within a polarized rural structure the limitations on the pricing mechanism vis-à-vis distinct types of producers imply a serious risk for the state. That risk is accentuated to the extent that a big component of the SAM is focused on consumption in an effort to put a basic food basket within the reach of the great mass of the population. Thus price increases translate into subsidy increments that occur far in advance of any effects on production. Nevertheless, the control of prices appears to be the most efficacious means of influencing production in the short run. Its effects and utilization, though limited, will thus be critical in the immediate future.

Other direct measures emanating from the SAM, such as shared risk, association between private farmers and *ejidatarios*, bringing idle lands or pasture into cultivation, and mechanization—all of which are contained in the Crop and Livestock Promotion Law (*Ley de Fomento Agropecuario*)—have as yet taken on no concrete content, nor do institutional mechanisms yet exist for their implementation. Nevertheless, with due reservation, it seems evident that these measures are intended to "modernize" the process of production of basic crops. In other words, they aim to raise productivity through the increasing incorporation of purchased inputs and "advanced technology." This implies the concentration of land resources in complex production units permitting the profitable adoption of the technology stemming from the Green Revolution. The same orientation may be ascribed to the other measures already taken.

In its initial documents, the SAM acknowledged the existence of social and economic problems as contributing, but not determining, factors, in the agricultural crisis. In its implementation, however, priority is granted to technical problems of productivity. Although the Mexican Food System makes constant references to increasing peasant incomes, it grounds this possibility in the better distribution of an additional income increment, i.e., of a new value added through modernization of the productive process. In this strategy no measure of redistribution of income or of resources currently in use has been considered, but only a better distribution of future earnings. In practice this increase is considered to be a variable that depends on greater and more technically advanced use of capital, to be supported basically by public-sector investment.

The strategy of the SAM, in its present form, thus repeats tactics that have already been attempted in previous administrations, leading one to suspect that there will be serious limitations on its effective implementation. Such limits may be analyzed at two levels. In the first place, the crisis includes crops that are already fully "modernized" in terms of their technique of cultivation. The case of wheat, mentioned earlier, serves to illustrate this process. Production beyond the level of self-sufficiency to the creation of exportable surpluses was achieved on the basis of subsidies that covered not only high costs of products but also very high profits for the commercial producers, who control the resources needed for production. The impressive increase in wheat productivity was thus made possible by the transfer of public resources to a small number of private wheat farmers. Modernization, however, turned out to be contrary to the national interest, as were the subsequent countermeasures that led to wheat imports. An increase in production and productivity based on subsidies, which translates into excess profits for entrepreneurs, therefore offers few alternatives, and those only over a very short period of time.

The other contradictory dimension of modernization applies to the peasant producers, who are the ones who have maintained production of basic grains. For them "technical change" (*tecnificación*) along entrepreneurial lines is a costly alternative that is seen to work against their interests.[18] Peasants without capital, capable of producing goods only on a reduced scale, cannot depend for their subsistence on risky return to capital. On the contrary, they live from their labor, which may even be recompensed below the subsistence level. Peasants compete in the market to monetize their labor, not to realize a profit. In view of such a situation, modernization cannot take place in basic crops, which require only a small labor force and promise low profits at best. Such modernization would require high intensity, of both labor and capital, in order for the payment to labor plus profits to be more than that obtained in the processing of subsistence crops plus a very small remuneration to labor from traditional cultivation. In order to achieve this intensity, what peasants require is not the operating capital for purchased input that has been offered them and that frequently competes with their own labor, but rather

[18] For a broader exposition of these contradictions, see Arturo Warman, "La colectivización en el campo; una critica," in *Cuadernos Políticos*, no. 11 (Mexico, January–March, 1977).

more and better land and capital. This naturally entails a process of re-distribution. The other alternative demanded by peasants—simple territorial extension for the purpose of expanding their current methods of subsistence cultivation—would also require redistribution, i.e., a continuation and broadening of the process of agrarian reform. The securing of a new agricultural frontier is in fact the peasants' most urgent and immediate demand.

The SAM has repeatedly avoided confronting the basic agrarian problem that is currently impeding the development of the rural productive process. On the other hand, it does attempt to renew the state-peasant political alliance, which is based in a certain set of agrarian relationships. On the political plane, the Mexican Food System clearly does not respond to the central demands of the peasants and presupposes their passive compliance rather than any active participation. In spite of this contradiction, which hinders if it does not actually obstruct any alliance being sought, it is precisely in the political sphere that one of SAM's immediate effects has occurred, and this despite the peasants' absence from that arena. Recognition of the agricultural crisis and of the problem of the countryside, as well as dependence on imports, has led to the reopening of discussion about the overall development model that had previously been considered closed. The need for representation of the peasant class in a national development program has also provoked novel realignments in the public sector. Food dependence, in all its severity, has thus introduced a new dimension to the prospects for national development over the short term. Self-determination, independence, and national security must now be discussed not only in terms of barrels of oil, but also in terms of tons of corn and beans.

Over the medium term the strategy of the SAM, in its formulation and current implementation, does not provide the basis necessary for modifying present tendencies toward increasing external dependence in the provisioning of basic foodstuffs for the population. The strategy's deliberate refusal to face up to the most profound rural problems—especially the problems of land and of the extreme concentration of resources—gives rise to the suspicion that its programs actually serve mostly to reinforce existing structures through an injection of new resources on an unprecedented scale. There is evidence that the present structure of agricultural production possesses neither the capacity nor the proper orientation for resolving the problem of basic food supply. The new resources are simply insufficient in magnitude and in the mode of their investment to alter the deep-lying roots of the crisis.

There may be some validity in the forecasts to the effect that, in the short run and in specific products or branches of activity, SAM and the concomitant resources will produce violent and even profound changes. It is probable that some of its concrete objectives can be realized and that it will manage to reduce dependence on some crops even as dependence increases on others. The mobilization of the state that SAM has achieved is by no means insignificant even though, as we have seen, it does not constitute a coherent global strategy. SAM tends to strengthen and deepen the state's intervention in the agricultural production process and even converts that intervention into one of its decisive elements.

The state, however, has not yet become the dominant force in the rural areas. Internal contradictions exist, and other groups and processes are operative in the same arena, in particular, the international division of labor, and the increasing "food power" of the industrial countries and their primary institutional expressions, the transnational corporations. The framing of a new order in the international marketplace may lead countries like Mexico to rethink radically the costs of their dependence, just as peasants are doing to mobilize and voice their demands. Pressures from the peasants are having an increasing input in the national political arena. Their presence can no longer be ignored except at great risk.

In few areas is it as difficult to make projections or predictions as in the area of agricultural production, inasmuch as the crisis is causing new problems and new forces to emerge with great rapidity. The necessity for change is evident; the possibility of carrying it out is a question that has no clear or obvious answer. The decade that has begun may perhaps supply an answer. For now, however, I believe it is possible only to confirm the movement.

The Design and Redesign of Strategies for Agricultural Development: Mexico's Experience Revisited

Bruce F. Johnston

ON OTHER occasions I have compared Mexico's bimodal pattern of agricultural development with the unimodal strategies pursued in Japan and in Taiwan.[1] In an effort to assess the advantages and disadvantages of those alternative strategies for contemporary "late-developing" countries, the principal conclusion, on which there is now substantial agreement, is that for low-income countries, where some 60 to 80 percent of the labor force still depends on agriculture for employment and income, a unimodal strategy has important economic as well as social advantages.[2]

It is generally recognized that if a late-developing country concentrates its agricultural investment and its increases in farm productivity and sales within a subsector of large, relatively capital-intensive farm units, most of its small-scale units will be bypassed, and rural poverty will be widespread and persistent. In contrast, the pursuit of unimodal strategies for modernizing the small farm units progressively, by means of divisible, yield-increasing innovations that are neutral to scale, can achieve widespread increases in rural incomes and well-being.

[1] Bruce F. Johnston, "Agriculture and Economic Development: The Relevance of the Japanese Experience," *Food Research Institute Studies*, 6, no. 3 (1966), 251–312, and "The Japanese 'Model' of Agricultural Development: Its Relevance to Developing Nations," in *Agriculture and Economic Growth: Japan's Experience*, ed. Kasushi Ohkawa et al. (Tokyo, 1969), pp. 58–102; Bruce F. Johnston and Peter Kilby, *Agriculture and Structural Transformation: Economic Strategies for Late-Developing Countries* (New York, 1975), ch. 6; also published as *Agricultura y Transformación Estructural: Politicas económicas para los paises en desarrollo tardío* (Mexico, D.F., 1980).

[2] See, for example, World Bank, *The Assault on World Poverty: Problems of Rural Development, Education, and Health* (Baltimore, Md., and London, 1975), and *World Development Report 1978* (Washington, D.C., 1978); Asian Development Bank, *Rural Asia: Challenge and Opportunity* (New York, 1978); Government of India, *Draft Five Year Plan 1978–83* (New Delhi, 1978); Republic of Kenya, *Development Plan: For the Period 1979 to 1983*, pt. 1 (Nairobi, 1979).

The objective here is to examine and seek to understand the factors that have shaped Mexico's dualistic agricultural strategy. Why have its resources been concentrated in a subsector of large, highly commercialized and mechanized farm units, especially in the North and Pacific North regions? Why has it neglected to a considerable extent the small-scale units in both the *ejidal* and the private sectors? The issues are timely, since Mexico's policy makers have been devoting special attention to problems of low productivity and poverty among small-scale farmers, as reflected in major programs such as PIDER and the Sistema Alimentario Mexicano (SAM).[3] Better understanding of the reasons for past shortcomings may contribute to the success of current efforts to redesign Mexico's rural development strategy. Achieving increases in productivity and income among the small-scale farm units that appear to have benefited so little from Mexico's generally impressive economic growth of the past three or four decades will be a difficult undertaking.

Experience in other countries—by no means limited to Japan and Taiwan—can be of some value. I recognize, however, that the analysis of factors responsible for Mexico's dualistic pattern of agricultural development is in itself a complex and speculative exercise. Needless to say, it is for those who possess detailed knowledge and understanding of Mexican agriculture to judge whether the interpretations and ideas presented here are of value. It seems probable that a shift to an essentially unimodal agricultural strategy would be neither feasible nor desirable. The advantages of relying on the progressive modernization of small-scale farm units by means of labor-using, capital-saving technologies are reduced when the opportunity cost of labor rises as nonfarm employment opportunities expand. According to recent estimates, the share of agriculture in Mexico's labor force had declined to only 39 percent in 1978, compared to 55 percent in 1960 and 65 percent in 1940.[4] Although this structural change may have raised the opportunity cost of labor in rural areas, the effects may have been negated by the tremendous increases in total population and labor force. It is in any event questionable to speak in terms of *the* opportunity cost of labor in Mexico, since there appear to be large regional variations in the price of unskilled labor. Furthermore, with an estimated 20 percent of the country's labor force employed in the United States, wage

---

[3] August Schumacher, "Agricultural Development and Rural Employment: A Mexican Dilemma" (paper prepared for the Binational Consultation on U.S.-Mexican Agricultural Relations, San Diego, February 25–27, 1981); Office of the President (Oficina de Asesores), *Sistema Alimentario Mexicano* (Mexico City, March 1, 1980).

[4] World Bank, *World Development Report, 1980* (Washington, D.C., 1980), p. 147; D. Colosio, "Urbanization and Economic Development in Mexico," WP-79-19 (Laxenburg, Austria, June 1979), p. 60.

rates across the border obviously exert a considerable influence on the opportunity cost of labor in Mexico.[5]

The evidence seems all too clear that there is still a great deal of poverty in rural Mexico. Between 1940 and 1960, for example, the combined number of landless and small, marginal farm units of less than five hectares more than doubled.[6] Considering the rapid rate of growth of the total labor force in Mexico, it seems likely that the number of landless workers and marginal farmers has continued to increase in spite of the decline in agriculture's share in the total labor force. Estimates of the agricultural labor force in Mexico are unsatisfactory, but those for urban and rural population appear to be more reliable. According to the latter, the rural population living in places with fewer than 2,500 inhabitants virtually doubled between 1940 and 1960 in spite of a sixfold increase in the urban population (see Table 4). In addition, a study of agricultural employment indicates that from the mid-1960s the rate of growth of demand for labor in Mexican agriculture has fallen sharply as compared to the 1940–60 period and that underemployment has increased considerably.[7] Collateral evidence of an increase in rural poverty is provided by estimates of food intake based on surveys carried out by the National Institute of Nutrition. Data for 1959 and 1974 indicate that in the North there was a modest increase, but in the Center and South energy intake fell from an estimated 1,900 to 1,750 calories; and in the Southeast there was a sharp decline from 2,000 to a grossly inadequate 1,575 calories.[8]

FACTORS CONTRIBUTING TO MEXICO'S DUALISTIC PATTERN OF AGRICULTURAL DEVELOPMENT

Fundamental to an examination of the factors deemed responsible for Mexico's bimodal pattern of agricultural development is the evidence concerning the extent of the dualism that exists. Between 1950 and 1970, there was an increase in the number of farm units, including both the *ejidal* and private sectors, from 2.4 to 2.9 million (Table 1). Virtually all of this 20 percent increase occurred during the 1960s and was influenced by the creation of a large number of new *ejidos*; the number of farm units

[5] Clark W. Reynolds, "Labor Market Projections for the United States and Mexico and Their Relevance to Current Migration Controversies," *Food Research Institute Studies*, 17, no. 2 (1979), 5.

[6] Shlomo Eckstein et al., *Land Reform in Latin America: Bolivia, Chile, Mexico, Peru, and Venezuela*, World Bank Staff Working Paper no. 275 (Washington, D.C., 1978), p. 17.

[7] Teresa Rendón, "Utilización de mano de obra en la agricultura Mexicana, 1940–1973," *Demografía y Economía*, 10, no. 3 (1976), as reported in Joel Bergsman, *Income Distribution and Poverty in Mexico*, World Bank Staff Working Paper no. 395 (Washington, D.C., 1980), pp. 32–33.

[8] Office of the President, *Sistema*, p. 9.

TABLE 1

Mexico: Percentage Shares in 1960 Agricultural Output
and 1950–60 Output Growth of Farms
(by value of output), and Number of Farms, 1950–70

Farm classes: mean value of annual output (1960 U.S. dollars)	Percentage shares in:			Number of farm units (thousands)		
	Number of farms 1960	Value of output 1960	Growth in output 1950–60	1950	1960	1970
A. Less than 80	50%	4%	−1%	1,312	1,241	1,358
B. 80–400	34	17	10	800	821	966
C. 400–2,000	13	26	11	289	307	468
D. 2,000–8,000	3	22	35	27	67	85
E. Over 8,000	0.5	32	45	8	12	14
TOTAL	100%	100%	100%	2,437	2,448	2,911

SOURCE: Eckstein et al., *Land Reform*, p. 38; based on Serges Reyes Osorio et al., *Estructura agraria y desarrollo agrícola en México*, I (Mexico City, 1970), 197ff.
NOTE: Arithmetic errors and categories in the original.

TABLE 2

Mexico: Output, Area, Inputs, and Yields of Ejido *Farms, Averages for Size Classes, 1960*

(money values in 1960 U.S. dollars)

Farm classes: mean value of annual output	Ejido (000)	farms (pct.)	Value of output ($)	Crop-land (ha.)	Irri-gated (ha.)	Ma-chinery ($)	Produc-tivity ($/ha.)
A. Less than 80	670	46%	45	2.8	0	8	16
B. 80–400	530	38	270	7	0.2	25	39
C. 400–2,000	200	14	900	15	4	200	60
D. Over 2,000	35	2	3,500	17	16	1,200	206
TOTAL	1,435	100%					

SOURCE: Eckstein et al., *Land Reform*, p. 41.
NOTE: Categories from the original.

is based not on the number of *ejidos* per se, but on the number of *ejido* members, most of whom were operating individual family farms.[9] It is striking that the two largest size categories, which represented only 3.2 perent of the total number of farm units, accounted for 54 percent of the value of agricultural output in 1960 and an astounding 80 percent of the increase in output between 1950 and 1960. At the opposite extreme, the small farmers with annual output of less than $80 (1960 U.S. dollars) represented half of the total number of farm units but accounted for only 4 percent of farm output in 1960.

It is apparent from the data in Table 2 that dualism is operative in the *ejidal* as well as in the private farm sector. The two groups of small "traditional farmers" accounted for most of the *ejidal* households, but their annual output amounted to only $45 and $270 respectively (in 1960 U.S. dollars). This was a consequence of the small size and low output per hectare of the farm units in those categories, which in turn was related to an almost total lack of irrigation and a minuscule investment in farm machinery and other purchased inputs. The two groups of large "modern" farms, with greater access to land, had an annual output of $900 and $3,500 respectively. Especially in the largest size category, this was a consequence of the fact that, with virtually all of the crop land irrigated, yields were four to six times as high as those in rainfed areas.[10] The yield differential was also associated with greater use of purchased inputs, especially farm machinery. On the largest farms its average value was some

[9] Eckstein et al., *Land Reform*, p. 38.
[10] Ibid., p. 40.

TABLE 3

Mexico: Maize Output on Ejidos, *1950–70*

Category	Traditional farms (A+B)		Modern farms (C+D)		Total
	No. (*000*)	Pct.	No. (*000*)	Pct.	No. (*000*)
Ejido farms (*000*)					
1950	1,146	87%	180	13%	1,326
1960	1,200	84%	235	16%	1,435
1970	1,492	78%	422	22%	1,914
Percent of output represented by maize					
1950		48%		52%	
1960		36%		64%	
1970		26%		74%	
Increase in output per farm (*percent*)					
1950–60		20%		62%	
1960–70		−15%		−7%	

SOURCE: Eckstein et al., *Land Reform*, p. 41.
NOTE: See groupings of *ejido* farms in Table 2.

150 times that on the smallest *ejidal* farm units, where the investment amounted to a paltry $8. The *ejidal* households in the two smallest groups received virtually no credit from the Ejidal Bank, which concentrated its lending in the larger collective *ejidos* in northern Mexico. For the small private farm units the situation was little different.

The greater value of output in the large-size categories was further influenced by the greater importance of wheat and cotton, relatively high value crops that have benefited greatly from research and yield increases. It is clear from Table 3, however, that even in terms of maize the large-size categories accounted for a disproportionate share of the increase in output between 1950 and 1970. By 1970 just over one-fifth of all of the *ejidal* farms were in the two groups of large farms, but they accounted for three-fourths of the total maize output in the *ejidal* sector. Because bad weather rendered 1970 an especially poor year for maize production, the data for that year probably exaggerate the dominance of the large-scale holdings where irrigation was available to help sustain yields.

This tendency for the value of crop production per hectare of harvested land to be significantly higher on large farms applies to the private as well as the *ejidal* sector.[11] It is important to emphasize, however, that

[11] Ibid., app. C.

evidence in developing countries other than Mexico consistently indicates the significant inverse relationship between farm size and productivity. The recent monograph by Berry and Cline brings together a mass of empirical evidence and analyzes the factors that seem to explain this general tendency for yields and productivity to decline as farm size moves from small to large.[12] The fact that Mexico is an exception seems to be primarily a result of the concentration of irrigated land in the areas where large-scale private and *ejidal* farms predominate. On irrigated land, also, cropping patterns tend to show a larger percentage of high-value crops. From 1926/28 through 1968 public investment in support of agricultural development concentrated some 80 percent of its resources in large-scale irrigation projects that have benefited primarily these high yield enterprises.[13]

There are numerous differences between Mexico and Japan or Taiwan that seriously limit the relevance of comparisons. Particularly striking are the historical contrasts betweeen a long tradition of small-scale farming in the two East Asian countries and the dominant position of large *haciendas* in Mexico prior to the Revolution. Political factors, which are inseparably linked with Mexico's historical experience, also merit attention in exploring agricultural dualism. Their influence seems to have been reinforced by some ideological or attitudinal factors. Because the dualism of Mexico's agriculture is so closely linked with geographical regions with different agroclimatic conditions, technical considerations also are extremely important in explaining the differential rates of growth of agricultural output and incomes between the large-scale and the small-scale agricultural sectors. Several economic factors, in turn, have buttressed those technical factors. Finally, there are organizational and other institutional pressures that appear to bear some responsibility for the relatively limited agricultural progress among the great majority of Mexico's farm households.

Historical Factors

The prospects for successful pursuit of a unimodal strategy based on the progressive modernization of small-scale farm units in the post-Revolutionary period have been compromised by many factors. One of the most fundamental considerations is that by 1910 there were virtually no small farms to modernize. Hansen suggests that, in adopting the Lerdo Law of 1856, "liberals had hoped to create a class of yeomen farm-

---

[12] R. Albert Berry and William R. Cline, *Agrarian Structure and Productivity in Developing Countries* (Baltimore, Md., 1979).
[13] Osorio et al., *Estructura*, pp. 208, 215.

ers." The outcome bore no relation to the hope. Through confiscation, debt peonage, and other processes, virtually all of the country's agricultural land came under the control of *haciendas* that were seldom under a thousand acres in size. By 1910, according to Hansen, "about 90 percent of Mexico's rural families owned no land, and approximately 85 percent of the country's Indian communities had lost all their holdings." In addition, the *hacendados* often refused to rent any land to *campesinos*.[14] Indeed, rental of land to smallholders was probably very rare. The privileged position of the landowners, which enabled them to bind the peasants to the *haciendas*, would clearly have been favored by combining their monopoly over farmland with a monopsonistic position as employers of a rural labor force that was denied the alternative of subsisting on rented land.

Historical factors, and especially Mexico's experience in the nineteenth and early twentieth centuries, appear to have shaped the implementation of the land reform goals of the 1910 Revolution. First, the significance attached to reestablishing the traditional Spanish/Mexican concept of communal landholding seems to explain the emphasis on linking land distribution with the creation of *ejidos*. Second, the existence of powerful landed interests, together with the political tradition that they reinforced, contributed to a policy of permitting landowners to retain much-reduced but still large operational units. Third, emphasis on the political dimension of land reform seems to have encouraged a tendency to stress the political and social advantages of redistribution; it also lent support to the view that the creation of new farm units, however inefficient economically, was justifiable by reason of its indirect effects. Reynolds, for example, has argued explicitly that the "dualistic structure" was advantageous because the redistribution of land in small parcels to ejidos "satisfied income security and distribution criteria essential to maintain political stability, while the policy of public investment satisfied productivity criteria designed to spur the rate of growth of agricultural production." In a similar vein, Edmundo Flores stressed the indirect contribution of land reform to economic growth by means of destroying the feudal-type caste system, increasing mobility, and helping to create a climate of opinion favorable to road-building, large investments in irrigation, and industrialization. Hansen has argued in greater detail that both the actual distribution of land to the landless and their continuing hope for future distributions were important in minimizing rural discontent and

[14] Roger D. Hansen, *The Politics of Mexican Development* (Baltimore, Md., and London, 1971), pp. 25, 28, 147. For *hacienda* control, see especially F. Tannenbaum, *The Mexican Agrarian Revolution* (New York, 1929), and N. L. Whetten, *Rural Mexico* (Chicago, Ill., 1948).

protests that might have interfered with the Revolutionary Coalition's emphasis on industrialization and large-scale commercial agriculture.[15]

The success of Japan and Taiwan in implementing unimodal agricultural strategies is sometimes attributed to land reforms carried out following World War II that brought about greater equality in the size distribution of farm ownership units. This view, however, ignores the fact that the unimodal pattern was well established in both countries long before the postwar land reforms. In spite of a highly skewed pattern of land ownership, the size distribution of *operational* units was unimodal because large landowners found it more profitable to rent out their land in small parcels, to be cultivated intensively by tenants or part tenants, rather than to undertake direct cultivation of large operational units. In the case of Japan, T. C. Smith has documented the historical process by which farming came to be organized in small, single-family units. These individual holdings had a comparative advantage in applying the more productive and more intensive farming techniques that had evolved slowly over a century or more prior to the Meiji restoration of 1867 and more rapidly during the post-Meiji period.[16] The high level of farm prices that is emphasized in commentary on postwar Japanese agriculture is a phenomenon of that particular period. In prewar Japan, and in prewar and postwar Taiwan, it has been the flow of technological innovations, not subsidized prices, that has provided the basis for widespread increases in farm productivity and income.[17]

Mexico's historical pattern of landowning limited the opportunities of the rural population to acquire the managerial and technical skills developed by the widespread learning-by-doing that characterized the process of agricultural development in Japan and Taiwan. It would have affected the attitudes toward work and management among the 1.2 million farm households in Mexico that were beneficiaries of land redistribution between 1920 and 1940.[18] Perhaps of equal importance was the influence of these historical antecedents on the attitudes of those responsible for determining and administering agricultural policies and programs. Because

---

[15] Reynolds, *Mexican Economy*, pp. 154–55; Edmundo Flores, *Land Reform and the Alliance for Progress*, Princeton University Center for International Studies, memorandum no. 27 (Princeton, N.J., May 1963); Hansen, *Politics*, ch. 7. See also François Chevalier, "The *Ejido* and Political Stability in Mexico," in *The Politics of Conformity in Latin America*, ed. C. Veliz (London, 1967), p. 187: "The peasants are still as poor as ever but they remain attached to the revolution which gave them what they desired most: a patch of ground. . . . They remember Cardenas and they wait patiently for better days. As . . . Moisés de la Peña has said, 'They live in hope.'"

[16] T. C. Smith, *The Agrarian Origins of Modern Japan* (Stanford, Calif., 1959).

[17] Yujiro Hayami and Vernon W. Ruttan, *Agricultural Development: An International Perspective* (Baltimore, Md., and London, 1971), chs. 6, 7, 9, 10.

[18] Hansen, *Politics*, p. 34.

of Mexico's proximity to the United States, policy makers, large farmers, agricultural scientists, and other groups in Mexico are constantly exposed to the flow of ideas and information between the two countries, which surely exerts a major influence on their attitudes. The direct transfer of technologies for cotton production from the American Southwest to northern Mexico was also of major importance in shaping attitudes toward farm size and choice of technology.

Political and Ideological/Attitudinal Factors

Lasswell's definition of politics as "who gets what, when, and how" underscores the decisive importance of political factors—themselves conditioned by the country's heritage—in shaping Mexico's bimodal pattern of agricultural development. Hansen's perceptive and well-documented analysis emphasizes that the Revolutionary Coalition continued the behavioral norm that power should be used by those who wield it to amass wealth, with wealth in the form of land being a favored form. Most of the "political generals" or "military politicians" who were so powerful during the post-Revolutionary period acquired large holdings of land, as did many state governors and other members of the elite who dominated the Revolutionary Coalition and the PRI, but by illegal means.[19]

Some students of Mexican politics emphasize the fact that the "agrarian sector" is one of the three sectors included in Mexico's ruling party, and they depict "the PRI as effectively representing its component sectoral groupings in the struggle over who gets what, when, and how." Hansen, however, argues persuasively that "the burden of evidence clearly suggests that the PRI is better conceptualized as an apparatus through which the Revolutionary Coalition controls Mexican politics than as a mechanism for representing and implementing the demands of its component interest groups." It is therefore hardly surprising that there has been "at best an ambivalent commitment to the principles of agrarian reform as stated in the Mexican constitution" and that the implementation of land reform legislation has not prevented the emergence of a subsector of large-scale, highly commercialized, and capital-intensive farm enterprises.[20]

Between 1935 and 1953 a large share of public investment was devoted to agriculture and to the building of roads and railroads. As noted earlier, investment in agriculture was concentrated heavily on large-scale irrigation projects that mainly benefited the high yield subsector of agriculture,

[19] Ibid., chs. 5, 6, 7.
[20] Ibid., pp. 107, 108. The military was included as a fourth "sector" in the four-sector system initiated by President Cardenas in 1937 but soon dropped (ibid., p. 103).

to which the improvements in the transport network were also of great value. The concentration of irrigation projects was of course influenced by the physical characteristics of the North and the Pacific North—an arid climate, large areas of potentially productive land, and nearby mountain ranges with snow and rainfall to be exploited for irrigation. The priority in the allocation of public funds was, however, also influenced by the fact that President Calles and a number of the other powerful "political generals" were from those northern regions.

Attitudes and ideology, defined as a body of concepts or a manner of thinking characteristic of particular social groups, also seem to have contributed to the policies that resulted in Mexico's dualistic pattern of agricultural development. Influential groups within the Revolutionary Coalition, for example, were inclined to tout the importance of economies of scale in agriculture. After all, many of them had profited directly and handsomely from the large-farm units that were permitted and indeed fostered by official policies and programs. Of greater significance, however, is the fact that the most influential groups opposing the emphasis on large private farm enterprises were committed to a socialist, and often Marxist, view of agricultural development. There is in Marxist thought a strong tradition—going back to Marx, and evident also in Kautsky and Lenin—that emphasizes the superiority of large-scale farm units.[21] In the Mexican context, the socialist view of rural development also seems to have emphasized the virtues of "cooperativism" and to have been hostile to individualism. Its main impact was on the policy of promoting collective *ejidos*, which had considerable support from member groups within the PRI's loose coalition.[22]

The prevalent tendency to exaggerate the importance of economies of scale in agriculture is often associated with a low opinion of the capacity of the *ejidatarios* and other cultivators of small holdings to acquire rea-

[21] Karl A. Wittfogel, "Communist and Non-Communist Agrarian Systems, with Special Reference to the U.S.S.R. and Communist China: A Comparative Approach," in *Agrarian Policies and Problems in Communist and Non-Communist Countries*, ed. W. A. Douglas Jackson (Seattle, Wash., and London, 1971), pp. 3–60.

[22] Most of the collective *ejidos* are concentrated in five highly commercialized areas, three of which are located in northern Mexico: the wheat- and cotton-producing region of Laguna, which overlaps parts of Coahuila and Durango; the Yaqui Valley in southern Sonora, which produces wheat, rice, and flax; and Los Mochis in northwestern Sinaloa, which produces winter vegetables and sugarcane. The five areas included only about 15 percent of all *ejidatarios* cooperating with the Ejidal Bank in 1944, but received 57 percent of all funds in that year (Whetten, *Rural Mexico*, p. 215). The establishment of the collective *ejidos* in the Laguna region resulted from the expropriation of a number of large commercial farm units in the fall of 1936, when nearly half a million hectares were distributed to some 300 *ejidos*, including almost 35,000 *ejidatarios*. Whetten, who describes this operation in some detail (ibid., pp. 216–24), draws heavily on a study carried out in 1940 by the Liga de Agrónomos Socialistas.

sonable competence in managing their enterprises. Having been viewed for so long as "peon labor," they were apparently the object of considerable skepticism: could they ever acquire the managerial and technical skills that are so evident among the small-scale farmers, for example, of Japan and Taiwan? A *hacendado* would tend to regard the *campesinos* who benefited from the expropriation of much of his land "as lazy, incompetent, and incapable of making adequate use of the land he so badly needs." Whetten clearly shares that view to some extent. He speaks of "the culturally retarded status of the *ejidatarios*" and also notes the tendency for the *ejidatario* to grow only subsistence crops, notably maize, to insure his family's food supply. He further asserts that, in general, "his methods of production are backward and, without a great deal of supervision, he is likely to produce little beyond his subsistence needs."[23] More significant than the attitudes of *hacendados* and of a foreign scholar is the attitude of paternalism and the policy of attempting to usurp managerial responsibilities of the *ejidatarios* by dictating cropping patterns that was characteristic of the Ejidal Bank.[24] Mexican economists also seem generally to have held the view that small-scale farm units could not be expected to be as efficient as large-farm enterprises. Of the economists whose views are reported by Solis, only Flores de la Peña emphasized the economic advantages of small farmers because of their intensive use of labor.[25]

In part, the negative attitude toward the capacity of small farmers to become reasonably competent managers can probably be explained by a common tendency to equate technical efficiency with economic efficiency. Recent studies that have attempted to compare the total factor productivity (i.e., output per unit of all inputs) have reached conclusions much more favorable to the economic efficiency of small farmers—both individual *ejidatarios* and small private farmers. Those results are sensitive, however, to the valuation of inputs of family labor. A statistical analysis of census data for individual states indicates clearly that in crop production the small-scale farm units are more efficient than large farms in their use of purchased inputs, and their superiority by that measure increased between 1959 and 1969. The rate of growth of crop output in the *ejidal* sector in that same period was also considerably greater for small farms than for large. Although the former group obtained higher returns per unit of scarce resources, this must be attributed in large mea-

[23] Ibid., pp. 204, 223.

[24] Hugh Stringer, "Land, Farmer, and Sugar Cane in Morelos, Mexico," *Land Economics*, 48, no. 3 (August 1972), 301–3.

[25] Leopold Solís, "Mexican Economic Policy in the Post-War Period: The Views of Mexican Economists," *American Economic Review*, 61, no. 3, pt. 2 (June 1971), 2–67.

sure to their restricted use of purchased inputs because of limited access to credit.[26] Incomes per worker in the *ejidal* sector have, of course, remained very low.

A 1967 survey by Eckstein of 313 relatively large, irrigated farms in nine regions indicated a sharp increase in the value of output per hectare in moving from small to large farms, and a considerable but lesser advantage for the large farms in terms of total factor productivity. The findings also indicated higher productivity for the ejidos than for the private farms in each of the three size classes compared—a phenomenon that, as Eckstein notes, "seems to be strongly contrary to trends in the rainfed areas, where *ejidos* show lower efficiency than private farmers of similar size." The tentative explanation offered is that in the irrigation districts *ejidos* have equivalent access to credit and inputs, whereas in rainfed areas they have little access to those resources. Eckstein's more general conclusion—that, on a national basis, the higher value of output per hectare on large private farms than on small private farms or on *ejidos* is due mainly to differences in crop mix and greater access to irrigated land—is based on analysis of data for the 1940 and 1960 Agricultural and Ejido Censuses of Mexico.[27] In my judgment the most significant agricultural problem in Mexico is the persistence of low levels of productivity and income on the numerous small *ejidal* and private farm units in the rainfed areas of central and southern Mexico.

Technical, Economic, Social, and Demographic Factors

The widening gap between income levels in the large-scale farm enterprises in northern Mexico and the majority of small-farm units in other regions was the result, to a large extent, of technical and economic factors. In the North and Pacific North the rapid expansion of irrigation opened up the possibility of similarly rapid expansion of crop area and of output. This provided a powerful incentive to mechanize in order to exploit that potential as rapidly as possible. The rapid rise in land values, in turn, provided an additional incentive to extend control over farmland.

Much of the land in northern Mexico was suited to irrigated cotton

[26] See D. T. Nguyen and M. L. Martinez Salvidar, "The Effects of Land Reform on Agricultural Production, Employment, and Income Distribution: A Statistical Study of Mexican States, 1959–69," *Economic Journal*, 89, no. 355 (Sept. 1979), 628–33; Folke Dovring, "Economic Results of Land Reform," Agency for International Development, Spring Review of Land Reform (Washington, D.C., June 2–4, 1970); Eckstein et al., *Land Reform*, pp. v, 61–67, and app. C, for an analysis based on different size and tenure groups. According to P. Lamartine Yates, *Mexico's Agricultural Dilemma* (Tucson, Ariz., 1981), pp. 160–61, the large private farms have been much more efficient than the *ejidos* in livestock production.

[27] Eckstein et al., *Land Reform*, pp. 83–85 and app. C.

production, and during the 1940s and 1950s U.S. price support policies and acreage restrictions on cotton provided an additional stimulus for increased production and exports in Mexico. Large cotton merchandising firms, such as Anderson-Clayton and Company in the United States, had an incentive to further expansion south of the border. The expertise, and the capital provided by their field offices in Mexico, facilitated the transfer of production technologies from the American Southwest to northern Mexico and contributed to a large increase in cotton yields as well as the rapid growth of both crop area and mechanization. Likewise, the cooperative research program of Mexico's Ministry of Agriculture and the Rockefeller Foundation made possible a nearly threefold increase in wheat yields between the early 1950s and the late 1960s. The cost-reducing innovations also enhanced the profitability of increasingly mechanized production in the irrigated areas. Because the large producers, whether of wheat or of cotton, maintain communication with agricultural research workers and thus have access to current technological information, they gain a competitive advantage over the small farmers, who suffer from the inadequacy of the agricultural extension programs available to them.[28]

Another factor to be considered in comparing the growth rates of the regions and their respective farm sectors derives from the characteristics of the wheat and of maize plants. During the 1950s and 1960s wheat production in northern Mexico was increasing, whereas elsewhere maize continued to be the dominant crop on most of the small farms. Diffusion of new, higher yielding varieties of wheat was relatively easy because of the information shared by the large growers and the scientists, who were striving for improvements in agronomic practices. In addition, since wheat is self-pollinating, the farmer could buy a small quantity of improved seed, multiply it himself, and use it for a number of years. A case in point is the success of both small and large farmers with the high-yielding semi-dwarf varieties of Mexican wheat that were introduced in Pakistan and India in the late 1960s.[29]

The maize improvement program in Mexico, on the other hand, concentrated for many years on developing pure-line hybrids, which were then multiplied and distributed by the National Corn Commission. Implementing the program was a difficult task because of the nature of the

[28] See Johnston and Kilby, *Agriculture*, pp. 259–67, for further discussion of cotton and wheat production.

[29] Michael Lipton, "Inter-Farm, Inter-Regional and Farm-Non-Farm Income Distribution: The Impact of the New Cereal Varieties," *World Development*, 6, no. 3 (March 1978), 319–37; Vernon W. Ruttan, "Induced Innovation and the Green Revolution," in *Induced Innovation: Technology, Institutions and Development*, ed. Hans P. Binswanger and Vernon W. Ruttan (Baltimore, Md., 1978), pp. 358–408.

hybrids. If a farmer replants those of a single cross, yield is reduced drastically and seed must be replaced annually. In addition, the pure-line hybrids were very location-specific, so that each year farmers had to obtain new seed adapted to local environmental conditions. The problem has become less acute in recent years, as plant breeders have begun to emphasize varietal hybrids that are adapted to a wider range of environmental conditions and do not lose their yield advantage as rapidly. Since the late 1960s several developing countries, notably Kenya and El Salvador, have achieved considerable success in diffusing high-yield hybrids among small-scale farmers.[30] Success in those countries has, however, been uneven. Very rapid diffusion has occurred in areas with adequate and well-distributed rainfall, but in areas where environmental conditions are less favorable, the rate of adoption has remained very limited, with the result that the yield advantage of the new varieties is also limited.

Promoting technical change among small farmers is considerably more difficult in areas that are rainfed than in those that are irrigated. In the former, environmental conditions are so diverse that improved varieties and practices must be adapted to fit a variety of local conditions. Moreover, the increases in yield and output that can be obtained by the introduction of improved seed-fertilizer combinations, which played such a decisive role in expanding agricultural output in Japan and Taiwan, are limited, especially in areas where the level and seasonal distribution of rainfall may give rise to problems of water stress. Under such conditions, which apply to many of the farming regions where the majority of Mexico's small-scale cultivators are located, improved seed-fertilizer combinations need to be supplemented by equipment and tillage innovations. Better soil and water management is needed both to realize the potential of improved varieties and to reduce the magnitude of the year-to-year variations in yields. Unfortunately, the research efforts devoted to such problems have been limited—in Mexico, and in other developing countries as well. Tillage methods and associated equipment for areas of marginal and uncertain rainfall have been evolved in several developed countries, but those technologies are so highly mechanized and capital-intensive that they are ill adapted to the socioeconomic conditions that prevail in Mexico's rainfed areas, where a large rural population is dependent on agriculture for its livelihood.

Experimental work carried out by ICRISAT, the International Crop Re-

---

[30] John Gerhart, *The Diffusion of Hybrid Maize in Western Kenya* (abridged by CIMMYT, Mexico City, 1975); Thomas S. Walker, "Decision Making by Farmers and by the National Agricultural Research Program on the Adoption and Development of Maize Varieties in El Salvador" (Ph.D. diss., Stanford University, 1980).

search Institute for the Semi-Arid Tropics, has demonstrated that improved systems of land and water management can be devised which are suitable for adoption by small-scale farmers and capable of yielding large increases in output and in net income. The farming systems work at ICRISAT has been based on the use of animal draft power in the belief that it will be many years before the small farmers who predominate in the semi-arid farming areas of developing countries will be able to afford tractor cultivation. The results obtained at ICRISAT serve to underscore yet another variable: that the new tillage methods permit large increases in production and profits only on certain types of soil.[31]

There is no doubt that the substantial growth of Mexico's farm and rural population since 1940 has slowed progress in raising per capita incomes. Between 1910 and 1940 the number of marginal holdings, i.e., of less than 5 hectares, was reduced from 1.2 million to 630,000, followed by a further, modest decline to 470,000 in 1960. For landless households, however, a dramatic decline from 1.1 million in 1910 to 200,000 families in 1940 had been reversed by 1960, when the number of landless reached 1.3 million. Changes at the regional level may be illustrated by estimates for the Laguna Basin, where there were 38,000 *ejidatarios* in 1940 and 6,000 landless workers. By 1960 the number of *ejidatarios* had increased moderately (by 10.5 percent) to 42,000, but "there were by then over 40,000 landless rural workers dependent on employment which had hardly increased."[32]

Because of inconsistencies in the farm labor force statistics, it may be useful to examine changes in the urban and rural population—the latter defined as the population living in places with fewer than 2,500 inhabitants.[33] Table 4 shows the changes in Mexico's urban, rural, and total populations between 1940 and 1980, and projects the figures to the years 1990 and 2000, on the basis of two alternative sets of assumptions. Projection A assumes that fertility and migration rates remain unchanged at the 1970 rates; projection B is based on a considerable reduction in fertility and a large increase in the rate of migration out of agriculture. According to these stylized figures, a nearly fourfold increase in Mexico's urban population was associated with a 74 percent increase in the rural

[31] James G. Ryan et al., "Assessment of Prospective Soil-, Water-, and Crop-Management Technologies for the Semi-Arid Tropics of Peninsular India" (paper prepared for the ICRISAT Workshop in Socioeconomic Constraints to Development of Semi-Arid Tropical Agriculture, Hyderabad, India, February 19–23, 1979).

[32] Eckstein et al., *Land Reform*, pp. 17, 67.

[33] Some of the estimates of farm labor force indicate a very large increase between 1940 and 1960, then a decline in 1970 (ibid., app. A). Colosio presents figures, adjusted by Oscar Altimir and published by Francisco Alba, that indicate a more gradual increase between 1940 and 1960, but continuing growth through 1970 ("Urbanization," p. 60).

TABLE 4

Relative Sizes of Mexico's Urban, Rural, and Total Populations, 1940–80, with Two Alternative Projections for 1990–2000

(1940=100)

Year	Urban population	Rural population	Total population
Historical projections			
1940	100.0	100.0	100.0
1950	148.9	122.2	131.6
1960	233.0	147.8	177.7
1970	378.9	173.8	245.8
1980	611.5	196.7	342.3
Future projections			
A. 1990	945.4	224.1	477.2
2000	1,429.4	257.3	668.6
B. 1990	882.8	213.7	448.5
2000	1,166.6	219.1	551.6

SOURCE: Based on Andrei Rogers, *Migration Patterns and Population Redistribution*, RR-80-7 (Laxenburg, Austria, March 1980).

population between 1940 and 1970. If the population in localities of 15,000 or more is classified as urban, then the growth between 1940 and 1970 appears to have been even greater: close to a sixfold increase from 3.9 to 22.0 million; by that definition, however, 55 percent of the 1970 population was still rural.[34]

Particularly with projection B assumptions of reduced fertility and an increased rate of rural-urban migration between 1970 and 2000, the growth rate of rural population will be considerably reduced. The concomitant increase in urban population, which would be staggering, calls to mind the oft-quoted projection that Mexico City's population alone may approach 32 million by the year 2000.[35] There will be a considerable lag before declines in the birthrate are fully reflected in a reduced rate of growth of the country's labor force, and the prospect of its continuing expansion has significant implications for the design of strategies for agricultural and rural development. Expanding employment opportunities within agriculture will continue to be important, expansion of nonfarm job opportunities even more essential. The principal hope for avoiding intractable problems of urban growth in Mexico City may be the de-

[34] L. Unikel et al., *El desarrollo urbano de México: Diagnóstico e implicaciones futuras* (Mexico, 1976), p. 27.

[35] United Nations, *Global Review of Human Settlements: A Support Paper for Habitat*, II (Oxford, 1976), 77–83.

centralized growth of employment in secondary and tertiary industries in towns and smaller cities.

A period of relative stagnation followed the rapid expansion of agricultural output in Mexico in the period 1940–70, when there had been, at first, a particularly swift extension of irrigation systems. Then, between 1955 and 1970, the pace of development of acreage under irrigation slowed, but yields—especially for wheat—rose dramatically with the introduction of high-yield varieties. Since the late 1960s expansion of the irrigated area has continued on a limited basis, while yield levels have been relatively stagnant and the prices of the major staple food crops less attractive to producers.[36]

Various social factors—some of them related to Mexico's traditional peasant culture—have also contributed to the uneven development of agriculture in the large-scale modern subsector as compared with the small-scale farming sector. Among a number of Indian communities, for example, the spread of Spanish is limited, and there persists a certain amount of hostility to outside influences. Perhaps more important has been the tendency for government officials to look upon peasant cultivators as "backward" and to view the role of government as a top-down process of "delivering" superior knowledge and technologies to an ignorant and passive peasantry. Successful programs of agricultural development, however, have proved that research and extension must be based on a two-way flow of information and ideas. Identification and diffusion of feasible innovations among small farmers requires an understanding of the problems, constraints, and opportunities that they face; and research workers and extension staff must listen and learn, not merely pontificate about "superior" technologies that may or may not be relevant to local conditions. A sensitivity to these issues as well as to the more conventional questions of structure and managerial procedures is a prerequisite for any organization program.

Organizational Factors

The literature on economic development has tended to ignore questions of organizational design and management. But effective development clearly requires organization. Brewster has described this as "the capacity for concerting reciprocally helpful behaviors into a continually widening network of larger, specialized units of collective action neces-

---

[36] The SAM reports that since 1960 the guarantee prices for "basic foods" (notably maize, beans, and wheat) have declined in real terms by 34 percent (Office of the President, *Sistema*, p. 27). Some displacement in the acreage planted to basic food crops has undoubtedly resulted from the rapid increase in sorghum production for livestock feed.

sary for enabling people to . . . transform their physical and biological world into a place of ever increasing goods and services."[37] Success in fostering technical progress and increased output among small-scale farmers is especially dependent on effective support institutions for agricultural research and extension, and for the construction and management of irrigation facilities and other types of infrastructure. These all provide "public goods" characterized by indivisibility, externality, and jointness in supply and distribution, not available at socially optimal levels without intervention by publicly supported organizations.[38]

Until about 1970 there appears to have been very little effort to promote increased productivity among small-scale farmers in Mexico: the ratio of agricultural extension agents to farm families was only about 1:10,000, compared to 1:1,900 in Nicaragua, 1:3,200 in El Salvador, and 1:5,000 in Honduras.[39] Support for research was not oriented to the needs of small-scale farmers. It is therefore not surprising that Wellhausen, a former director of the cooperative research program of the Rockefeller Foundation and Mexico's Ministry of Agriculture, argued in 1976 that "the lack of a dynamic on-farm research program and the lack of an adequate farmer-education system have been the primary factors in preventing the spread of modern technology to a greater number of farmers."[40]

Recent programs such as PIDER and the Sistema Alimentario Mexicano point to a significant shift in government policy, giving a higher priority to measures that will promote increases in productivity and income among Mexico's small-scale farmers. The creation of Banrural in 1975, and the concurrent elimination of collateral requirements in making loans to *ejidatarios*, is also a promising sign. The decentralization of many development programs and the creation of coordinating commit-

[37] John M. Brewster, "Traditional Social Structures as Barriers to Change," in *Agricultural Development and Economic Growth*, ed. Herman M. Southworth and Bruce F. Johnston (Ithaca, N.Y., 1967), p. 69.

[38] Hiromitsu Kaneda, "Growth and Equity in India's Agriculture in Recent Years," Working Paper series no. 155 (Davis, Calif., September 1960), p. 27. In the East Asian countries of Japan, Taiwan, South Korea, and also in the People's Republic of China, unusual attention has been given to creating a network of organizations capable of providing these support services.

[39] Hansen, *Politics*, p. 86. See also Eduardo L. Venezian and William K. Gamble, *The Agricultural Development of Mexico: Its Structure and Growth since 1950* (New York, 1969), pp. 165–67, and Cynthia Hewitt de Alcantara, *Modernizing Mexican Agriculture: Socioeconomic Implications of Technological Change 1940–1970* (Geneva, 1976), pp. 42–43.

[40] Michael Redclift, "Production Programs for Small Farmers: Plan Puebla as Myth and Reality," Ford Foundation, Office for Mexico and Central America (Mexico City, January 1980), p. 23.

tees at the state level seem to be significant steps toward the implementation of rural development. There is, however, a need for both a new approach to small farmer development and an increase in the priority given to it.

SPECULATION ABOUT THE REDESIGN OF
RURAL DEVELOPMENT IN MEXICO

The shift in attention of policy makers and the strengthening of the economic situation offer significant opportunities for reducing the poverty still so pervasive in rural Mexico. Given the difficulty of the task, it would be foolish, however, to be highly optimistic about the outcome. Even the required change in priorities with respect to resource allocation is likely to be difficult.[41] A first step toward the objective has been a substantial increase in public investment in agriculture and rural development—from 15 percent of total federal public investment in the early 1970s to 20 percent in 1979, and authorizations for 1980 equal to 25 percent of total public investment.[42] Redistribution of land suitable for arable farming remains one of the most direct means of raising incomes of landless and marginal farmers, but prospects for it are uncertain. Although the SAM refers to 3 million hectares of good land that "is simply unused, is underutilized in extensive ranching, or has reverted to bush fallow,"[43] there will undoubtedly be strong political resistance to further redistribution to the marginal and landless farmers.

Success in reducing rural poverty will depend primarily on increasing agricultural productivity in the rainfed regions, where the bulk of the farm population is located. The SAM, which expresses an optimistic view of the prospects for achieving self-sufficiency in food, suggests that the strategy should involve active state participation in three areas: (a) sharing the risks of food production in order to avoid the deterrent effect on farm investment and use of inputs because of the large discount applied by farmers for risk and uncertainty; (b) subsidizing farm inputs and providing public support for research and extension work; and (c) strengthening *campesino* organizations and fostering a partnership between the government and them (with particular emphasis on participation in agroindustries so as to increase the value added retained at the local level).[44] New emphasis would be directed to stimulating technical change in the rainfed areas, as a means of fostering progress among small farmers there.

[41] Ibid., p. 27.
[42] Schumacher, "Agricultural Development," annex 1.
[43] Office of the President, *Sistema*, p. 24.
[44] Ibid., pp. 24–25.

Technical Change in Rainfed Areas

Promoting technical progress in these regions is more difficult than under irrigated conditions because of the need for simple, inexpensive equipment and for tillage innovations to supplement improved seed-fertilizer combinations. Research on such problems has been limited, and there exists no established methodology for identifying the innovations most effective under a variety of local agroclimatic and socioeconomic conditions.[45] Thus it is a problem not merely of "stimulating technological change" but also of calling for an enlarged program of research and "farmer acceptance trials" to identify specific equipment/tillage combinations suited to a variety of local environments.

INIA has recently taken a first step by importing a "bullock tractor," the well-designed, animal-powered tool carrier being used in the farming systems research at ICRISAT. Trials are being carried out to test the value of this tool in implementing tillage systems to improve water and soil management, e.g., by reducing runoff of rainfall and improving water retention.[46] Under some circumstances small tractors may offer greater promise. In a number of areas, construction of irrigation facilities—probably small-scale, communal systems—will also play an important role in increasing the level and stability of crop yields.

In brief, achieving significant technological progress in Mexico's rainfed areas involves much more than simply "facilitating the work of experts in introducing technological change and the distribution and application of inputs."[47] The SAM rightly emphasizes the importance of questions of organization. Both the organizational and the management aspects of rural development merit serious and sustained attention. If the complexity of these issues is underestimated, the high risk of frustration and failure may be expected to escalate accordingly.

Organizational Issues and Agricultural and Rural Development

An important lesson from past programs of rural development concerns the design and performance of two types of organizations—(a) small farmers' and women's groups at the local level, and (b) "facilitator organizations" for providing research, agricultural extension, and health services. The success of rural development depends not only on individ-

[45] Bruce F. Johnston, "Socio-Economic Aspects of Improved Animal-Drawn Implements and Mechanization in Semi-Arid East Africa" (paper prepared for the ICRISAT Workshop, as in n. 31, above).

[46] Personal communication from Dr. Antonio Turrent Fernandez, the Colegio de Postgraduados, Chapingo and INIA, Mexico City, June 1980.

[47] Office of the President, *Sistema*, p. 37.

ual organizations but also on the establishment of effective vertical and horizontal linkages so as to achieve a good "fit" between the competence of various organizations, the programs that are being implemented, and the needs of the people in rural communities who are the intended beneficiaries.

The process of increasing the organizational "capacity for coordinating reciprocally helpful behaviors" poses difficult problems whether one is considering the small, local organizations of farmers or the development bureaucracy.[48] Organization is a central element of a successful strategy because attempts to change *what* things are done must be accompanied by appropriate changes in *how* things are done. It is useful to view organization as providing a framework for "calculation and control" through which groups of individuals determine what each is to do and seek to assure that each does what is expected of him. Techniques to this end may include informal, face-to-face bargaining within small groups, hierarchical procedures that are characteristic of "facilitator organizations," and exchange transactions such as price and market mechanisms.

The general neglect of organizational issues in the literature on development seems to reflect the view that they are either unimportant or unsuitable for governmental concern. In fact, they are subject to both experimentation and government action. It is imperative, however, that government efforts to influence the design and management of develop-

[48] William Clark and I have recently examined those problems in considerable detail (Johnston and Clark, *Redesigning Rural Development: A Strategic Perspective* [Baltimore, Md., 1982]). Our analysis draws heavily on empirical studies of organization experience in developing countries by David C. Korten ("Toward a Technology for Managing Social Development," in *Population and Social Development Management: A Challenge for Management Schools* [Caracas, 1979], pp. 20–57; "Community Organization and Rural Development: A Learning Process Approach," *The Public Administration Review*, 40, no. 5 [September/October 1980], 480–511; "Agricultural Planning and Management for Rural Development: A View from the Field of Management" [presented at the Instituto Interamericano de Ciencias Agricolas, Mexico City, September 1980]), David K. Leonard (*Reaching the Peasant Farmer: Organization Theory and Practice in Kenya* [Chicago, Ill., and London, 1977]), Robert Chambers (*Managing Rural Development: Ideas and Experience from East Africa* [Uppsala, 1974]), Guy Hunter (*The Administration of Agricultural Development: Lessons from India* [London, 1970] and "Report on Administration and Institutions," in Asian Development Bank, *Rural Asia: Challenge and Opportunity*, Supplementary Papers, IV, *Administration and Institutions in Agricultural and Rural Development* [Manila, 1978]), and Norman T. Uphoff and Milton J. Esman (*Local Organization for Rural Development: Analysis of Asian Experience*, special series on Rural Local Government, RLG no. 19 [Ithaca, N.Y., 1974]), and on the earlier analysis of organization by Robert A. Dahl and Charles E. Lindblom (*Politics, Economics, and Welfare* [New York, 1953]). Although our *Redesigning Rural Development* is a collaborative enterprise, Clark was mainly responsible for the preparation of chapter 5, "Organization Programs." I am indebted to him for whatever merit this summary treatment may have. I am also aware that it does not do justice to his extended analysis of the issues.

ment organizations be informed by an understanding of the constraints and opportunities operative within them, lest a bad situation be made worse.

The most effective approach to the complex problems of rural development promotes a mutual learning process involving local people and the field staff and specialists who man the facilitator organizations. There is a growing body of evidence that demonstrates the fallacy of a "blueprint approach"—one that views local organizations from above, as essentially means of assisting planners at higher levels in implementing their plans. The potential benefits of organization at the local level will be realized only if there is provision for tapping local knowledge and understanding and for giving maximum support for the development of local problem-solving capabilities.

The basic idea involved in dealing with local groups is simple: link appropriate groups of people into a "continually widening network of larger, specialized units of collective action" through which they can better solve local problems, make demands on the broader system, and generally become involved in the design and implementation of development programs. At the local level people are linked "horizontally" and, through their organizations, "vertically" at the same time into the larger administrative or economic structure. Emphasis on local participation has become extremely fashionable in this context in recent years, but unfortunately most of the discussion has not gone beyond the level of rhetoric. In particular, there is a tendency to treat participation as a free good, desirable in unlimited quantities. In fact, it requires an investment of time and energy by the participants, and cannot be commanded by policy makers or administrators. It must be induced. The facilitator organizations must learn to recognize and design programs capable of mobilizing participation and also to abandon those programs that fail to attract that investment.

Clark suggests that the ability to attract effective participation will depend mainly on three features of local organizations: the attractiveness of the benefits expected from participation, a relative consensus on the objective, and simplicity of technique. In the first instance, local participants cannot be expected to invest time and energy in a local organization unless it offers highly desirable and tangible benefits not otherwise available at similar cost. Second, collective social action requires an ability to air and resolve conflicts among participants; without it, and without sufficient agreement about objectives, a local organization can easily become immobilized by struggles for power.

Simplicity of technique appears to have an especially important bearing on organizational issues in rural Mexico. The general proposition seems persuasive: local organizations are more likely to be successful if the demands for calculation and control are relatively simple. In particular, two characteristics of an organization merit attention. First, the larger the organization, the more complex and difficult is the task of determining individual responsibilities and rewards from the collective social action. The second factor concerns what Clark refers to as "communality." When participants contribute their labor or other resources to a common productive activity, calculation and control become inevitably more complex than when each individual's contribution is directly reflected in his own reward.

The great practical advantage of the individual family farm is, of course, that the cultivator and his family have a clear-cut incentive to invest their labor, knowledge, and skill in the enterprise because of their direct interest in the outcome of their efforts. Chevalier suggests that in rural Mexico "individualism has made slow and steady progress"; and it is his "impression that the mental outlook of the *ejidatarios* continually evolves towards the smallholder rather than towards a form of socialism" emphasizing cooperation within the traditional community.[49] Now, fifteen years later, it appears that the overwhelming majority of *ejidatarios* have not yet found the ideal of joint production within collective *ejidos* very attractive.

The point that bears emphasis here is that the success or failure of organizational efforts will be determined more by the attitudes and the response of participants, and in turn by their perception of the balance between costs and benefits, than by the ideological predilections of policy makers. A communal irrigation system, for example, would attract greater participation from a group of farmers than would a scheme for joint cultivation of crops.

A strategy for rural development must also give high priority to ensuring that the mass of the rural population has access to essential social services, notably education, health, and family planning. Mexico has made substantial progress in expanding education in rural and urban areas. It is estimated, for example, that adult literacy increased from 65 to 76 percent between 1960 and 1975. There has been a large increase in the percentage of school-age children enrolled in primary school, an impressive achievement considering the enormous increase in their number. Mexico's rate of natural increase reached 3.3 percent in 1960 and was still as high as 3.0 percent in 1978 in spite of a decline in fertility from 45 to 38 per thousand.[50]

[49] Chevalier, "*Ejido*," pp. 182–83.
[50] World Bank, *World Development Report* (1980), pp. 145, 155.

Mexico appears to have made considerable progress also in improving health conditions, and efforts to promote the spread of family planning are now vigorous and comprehensive. It is estimated that between 1960 and 1978 infant mortality declined from 78 to 60 per thousand, and mortality in the 1–4 age group dropped from 14 to 6 per thousand.[51] Those estimates are fairly rough approximations, and in rural areas, which have been largely bypassed by the economic growth of recent decades, the rates are well above those national average figures. In educating for family planning, progress will inevitably be more difficult in rural than in urban areas. The National Family Planning Program, presented to the president and members of the National Population Council in October 1977, acknowledged this fact in establishing its goal at 25 percent coverage of women in urban areas by 1982, but for rural areas at only 14 percent.[52]

There is considerable evidence to demonstrate that active participation by local groups can make a significant contribution to the effectiveness of rural health programs and of efforts to promote family planning.[53] The quality of life in rural Mexico can be improved significantly by health programs that emphasize immunization, promotion of better child-feeding practices, hygiene and environmental sanitation, and the simple but effective technique of oral rehydration (for minimizing the adverse effects of frequent bouts of dysentery that are such an important cause of morbidity and mortality among small children). A substantial reduction in fertility, which can be facilitated by improving child survival prospects, will also yield important, direct benefits for the health of mothers and children. The medium-term benefits from improvement in family diets and in the coverage and quality of social services are also significant. And, in the long run, a slowing of the growth of the country's rural population and labor force can be expected to increase returns to labor as the supply/demand situation in labor markets tightens and per capita incomes increase.

A feature common to both the production and the social service programs under discussion is the need for much trial-and-error learning. Achieving a "fit" between the needs of rural people, the benefits of a program, and the competence of the supporting organization must therefore

---

[51] Ibid., p. 151.

[52] Government of Mexico, *National Family Planning Program* (Mexico City, 1977), pp. 12, 18.

[53] See, for example, David F. Pyle, *Voluntary Agency-Managed Projects Delivering an Integrated Package of Health, Nutrition, and Population Services: The Maharashtra Experience* (New Delhi, March 1979), and David C. Korten, *Integrated Approaches to Family Planning Services Delivery*, Development Discussion Paper no. 10 (Cambridge, Mass., December 1975).

be viewed as a dynamic learning process. Analysis of past experience suggests that successful programs have evolved through three phases.[54] First, each program had to learn to be effective by identifying activities that were feasible in terms of existing resource, organizational, and political constraints, and at the same time capable of yielding significant benefits. Second, each program had to learn to be efficient by reducing the input requirements per unit of output. Third, each program had to learn to expand in order to achieve wide coverage. Transmitting the fruits of one learning sequence to other people and areas is a tricky business. If too much is attempted too quickly, there is apt to be a large loss of both effectiveness and efficiency.

An encouraging feature of PIDER is that the design of this large investment program for rural development in Mexico recognized that rural development needs to be viewed as a continuing, dynamic learning process. From its inception in 1973, provision was made for monitoring and evaluation, to draw lessons from ongoing experience and to guide the design and redesign of future activities. The creation of CIDER, the Research Center for Rural Development, was an interesting attempt to institutionalize applied research and evaluation to support that learning process.[55] The mid-term evaluation of PIDER emphasized that an important shortcoming of the program was the lack of feasible and profitable technological "packages" adapted to small farmers in Mexico's rainfed areas. The "Rainfed Agricultural Development Project" now under way offers promise of helping to overcome that serious deficiency. The additional resources now becoming available in the Mexican economy will surely bolster the efforts to reduce rural poverty, but they will not eliminate the need for time and persistence.

[54] Korten, "Community Organization," pp. 499–501.
[55] Michael M. Cernea, *Measuring Project Impact: Monitoring and Evaluation in the PIDER Rural Development Project—Mexico*, Staff Working Paper no. 332 (Washington, D.C., 1979).

The World Food Economy: Recent Lessons for the United States and Mexico

Walter P. Falcon

THE IMPORTANCE of Mexico and the United States in the world food economy includes three factors especially relevant to this conference. First, Mexico and the United States are each increasingly involved with an interdependent food system—the latter a dominant force, and Mexico of increasing importance, particularly in this past year. Indeed, the two major entrants this last year in the world food and feed economy were Mexico and the People's Republic of China.

Second, there are important lessons to be learned from the 1970s about the involvement of U.S. agriculture in the international feed grain market, the role of macroeconomic policy in U.S. agriculture, and the escalating role of the middle-income countries in the derived demand for feed grains.

Third, there are reasons for optimism about using agriculture and agricultural trade as a means for decreasing, rather than increasing, some of the tensions between Mexico and the United States.

AGRICULTURAL DEVELOPMENTS IN THE UNITED STATES

International events of the 1970s, such as the rise in oil prices, the Russian wheat failures of 1972/73 and 1975/76, and the U.S. trade embargo against Russia have tended to cloud what has happened in the U.S. domestic agriculture. There are well-founded doubts about the capacity of U.S. agriculture to supply ever-increasing amounts of food to the world. This concern is not in the tradition of the "Famine '79" literature, but it is based on the judgment that U.S. agriculture will not be able to double its grain exports in the 1980s as it has done in each of the three previous decades. The expected growth in output of U.S. agriculture will be lower for several reasons.

The migration process in U.S. agriculture is basically over. The United

Transcript of informal remarks presented at Stanford University, November 1980.

States has become a nation of part-time farmers; more than half of the income of farmers in the United States comes from nonfarm sources. The rural labor force has stabilized, and there will be no more easy gains from further removal of excess labor from the U.S. agricultural scene.

Second, fertilizer is already used at fairly high rates in the United States, and further increases in output from increases in fertilizer applications will probably not occur. If relative prices change substantially between outputs and inputs, more productivity can be obtained from chemicals. In general, however, a continuing fertilizer revolution in the 1980s is not a reasonable prospect for U.S. agriculture.

The major economies of scale from mechanization have been reaped already. Farm size is well beyond the 160-acre unit, and much of the good farm land has already been consolidated. Most current expansion in farm size is in response to tax laws, not to underlying technical relationships or requirements. In short, there will be fewer major productivity increases from mechanization.

There are few prospects for new seed technology in the immediate future. Basic genotype selection may lead to some increases in yields, and a few advances may be made in animal husbandry as well. But major breakthroughs in seed technology are probably ten years away and will involve radically new applications of science such as recombinant DNA, photosynthesis enhancement, and nitrogen fixation of grasses. With additional regulation, problems will increase in the development of new biochemical technologies. Regulation may be necessary and desirable, but it will restrain future technological advancements in agricultural productivity.

Increased irrigation, which has been the source of considerable growth in the last three decades, is also slowing. This trend will continue as the cost of energy for pumping increases and water tables fall.

Finally, the transportation system will have difficulty in moving ever-increasing tonnage to the ports. Rapid progress has been made in solving some of the bottlenecks, mainly by large private firms since 1978, but ready port access still remains a great problem in the upper Midwest.

In short, a combination of elements are hampering agricultural productivity and total growth of farm output in the United States. There was little underutilized capacity in U.S. agriculture in 1980, and the idea that the United States can increase agricultural output at 10 percent a year is wrong. Even with a 15 to 20 percent rise in real prices of grain, large increases in American agricultural production will not be forthcoming.

Some evidence of these trends is given by post-1975 productivity data. Total inputs into U.S. agriculture have changed very little since 1930, and virtually all of the increased output has come from technological change

TABLE I

Indexes of Farm Output, Input, and Productivity, United States, 1930–80

(1967=100)

Year	Output	Input	Produc-tivity[a]	Year	Output	Input	Produc-tivity[a]
1930	52	101	51	1955	82	105	78
1931	57	101	56	1956	82	103	80
1932	55	97	57	1957	81	101	80
1933	51	96	53	1958	87	100	87
1934	43	90	48	1959	88	102	87
1935	52	91	57	1960	91	101	90
1936	47	93	50	1961	91	100	91
1937	57	98	59	1962	92	100	92
1938	57	96	59	1963	96	100	96
1939	58	98	59	1964	95	100	95
1940	60	100	60	1965	98	98	100
1941	62	100	62	1966	95	98	97
1942	70	103	68	1967	100	100	100
1943	69	104	66	1968	102	100	102
1944	71	105	67	1969	102	99	103
1945	70	103	68	1970	101	100	102
1946	71	101	71	1971	110	100	110
1947	69	101	68	1972	110	100	110
1948	76	103	74	1973	112	101	111
1949	74	105	71	1974	106	100	105
1950	74	104	71	1975	114	100	115
1951	76	107	71	1976	117	103	115
1952	79	107	74	1977	119	105	114
1953	79	106	75	1978	122	105	116
1954	80	105	76	1979	129	108	119
				1980[b]	122	106	115

SOURCE: United States Department of Agriculture.
[a]Data computed from unrounded index numbers.
[b]Preliminary.

(Table 1). Since 1975, however, productivity growth has stagnated, a trend that could continue into the 1980s and beyond.

Looking to the United States as the infinite breadbasket, and as a compensating source for agricultural shortfalls in the rest of the world, is unrealistic. This conjecture, in turn, has important implications for the world food economy in which Mexico now finds itself.

ADDITIONAL LESSONS OF THE 1970S

International events in the 1970s other than productivity growth also hold lessons for the 1980s. The United States is the major participant in the world grain market. In the last twenty years it has moved from supplying 30 percent of the world grain exports to providing about 50 percent, shipping about 40 million tons in 1960, but about 130 million in 1980 (see Table 2). These exports are extremely important for U.S. agriculture as well as for the world food economy, but they are unlikely to continue increasing at a similar rate in the 1980s and 1990s.

Recent growth in export supplies was matched by new demand pressures on the world food system, exerted mainly by middle-income countries. Mexico should heed the lessons of the 1970s of other middle-income countries very carefully, for they are sobering to any rapidly growing oil economy seeking food self-sufficiency. In 1980, the middle-income countries had 250 million more people living in the cities than they did in 1960. Half of the urban food consumption in middle-income countries is now supplied by imports. Sixty percent of the increase in grain exports over the last three years went to middle-income countries, and that percentage is projected to rise to 75 percent by 1985.

The middle-income countries' imports have been made necessary by the direct demand for grain as food, but will increase because of the derived demand for feed grains. Meat, poultry, and milk demand, not the 800 million people who suffer moderate to severe malnutrition, has become the driving force of the world food economy.

Another lesson of the 1970s is the importance of general macro policy

TABLE 2

The Changing Pattern of World Grain Trade: Net Grain Movements by Region

(millions of metric tons)

Region	1948 to 1952	1960	1970	1980
North America	23	39	56	131
Latin America	1	0	4	−10
Western Europe	−22	−25	−30	−16
Eastern Europe and the Soviet Union	0	0	0	−46
Africa	0	−2	−5	−15
Asia	−6	−17	−37	−63
Australia and New Zealand	3	6	12	19

SOURCE: Lester Brown, "World Population Growth, Soil Erosion, and Food Security," *Science*, 214 (Nov. 27, 1981), 998.
    NOTE: Minus signs indicate net imports.

on agriculture. Macroeconomic policy variables, such as interest rates, balance of payments, and labor policy issues, are becoming a much more dominant force in U.S. agriculture than traditional commodity programs. Although agriculture in the United States supplies only 3 percent of GNP, 20 percent of total exports come from agriculture. Hence, interest rates and dollar exchange rates have an important impact on the entire U.S. economy through their effects on agricultural trade.

The 1970s hold two more international lessons. One is the inability of the international community to agree on anything related to food. There have been few developments on international reserve schemes or buffer-stock operations. This slowness has occurred in part because the North has not been serious about those negotiations, but disagreement is also deeply rooted in the political economy of agriculture in the individual countries. Little progress on negotiations can be foreseen for the 1980s.

Finally, there are increasing problems for the United States as the result of its very open agricultural economy. U.S. agriculture has largely borne the shocks of international events. For example, the crop failures in Russia and the concomitant change in Soviet policy not to destroy livestock herds or raise prices, but to go instead to the international grain market, were absorbed principally by changes in U.S. stocks and export flows. As a consequence, the livestock sector in the United States suffered in particular during the 1970s as the United States tried to react to international events. International shocks create serious problems for countries that try to keep open economies, and the larger the number of countries that do not adjust, the greater will be the instability for all. Among major importers, Europe adjusts little and the Soviet Union and Japan are only slightly more responsive to international prices. Thus, an important question for the 1980s is how long open economies can continue to react to world price fluctuations without creating some form of export policy to minimize the internal impact of these shocks.

TRENDS IN THE 1980s

What will be the trends in the 1980s, and what do they mean to the United States and Mexico? Continuing increases in expenditures on livestock products by the middle-income countries will be the most significant component of rising import demand, and the tapering off of U.S. agricultural productivity growth will affect export supplies. As a consequence, world grain prices will probably rise and become increasingly unstable. The amount of the price rise will depend to some extent on supply responses in a number of countries, such as Brazil; on the strength of the global economy; and on weather, particularly in the United States and the Soviet Union.

In addition to feed grain demands, a new pressure could be exerted on the world grain economy as a direct consequence of energy policy. There are understandable policy concerns about energy use in U.S. agriculture and the United States' dependence on fossil fuels. Even more important, however, is the potential threat created by the new Synfuels Bills in promoting gasohol production from agricultural products, especially corn. The potential effects on U.S. agriculture are very great. This past year, fifteen new alcohol plants were established. A 10-billion-gallon target has been set for ethanol in 1990, which when converted to gasohol would supply 10 percent of the U.S. gasoline requirement. It would also require 100 million tons of grain, an amount about equivalent to current grain exports.

The corn-belt politics of gasohol in the United States are understandable; the basic economics of corn-belt gasohol are not. Gale Johnson has calculated the costs of producing the corn and converting it into alcohol and has suggested that gasoline, after refining and before distribution and taxation, would have to cost about $1.80 a gallon to make corn-based ethanol pay without subsidy.[1] But astonishing things can happen in the United States. Twenty-two states now have a combined federal and state subsidy on ethanol of $1.40 to $1.50 a gallon, and the federal government is now prepared to provide loan guarantees for plant construction. Although it is doubtful that the United States will in fact produce 10 billion gallons of ethanol by 1990, several private companies indicate that they anticipate 20 percent of the U.S. corn crop in 1990 going to ethanol production. As a result of shifts in demand for corn, the 1980s may be the decade in which substantially more wheat is fed to livestock.

UNANSWERED QUESTIONS FOR MEXICO
AND THE UNITED STATES

The United States now is faced with three fundamental issues with respect to its agricultural policy. First, will it retain its open, privately operated, market-oriented agricultural trade policy, or will the pressures be such that the United States will move toward more government sales? Will export bans be imposed in critical situations to avoid domestic problems of income instability for U.S. farmers and price instability for U.S. consumers? In short, will the United States be able and willing to absorb shocks from the international system?

Second, will the United States continue to subsidize the gasohol program? If heavy subsidies continue, price pressures on corn will increase, which could also be important for Mexico.

---

[1] D. G. Johnson, "Agricultural Policy Alternatives for the 1980s," paper presented at a conference on Food and Agricultural Policy, Washington, D.C., October 3, 1980.

Third, will the United States make hunger alleviation its focus with the Third World? There is no doubt that the United States should adopt such a stance, but it is unlikely that the country will do so as a matter of official policy. The nature of our food relationships with middle- and low-income countries is a fundamental question for U.S. foreign policy, but those relationships appear now to be in serious disarray.

The answers to the foregoing questions will determine the shape of the world food economy in which Mexico will operate during the next decade. Whatever is done to increase grain supplies in Mexico, much more concern and analysis is needed on what will happen to the *demand* for grain within Mexico. This analysis is needed particularly for corn, and less for corn as food than for its role in meeting meat and poultry demand. Unrestrained, the rising rate of grain consumption by livestock will jeopardize Mexico's political, economic, and agricultural plans for self-sufficiency.

The second fundamental question for Mexico is whether the self-sufficiency program for corn can solve issues of both production and distribution. Productivity increases will undoubtedly lag in rain-fed agricultural areas. The technology for these areas has not been fully adapted, although progress is being made. The danger in aiming for self-sufficiency is that the zeal for increasing production might supplant distributional goals. Production concerns may cause important regions of the country to grow corn where it should not be grown, and an intense self-sufficiency program might also hinder broad-based development programs for agriculture. A large enough increase in corn prices and a reduction of the restrictions on irrigating corn crops might achieve self-sufficiency—probably, however, at the expense of real increases in per capita income. A Mexican agricultural program that succeeded in complete food self-sufficiency would almost surely be counterproductive for Mexico.

CONCLUSIONS

What can be postulated as the optimal solution for the food system in Mexico and in the United States, and for trade relationships between the two countries? Clearly Mexico has substantial oil reserves in an unstable oil market, and the United States has abundant food resources in an unstable food market. Might they have a basis for negotiation? This idea, especially in Mexico, is not very popular. Yet corn could be a central element in a new trade relationship between the United States and Mexico. For example, if self-sufficiency in corn production is not an overriding concern in Mexico, a new trade relationship in agriculture could evolve with the United States increasing corn sales to Mexico and easing restrictions on labor flows and trade in specialty products. Oil could be a part of the negotiations, but even within agriculture there is a basis for further discussion.

There is room for optimism about trade possibilities if both sides will approach the negotiations seriously and as equals. Mexico is wise to move toward grain self-sufficiency at the margin. Demand will rise rapidly, however, and the self-sufficiency target will be a rapidly moving one. Under these circumstances, new approaches to U.S. and Mexico agricultural trade relations offer possibilities for the 1980s that did not exist in the 1970s.

Mexican Migration: The Political Dynamic of Perceptions

Jorge A. Bustamante

THE PHENOMENON of undocumented Mexican migration to the United States has at times been analyzed in a confused and frequently emotional manner. One reason may be the lack of an analytical differentiation between two dimensions of the problem—first, the public perceptions of the phenomenon in Mexico and in the United States, and, second, the structure of the international labor market in which the phenomenon takes place.

The presupposition here is that each aspect has its own dynamic, whose characteristics are not necessarily dependent on that of the other. The fundamental distinction between the two is that the one changes with the internal politics of each country, and the other responds to structural factors pertaining to an economic system that includes both Mexico and the United States.

This paper will focus only on the first of these dimensions, inasmuch as the structural dimensions of the labor market have been treated elsewhere. The periodic attention to the theme of undocumented migration of Mexicans in the U.S. mass media has been observed by various authors and documented by researchers in the communications field, such as Félix Gutiérrez of California. It has also been observed that this intermittence coincides demonstrably with periods of economic crisis in the United States, and particularly with periods of increasing rates of unemployment there. The coincidence appears to be the result of a process that may be characterized as follows:

1. In situations of an increase in unemployment beyond limits that powerful sectors of U.S. opinion find tolerable, the voice of some public authority proceeds to define for public opinion a causal connection between the presence of immigrants and the increase in unemployment.

2. This definition of the unemployment problem implicitly carries with it the message that there is a factor external to the U.S. system, the

immigration of foreign workers, that is disequilibrating the supply and demand for labor power in the United States. Also implicit in the message is the idea that, in the absence of that external factor, unemployment would diminish considerably and the domestic labor market would function in a more equilibrated fashion. Such a definition serves political ends and lacks substance insofar as it proceeds not from scientific findings but from a political interest in diverting the attention of the public away from the increase in unemployment and away from any examination of factors internal to the national economy that might be associated with it, toward an external factor such as the immigration of workers from foreign countries.

3. The public in general, and pressure groups in particular, accept the explanation that the unemployment situation is provoked by the presence of migrants, and bestow credibility to that explanation by demanding that the migrants be excluded and the frontiers closed to them. This demand implies that the message alluded to under point (2) above has been understood and that the external factor, identified publicly as the cause of the problem, should be removed so that domestic labor market conditions can return to normal.

4. Those responsible for policy in the United States take up the public demand against immigration and respond in turn by setting the official apparatus of decision making in motion toward the end of either expelling the immigrants or in some way barring their entry.

5. This process is maintained until the economy recovers and rates of unemployment are reduced to politically tolerable levels.

6. The visibility of undocumented immigrant workers in the mass media then diminishes almost to the zero point.

With some variations, this process has functioned with "political success" throughout most of the course of labor migration to the United States. Temporary victims of the process have been the numerous ethnic groups who at various moments in U.S. history were defined as the "external factor" that was "causing" problems. As has been documented elsewhere, the role of scapegoat for epochs of crisis fell to the Irish to play from 1830 to 1840, to the Germans from 1848 to 1860, to immigrants from the countries of Southern and Eastern Europe from 1870 to 1914, and on the West Coast to the Chinese from 1850 to 1890, the Japanese from 1890 to 1903, the Filipinos from 1900 to 1921, and the Mexicans throughout this century. The roles that these great groups of immigrants have played in the United States have varied in that those proceeding from Europe always found roads to assimilation and access to structures of opportunity in U.S. society, whereas Asiatic immigrants were finally expelled and Mexicans have been kept in proximity to a revolving door through which they can be enticed or expelled, depending on the state of the U.S. economy.

Throughout this century the immigration of Mexican workers to the United States has served as a scapegoat in times of crisis and of increasing unemployment—in 1919, 1921, 1930–35, 1954, 1974, 1975, and 1980—and has been blamed as well for such economic or social evils as the increased cost of public services, jumps in indices of criminality, and growing health problems. This scapegoat function has had nothing whatever to do with the practical, day-by-day conditions prevailing in the hiring of undocumented workers, but instead has been related to the political situation associated with each crisis.

The "political success" of officials who have provoked or responded to this situation derives from the publicly accepted view that anyone in the United States who attempts to counter undocumented immigration during periods of economic crisis is demonstrating sensitivity to the problems of the voters or to broad sectors of opinion. Although U.S. public opinion has never been unanimously against such immigration, even in the worst moments of crisis, it can be said that the tendency for correlation of severity of crisis and joblessness with a preponderantly negative view of immigration appears to be a historical constant.

A key element in the formal political aspect of the process is the de facto independence between the result of this process (i.e., its conversion into some measure restricting immigration—massive deportations, restrictive legislation, reinforcement of the border fences, for example), and the persistence of demand for migrant labor inside the country. Even if the overt manifestations are oriented toward penalizing the supply of immigrant labor, the demand from the U.S. side persists without experiencing any significant change either during or after the economic crisis that provokes the reaction against the immigrants' presence.

De facto independence between anti-Mexican perceptions and demand for supplies of cheap labor also embraces the paradox that a real demand for migrants as a labor force exists alongside their rejection as subjects with rights or as members of U.S. society. This paradox is explainable only when one analyzes the history of Mexican immigration and its role in the expansion of the U.S. economy, which has enjoyed its benefits without being willing to pay the costs associated with the contribution it makes.

In fact, the activation of the political apparatus toward restricting immigration has never succeeded in closing the door to immigration from Mexico. Legislation to that end—head taxes, literacy tests at the beginning of the century, selective immigration "quota" laws of 1921 and 1974, creation of the border patrol in the latter year, the bracero agreements signed between 1942 and 1964, and the McCarran-Walter Act of 1952—have never in practice made it impossible to maintain the flow of undocumented laborers from Mexico to the United States. Despite massive deportations during various periods of unemployment crisis, these measures have translated into pressures exerted on the supply without substantially affecting the conditions of demand for undocumented labor.

On this basis one can affirm that the perceptual dimension of the phenomenon on the U.S. side has arisen within a definite domestic political context, and has never gone beyond that context so as to influence in any important way the structural labor-market situation faced by undocumented Mexicans. In other words, the dynamic of this perceptual dimension has been kept within bounds marked by a political definition of the problem. The intermittence of undocumented immigration in the public media corresponds to that definition. Whereas undocumented immigrants have emerged into public view and then disappeared according to the state of the U.S. economy throughout this century, the government has in fact maintained a constant policy toward Mexico aimed at assuring interested business sectors of a supply of Mexican labor at the lowest cost possible, independent of the conditions of the domestic political milieu.

The most voluminous report on immigration to the United States was published in 1911 for the federal government by the Dillingham Commission. It showed that the immigration "problem" in the Northeast consisted of the pejoratively labeled "new immigration" coming from southern and eastern Europe. From this one may deduce that in the West the problem was Asiatic immigration. Some years earlier the United States and Japan had signed a gentlemen's agreement by virtue of which Japan would repatriate its citizens residing in the United States wherever they were accused of either causing unemployment or provoking a drop in wages.

The businessmen who had originally encouraged the immigration first of Chinese, then of Japanese, were worried over not being able to find labor to substitute for the Asians who were being expelled after having been made scapegoats for unemployment and low wages. The streets of San Francisco and Los Angeles had been the theater for mass hysteria against the "yellow peril," which resulted in massacres of Chinese and Japanese at the hands of mobs of enraged unemployed who blamed the defenseless Asiatic immigrants for having stolen their jobs. Already at that time, then, the system had found a way of maintaining its legitimacy among the poor and unemployed by searching outside the system itself, where migrants were seen to be, for "causes" for its crisis, in which workers were always those most deeply affected. Having blamed Asian immigrants for the first economic crisis of the century and having produced a populist reaction that led to their expulsion en masse, business then had to find another source of cheap labor, and searched for it in Mexico.

The entrepreneurs' interest in obtaining the backing of the federal government through a policy of attracting migrant workers from Mexico was openly expressed in Washington. The Dillingham Commission report recounts the case of a congressman from California who, speaking of the advantages of Mexican workers vis-à-vis workers from other countries, had argued in 1907 that the "Mexican race" (as it was officially called in the United States until 1942, when by presidential decree Mexicans stopped being non-whites and passed to the euphemistically described category of "Caucasians") was "physically constituted" for agricultural labor. The legislator tried to convince his colleagues in Washington of the argument that, just as the white race was physically and mentally constituted for industrial labor, so the Mexican race was for work in agriculture. Proof of this was the fact that, being shorter in stature than whites, Mexicans were closer to the ground and hence it cost them less effort to bend down. Another thesis sustained by the California legislator was that Mexicans would not stay in the United States, because their cultural values included a certain "gypsy spirit" that always compelled them to return to their places of origin after having worked in the United States for a time. The same ideas were utilized in the 1960s by California Senator George Murphy to defend the renewal of the bracero contracts.

Such a simplistically racist vision, of course, did not persist in a vacuum, either in 1907 or in the 1960s. On both occasions it represented an idealization of the demand for cheap labor, one which has so often, down to our own times, been disguised as a policy of good neighborliness—an immigration policy that is in reality a labor policy. Take the case of the immigration law currently in force in the United States. In 1952 it was modified by what came to be known as the "Texas proviso." This amendment basically exempted employers from criminal responsibility upon hiring any person who had entered the United States in violation of immigration laws. In practice it gave the employers the power to decide when to treat the undocumented as workers and hire them, and when to treat them as criminals and denounce them to the immigration police as violators of the laws. This power, which derives from the immigration legislation now in effect, continues in 1980 to operate in labor relations between employers and undocumented workers.

The circumstances created by such legislation place the employer in a position of absolute power to determine if a person who asks him for a job should be in the United States or not. Such power is concomitant with a lack of labor rights for the undocumented vis-à-vis employers, for the Mexican has no documents and is, in practice, by virtue of the immigration laws a worker *sui generis*. That is, he or she is a worker, in the sense of offering labor power and being contracted to work in the United States, but does not possess the rights that the laws of the country concede to native workers. The reason why the undocumented enjoy no rights as workers derives precisely from the immigration laws: the undocumented status produces definite effects on the work relations of those who are pinned with this label as a condition of access to labor contracts. It is not by accident, then, that the so-called problem of the undocumented in the United States refuses to disappear despite the fact that their presence is supposedly associated with all sorts of social evils.

THE PERCEPTUAL DIMENSION IN MEXICO

In the Mexican political context, the emigration of workers to the United States has never had the visibility, in terms of either intensity or frequency, that it has achieved in the United States. For one thing, it has never become a theme whose treatment presented an opportunity to obtain support from influential groups for the mobility aspirations of Mexican politicians. Nor has it been an issue of national political debate to the degree that it has, for very different reasons, in the United States at various times during this century. Nevertheless, such emigration has not been absent from the purview of public commentators, as is evident in an article that appeared in a Mexican news weekly during the dictatorship of Porfirio Díaz.

We have already dealt on other occasions with the mistreatment suffered by Mexicans who emigrate to the United States of the North. Our envoys in the United States worry little or not at all about the Mexicans who have emigrated to that Republic and for that reason many of our countrymen wander through American cities naked and dying of hunger. For the mistreatment that Mexicans suffer outside the country the government is to blame, on account of its lack of energy. Our government must demand respect for the man who emigrates because the dignity of the nation requires it.[1]

This commentary, written in 1905, is eloquent in its message that the phenomenon of Mexican migration has roots stretching back to the beginning of this century; that in the Mexican capital consciousness had been generated concerning the conditions in which emigration was taking

[1] *El Colmillo Público* ("The Public Eyetooth"), March 8, 1905, p. 30.

place; and that both the complacency of the government and the perception of the migration phenomenon could be cited in organs of public opinion in the urban Mexico of 1905.

This commentary did not, however, reflect any current of opinion that necessitated a response on the part of the Mexican government. The explicit reasons for the overthrow of Porfirio Díaz some years later would lie elsewhere. Within his government the dominant perception in regard to emigration of workers to the United States was positive as long as it did not represent the flight of peons from the large *haciendas*, or of workers from mines in the Mexican North. The governing group at that time, the so-called *científicos*, touted the advantages for Mexico of a migration that would bring in skills and foreign exchange to accelerate Mexico's development, just as European immigration would provide a way of "improving the race."

During the revolutionary period the problems of regime survival and institutionalization caused the issue of migration to the United States not to be perceived as critical or as requiring governmental action. As has been documented by Mercedes Carreras de Velazco in her book, *Los Mexicanos que devolvió la crisis*, emigration was not viewed as a serious problem even though lamenting references to its occurrence were made from time to time. The state of Mexican legislation concerning emigration reflected this situation in the population laws of both 1908 and 1926. It was not until 1930 that Mexican laws reflected a change of perception in regard to emigration, describing it as something to be averted through inquiry into its causes, toward which end the law created the Consultative Council on Migration. One of the tasks of this commission was to prevent depopulation by way of emigration. An important element in the process of perceptual change at the government level was provided by the research and return to Mexico of Manuel Gamio, whose works comprise rays of wisdom within a general ambience of ignorance and indifference. He was the first, and for many years the only, author to carry out scientific research on the phenomenon of Mexican labor migration to the United States.

Notwithstanding their breadth and profundity, however, Gamio's studies on the issue provoked more debate in the United States than in Mexico. In the postrevolutionary period there emerged anew in the government's political rhetoric the idea of the "safety valve," associated with emigration to the United States, which had been heard incipiently in the period of Díaz. The emigration of Mexicans to the country to the North began to be viewed more as a solution than as a problem. Not until the government of Lázaro Cárdenas (1934–40) did the trend of the issue change in the perceptions of Mexican politicians—politicians who had emerged from the political upheaval unleashed by the 1929 recession in the United States, and who for the first time converted migration into a dominant theme in the Mexican media. These perceptions were basically connected to the abuses and violence that characterized the deportations of the period. A popular clamor was generated in those years—and reflected in the printed media—demanding protest action by the Mexican government toward the United States over the brutal and discriminatory treatment coming to light in the denunciations and tales of the migrants and of some United States citizens of Mexican origin who had been expelled for no reason other than their physical resemblance to Mexicans. The flow of Mexican returnees provoked by these conditions has been measured at approximately one half million persons.

The government of President Cárdenas responded to this clamor with a repatriation program, which consisted of orienting the exiles toward various centers of *ejidal* agricultural production. At the political level the program was considered to be the result of a new policy that had given birth to the General Law of Population drawn up in 1936, which explicitly proposed that repatriation of Mexicans be incorporated into the tasks of national development. Albeit belatedly in regard to the mass expulsions of the early 1930s, the government of General Cárdenas was responding to the U.S. migration policy of that era with dignity and in adherence to law. However, the institutional response was not maintained for long. Shortly thereafter, the events that culminated in the oil expropriation of 1938 completely displaced the question of migrant workers from the Mexican political scene. Moreover, provoked by the onset of the Second World War in Europe in 1939, the U.S. economy took a quick turn toward expansion. The anti-Mexican climate that had accompanied the mass expulsions a few years before was replaced in the U.S. political scene by a change in the public's perception of Mexican workers toward that of "hard working people," the same perception that had served as the political justification for the organized efforts to recruit Mexican labor in previous periods of economic expansion.

In 1940 the government of Mexico passed into the hands of a new administration, with a new political and economic orientation. Emphasis in government action toward national development was henceforth placed on industrialization. President Ávila Camacho's (1940–1946) economic advisors prompted him to discern the opportunity that the war was opening up to develop industrial production in Mexico for export. The government then took the political decisions necessary to exploit the opportunity and, in the space of less than two years, had managed to increase industry to an extent that was spectacular. The U.S. entry into the conflict against the Axis powers thus found Mexico with an unprecedented capacity for industrial production, and in 1942 a takeoff began in the country's development and modernization. Along with the new industrial plant came not only technology but also capital from the United States, eager to associate itself with a Mexican industrial bourgeoisie undergoing expansion of its economic power and political influence. In this new project of development, the rural sector was abandoned in favor of the urban. Nevertheless, the standard of living of the greater part of the population began to rise, with effects on the patterns of demographic increase. After 1940 a decline in infant mortality, a lengthening of life expectancy, and a notable growth of cities took place.

Coinciding with Mexico's formal entry into the war in 1942, there appeared once again an initiative by the United States to attract Mexican workers. This time it was the Department of Defense that requested the government of Mexico to collaborate with the Allied cause through a contribution of labor power. Production of food had acquired military-strategic importance at the same time that the domestic work force had been converted into an army, and agricultural production ran a serious risk of being lost for lack of labor. Recruiting labor was thus considered an "emergency war measure" of the highest priority for the U.S. national interest, and the government resorted to asking the Mexican government for *braceros* as a form of cooperation in the war effort against the Fascist powers aligned in the Berlin-Rome-Tokyo axis. The Mexican government agreed to send braceros in accord with a convention that established annual quotas for temporary hiring under stipulations guaranteeing protection of the labor rights of Mexicans working in the United States.

In the bracero agreement the U.S. government, under the exigencies of war, accepted labor rights that had not been conceded to agricultural workers in the United States itself. When the war ended, however, Mexican migratory workers ceased being the subject of a program defined strategically in national-security terms, and in practice ended up in the hands of agricultural employers' associations. With this change, the presence of Mexican workers in the United States was placed once again within the framework established before the war: the ability to count on a ready source of cheap labor.

In spite of innumerable denunciations of discrimination and of the growing phenomenon of undocumented workers who crossed the border attracted by news of the bracero agreement, by 1964 the Mexican government had adopted an attitude of acceptance toward sending workers to the United States and was already beginning to negotiate appropriate bracero accords. The series of concessions that the government began to make to U.S. agricultural employers reached the point of shameful indifference toward the mass expulsion of a million undocumented workers in

1954. Even after the culmination of the infamous "Operation Wetback," from which the expulsions of that year occurred, the government of Mexico continued to see no alternative for its migrant workers than the "escape valve" of bracero contracts.

By 1964 the predominance of the migrant worker theme had been extended to bilateral discussions, and the last of the bracero accords was signed, only to expire the same year. Also in 1964 a new Mexican ambassador arrived in Washington, whose principal mission was to seek the renewal of the bracero agreements. However, both U.S. agricultural employers and the Mexican ambassador failed in their efforts, owing to the power of the AFL-CIO, which had always been opposed, even during the Second World War, to the importation of workers into the United States.

Starting in 1965, the issue of migratory workers practically disappeared from the agenda of bilateral discussion. Technically speaking, there were no more bracero-workers legally contracted for temporary labor in the United States. Although official emigration declined considerably after the agreements were terminated, the number of Mexican workers who emigrated without documents began once again to increase. By 1970 the number of undocumented workers deported had reached a quarter of a million. In 1971, Congressman Peter Rodino organized congressional hearings in various cities, in which debate was begun and still continues—over the significance of the undocumented immigrants' presence.

While the issue took on a political character in the United States, in Mexico it was ignored almost completely. With the imminent visit of President Echeverría to Washington in 1972, the Mexican government was forced to gather information about the topic, which was acquiring importance in U.S. politics and which affected hundreds of thousands of Mexicans. Although the salinity of the waters of the Colorado occupied the highest priority in this presidential meeting, the treatment of undocumented Mexican migrants was discreetly included on the agenda. By the time of the meeting between Presidents Echeverría and Ford in October 1975, the migrant worker theme had attained highest priority on the agenda for discussion—and, just as in 1942, at the initiative of the U.S. government. In 1975, however, the objective was to get rid of Mexican workers in view of the economic recession that had begun in 1974.

In interviews with all the Mexican consuls in the cities bordering on the United States and Mexico in 1969, it was surprising to find that every one of them denied the existence of any problem with undocumented Mexican workers. One, however, who wished to remain anonymous, could not resist the evidence adduced by the official statistics on apprehensions of the U.S. Immigration and Naturalization Service (INS), which showed a notable growth in the number of apprehensions of Mexicans, which by 1967 had already exceeded one hundred thousand. In an interview the consul related that all Mexican consuls in the United States had instructions from the Ministry of Foreign Relations not to talk about the "wetbacks" or to respond to references to their existence. The consul explained that the government of Mexico did not desire to enter into discussions about the undocumented that might become embarrassing or might hinder the government's efforts to renew the bracero convention suspended in 1964.

The official Mexican policy toward undocumented migrant workers from the beginning of the bracero program manifested itself in two contrasting ways. Public opinion was kept in almost complete ignorance with respect to both the content of the negotiations and the complaints that the government was making to the United States in the context of the bracero agreements. At the negotiating table, however, the Mexican government took a position of energetic protest in the face of evidence of mistreatment and abuse of braceros. An office was also established at the *Dirección* level within the Ministry of Foreign Relations whose function was to exercise official protection for Mexican workers in the United States.

These foreign policy decisions had no counterparts, however, in the domestic policy sphere. The government did nothing to discourage emigration; quite the opposite. Despite the fact that it spoke at the negotiating table of preventing emigration to places where there was evidence of discrimination, in practice this could not be implemented, in part because of the ambivalence of foreign policy with respect to domestic policy. Internal policy continued to be congruent with the notion of keeping the escape valve of emigration open, even at the cost of the increasing exploitation to which a number of Mexicans were being subjected as a result of the saturation of the labor market both for braceros and for wetbacks.

The Mexican government's negotiating posture appeared to pursue the objective of getting the United States to accept guarantees for the workers, even if only on paper (i.e., in the bilateral documents). In practice, no preoccupation over the implementation of such guarantees was demonstrated beyond the actions taken by consuls. As has been documented by Ernesto Galarza, braceros did not have access to the courts because they were not recognized as parties to the agreements. Only the consuls could take action in cases of negative effects stemming from the nonenforcement of the agreements, which in general signified a relation of tutelage toward migratory workers that impeded them from exercising their rights by themselves.

Examining the negotiations of the latter half of the 1940s, one may verify the great political error of the Mexican government in declaring itself an enemy of illegal migration. It departed from a formalistic, purely theoretical assumption that the act of crossing the frontier without documents was the individual responsibility of the person undertaking it. The lawyers negotiating the bracero accords thus committed the error of applying to the undocumented the doctrine of penal law that presumes the criminal individually responsible for his actions. No consideration was given to the responsibility of those actors who created and maintained the system and who profited with impunity from it. Such is the case with the "Texas proviso," by virtue of which employers have been permitted since 1952 to hire undocumented workers, who are punished under the same law for violations of the immigration statutes.

The apparent ignorance on the part of the Mexican negotiators of the social and economic context in which the structural conditions of the labor market for migratory workers were formed led them to become partners in the U.S. policy of persecuting the undocumented. It would be difficult to erase the historic shame deriving from the fact that the government of Mexico accepted and cooperated in the infamous "Operation Wetback" in 1954. The only explanation for the policy lies in a legalistic error of judgment on the part of the Mexican negotiators, who viewed undocumented workers as delinquents and not as victims of labor market conditions designed to facilitate their entry as workers and their expulsion as migrants and human beings.

During the decade 1950–60, the internal political context in Mexico coincided with a large expansion of the industrial sector, a turn toward land concentration (above all, lands endowed with water by new public irrigation works), an insistent policy of attracting U.S. investment, and great harmony in intergovernmental relations between Washington and Mexico City in spite of the fact that Mexico decided to maintain relations with Cuba.

While the economic development plans of Mexican governments after Ávila Camacho up through Díaz Ordaz (1964–70) went on giving priority to the industrial sector at the expense of the peasantry, income concentration increased the distance between rich and poor, to the point— sadly—of putting Mexico in the runner-up spot in the hemisphere, after Brazil, in indices of concentration of wealth. The increasing growth of population, coupled with a model of development based on the use of U.S. technology designed to save labor, and the neglect of the situation of the peasants, also produced increasing rates of unemployment. Nonetheless, the country's political stability was the object of widespread international recognition. One of the least explored causes of that stability, which coexisted with increasing unemployment and wealth concentration, has been the emigration of workers to the United States. The major hypothesis deriving from such an explanation would be that the increasing migratory flow to the United States functioned as a political solution or safety valve for pressures that would otherwise have been generated by unemployment and concentration of wealth. Taking this hypothesis to an extreme, one might argue that emigration to the United States, maintained over several decades by an unbalanced social development, has contributed to preventing another revolution in Mexico during this century. Put another way, the phenomenon of labor migration to the United States has been a factor favoring political stability in Mexico. From this stability U.S. industrialists and investors have obtained as much advantage as have their Mexican partners.

The association of interests between foreign investors and capitalists in Mexico is of great significance and must be pointed out when attempts are made to explain the phenomenon of undocumented migration as a simple result of the existence of "factors of attraction and expulsion."

The use of capital and technology from the United States in the evolution of Mexico's development model makes it necessary to recognize that the so-called expulsion factors are not necessarily endogenous to the economy or society of origin of the migrants. In the circumstances of a developing country highly dependent economically on its neighbor to the north, the indiscriminate use of technology designed to save labor power is less rational than it would be when applied to the conditions of an economy that is highly developed in all sectors. When such foreign technology was utilized in a country like Mexico from 1940 to 1970, particularly in agriculture, a displacement of labor power was produced that could not be absorbed by other sectors and that ended up emigrating to the United States. In no way do I mean to suggest that this occurred in all branches of economic activity where foreign technology was employed or that such technology is anathema; in some branches, however, decisions taken in the United States, with the consent of some Mexicans, to use a certain technology in a production process did often result in unemployment and in emigration to the country whence the technology and capital came. In such cases the resultant unemployment could not be considered a factor of expulsion operating independently of what was occurring in the country that became the unemployed migrants' destination.

The analytical risk involved in not recognizing the lack of independence that may exist between factors of expulsion and those of attraction is that one may fall into biases that imply dissociating politically the responsibility of the country of destination from its participation in generating the causes of migration. With this consideration in mind, it may be said that there have been economic interests on the part of groups in both countries that have determined public perceptions of the phenomenon of undocumented migration. Nevertheless, those perceptions do not emerge with the aim of affecting, nor do they manage to affect, the structural conditions of supply and demand for the labor of the undocumented, conditions that have remained independent and relatively constant from the beginning of the century down to the present.

A notable alteration in the political view of undocumented migration in Mexico, which had not changed since the era of President Cárdenas, occurred during the regime of President Echeverría (1970–76). As he received information from nongovernmental sources concerning the condition of undocumented migrants from 1972 onward, he altered his previous posture in favor of the escape valve, which had been equivalent to favoring a renewal of the bracero contracts. Within his cabinet, however, this change of view was not shared to any significant extent. The ministers of Foreign Relations and Interior (*Gobernación*) did not slacken in their open insistence on the traditional posture of fighting for the renewal of the bracero agreements before both foreign and national public opinion. Only the newspaper *El Día* of Mexico City commented favorably on Echeverría's first public declaration against renewal of the agreement in his speech on "Freedom of the Press Day" in 1974. Nevertheless, as became evident some weeks later, Secretary of Foreign Relations Lic. Emilio Rabasa continued his negotiations with Dr. Kissinger in spite of such a renewal.

On the eve of the meeting between Presidents Echeverría and Ford in Arizona in October 1975 the Mexican president's interest in learning about the history of the bracero agreement's functioning in practice (the written text had been familiar to him long before he became president) intensified. Pursuing this interest, he invited to Los Pinos Dr. Ernesto Galarza, author of the most important study of the labor practices deriving from the bracero accords. Without comment from Echeverría or any indication of his personal evaluation of the information and analysis that Dr. Galarza had related to him over the course of several hours, the interview between the two presidents was held three days later. To the surprise of many, Echeverría told Ford at the first opportunity that the Mexican government did not desire the renewal of the bracero agreement, and the statement appeared in the headlines of all the principal dailies in Mexico the next day. Eloquent too was the fact that the following day the *Los Angeles Times* and the *San Antonio Light* reported precisely the opposite, affirming expressly that President Echeverría had requested from President Ford the renewal of the contracts. Some days later, in an inside page note, the *Los Angeles Times* rectified its error.

A few weeks after this presidential encounter, Secretary Rabasa presented his resignation, for reasons that clearly had nothing to do with President Echeverría's new posture vis-à-vis undocumented migrants. What is certain is that after Rabasa was replaced in office by Ambassador García Robles, the government of Mexico did not go back to insisting on renewal of the bracero accords. Its new thesis, oriented toward the protection of the human and labor rights of the undocumented, had been strengthened by the strong indignation provoked in Mexico by the incident involving Arizona's Harrigan brothers, who had subjected to sadistic torture two undocumented migrants who later denounced them from a hospital in Sonora, supported by the testimony of doctors who attended to their wounds.

THE PROPOSED "SOLUTIONS"

The spectrum of proposed solutions currently at the forefront of the debate over undocumented migration can be completely understood only if one is aware of the domestic political contexts within which the dominant perceptions of the most vocal interest groups have been generated. This spectrum includes the following alternatives (which are not mutually exclusive): (1) renewal of the bracero accords; (2) broadening the H-2 visa program (this is a unilateral hiring program carried out under section H-2 of the immigration law in force in the United States, which requires prior certification by the Department of Labor of the lack of locally available native workers); (3) an increase in the quota of resident visas conceded to Mexican citizens by the U.S. government; (4) creation of a new program of visas for "guest workers" along the lines of the model followed in Europe and practiced especially by West Germany; (5) "legalization," "regularization," or "adjustment of migrant status," commonly subsumed in the United States under the notion of "amnesty," by virtue of which a certain number of undocumented who have resided in the United States for a period of years could continue their stay and work in the country legally; (6) an increase in the number of border police on the part of the U.S. government; (7) massive deportations in the wake of police roundups.

Such measures head proposals that generally include others in combination—for example: (8) U.S. financial aid for development programs tending to strengthen migrant workers' roots in Mexico; (9) sanctions against employers who hire undocumented workers; (10) cooperation from the government of Mexico in police actions tending to impede the outflow of undocumented migrants; (11) temporary visas of a *sui generis* nature, such as those mentioned in the Carter plan. All these measures are known to have been proposed publicly by some official of the U.S. government.

On the Mexican side, with the exception of Licenciado Hugo B. Margáin, Mexico's ambassador in Washington, who has conspicuously proposed a form of renewal of the bracero agreements following the 1942 model, no official has advocated any solution at all. Since the meeting between Presidents López Portillo and Carter in February 1979, the Mexican head of state has declared repeatedly that his government is not prepared to propose or to accept any solution to the problem of undocumented migrant workers. Both President López Portillo and the current secretary of foreign relations, Jorge Castañeda, fall back on the fact that the government, through the ministry of labor, is carrying on a complex, in-depth investigation of the problem, from which results are expected to be obtained in the course of 1982 (see the paper by Manuel García y Griego). The absence of proposals on the part of the Mexican government has been justified by the promise that the investigation will produce reliable data with regard to both the quantitative and the qualitative characteristics of the migration of Mexicans, on the basis of which that government will be able to design domestic and foreign policy actions concerning the issue.

The notion of a solution implicit in the statements of President López Portillo and Secretary Castañeda does not coincide with those habitually put forward in the United States—it does not refer to avoiding the migratory flow to the United States, but rather to rationalizing the conditions in which it takes place through measures that would prevent the abuse of, exploitation of, or discrimination against Mexican workers. The set of solutions to the question of the undocumented may be grouped under three courses of action: (1) a conditional opening of the U.S. border to immigration of Mexican workers; (2) a relative closing of the U.S. border to such immigration; (3) rationalization of the flow of migratory workers, starting from a recognition of the real demand for foreign labor from the U.S. side and an excess supply of unskilled labor in Mexico, a problem correctable only in the long run.

Course (1), which groups those who have proposed the measures described in clauses (1) through (5), and (8), begins from a different set of assumptions, which for the purposes of bilateral negotiation may be enunciated as follows: First, the securing of a permanent supply of cheap labor from Mexico is conditional upon some form of legalization for a limited number of undocumented workers in the United States, which is equivalent to offering "amnesty." Second, it is necessary to help the Mexican government to keep open the safety valve for the tensions created by unemployment and concentration of wealth; otherwise, political instability and a "turn to the left" on the part of marginal groups might be produced similar to those that occurred in Nicaragua and El Salvador, something contrary to U.S. interests.

Course (2), characterized by proposals (6), (7), and (10), derives from the assumption that the migration of undocumented workers to the United States is its internal problem, which requires domestic solutions defined by the "domestic" political context to the exclusion of the international. This current of thought does not favor bilateral negotiations and labels as "consultation" with the government of Mexico what in reality is nothing more than a unilateral decision on the part of the United States (when the possibility of acting with the Mexican government is considered, those supporting this course also seek out option [10]).

Course (3) is characterized by the assumption that, even though a diminution in the economic and demographic conditions promoting the migration of Mexicans to the United States could occur, it will not occur in less than several decades. Furthermore, this course presupposes a broad recognition among powerful sectors in the United States of the real demand for Mexican labor and of the physical and political impossibility of closing the frontier to the immigration of undocumented Mexican workers.

The thesis offered here to help understand this array of solutions is that they all involve a contradiction that ends up inhibiting any structural change in the conditions of demand for Mexican labor in the United States. The contradiction occurs between the economic interests of the employers who benefit from the circumstances in which undocumented labor power is contracted and the political interests of those who seek to preserve the legitimacy of the U.S. economic system by blaming immigrants—defined as a factor external to the system—as the cause of their own crises. This contradiction exists because economic crises do not affect all members of the system in the same way.

If the crisis is manifested by unemployment and/or inflation, the workers—having fewer options for eluding it—are those who end up being most affected. As was demonstrated first in the 1920s, and later in the 1930s, the legitimacy of the system becomes vulnerable precisely among the workers. Those most affected by economic crises are the ones who begin to question the design of a system that produces such crises. Thus it is to the workers that the idea of a solution through closing the border to immigration is directed. It is not by chance that from Samuel Gompers in the 1920s to George Meany in 1979 the American Federation of Labor (AFL) has been the principal organization advocating massive expulsions and restrictions on immigration as the solution for unemployment. Although employers are also interested in preserving the system's legitimacy, they are not interested in a real closing of the border to workers from Mexico. Hence they search for migratory formulas that will produce a political impact on dominant perceptions without in practice affecting the structural features of the migrant labor market.

Although its effects were ephemeral, a politically successful example of such a formula was the so-called tortilla curtain. Another example, this one unsuccessful, was represented by President Carter's proposed 1977 immigration policy, which aimed to give something to everyone according to the interest of each. It was the contradictions among those interests that made the plan a total failure. However, the context of those contradictions has not been sufficiently analyzed. None of the proposed solutions gets at the structural roots of the phenomenon of undocumented migration. All respond in some fashion to the perceptual context and not to the context of the labor market structures that operate across the frontier.

The solution to the problem depends on how it is defined. As long as one keeps on disguising a labor problem as a "problem of sovereignty" represented by the enforcement of an immigration law, the solution will have no relation to the true problem. It is understandable that the phenomenon of undocumented migration is not seen as a problem from the perspective of the workers in the same way that it is from the perspective of employers; nonetheless, there is a long experience of ways to reconcile such conflicts of interest. Within the capitalist system that experience is none other than the union organization of international migratory workers. This will take place only when the discrepancies between the dimension of perceptions and the dimension of reality in the understanding of the phenomenon of undocumented migration disappear.

The Problems of Planning for the Expected: Demographic Shocks and Policy Paralysis

Warren C. Sanderson

IT IS a commonplace among those who design complex systems that prudence requires them "to expect the unexpected"—to build into their plans a certain amount of redundancy in case something unforeseen happens. Experience has proven the importance of such a philosophy. Unexpected things do indeed go wrong and, without some backup capability and contingency planning, the entire system can fail. Not only are such complex items as nuclear reactors, electric power grids, and spacecraft constructed with attention to the possibility of failure, but more mundane, down-to-earth products also are similarly protected. Automobiles, for example, usually carry spare tires and jacks; sinks and tubs generally have emergency drains built in near their tops.

Prudence requires that people who design complex government policies also expect the unexpected—that they have some plans to detect and correct the unanticipated, undesirable consequences of their decisions. Such prudence is rarely observed, however, in the design of governmental policies. It is clear to a designer of a nuclear reactor that all precautions must be taken to prevent a core meltdown. A meltdown is a design failure. There is no ambiguity about it. An economic policy in the United States that led to a 12 percent rate of inflation and a 7 percent unemployment rate was also a design failure, yet there were no contingency plans about what to do when the economy first showed signs of getting out of control.

A partial explanation for the comparative lack of planning for the unexpected in governmental decision making is easily come by. Nuclear power plants and spacecraft are simple, compared with the systems politicians attempt to manipulate. It is easier to know, for example, when a spaceship is out of control, than to know when an economy is dangerously off course. Also, the successes of governmental policies are often hard to distinguish from the failures. Does the current stream of migrants from Mexico into the United States indicate that the policies of the Mexican government have succeeded or failed? Such questions are difficult to answer.

Public policies are often the result of fuzzy decisions applied to poorly understood systems. When decision makers try to balance numerous conflicting goals subject to poorly understood constraints, it is no wonder that there is no redundancy designed into the policy and no contingency planning.

Not only has public policy had difficulty in expecting the unexpected, it often fails to expect the expected as well. For example, it is well known that certain regions of California will experience severe earthquakes in the foreseeable future. Yet planning for these events is quite poor, and people are neither educated in proper responses to various degrees of increased earthquake risk nor in appropriate responses to a totally unforeseen earthquake. The reason for the lack of preparation for a nearly certain disaster is that the very act of planning itself is difficult and loaded with conflict and uncertainty. Government officials are extremely reluctant to pay the political costs of serious planning for future earthquakes when the benefits of their actions may only become apparent a decade in the future when they are long out of office.

The complexities, uncertainties, and costs associated with the formulation and implementation of a meaningful policy concerning earthquakes in California has kept such a policy from being developed—even though we know with virtual certainty that one day there will be a fearfully pressing need for it. This is an example of policy paralysis. One day, when an earthquake does occur, the policy paralysis will become a policy failure, one which is even more injurious to the population than would be a meltdown in the core of a nuclear reactor.

This example clearly indicates how coping with complex and uncertain future events can lead first to policy paralysis, and then suddenly to policy failure. It is difficult to avoid the paralysis, but one curative action is to assess realistically the cost and probability of failure. If both are high, policy makers are occasionally jolted back to the reality of having to find solutions today to problems that are likely to be upon us tomorrow.

The phenomenon of Mexican migration to the United States has caused a particularly complex form of policy paralysis, both in Mexico and in the United States, which, if not cured, must lead to a policy failure that could be unfortunate from the viewpoint of both countries. This is the central proposition I shall develop here. The nature of the problem itself is such that there are no easy solutions. There are, however, ways to lower the probability of impending failure—of planning for the expected shock of vastly increased Mexican migration into the United States—so that if it does occur, we can deal with it in an orderly and carefully considered manner which would benefit both countries.

THE ANATOMY OF POLICY PARALYSIS

For different reasons both the Mexican and the United States governments find themselves in a policy paralysis over the issue of Mexico–United States migration. It is crucial for us to understand the anatomy of the policy paralysis in each case to know which parts of the body politic are affected and why. Only then can we make an assessment about whether it is possible to envision movement in public policy or whether the paralysis should be considered permanent.

Policy Paralysis in the United States

There are three basic positions with regard to illegal immigration from Mexico that enjoy some support in the United States today. The first may be broadly called the Carter administration policy. It favors giving amnesty to undocumented aliens currently in the United States, while vigorously attempting to discourage future migrants from entering the country. The second position favors the introduction of some form of guest-worker program into the United States. Such a program would, in essence, transform the illegal migrants into a group of workers who had the right to remain in the United States for some prespecified, but presumably rather short, time. The Reagan administration has already proposed a pilot guest-worker program to Congress.* The third alternative—the policy of maintaining the status quo—may be viewed either as a policy in its own right or as a failure of the other two policies. In either event, we must also analyze the benefits and costs of not budging from our current position.

The Carter Administration Policy. Although the Carter administration has now been soundly dismissed by the electorate, its proposals are worth discussion. In the first place, they were drafted in response to perceived pressures from the public and from the American labor movement. Those pressures still continue, to some extent, during the Reagan administration. Secondly, a legacy of the administration, the Select Commission on Immigration and Refugee policy, reported its recommenda-

* Editors' note: This proposal was not developed into legislation, nor did similar elements in the currently pending Simpson-Mazzoli bill go beyond discussion in the Congressional committee in recession-plagued 1982, though the bill itself, which imposes tighter controls on migration and employer sanctions, is said to have a good chance of enactment into law. This is notwithstanding the fact that it does not address the fundamental structural questions of labor market interdependence raised by this and other papers in this section.

tions to Congress in March 1981, and they remain, at this writing, at the center of the U.S. policy debate. Some of these recommendations have even been accepted by the Reagan administration.

The Carter administration proposals originally submitted to Congress in August of 1977 and, roughly speaking, reiterated by the Select Commission in 1981 have essentially two parts: (1) the amnesty for illegal migrants who have been in the United States for a few years and who have broken no laws, and (2) sanctions against employers who hire illegal aliens. Both legs of the proposal have severe weaknesses. It is not at all clear whether this proposal will come to represent a serious U.S. government policy.

The amnesty proposal has been criticized as rewarding those who broke the law and migrated illegally. If there is one general amnesty now because illegal migrants have grown too numerous to deport, might there not be another amnesty in five years or so?[1] If this perception were to become widespread, it would perhaps encourage a new wave of migrants to come and await the next amnesty. On the other hand, groups representing the interests of the migrants generally criticized the amnesty proposal as not being lenient enough—it did not make citizens or even legal immigrants of the illegals. Instead, those who had entered the country within the past seven years were to be put into a new immigrant class called temporary resident aliens. These people would be allowed to work in the United States for a period of five years. What would happen to them after five years remained intentionally vague. Since it is possible that all the new temporary resident aliens would be deported after five years, it is understandable that some groups doubted the good faith of the Carter administration.

The amnesty proposal also offered little incentive for the illegals to reveal themselves. The temporary resident aliens would not be allowed to bring family members into the country and would not be eligible for Medicaid, food stamps, Aid to Families with Dependent Children, or Supplemental Security Income. Illegal immigrants who had been in the United States for some time would be faced with a difficult decision. If they registered under the amnesty plan and gave all the information the government required, it could then deport some of them immediately on various technicalities of health, moral character, or criminal behavior. The remainder could be deported in five years.

Given the risks faced by the illegal migrants in registering for the amnesty program and the uncertain gains they would obtain, it is probable that it would fail to enroll the majority of illegal migrants. The U.S. gov-

---

[1]The discussion on the Carter administration proposals is based on C. B. Keely, *U.S. Immigration: A Policy Analysis* (New York, 1979), pp. 53–59.

ernment would then be faced with the situation of what to do with those migrants who had refused amnesty. Clearly, any policy that leaves the U.S. government with such a dilemma is hardly desirable.

The other leg of the Carter administration proposal is hardly stronger. Employers were to be fined $1,000 for each illegal alien whom they hired. This, of course, puts on employers the burden of determining who is legal. They would need guidelines—to be provided at some future date by the attorney general—as to what evidence constituted proof of legality. The AFL-CIO criticized this portion of the proposals on the grounds that a $1,000 fine was too small to be effective; they are probably right.

Employers are generally against policing the labor force, particularly if their performances as policemen are monitored by the government. Also lined up against the idea of employer sanctions is a coalition of groups with an interest in civil rights. Effective enforcement of the law would require that employers somehow distinguish between illegal Mexican migrants and all other people of Spanish heritage. To do so would probably require a national identity card—an idea that is anathema to many Americans.

Indeed, for the purpose of deploying effective employer sanctions, the Select Commission on Immigration and Refugee Policy proposed the establishment of a national identity card system to the Congress in March 1981. Even though the card would presumably be difficult to forge, one can easily imagine the cost and the bureaucracy associated with administering such a system.

The proponents of national identity cards, of course, want strict limitation as to the amount of information that could be included. Nonetheless, the existence of such cards would be a constant temptation for the government. Politicians, for example, would certainly find it expedient if employers were not allowed to hire males who had not registered for the draft. Would minorities who were eligible for special employment programs have a special code on their identity cards? It is easy to see why civil rights groups view a national program of this nature with horror and anxiety. For them, and for many of us, this cure is considerably worse than the disease.

The Select Committee proposals are still alive. The two discussed have even been adopted in somewhat altered form by the Reagan administration. Nonetheless, the committee's proposals are opposed by almost every group involved in the problem, from those interested in the well-being of the migrants, to those interested in the well-being of their employers. There is little movement to be expected here.

The Guest-Worker Option. The Reagan administration has proposed a pilot guest-worker program and may even be able to get it enacted into law. Yet the problems with such legislation could be staggering. The pilot program would allow 50,000 Mexicans to enter the United States for a year at a time. The temporary migrants would be allowed to work only in those sectors of the economy where there was a certifiable shortage of labor. Once their time was up, they would be expected to return to Mexico. The details of the program, and even its passage by Congress, are uncertain at this writing, so rather than speculate about them, let us turn to what the literature has to offer concerning guest-worker programs.

A good starting point is the recent paper by Martin and Sehgal who maintain that a guest-worker program would have a number of problems.[2] The first concerns civil rights. In the view of the authors, guest workers would become *de jure* second-class citizens, with their rights severely limited. Certainly, the exact extent of their rights and obligations under law is unclear and would need to be worked out in the courts. One need not strain to think of complex cases. For example, suppose a guest worker, who has been in the United States for his prescribed duration, buys an automobile in preparation for his return to Mexico. He gets into an accident in which someone is killed, and a suit is filed against him by the decedent's spouse. Will the defendant then be allowed to leave the country? Problems clearly arise, whether or not he is allowed to leave.

It seems likely that a guest-worker program would cause innumerable legal tangles. The courts could be jammed with cases concerning the rights and obligations of the guest workers. It would be difficult to predict a priori whether the cumulative effect of such rulings would be to define the rights and obligations of the new class of temporary residents in a manner acceptable to the majority of Americans. As with any guest-worker scheme, this would be a social cost that must be included in any final reckoning of the desirability of this type of program.

Another problem that Martin and Sehgal broach is more basic. It is unclear whether employer access to massive flows of guest workers would help solve a long-run labor shortage problem. The argument goes roughly as follows. In the long run, both the techniques of production and the nature of technical change depend on the relative availability of each factor of production. A large increase in the availability of low-skilled labor could lead U.S. industry, in the long run, to create jobs suitable for low-skilled labor. This, in turn, may cause two sorts of problems: an "addiction" to low-wage, low-skilled labor, and a redirection of research and development efforts away from those areas most likely to be highly productive in the long run.

[2] P. L. Martin and E. F. Sehgal, "Illegal Immigration: The Guest Worker Option," *Public Policy*, 28, no. 2 (spring 1980), 207–29.

The addiction hazard is based on the notion that in the long run there is a relationship of simultaneous causation between factor availabilities and utilized technology, but that in the short run painful imbalances can occur. By this reasoning, the availability of guest workers from Mexico would lead U.S. businesses either to design jobs that effectively utilize these workers or simply to refrain from upgrading current jobs. Thus, in the long run, U.S. businesses would develop a need for low-skilled workers. Perhaps a short-run labor shortage can be cured with a guest-worker program, but a long-run shortage, so the argument goes, could not be because of the long-run adjustment process. In the short run, however, businesses that have developed a need for large numbers of low-skilled workers can be hard pressed if the supply of such workers diminishes.

The implications of this addiction to low-wage labor require careful consideration. If for one reason or another the supply of guest workers from Mexico diminishes sharply, U.S. businesses will have a strong incentive to lobby for guest workers from other countries. A guest-worker program, then, would be difficult to end, even when the supply of guest workers from Mexico diminishes. Such a program, even if instituted to cope with a short-run labor shortage, would have no natural long-run terminus. The potential for addiction is clear, but what could subsequently be done about it is not. Here again the difficulty of planning for the expected becomes painfully evident.

The second aspect of the issue, concerning technology, is more subtle, but potentially of great importance. The kinds of industrial techniques in place determine in part the nature of technological progress. This is true because a portion of technological change comes about as a by-product of experience with techniques in actual use and concerns how to improve those techniques. There is an interaction, therefore, with the techniques in place and the sorts of technical progress resulting from advances in science and engineering. A brief example, perhaps, will help to clarify this point. Japanese automobile manufacturers facing a relative shortage of labor have been assembling their automobiles with the use of industrial robots. In the United States, in contrast, comparatively high unemployment and scarce capital have led to far less use of such robots. A guest-worker program that provided a large pool of low-wage, low-skilled workers would be another inducement for U.S. automobile manufacturers to maintain their relatively labor-intensive methods of production. To date, even the development of microcomputers, which have greatly increased the productivity of industrial robots, has had little impact on U.S. automobile production techniques.

There are additional feedbacks that must also be considered here. Microcomputers surely influence the productivity of industrial robots, but, in the long run, the use of microprocessors in industrial robots will influence the design of new generations of microprocessors. If the industrial robots are mainly Japanese and the new robot-oriented microprocessors are also Japanese, the United States will find itself no longer in the technological vanguard of two important industries.

The point here is a general one. It is unclear whether developing more jobs for low-skilled individuals is the direction that is best for U.S. technology. Perhaps the best long-run strategy is to follow the lead of the Japanese and utilize more labor-saving techniques of production. A guest-worker program will probably affect U.S. productivity growth. The precise effects will depend on the details of the program, but there are some a priori suspicions that the effects may be detrimental. How should this factor be weighted when we consider the desirability of a guest-worker program?

Another problem raised by Martin and Sehgal concerns whether the guest workers would really remain in the United States temporarily or whether they would form a de facto group of permanent migrants. This question must be dealt with from a number of different perspectives. Guest-worker programs are by their nature temporary worker programs. Their attractiveness to employers stems in part from their impact on wages. In addition, the elasticity that the guest workers provide to the labor supply gives employers considerable leverage in administering discipline by means of firings. When all is said and done, however, the employees must still produce output—and to this end some form of training is necessary. European experience suggests that once hard-working, low-wage trained workers are identified, firms try to avoid sending them back to their country of origin. This was often possible because of loopholes written into the law, which allowed employers to appeal on various grounds. The guest workers could also appeal, and the result was a temporary labor force that grew progressively more permanent.

Consider for a moment the circumstances of a guest-worker who has done well in the United States. He will have acquired training that is valuable in the U.S. labor market, and the respect of his employer. Suppose now that the U.S. government wants to send him home, but his company wants him to remain. Some workers would leave, but some would certainly go underground and remain. If the guest-worker program were a large one, the number of those who went underground could be substantial.

Many problems could arise because workers, originally thought to be temporary, turn out to be permanent. A somewhat less direct variation on this theme is that the number of temporary workers admitted into the

United States may, for political reasons, be somewhat inflexible. Envision for the moment a world-wide recession like the one experienced in 1974, and consider the effect of a substantial increase in unemployment on the programs. Initially, many politicians would try to lower the number of guest workers in the country, which is exactly what many European countries did in 1974. Now envision the response of the Mexican government to the plan of returning the guest workers just at the time when unemployment in Mexico was also particularly high. If the United States were to move unilaterally, Mexico could retaliate in a number of ways. If the United States and Mexican governments were to negotiate over the number of workers, the issue might not be resolved for years. Even if it were, there would probably be less flexibility in the number of guest workers than the United States would wish for.

Two conclusions follow from this discussion. First, during recessions guest workers may not leave the United States fast enough to avoid causing substantial unemployment in certain local labor markets. Since the government will have admitted the guest workers, people would first put pressure on it to remove them and might then show frustration with the government's seeming impotence in achieving any action. Second, for some time, the numbers of guest workers might follow a ratchet-type pattern, increasing during business expansions, but not decreasing during contractions. Thus, the questions of permanence and flexibility further bedevil any attempt to implement a guest-worker program.

Martin and Sehgal raise one more broad question about guest-worker programs that is of central importance. Would they bring an end to large-scale illegal migration into the United States? The answer depends, naturally, on the details of the program, but it seems unlikely that illegal migration will be completely halted by any such device. The program could just change the balance between the legal and the illegal flows.

This assessment is based on several factors. First, if the number of temporary workers admitted to the United States is less than the number of those who would like to come, there will always be an incentive for some people to enter illegally. Second, for those who want to settle permanently, it is unclear whether it is preferable to enter illegally at the outset or to enter legally and then not return as required. Some people will choose the first strategy, and some the second. Whatever strategy is elected, the end result will be the same—they stay in either case. Third, there will always be those whose intention had been to return to Mexico, but who have been so successful that they opt to stay in the United States even without a legal status. Fourth, the larger the group of guest workers, the easier it is for illegals to go underground. Even the massive programs in Europe were accompanied by sizable illegal flows estimated as being between 10 and 20 percent of the legal flow. Thus, a guest-worker program probably would not eliminate illegal migration from Mexico to the United States, but it might make the flow more manageable.

It would not be extreme to say that guest-worker programs are fraught with difficulties and uncertainties that could lead to policy paralysis in coping with undocumented migration. Difficulties and uncertainties do not, however, stand in the way of program implementation. People propose or reject programs, just as people stand to gain or lose from the implementation of a given program. In the case of a guest-worker program, the gainers and the losers are easy to identify. Employers gain from having a large volume of low-wage domestic labor available, and laborers lose from having more competition. The distribution of benefits is of course more complex, for not all employers gain from a guest-worker program. If a particular employer cannot hire guest workers and his competitors can, the employer who cannot hire guest workers is put at a comparative disadvantage vis-à-vis those of his competitors who can; he may even be put out of business. Further, there are some employers who use the migration system as a means of breaking U.S. labor laws. They do not pay social security tax, health or unemployment compensation insurance, and, to boot, they pay the illegal migrants less than the minimum wage. A guest-worker program could make such violations of the law more difficult and thus hurt the employers who commit them. On the whole, large corporations who currently pay minimum wages and social security taxes will have a short-term gain from the guest-worker programs.

In the same way, not all workers would be harmed by a guest-worker program. Professionals and managers will find that the guest workers do not compete vigorously with them. Indeed, their standard of living may increase because the prices of various commodities they consume, such as maid service, may fall. The poor in the United States are those who will suffer if there is a guest-worker program because the immigrants will compete directly with them for jobs.

A guest-worker program, then, would not provide a trouble-free solution to the problem of undocumented migration from Mexico to the United States. Any such program would be fraught with such political and social difficulties that it would be unattractive to the unmotivated social reformer. It is precisely in such configurations of potential problems that policy paralysis is most likely to occur.

The Status Quo Option. The Carter administration proposals concerning amnesty and employer sanctions have been accepted by the Reagan administration and the pilot guest-worker program added to them. The result, of course, is the recurring question: what's wrong with the status quo? In fact, it does have a number of advantages. For example, although the employees of the Immigration and Naturalization Service do indeed have to work very hard, we in the United States do not have a gigantic government bureaucracy administering either a guest-worker program or a national identity card system. And, since illegal migrants enter and leave the country largely as economic conditions dictate,[3] there is also no government bureaucracy telling the migrants in which industries to work or not to work. Furthermore, the migrants often pay taxes for which they receive few benefits, and the poor with whom they compete cannot complain to the government as long as it is ostensibly trying to keep the migrants out.

Who loses under the present system? Clearly, the working poor, but perhaps not as much as under a formal guest-worker program. The migrants themselves gain, or they would not come to the United States. Their gains are offset to some extent by the lack of legal status and the poor working conditions they experience. Their employers gain from their very presence. Under a guest-worker program the gains might shift, but they would persist.

Who stands to make a dramatic gain if the status quo is altered? The Carter administration proposals would perhaps have aided the U.S. working poor at the expense of the Mexican migrants and the U.S. business community. A guest-worker program could perhaps aid the U.S. business community somewhat and the Mexican migrants at the expense of the poor. The combination proposed by the Reagan administration has elements that offend both the labor and business communities, and it remains to be seen whether the benefits of a change outweigh its costs to any group.

The status quo option is an attractive one for the U.S. government, partly because it avoids dealing with migration policy and partly because of the difficulties and uncertainties associated with other options. In the Carter administration, policy paralysis developed because the government posed only unworkable and unattractive alternatives to the status quo. The November 1980 political shock to the American political system may have temporarily reduced the paralysis, but a long-run cure for it is not yet at hand.

Policy Paralysis in Mexico

My treatment of policy paralysis in Mexico will be briefer than my treatment of that condition in the United States. There was, until recently, only one position regarding Mexican migration to the United States—

---

[3] Since it is risky for undocumented migrants to claim unemployment compensation, there is a clear economic incentive for them to leave when jobs for them disappear.

that it was a solution to a problem, not a problem itself. The analysis which led to that position is easily stated and is interesting from the point of view of policy paralysis. Mexico has followed a development strategy that has been remarkably successful. Development has proceeded in a capital-intensive manner, with much of the growth concentrated in a few regions. This has caused two interrelated and potentially severe problems. First, many rural poor were left out of the internal dynamics of the Mexican development process. This left them, by and large, with three operative choices: to remain on the land and suffer, to migrate to a large city in Mexico, or to migrate to the United States temporarily and return with some money for capital improvements. The different options people chose are interrelated, and here the second problem enters. Migration to major Mexican cities, particularly Mexico City, may have begun to produce diseconomies of scale. Faster, and some even say further, growth of Mexico City may be economically quite costly.

Migration, then, has helped Mexican development in a number of ways. First, in several Mexican states, the United States has been a provider of capital for rural development. This capital has come not from aid programs, but from the hard work and savings of energetic people. In and of itself, it has been important to Mexican economic growth. It has freed the Mexican government to concentrate on urban economic growth without thoroughly alienating the rural populace, and it has aided rural economic development. Had migration to the United States not been possible, many of the migrants would probably have moved to Mexican cities, where they might have aggravated urban congestion and would perhaps not have been able to save as much money as in the United States. The result would probably have been more urban problems, still more unequal economic growth, and lower per capita income growth.

All in all, then, migration to the United States may have been a solution to a problem and may continue to be. This does not mean, however, that of itself it has not caused problems. First, its very success has meant that a substantial segment of the Mexican population has enjoyed what might be called a migration dividend—extra disposable income derived either from work in, or from the remittances of family members who work in, the United States. This income is a problem in the sense that a U.S. anti-migration policy would have important destabilizing effects both on Mexico's economic and on its political life. Second, a substantial number of Mexican citizens are now poorly treated each year in the United States. The Mexican government feels that the undocumented migrants should be treated better, but has not pushed the point vigorously.

The Mexican government, then, has two priorities with respect to migration: the first economic, and the second political. On the economic side the Mexican government wants to continue the current policy of relatively free access of its citizens to the U.S. labor market. To do this it tries to block U.S. policies, aimed at reducing the migration flow. On the political side, and thus of secondary priority, is the attempt to ameliorate the working and living conditions of Mexican citizens in the United States.

The reasons for policy paralysis in Mexico are clear. The present policy is not bad, and there are no effective unilateral options open to the Mexican government that could make the situation much better. Mexico can give the United States certain oil concessions in exchange for better treatment of undocumented migrants, but this would not address the main issue of concern to the Mexican government, a guarantee that the flow of migrants can continue more or less unhindered. The real bargaining must be over the access of Mexican nationals to the U.S. labor market.

In this perspective the status quo may seem adequate. Even without negotiations or concessions Mexicans have access to the U.S. labor market, although perhaps not on optimum terms. Thus there is little to be gained—and perhaps much to be lost—from altering the status quo.

Joint Paralysis in United States–Mexico Migration Policies

Under the Carter administration there was no joint Mexico–United States action on migration because the United States wanted more restricted migration and Mexico wanted no new restrictions. The administration might perhaps have forced the issue if it had found a formula that was domestically acceptable. The goals of the Reagan administration and the Mexican government are not so diametrically opposed. The former would like to assure a controlled flow of low-wage labor to U.S. industry and the latter would like to assure that the United States does not suddenly disrupt the migration and remittance flow. The difficulty with cooperation lies in the locus of control. The U.S. government would like effective control over the annual migration flows in order to tailor the flows to U.S. labor market and social conditions. The Mexican government would like effective control over the annual migration flows to tailor these flows to Mexican labor market and social conditions.

Can the policies of the two governments be reconciled? Will the partial losses of control inherent in such a compromise be acceptable to the two governments, or will the status quo prevail? In order to answer this question, it will be necessary to determine both the costs of not compromising—of allowing the paralysis to persist—and the true costs of such a compromise.

POLICY PARALYSIS AND POLICY FAILURE

What will happen if the current policy persists? Even though the question cannot be answered with precision, we can at least analyze some of the determining factors. Within the next few years the demographic situation of young people in the United States will alter dramatically. Instead of growing larger every year, the absolute number of young workers between the ages of twenty and twenty-nine will shrink between 1980 and 1990 at a rate of 0.4 percent per year, and between 1990 and 2000 by an average of 1.3 percent per year, if labor-force participation rates are held constant at their 1977 levels. Unless the participation rates for young females increase dramatically, the shrinkage in the number of young U.S. workers between now and the year 2000 will be a jarring demographic shock that will have a potent effect in inducing young Mexican adults to migrate to the United States.

The precise magnitude of the migration response is difficult to predict. We do know that in this same period the number of twenty- to twenty-nine-year-old males will be growing rapidly—by about 1.9 percent per year from 1980 to 1990, and by about 1.7 percent per year from 1990 to 2000.[4] Although we do not know what the performances of the respective national economies will be, we may presume that, other things being equal, the migration flow will be positively correlated with the rate of U.S. economic growth and negatively correlated with the rate of Mexican economic growth.

Even such simple theorizing, however, does not move us much closer to the goal of understanding the reaction in the United States to increased migration from Mexico. This reaction itself depends in a complex way on the same economic conditions. Migration may generate less hostility when the labor market is slack than when it is tight. On the other hand, if the migration wave itself causes the market for unskilled labor to be weak, while other labor markets in the country are tight, the reactions of the affected unskilled laborers may be quite strong.

Consider for a moment the following scenario. Communities where the illegal migrants flock can welcome them with open arms. They can commend the migrants for breaking U.S. law and providing the labor necessary for the factories, restaurants, and hotels in their area to make large profits. They can raise their taxes so that the local school district can afford to hire a few extra teachers who specialize in bilingual education. And when the migrants leave, taking with them the money they

[4]Secretaría de Programación y Presupuesto, "Proyecciones de la población Mexicana, 1970–2000," *Evaluación y Análisis*, ser. 3, no. 8 (Mexico, 1978), 61.

have not spent locally, the community banks can provide them with free peso-denominated travelers' checks.

That scenario, however, is about as likely as that everyone in the San Francisco Bay Area would react calmly to the news that there will probably be a major earthquake in the next seventy-two hours. The more likely reaction in the case of the earthquake warning is panic—in the case of a massive wave of illegal migration, antagonism and violence and strong pressure on the government "to do something about it." It will not matter much, at this point, what action the government takes. If U.S. citizens feel resentful toward those Mexicans who have entered their country illegally, their feelings will be mirrored by the Mexicans, who will feel unjustly betrayed and maligned.

The point of mutual bitterness and antagonism is the point of policy failure—a point of discontinuity in the relations between the United States and Mexico, affecting trade and investment as well as migration. Once we have reached the point of policy failure, it would be very difficult to return to the *status quo ante*, because the ensuing interrelated domestic ramifications, in both countries, will tend to exacerbate the situation. For example, suppose, in response to anti-Mexican incidents in the United States, the Mexican government decides to limit oil exports to the United States. Such action would in turn increase anti-Mexican sentiment. On the other hand, if the policy failure led to a reduction in the migration flow, many facets of the Mexican economy might be negatively affected, and the resulting difficulties would add to anti-United States feelings. In this way, the policy failure could trigger a self-reinforcing set of events that would severely strain relations between the two countries.

The foregoing scenario is not meant as a prediction of the future, but rather as a statement of a potential problem with our existing institutional technology. We know that a demographic shock is coming, but we do not know how the system will react to it. Perhaps the rapid demographic changes will cause no serious problems. It seems possible, however, that the shock could cause a grave rift in Mexico–United States relations. The lack of a backup procedure designed to prevent the shock from causing a "systems failure" is a deficiency in the current institutional technology.

It is important to note in passing that this deficiency is not solely the responsibility of the United States. If a policy failure occurs, Mexico can play the part of the aggrieved mate and win some public relations points at the expense of the United States. Certainly, both the right wing and the left wing in Mexican politics will use the anti-United States feelings for whatever short-run political gains they can muster. Still, there would be no escaping the fact that the Mexican government's policy of assuring access to the U.S. labor market for its citizens would have failed. Indeed, the consequent economic, social, and political disruptions in Mexico would represent policy failures as well.

If antagonism over undocumented migration were to cause a serious deterioration in their relationship, both Mexico and the United States would suffer. It follows, then, that both parties stand to gain from planning for the expected and protecting that relationship against pending demographic changes. There are also potential losses from such planning, as the discussion concerning policy paralysis amply illustrates. Should Mexico and the United States gamble that all will be well? To answer this question requires that we shift to a somewhat lower level of abstraction in order to gain some insight into the nature of Mexican migration to the United States.

SOME FACTUAL DETAILS

A Brief History of Mexican Migration to the United States

The migration of Mexicans to the United States began in earnest in the late nineteenth century, with the coming of rapid economic development to the U.S. Southwest. In the first two decades of the twentieth century, Mexicans found employment chiefly in three lines of work: railroads (particularly construction and maintenance), agriculture, and general, unskilled manual labor. The strong demand for labor in the Southwest in the decades before the First World War clearly determined the timing of the first substantial wave of migration from Mexico and probably influenced the level of the flow as well.

Demand factors, however, were not the only operative forces. The Mexican Revolution, which began in 1910 and continued sporadically for over a decade, provided both economic and noneconomic motives for migration to the United States. The movement was made easier in the early twentieth century by the completion of railroad lines linking Mexico's populous central plateau region to the U.S. Southwest.

The concern over "illegal" migration began in 1917 with the implementation of the Immigration Act of that year, which required that every immigrant who was over sixteen years old be literate in at least one language and pay an $8.00 tax upon entry. The results were wholly predictable. The first "undocumented" migrants crossed the border from Mexico, and immigration officials began complaining that they had too few employees to police the border. Also, as one would expect, employers of Mexican migrants began a vigorous lobbying campaign to exempt their employees from the new rule. This campaign met with temporary success during the war, and after the war the reinstitution of the old rules caused no hardship to employers. The border remained essentially unpatrolled, and the tradition of undocumented migration was already well established.

The postwar recession of 1921–22 was the first serious recession to have affected the fledgling Mexican community in the United States. What happened was, of course, not one of the finer moments in U.S. history. Racist acts of violence and terrorism abounded. In Fort Worth, Texas, unemployed Mexicans were arrested for vagrancy, taken to jail by the truckload, and sentenced to work on chain gangs; in Ranger, Texas, Mexican families were beaten by a gang of masked thugs and ordered out of town; and these stories can be multiplied many times. What transpired is an all too common response—a majority group taking out frustrations over its economic setbacks on a weak and destitute minority. With the coming of better times in 1923, the hostility toward Mexican immigrants abated and the flow of migrants from Mexico resumed.

The unfortunate circumstances of the early 1920s were replayed in the Great Depression of the 1930s—and with a vengeance. The novel element here was the concept of "voluntary deportation," applied on a local level to Mexican-American communities. Between 1931 and 1934 over 13,000 Mexicans were returned from Los Angeles County alone. For the country as a whole the number may well have been several hundred thousand, though no data were systematically collected on these cases of voluntary deportation.

The depression brought with it a temporary halt in migration. With the onset of the Second World War and the initiation of the *bracero* program in 1942, substantial migration from Mexico resumed. The termination of the program in 1964, however, did little to retard the flow of migrants. The U.S. labor market was relatively tight, and individuals who wanted to migrate simply did what similar people had been doing since 1917— they became the army of undocumented migrants.

Undocumented Migration Today

Recent quantitative studies of the phenomenon of undocumented migration from Mexico have now yielded a set of fairly consistent estimates for the mid-1970s. García y Griego (1980), in a pathbreaking study, has derived estimates of the net and gross annual flows of undocumented migrants for the years 1972 through 1976.[5] These data, based on informa-

---

[5] M. García y Griego, *El volumen de la migración de Mexicanos no documentados a los Estados Unidos (nuevas hipótesis)*, ser. ENEFNEU, subser. Estudios 4 (Mexico, 1980), p. 527. See also the paper by García in this volume.

TABLE I

Estimates of Annual Gross and Net Flow of Deportable Mexicans
into the United States, 1972–76

(thousands)

Year	Gross flow[a]			Net flow[b]		
	Low	High	Average	Low	High	Average
1972	465	1,497	981	12	39	26
1973	545	1,770	1,158	28	131	80
1974	651	2,139	1,395	20	77	49
1975	680	2,239	1,460	75	256	166
1976	799	2,591	1,659	113	284	198
Average	628	2,043	1,331	50	157	104

SOURCE: García y Griego, El volumen de la migración de Mexicanos no documentados a los Estados Unidos (nuevas hipótesis), ser. ENEFNEU, no. 4 (Mexico, 1980), ch. 5, table 5.2.
[a]Entries into deportable status.
[b]Difference between entries and exits from deportable status.

tion produced by the INS and on information gathered from a border survey taken in the autumn of 1977, show a clear relationship between net
and gross flows (Table 1). The average annual net immigration flow between 1972 and 1976 from Mexico to the United States was between a
low estimate of 50,000 and a high of 157,000 people, while the average
gross flow was more than twelve times as great—between a low of
628,000 and a high of 2,043,000.

The same phenomenon is evident in the data on the distribution of deportable Mexicans, based on their length of stay in the United States (as
of January 1, 1977). Of that group roughly 45 percent had been in the
country for less than one year, and only about 10 percent continuously
for five years or more.[6]

The thrust of García y Griego's computations is supported by a number of studies using other methodologies. Heer and Robinson, in two
very different studies, have found relatively low net migration figures
which are roughly consistent with García y Griego's. Studies by Reichert
and Massey and by Cornelius provide interesting and consistent data on
the return flow. According to a sample collected by Cornelius among
families with some history of migration to the United States in the period
1930–76, temporary migrants outnumbered permanent settlers by a
ratio of 8 to 1. Reichert and Massey found that 90 percent of the migrants from their study-village returned home for two to four months

[6]Ibid., table 5.1, p. 523.

each year.[7] All of these studies support the view that the bulk of the gross flow of undocumented migrants is temporary.

There is an implication of this large temporary flow of migrants back and forth across the border which deserves mention here. In their village Reichert and Massey calculated that 79 percent of the population was dependent in some way on wages earned in the United States. Clearly, the economic life of that village is closely connected with the experience of undocumented and temporary migrants. Cornelius suggests that perhaps two million such migrants work in the United States in the course of a year. If this is the case, more than 21 percent of the entire population of Mexico at the present time depends to some extent on income earned in the United States. Cornelius' estimate is corroborated by García y Griego's figures. Taking the midpoint of the low and high estimates of the gross flow for 1976 yields 1.7 million, and the current figure may be much higher. The policy of the U.S. government toward undocumented migrants, then, can potentially have an enormous impact on the economic well-being of the Mexican populace.

The current situation, then, appears to differ from the historical experience. Poor economic conditions in the United States were typically disastrous for Mexican migrants. Now that temporary migration is so common, however, U.S. government policy can influence more Mexican citizens than ever before, both directly and indirectly. An obvious corollary to this judgment is that policy mistakes on the part of the U.S. government will produce far more disgruntlement in Mexico than one might believe on the basis of the net migration figures.

TOWARD A JOINT POLICY

The migration statistics provide a new perspective from which to answer the question, whether planning for the expected was preferable to a continuation of the present institutional arrangements. Of particular relevance is the importance to the people of Mexico of money earned in the United States. The direct cost to them of a policy failure in the field of migration is probably greater now than ever before. It is significant, too, that the vast majority of undocumented Mexican migrants come for a brief period and leave of their own volition.

The first point suggests that the cost of noncooperation may be quite

[7]D. M. Heer, "What Is the Annual Net Flow of Undocumented Mexican Immigrants to the United States?" *Demography*, 16, no.3 (August 1979), 417–24; J. G. Robinson, "Estimating the Approximate Size of the Illegal Alien Population in the United States by the Comparative Trend Analysis of Age-Specific Death Rates," *Demography*, 17, no. 2 (May 1980), 159–76; J. Reichert and D. S. Massey, "History and Trends in U.S.-Bound Migration from a Central Mexican Town," ms., xeroxed (August 1979); W. Cornelius, *Mexican*

high, just as the second suggests that the cost of some sort of joint program may be relatively low. It would, naturally, be easier to administer a program of temporary labor market participation in the United States among individuals who themselves have chosen such a regime than among a group who are bent mainly on permanent residence. Together these two considerations, then, tilt the balance in favor of cooperation.

This is not the place to present the details of such a joint program which would meet the objections already discussed. The initial step is to achieve a recognition among policy makers in both countries that some sort of anticipatory migration program is desirable. To this end, a tentative set of principles can be suggested on which such a policy could be based. Once the principles are accepted, work on the details can follow.

In the first place, the number of temporary migrant permits (technically, we should deal in what might be called migrant-years because some migrants may not remain for an entire year) must be decided periodically by a joint Mexican-U.S. commission established for the purpose. This principle will please neither government fully, because in some sense it limits their sovereign powers. But the United States and Mexico are so interlinked that effectively neither country has control over the migrant flow, and joint control is certainly to be preferred to no control. Formal governmental recognition of this interdependence seems to be a crucial step toward an effective migration policy.

The second principle should be to provide positive incentives for the migrants to adhere to the policy. Positive incentives are more effective than negative ones, and a policy which enlists the voluntary cooperation of the migrants will be more effective than one which tries to influence them through compulsion. What kind of incentives are available? Among other possibilities, lump-sum payments to migrants upon their return to Mexico would have a positive effect. The U.S. government could transfer to the Mexican government the employee's share of social security tax payments made during his stay in the United States. This amount, about 8 percent of an individual's wage income, would accumulate to a considerable sum. The Mexican government, then, could implement the program for proper distribution of the funds. While in the United States the migrants should be allowed to participate in certain social benefit programs such as Medicaid. Priority treatment for future temporary stays in the United States might also be given to the migrant and his or her family members, as still another incentive.

One important positive element might lie in special consideration for

---

Migration to the United States: Causes, Consequences, and U.S. Responses, Migration and Development Study Group Monograph C/78-9 (Cambridge, Mass., 1978).

permanent admission into the United States. A set of regulations could stipulate that migrants who have successfully completed a certain number of work periods and who want to live in the United States permanently be considered as a special category for purposes of admission. This would provide an incentive to join the system rather than reject it; it would also provide a carefully controlled means of admitting permanent migrants from Mexico. Lacking the negative features which are currently prevalent, the new program would have a more positive impact. The border crossing would be safer, and migrants would not have to pay "coyotes" to help them cross it. They would also have a legal status and would not be hounded by the INS.

There are undoubtedly many other effective, positive incentives which could be implemented. A migration policy based on these incentives helps the Mexican government achieve its goal of protecting Mexican citizens in the United States. Further, such a policy is likely to elicit cooperation from the migrants and thus would require lower policing costs.

The third principle on which such a migration policy should be based concerns the maximum duration of stay which, with rare exceptions, should never exceed twelve months. Repeat stays after a suitable interval should of course be allowed. A work tour of three months every year might be allowed, for example, but not repeated work tours of a year separated by a month's vacation in Mexico. In general, the guiding notion here should be that the migration program give Mexicans the opportunity of working temporarily in the U.S. labor market. Employers should not be encouraged to become overly dependent on any one individual worker. However much they may dislike the idea of limiting to one year the duration of any given work tour, employers will gain significantly from the migration policy and must make some compromises to implement it.

Another tentative principle does not, unfortunately, go without saying: that the working conditions of the migrants meet the conditions mandated by law for U.S. workers. Migrants would have to be paid at least the minimum wage, and employers would have to apply to them the same health and safety guidelines as to natives. This provision too might bring objections from some segments of the business community, but it is imperative that the migrants be protected from the abuses of illegal employers.

The final principle for consideration is to provide relief for the poor in the United States. They are, after all, the ones who would be hurt most by the migration system. I propose that the employer's share of social security tax payments be put into a fund to be established for that specific purpose. The annual contributions would then vary with the magnitude of the controlled migration flow.

Implementation of these principles would result in a program that would satisfy the bulk of the current undocumented migrants from Mexico to the United States. It is a just program and one that the governments of both Mexico and the United States can endorse. Each side compromises to some extent in order to achieve some measure of joint control over the migration flow.

This still leaves those who want to remain permanently in the United States—some of whom will voluntarily participate in the temporary worker program if there is a meaningful chance that it would lead to citizenship. Some people, however, will still enter the United States illegally. This is inevitable. The INS, freed from some of its more onerous chores, could continue trying to find these individuals according to standard operating procedures. Perhaps, with the agreement of Mexico, this relatively small group could be given a punishment stronger than just being returned home.

CONCLUSION

The United States and Mexico have been suffering from policy paralysis. This paralysis could lead to a policy failure that would damage the relationship between the two countries. The cure for the paralysis is knowledge—knowledge both of the implications of a policy failure and of the costs of preventing it. For us, as responsible scholars, the agenda must be to agree on some common programmatic principles and to begin the work of educating policy makers on the need for action before a crisis—for expecting the expected, however difficult that task may be.

Comments on Bustamante and Sanderson Papers and on Research Project ENEFNEU

Manuel García y Griego

B EFORE summarizing the findings of some current research on Mexican immigration, I should like to comment on the provocative papers by Jorge Bustamante and Warren Sanderson. Both authors describe migration from Mexico to the United States within the context of the debate on current policy proposals in the United States; both are attentive to the long historical evolution of this migration; both contrast the perceptions of it as a social process and as a political problem; both stress the differences in the manner in which the political problem is perceived north and south of the border; and both examine the migration policies that have touched upon this process. Yet Sanderson and Bustamante differ sharply in their approach to the problem, in the manner in which they define it, and in their preferred policy prescriptions.

WHAT IS THE PROBLEM?

The most visible component of Bustamante's analysis emerges as a "scapegoat scenario," which can be described as a series of mutually connected propositions: the U.S. tendency to define immigrants as the cause of a domestic social problem in times of high unemployment; in response, the public demand for stricter immigration policies; subsequent U.S. government response, entailing coercive actions; and, finally, the subsiding of the problem as the economic crisis recedes. On another level, Bustamante stresses that crises and restrictive policies are an intermittent feature of U.S. government behavior. A constant feature—even during recession—is that the government has consistently "insure[d] the supply of Mexican labor at the least possible cost" to those most in need of it in the private sector. Thus, while Bustamante suggests that a paradox exists in U.S. immigration policies, he does not explain it. While the articulation of such policies, and their execution, has zig-zagged between opening and closing the door to immigration at various points in time, it is not clear how the U.S. government can act to restrict and at the same moment to promote migratory flows.

He identifies the U.S. desire to enjoy the benefits of Mexican migrant labor on the one hand, while on the other shunning or attributing social costs to it, as the root of the contradictory nature of the policy proposals presently being considered in the United States. Bustamante's allusion to the "conditional" opening and closing of the border is both apt and revealing. It reflects the author's view—which I share—that the paradoxical nature of U.S. policies and the present domestic political environment are not likely to yield long-term policy responses from the United States that either open the door very widely or close it very tightly. Although he does not offer a set of proposals to bring the U.S. policy-making process into touch with the realities of migration as a social phenomenon, one is left with the impression that Bustamante would argue that a step in the right direction would be for U.S. policy makers, like their Mexican counterparts, to recognize migration as a structural phenomenon, as a semi-permanent feature of United States–Mexico relations. Put in other terms, if the U.S. position were to shift away from conjunctural scapegoating and closer to the Mexican position, Bustamante would envision a more constructive approach that would "rationalize" the flow of migrant workers.

Sanderson's argument, by contrast, sees migration as that component most likely to fail in the complex, delicate mechanism that he considers Mexico–United States relations. Its failure would ultimately lead to a core meltdown, i.e., to a serious breakdown in the relations between the two countries across many issue-areas. In this context, Sanderson concludes that continuing on our present course without new policy responses or attempts at solutions is a prescription for disaster.

He projects an "escalation-to-disaster" scenario that can be described as a series of mutually connected propositions: a rapidly rising volume of undocumented immigration; a strong negative reaction by the U.S. public, and especially by "affected unskilled laborers"; the domestic responses to these perceptions, leading to U.S. unilateral and restrictive policies toward Mexican migration; escalation to a strong Mexican reaction against U.S. policies; and, as the ultimate outcome, a negative-sum condition for both countries, in which both lose substantially from a rupture in relations and as a result of the spreading of conflict into other issue-areas such as trade and investment. In Sanderson's view, what is needed is for both governments to recognize that inaction is inevitably leading toward disaster, that their societies are greatly interdependent, that each country is vulnerable to actions taken by the other, and that the only way to prevent disaster is to cooperate.

As we can see, the two views as to what constitutes the "problem" are quite different, though not altogether incompatible. Notwithstanding differences in approach and in emphasis, the two papers do share the view that migration can be "rationalized" in the interests of the principal actors concerned. Thus, both authors agree that the elements of a positive-sum condition exist, and even agree on some of the key ingredients that establish that condition. And, although they seem to differ sharply on the specific policy prescriptions they prefer, a close reading of their arguments suggests that some proposals not explicitly developed in these papers would largely coincide with the thrust of both approaches.

WHAT ARE THE POLICY PRESCRIPTIONS?

Sanderson proposes a guest-worker program jointly controlled by the Mexican and United States governments. Though well-intentioned, the proposal has a number of serious problems, which I will outline. Its basic fault is that it overlooks a relevant historical experience that will be cited by its opponents, both in the United States and in Mexico: namely, the lessons that can be drawn from the so-called bracero program, a mechanism administered by both governments to control the distribution of 4.6 million contract workers from Mexico to the United States during a twenty-two-year period. Ironically, the creation of the program was itself a response to a very different "disaster" scenario, one involving "severe" labor shortages—whether real or imagined—that persisted uninterrupted in U.S. agriculture between 1942 and 1964. Clearly, contemporary interpretations of the operation and demise of this program will influence future debate concerning the social costs and benefits associated with any temporary worker program similar to that proposed by Sanderson.

A review of some of the reasons why the program was terminated unilaterally by the United States in 1964 may be instructive.[1] Opposition to the program was led by the AFL-CIO, and, as one might expect, the most important argument raised against it was the notion that braceros displaced domestic workers, undermined agriculture strikes, and contributed to the deterioration of local working conditions. Although the composition and occupational distribution of the bracero labor force of the 1960s are quite different in some respects from that of the undocumented labor force in the 1980s, there is a marked similarity in the arguments used to oppose both. Indeed, it is the possible escalation of such opposi-

---

[1] For further analysis of the bracero program, see García y Griego, "The Importation of Mexican Contract Laborers to the U.S., 1942–1964: Antecedents, Operation and Legacy," Working Papers in United States–Mexican Studies, no. 11 (University of California, San Diego, 1981).

tion in the United States that leads Sanderson to predict future disaster and to consider that a need for serious action exists. Ironically, the kinds of concerns about worker displacement that led to the termination of the program in the 1960s are now evoked to justify the initiation of a new, and perhaps similar, program that would substitute controls on legally admitted workers for undocumented immigrants.

In my opinion, the logic behind such a proposal is flawed. It is based on the assumption that, while the U.S. public, and particularly the affected unskilled workers, may be strongly opposed to undocumented immigration, they will nevertheless be tolerant of foreign (legal and temporary) workers. My discussion of the termination of the bracero program suggests that this is not the case; instead, it appears that the immigration status of foreign workers is not itself at issue. This potential for backlash against immigrants, which apparently has worried Sanderson (and others, including myself) and which constitutes the basis for his prescription for disaster, may arise from the domestic economic environment and from the fact that these workers are foreigners, not from their lack of proper documentation per se. If correct, this deduction would be consistent with Bustamante's suggestion that not only do immigrants serve as scapegoats, but that in the process they legitimize a system that is to blame for the U.S. economic crisis. It would likewise be consistent with another argument, which is that, to the extent that Mexican workers are truly an external presence—as indeed they are to the vast majority of the U.S. public—such workers are more likely to be perceived as a threat.[2]

Another aspect of our experience with the bracero program suggests that, rather than serving as a basis for cooperation, such a program can be a divisive force in Mexico–United States relations. The contract labor agreement put the Mexican government in the position of acting as a bargaining agent for its workers and the United States as a representative of its employers. During the early years of the program, the Mexican negotiators acted—sometimes aggressively—to get higher wage concessions and improved conditions for the workers. The United States acted to oppose these actions and became increasingly successful as time wore on.

This intermittent conflict led to serious ruptures in bilateral relations in October 1948 and again in January 1954. What occurred then may seem anomalous to us now, but those events may be suggestive of future re-

[2]In "America in the Era of Limits: Nativist Reactions to the 'New' Immigration," Working Papers in United States–Mexican Studies, no. 3 (University of California, San Diego, 1982), Wayne Cornelius analyzes nativist attitudes in the United States and notes that it seems to be those persons who are least familiar with Mexican migrants (persons from the Midwest, Northeast, and South, as opposed to the West) and least affected (white, college-educated males) who are most vociferous in their opposition to Mexican immigration and most supportive of restrictive immigration policies.

sponses to a government-to-government contract labor program. In order to gain some concessions, Mexico acted (though unsuccessfully in these cases) to restrain the flow of workers to the north, going so far as to deploy troops along parts of the border on one occasion. The United States, on the other hand, opened its ports of entry to any Mexican who wanted to work in agriculture. Thus, the admission of workers through official channels may set the stage for a series of conflicts perhaps more, rather than less, likely than the status quo to lead to a "core meltdown." In other words, I argue that a program of the type that Sanderson proposes may actually lead to a variant of the disaster that he is trying to avoid.[3]

Finally, the idea that everyone benefits, or can be made to benefit, from such a program is likely to be challenged within the United States as well as in Mexico. If we were to hypothesize that the AFL-CIO position has not changed very much in twenty years,[4] we would expect to hear the argument that domestic labor stands to lose a great deal from the adoption of such a program. Other opponents will surely draw on the research and writings of Ernesto Galarza, who presented irrefutable evidence of massive violations of the terms of the binational agreement by employers during the bracero era.

One important lesson of the bracero program is that employers may be reluctant to participate in a program unless it is watered down to a point where it would be an attractive substitute for undocumented labor. Such employer reluctance was particularly visible during the early years of the bracero program. By 1954 it was considered necessary to launch an all-out attack, called Operation Wetback, on undocumented labor, in order to induce employers and workers to enter into contract labor agreements with the two governments. Thus the notion that, among others, workers will benefit from this alternative, depends to a great extent on how it is implemented and what kinds of actions are taken to make it function as a viable alternative to the status quo.[5]

Whether or not the experiences derived from the bracero program are directly applicable to a concrete proposal for the entry of temporary la-

---

[3] I would argue that the "disaster scenario" also assumes that United States–Mexico relations are notably less resilient than a reading of their long history of conflict and cooperation might suggest; I therefore assign a low probability to the escalation-to-disaster scenario. This does not mean, of course, that the initial steps might not occur, nor that the conflict that would result would not end in a negative-sum situation.

[4] See, for example, "'Extrema' oposición de AFL-CIO a un plan de braceros," in *Excélsior*, January 22, 1981, p.1.

[5] For a graphic discussion of a current preference by some employers for undocumented over legally available workers, a preference not dissimilar from that among farmers during the early phase of the Bracero Program, see Joseph Nalven and Craig Frederickson, *The Employer's View: Is There a Need for a Guest-Worker Program?* (San Diego, Calif., 1982), pp. 30–34.

bor, they will set the tone and shape the policy debate likely to occur with respect to a future guest-worker type program. While it seems theoretically possible to devise a temporary labor proposal that would benefit the principal actors concerned, the political reality is that any such proposal will be haunted by the failures and abuses of the program.

In terms of his preferred policy prescriptions, Bustamante is less explicit, and he does not offer a comparable, concrete proposal. Nevertheless, one does get the impression—from the statement that migration is the result of a "real demand for foreign labor and an excess of unskilled labor in Mexico which can only be corrected in the long run"—that in the short term he is pessimistic about solutions, even partial ones. Thus, ending the flow of undocumented workers will necessitate ending the structural U.S. demand for, and the Mexican supply of, such labor. One can easily see why Bustamante is pessimistic about short-term solutions. Indeed, other writings by him indicate that he would reject a guest-worker solution, even though perhaps for reasons other than those I have given.

While a guest-worker proposal may seem consistent with the acceptance of current migration as a structural phenomenon, I have attempted to show that it is not consistent with Sanderson's policy objectives of avoiding a disaster scenario and of giving something to everyone concerned. However, there are other policy directions, consistent with one or both of these objectives, that flow from other concerns raised by both authors in their discussion of the problem. None of the policy directions that I will discuss, however, implies other than incremental changes in the status quo.

Sanderson argues for a temporary worker program based on the quantitative argument, which I share, that undocumented immigration is largely temporary. However, other policy implications from this data should be considered. If we note, for example, that in the short term the volumes of legal and illegal migration seem to be inversely correlated,[6] one can infer that incremental additions to the number of Mexicans legally admitted will decrease the number of undocumented immigrants from Mexico,[7] and that such relatively small increases (in the tens of

[6] My research indicates that, as the number of Mexican legal immigrants has decreased from about 70,000 to about 40,000, the net flow of "settled" undocumented immigrants has increased by several tens of thousands per year. Manuel García y Griego, *El volumen de la migración de mexicanos no documentados a los Estados Unidos (nuevas hipótesis)* (Mexico, 1980), pp. 421–24, 441–44, 447–50, 452–55, 457–60.

[7] This argument assumes (a) that many of the persons who "settle" in the United States in undocumented status would prefer to have the status of legal immigrants and (b) that both legal and undocumented immigrants are drawn from the same pool of persons. Assumption (a) is supported by the evidence cited in the previous footnote. Assumption (b) is supported

thousands per year) of legal immigration from Mexico may have a significant effect in decreasing net undocumented immigration. One of the policy implications of Sanderson's analysis thus leads us to incremental change in the procedures used for admitting legal immigrants.

Incremental growth in the number of Mexican legal immigrants admitted is the key to this prescription. Such increases could be effected by marginal changes in the worldwide ceiling on "quota" immigrants, or by keeping the same global ceiling but eliminating the numerical limitations of 20,000 per year imposed on each country. Our laws apply this limit to each country, irrespective of its population size, its "supply" of emigrants, or its history of migration to the United States. For migrants from countries such as Mexico, whose number of applicants exceeds the quotas imposed by U.S. laws, the waiting period can be long—several years —whereas the applicants from other countries may have to wait only several months. Indeed, because of 1977 changes in the law some applicants—many who currently reside in the United States as undocumented "settlers"—though technically eligible for admission, may not immigrate within their lifetimes unless some changes are made in the current law. Though such a policy action would affect a relatively small component of the overall flow, it would alleviate some of the gross inequities imposed by current immigration procedures and would furthermore benefit U.S. citizens and residents as well.

Another policy direction would focus on the bulk of the migrant labor force that stays temporarily and works in unskilled jobs for marginal industries. It would call for the more strenuous enforcement of federal, state, and local fair labor standards and minimum wage laws. To the extent that it is marginal employers who hire undocumented workers because they cannot, or will not, offer wages and working conditions attractive to domestic workers, such enforcement would have the effect of either improving working conditions or driving such employers out of business. In the first instance, to the extent that undocumented workers remained in the labor force, the availability of such workers would not itself constitute the primary motivation for the operation of such businesses. In the second instance, jobs that served only to attract undocumented workers would be reduced in number. Thus, whether this action eliminated a real or an imagined problem, what would be clear—and very real—is that the local worker would stand to gain from the improvement in working conditions and wages that would result. Moreover,

by a 1973 survey of Mexican legal immigrants which showed that about 60% of those legally admitted had resided (without documents) in the United States prior to their admission. See Francisco Alba-Hernández, "Exodo silencioso: la emigración de trabajadores mexicanos a Estados Unidos," in *Foro internacional*, 17, no. 2 (1976), 163.

whether this action resulted in the return of thousands of workers to Mexico or not, it would seem unlikely that the Mexican government would oppose it or that it would be deleterious to Mexico–United States relations.

A third policy direction congruent with the views of both papers would be the recognition that many actions taken by the U.S. government and by the U.S. private sector in a general context have a direct effect on the condition of the Mexican economy and, to some extent, on the conditions that foment emigration to the United States. U.S. actions to strengthen, rather than weaken, that economy are likely to result in improvements in the employment situation and perhaps in the well-being of Mexicans who might otherwise migrate to the United States. Many of these actions, particularly those taken by the private sector, do not fall directly within governmental jurisdiction or the regulatory apparatus. But to the extent that the U.S. government acts to influence lending, trade, and investment policies toward Mexico, it may also have an influence on migration across its borders. These issue areas may constitute the basis for the kind of binational cooperation that both Sanderson and Bustamante seem to envision as constructive.

Finally, I should note that policy proposals in this issue-area have not always been subjected to the kind of theoretical and empirical testing that available information would permit. Moreover, the data base for engaging in such testing is rapidly expanding; much of the research presently being conducted has yet to find its way into print. Although some basic features about Mexican migration are known with confidence, many important questions remain to be settled. To discuss policy proposals in the near-vacuum of unanswered questions would be a serious error. The lack of consensus demonstrated recently by the close votes of the Select Commission on Immigration and Refugee Policy may be partially indicative of a lack of consensus among the "experts" on what the answers are or even what questions remain to be posed and considered. A more thorough airing of research questions and research findings may therefore significantly contribute to the on-going policy debate.[8]

PROJECT ENEFNEU: A SUMMARY

In that spirit, and taking note that I have been asked to summarize the preliminary results of a major research project with which I am associated, I now shift my attention to the National Household Survey for Emi-

[8] A pioneering effort in this direction is the monograph by Wayne Cornelius: *Mexican and Caribbean Migration to the United States: The State of Current Knowledge and Priorities for Future Research*, Monographs in United States–Mexican Studies, no. 1 (San Diego, Calif., 1982).

gration (ENEFNEU) of the National Center for Labor Information and Statistics (CENIET), an agency of the Mexican federal government.[9] This survey, based on a probabilistically drawn sample of approximately 62,500 households, is by far the largest effort to date to get a "representative" sample of Mexican workers who migrate to the United States.

The population on which the survey focuses can be described as the set of Mexicans, with or without immigration documents, that entered the United States and worked for a day or more between 1974 and 1978 (see accompanying figure, box 1). These people can be classified into three mutually exclusive categories: those who by the time of the survey in December-January 1978–79 had died or had established a usual place of residence in a country other than Mexico or the United States (box 2); those who had established a usual place of residence in Mexico (box 3); and those who had established a usual place of residence in the United States (box 4). The survey ignores persons who died or who reside outside of Mexico or the United States (box 2). Given that the survey was carried out in Mexico, the bulk of its attention was focused on persons habitually residing there at the time of the survey (box 3).

Migrants in the third category can in turn be classified into two mutually exclusive categories: those physically present in the United States, with a householder in Mexico who could have reported their absence from Mexico at the time of the survey (box 5), and those physically present in Mexico and exposed to the risk of being interviewed in the household survey (box 6). The former group is called "absent workers" or "population V" and was sampled with a questionnaire applied to a fellow householder for the purpose. There were an estimated 519,300 such workers absent from Mexico at the time of the survey.

The latter group is called "returned workers" or "population W" and was interviewed directly with a questionnaire designed for the purpose. There were an estimated 471,400 such persons in Mexico in the winter of 1978–79.

The data on absent workers (box 5) was necessarily gathered from second-hand sources. In the design of the questionnaire for this group we relied on the experience of our pilot surveys, which indicated that householders could not report reliably on some details of the absent workers' experience. For that reason, householders were not asked to report on the immigration status of absent persons. The 519,300 figure thus refers to absent persons irrespective of their status in the United States.

[9] Centro Nacional de Información y Estadísticas del Trabajo. The ENEFNEU project involved, in addition to the household survey of the same name, three border surveys of migrants expelled by INS (sample sizes of 10,000, 25,000, and 58,000, successively), and a series of background papers on related topics.

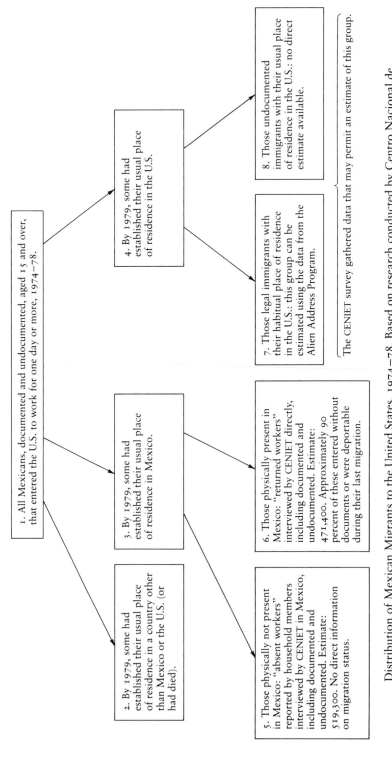

1. All Mexicans, documented and undocumented, aged 15 and over, that entered the U.S. to work for one day or more, 1974–78.

2. By 1979, some had established their usual place of residence in a country other than Mexico or the U.S. (or had died).

3. By 1979, some had established their usual place of residence in Mexico.

4. By 1979, some had established their usual place of residence in the U.S.

5. Those physically not present in Mexico: "absent workers" reported by household members interviewed by CENIET in Mexico, including documented and undocumented. Estimate: 519,300. No direct information on migration status.

6. Those physically present in Mexico: "returned workers" interviewed by CENIET directly, including documented and undocumented. Estimate: 471,400. Approximately 90 percent of these entered without documents or were deportable during their last migration.

7. Those legal immigrants with their habitual place of residence in the U.S.: this group can be estimated using the data from the Alien Address Program.

8. Those undocumented immigrants with their usual place of residence in the U.S.: no direct estimate available.

The CENIET survey gathered data that may permit an estimate of this group.

Distribution of Mexican Migrants to the United States, 1974–78. Based on research conducted by Centro Nacional de Información y Estadísticas del Trabajo, Mexican Department of Labor (Mexico City).

In contrast with this group, returned workers were questioned about the type of documents they had used during past migrations. About 90 percent of them reported that the last migration to the United States had been effectuated in a manner that would have classified them as deportable.

Those migrants with a usual place of residence in the United States (box 4) tend to fall outside the scope of the CENIET survey since only one question in the household short form applied directly to them. While the data collected may permit us to make a crude estimate of the size of this group—legal and illegal combined—the data remain to be tabulated and will not provide any detail. In order to secure comprehensive data on this group, therefore, it will be necessary to conduct a national survey in the United States.

Interviews of absent workers have yielded some results.[10] This population is made up largely of young adult males from rural areas, with little education by U.S. standards, whose principal employment in Mexico is in agriculture.[11] Surprisingly, only 3 percent were reportedly unemployed (actively seeking employment in Mexico) prior to their departure for the United States, although a larger proportion, approximately 20 percent, did not have a job in Mexico (economically inactive).

The lion's share (51 percent) of this population found its way to California, while another 21 percent was absorbed by Texas. Illinois, the state with the third-largest proportion of absent workers, was the destination for 8 percent of the population. Thus, migration to the United States has a high geographical concentration—80 percent of the migrants could be found in three states of the Union.

As we know, migrants go to the United States for the purpose of working, and many for the purpose of sending money home. The amounts remitted by this population have not been quantified in a manner that would permit us to indicate the volume of dollars sent per year, but the tabulations we have seen thus far suggest that the total remitted by migrants with a residence in Mexico (V and W) will be somewhat under one billion dollars per year, and not the several billion that had been supposed.

A large proportion of the absent workers had been gone for only a few days or months, as one would expect, inasmuch as all such persons are

[10] The data that follow are based on CENIET, "Informe final: los trabajadores mexicanos en los Estados Unidos (Encuesta Nacional de Emigración a la Frontera Norte del Pais y a los Estados Unidos, ENEFNEU," preliminary draft, unpublished report, Centro Nacional de Información y Estadísticas del Trabajo (Mexico City, February 1982).

[11] Of the total, 433,300 were males, and 86,000 females; two-thirds fell between the ages of 15 and 29; 90% had less than ten years of schooling; 62% were employed in agriculture; and almost 80% resided in rural communities (places with fewer than 20,000 persons censused in 1970).

relatively "temporary" migrants, still reported as habitually residing in Mexico. Indeed, it is surprising that a relatively high proportion, 28.5 percent, had been gone for a year or more. This datum is indicative in some respects of the temporary commitment that even long-term migrations may represent, since over one-fourth of the absent workers evidently intended to return, notwithstanding the fact that they had been gone for a year or more.

As previously indicated, these findings draw upon the first national, probabilistic sample of Mexican migrants. Nevertheless, the data analyzed thus far provide the answers only to general questions; the analysis of the data has thus far been descriptive. A discussion of summary characteristics, broad socio-economic profiles, and the analysis of aggregate data constitutes a first, but modest step. More detailed analyses are possible and will be carried out.

One should stress the limitations of the data collected by these surveys. The limitations of the border surveys are self-evident: some of the characteristics of expelled migrants differ significantly from those of undetected migrants, and expelled migrants enter a sample with unknown probabilities of selection. Border surveys do, however, provide data on an important subgroup of the undocumented population; they are relatively inexpensive to carry out; and it is easier to tabulate the unweighted sample results. Moreover, there is relatively little ambiguity with respect to the migration status of the interviewees.[12]

The limitations of the household survey are those generally associated with survey research, owing particularly to the fact that the survey was carried out in the place of origin rather than the place of destination. Thus, entire households that emigrated to the United States would be missed by this survey, and the data gathered that are most reliable—based on the absent and returned workers—are also the least interesting from a U.S. policy perspective, which would be most concerned about the population represented in box 8 in our schema. That these population groups are most interesting from the Mexican policy perspective should not be overlooked, of course, but the series of Mexican concerns—like those of the United States—constitutes only one part of a more complex whole.

Data from the CENIET survey permit some general inferences about the potential impact of labor migration on the U.S. society and labor market. More importantly, a comparative analysis of the population subgroups (V, W, X, Y, and Z)[13] will permit analysts to test hypotheses re-

[12] Nevertheless, during the First Border Survey (conducted in October-November of 1977), there were 14 persons who were expelled, even though they apparently qualified for registry (they had last entered prior to 1948) and were therefore not deportable.

[13] Populations V and W have already been defined. Populations X and Y refer to internal

garding the cause of outmigration, both to the United States and within Mexico, and for the first time to explore the connections between internal and international migration.

The principal criticisms of the results of the National Household Survey have thus far focused on the unexpectedly small magnitude of migration implied by the national estimates of "absent" and "returned worker" populations. In order both to clarify the meaning of the estimates and tentatively to defend them as valid I would like to respond to four possible variants of the criticism that the populations measured by the survey are "too small." [14]

The first variant could be expressed by the bald assertion that the numbers are simply too low. The reply is equally brief—we do not have an independent, "reliable" estimate that would permit one to assert that the estimates of absent and returned workers are too low. Indeed, analytical estimates of the general, undocumented population, irrespective of place of residence, are increasingly pointing in the direction of smaller numbers. Conjectural estimates that the number of undocumented Mexicans in the United States range in the several millions can be rejected out of hand—not because the numbers are too high per se, but because conjecture cannot substitute for measurement. The bald assertion that the numbers are too low is therefore equivalent to the argument that conjecture *can* be substituted for measurement.

The second variant could be stated thus: the estimate of absent workers is too low because of two considerations: first, the category includes both legal and undocumented workers; second, the 1979 Alien Address Program, administered by the Immigration and Naturalization Service, reported a relatively large number—480,000 legal immigrant workers—while CENIET's absent worker estimate, which includes both legal and illegal migrants, was only 519,300. On the basis of these two considerations some analysts have concluded that the CENIET survey simply "missed all the illegals."

---

migration to the northern border *municipios* and to the rest of the country, respectively. Population Z is the residual, non-migrant population.

[14] This criticism first appeared in a paper prepared for the Select Commission on Immigration and Refugee Policy by Jacob S. Siegel, Jeffrey S. Passel, and J. Gregory Robinson, "Preliminary Review of Existing Studies of the Number of Illegal Residents in the United States," in *U.S. Immigration Policy and the National Interest, The Staff Report of the Select Commission on Immigration and Refugee Policy*, Appendix E: "Papers on Illegal Immigration to the U.S." (U.S. Government Printing Office, Washington, D.C., 1981). The reader will note that the authors discuss a CENIET survey estimate of 405,000 absent workers, while our working figure is 519,300. Siegel et al. directed their criticisms at preliminary, unpublished findings. Since then, some corrections were made in the estimates of the sample weights, and the final number is somewhat larger. In any event, this slight change probably would not have altered their criticisms—nor this reply.

The problem with this argument is that those persons registered by the Alien Address Program are not strictly comparable to the persons counted in the survey—indeed, they are almost entirely mutually exclusive. The survey counted only persons who habitually reside in Mexico; the Address Program, with minor exceptions, counts persons residing in the United States. Thus, the population registered in the program (480,000) is not a conceptual subset of the population counted by the survey (519,300). Indeed, with the exception of the so-called commuters residing on the Mexican border who register with INS, the two populations are separate and additive. The total number of Mexican workers in the United States in early 1979 would be 519,300 plus 480,000 minus those persons habitually residing in Mexico who register with INS, plus those undocumented Mexican workers who habitually reside in the United States.

The third variant of this argument might state that the numbers are too low because the Immigration and Naturalization Service catches and expels nearly one million Mexicans each year. How is it possible that there were only 519,300 absent workers in the United States, not all of them undocumented, if a much larger number of deportable Mexicans are located by INS each fiscal year?

There are several problems with this argument. First, INS statistics represent events, not people; since some individuals are caught more than once each year, the nearly one million apprehensions do not represent as many different people. Second, the argument confuses stocks with flow; a population size (stock) refers to a point in time, apprehensions refer to a flow (over an interval of time). Thus, it does not matter that nearly one million persons are caught each year. By the same token, several million are caught in a decade, and only a hundred thousand in a month. What is so special about a year as an interval of comparison? Third, the bulk of INS apprehensions occurs shortly after entry—and while the figures may be an index of the level of vigilance exercised at the border, or of the general trend of the inflow of persons, they tell us nothing about the number of persons in the interior, and even less about persons who have been in the United States for some time. Although nearly a million apprehensions of Mexicans occur each year, only 50,000 approximately are caught who have stayed for a year or more.

There is, moreover, some evidence to show that the (relatively high) INS statistics are compatible with the relatively small emerging estimates of stock. A study I prepared recently arrives at (relatively small) estimates of the deportable Mexican population in the United States, using as its principal source the (relatively high) INS statistics on deportable Mexicans located. Because the volume of flow of exits from the deportable population is relatively small for lengths of stay of a year or more, however, the estimates that resulted were comparatively low. (For January of 1977 I estimate the "probable" range of stock to be between 480,000 and 1.2 million on the basis of this model.)[15] Thus, INS expulsion of nearly a million or more deportable Mexicans does not necessarily lead to the conclusion that the size of this population must be in the many millions.

The fourth variant of the argument could read: the numbers are too low because the survey was conducted in the winter, a time that corresponds to a seasonal low in migration to the United States. Had the survey been carried out during a seasonal peak, the numbers would have been much higher. While one cannot deny that winter represents a seasonal ebb in migration, it is difficult to see how that invalidates the survey results. Depending upon whether the season in which the survey was taken were summer or winter, the number of absent workers would be high or low, respectively, and the number of returned workers would conversely be low or high. In the winter, the absent population was at a minimum but the returned population was at a maximum—and both were estimated. Thus, at the seasonal peak in 1978, while one would have expected the size of the absent worker population to have been higher than 519,300, it still would have been lower than the combined total of absent and returned workers—990,700. The precise estimate of the stock at the peak season will require the reconstruction of migration histories and their representation in a cohort model that accounts for the multiple entry, exit, and re-entry of undocumented migrants. But clearly, the choice of winter to carry out the survey enhances, rather than invalidates, the results, since the number of persons that could be interviewed directly (returned workers, as opposed to absent workers) was maximized.

It is important to stress in my conclusion that these estimates of migrant populations and their characteristics have not been tested fully. This is what we got when we tabulated the results and weighted each questionnaire according to the estimated probability of selection of each case. Estimates of sampling error and an analysis of bias and response error will permit us to evaluate the quality of the data thus far presented.

CONCLUSION

One may infer that the project ENEFNEU is but one of many research efforts that seek to answer key empirical questions. Perhaps the most im-

[15] García y Griego, *El volumen*, pp. 429–30, 434, 522. The reader should note that, although the data collection and the publication of the results of this model were done under the auspices of CENIET, the data and their results are independent of the household survey results mentioned above. The estimates of stock are also not strictly comparable, since the conceptual definition of the population estimated with the model was Mexican migrants (of all characteristics) exposed to the risk of being expelled by the INS.

portant empirical questions that Bustamante's paper poses are: What are the determinants of U.S. and Mexican government policies toward migration? And what is the relationship between the perceptions and the realities of this social process? In the former case, a study of the lessons of the bracero program may be useful. In the latter sense, survey research that builds on the findings of previous work such as the ENEFNEU may help answer some basic questions about the role and impact of migration on the relations between Mexico and the United States.

At the heart of Sanderson's paper too are a set of political questions: Will "paralysis" lead—one is tempted to add, "inevitably"—to policy failure? How *does* migration fit in the context not only of social but also of government-to-government relations between the United States and Mexico? What other components are there in this "nuclear reactor" of United States–Mexico relations that are in danger of breaking down? How have Mexico and the United States handled core meltdown scenarios in the past?

One can easily see why the Bustamante and Sanderson papers are provocative. Among their many virtues, they make it easier to understand why important empirical and analytical questions related to undocumented migration are not limited just to the social and demographic characteristics of the immigrants themselves.

The Future of Relations Between Mexico and the United States

Mario Ojeda

THIS ANALYSIS of alternative near-term courses for Mexico–United States relations in the 1980s will focus particularly on the structural and conjunctural questions that may affect both the perception of U.S. objectives and Mexico's degree of freedom to negotiate, and thus the development of relations themselves. The general hypothesis is that at any given moment, regardless of concrete problems that might affect relations between the two countries, the relationship itself depends upon structural factors. These factors, even if susceptible to change, change only in a gradual manner and thus permanently condition the capacity of each country to negotiate over the issues or problems that emerge from the relationship. Internal and international events of a critical nature are also powerful factors that may affect relations insofar as they tend to alter not only the priority assigned to different issues but also the views about what the objectives of foreign policy should be over both the short and long run.

HISTORY

History shows that relations between Mexico and the United States have never been easy. In the past century and a half one finds conflict rather than understanding and cooperation. During the nineteenth century and much of the twentieth, relations occurred within a framework of permanent conflict, with the exception of a short period of cooperation that coincided in Mexico with the French intervention and in the United States with the Civil War. Throughout this long period Mexico has fared badly. The 1836 War, for example, resulted in the loss of Texas with Washington's tacit approval; the U.S.-Mexican War in 1847 entailed the loss of a vast territory that, including Texas, constituted more than half of the original territory of independent Mexico; and in 1854 the

Treaty of La Mesilla, the "Gadsden Purchase," legislated the forced sale of still more territory.

Conflict continued to characterize relations between the two countries during the first four decades of the present century. From the beginning of the Mexican Revolution the United States intervened openly in the internal political affairs of Mexico and, on at least two occasions, militarily as well—in 1914 with the occupation of Veracruz, and in 1917 along the northern border through the punitive expedition of General Pershing, sent to punish Francisco Villa for his assault on the town of Columbus, New Mexico.

Other sources of conflict during the Revolution were the various claims made by Washington over loss of life and damage caused to the property of U.S. citizens residing in Mexico, as well as the suspension by various revolutionary governments of payments on the foreign debt. These problems continued to muddy relations between the two countries in the 1920s and 1930s. In time the two issues that became constant sources of both conflict and cooperation were migration and petroleum. During the 1920s thousands of Mexicans, repelled by the revolutionary conflict in Mexico and attracted by the bonanza of the U.S. economy, emigrated to the United States, only to find that 300,000 of them would be deported between 1930 and 1933 in the wake of the 1929 depression.

During the 1920s petroleum came to be Mexico's most important export, owing to the growth of foreign investment (both U.S. and English) in the industry. Oil became a source of conflict as Washington tried to prevent Mexico from applying retroactively the new constitution that claimed national ownership of all subsoil resources. This conflict culminated in 1938 with the expropriation of foreign firms. In 1941 a general agreement was signed between Mexico and the United States to resolve the dispute.

World War II constituted a clear parting of the ways in Mexico–United States relations. In the 1930s the United States had replaced its former policy toward Latin America, typified by "big stick" intervention and dollar diplomacy, with a new one—the policy of the good neighbor. They sought the cooperation of Latin America in the imminent conflict and, in exchange, through a multilateral accord of 1936, to renounce any rights to intervene in the internal affairs of that region. Cooperation on three levels was the objective. On the military level, the United States wished to establish bases for its armed forces and to reinforce the capacity of the Latin American armies to combat possible attempts at internal subversion induced from abroad by the Axis powers. On the political level it sought to counteract Axis propaganda and the Nazi-Fascist Fifth Column in the hemisphere. On the economic level the goal was to keep open Latin American sources of raw materials strategic to the Allied cause and to prevent the Axis powers from obtaining access to them.

For Mexico, cooperation with the United States in the war effort was essential. The prevailing international situation, which involved all nations in the armed conflict, offered few alternatives, except perhaps neutrality "á la Argentina," which was hardly realistic inasmuch as economic chaos would be the result. If Mexico did not give determined cooperation, there was a real possibility of domestic subversion instigated by the United States, or even of occupation by the U.S. Army of certain zones of Mexican territory, such as Baja, considered vital for U.S. defense.

More important for Mexico was the wartime collaboration, which signified an opportunity to negotiate problems pending with the United States as a quid pro quo. And this is precisely what occurred. Mexico obtained recognition by the United States of the Revolution as an accomplished fact; the adjustment of the different claims stemming from the internal conflict; recognition that the expropriation of the oil companies had been an act of domestic sovereignty; and, finally, a warning from Washington to those companies to negotiate the corresponding indemnification on terms not far different from those advocated by the Mexican government.

Once the war had ended, a spirit of cooperation continued between the two countries notwithstanding the problems that presented themselves. Like other Latin American countries, Mexico had to confront the negative economic consequences of the immediate postwar period. She sought to resist pressures from the United States in order not to be dragged into Cold War adventures. During this period several specific bilateral problems surfaced, in such matters as standards in the campaign against hoof-and-mouth disease and the negotiation of a new bracero agreement in 1951. In general, however, no really important problems arose that could not be negotiated in a spirit of cooperation. The symbol of this new cooperation came to be the return of El Chamizal, Mexican territory lost when the course of the Rio Bravo changed during a severe flood. The repatriation of the territory had been denied Mexico since 1911, despite a judgment in her favor.

At the end of the 1970s bilateral relations changed abruptly with the resurgence of the two controversial issues of migration and hydrocarbons. Other recent problems have been the drug traffic from Mexico to the United States and the smuggling of goods and arms to Mexico. These issues, together with U.S. protectionist measures against Mexican exports, constitute the principal potential sources of conflict in future relations between the two countries.

THE STRUCTURE OF THE RELATIONSHIP

In analyzing bilateral relations one must distinguish between structure and process, that is, between the framework of political-economic realities within which relations take place on the one hand, and the questions or issues that form the substance of the relations, as well as the problems that arise from them, on the other. From the Mexican point of view, structure is the principal preoccupation. The structure of the relationship prevents Mexico from negotiating problems with the United States on an equal footing and frequently obliges Mexico to accept unilateral decisions from Washington without alternative.

The structure of the relationship between Mexico and the United States is characterized by at least three basic elements that tangibly affect the pattern of negotiations on various issues: geographic contiguity, which has military-strategic implications for Mexico and signifies an obvious limitation on her full de facto autonomy; power asymmetry, which signifies that Mexico is the weaker partner in the relationship; and Mexico's economic and technological dependence on the United States, which signifies a great vulnerability on Mexico's part to decisions taken by the government in Washington or by transnational firms.

From a geopolitical point of view, being a near-neighbor of the richest and most powerful country on earth makes Mexico part of the sphere of influence of that power. It means that the United States considers Mexico a key zone, a first line of national defense. According to some experts on military strategy, Mexico is located in a region considered a categorical imperative for the national defense of the United States. Not only is Mexico not entirely free to decide its international policy, but any Mexican government must be on good terms with Washington; otherwise it risks being destabilized or subverted from without. Finally, and most important, this proximity implies that the basic policies adopted by the Mexican government must be acceptable to Washington.

A second consequence of territorial contiguity is that Mexico offers clear advantages for trade with the world's richest market in comparison with other developing countries. One concrete result has been the excessive concentration of Mexican economic and political relations on a single country. Geographic proximity, coupled with a border highly porous to the transit of people, goods, and capital, has caused relations between the two countries to exceed markedly the framework of government-to-government diplomatic relations and traditional interchange. The relationship is so highly complex that policies designed to regulate it tend to be only partially effective.

The second, important element characterizing the structure of Mexico–United States relations is the power asymmetry that exists between them. Mexico is the weaker partner in the relationship. The United States is a colossus of over 200 million inhabitants, with a gross national product (GNP) in excess of a trillion dollars and a per capita income greater than $8,000. Mexico, by contrast, is a medium-size nation of more than 68 million inhabitants with a GNP of $70 billion and a per capita income of $1,110. In other words, the United States has a population about three times larger, a per capita income eight times higher, and an economic output twenty-five times that of Mexico in absolute terms.

To understand the extent and real limits of this power asymmetry, it is necessary to analyze it within a broader framework of world power—on a scale of 150 independent nations that constitute the present world conglomerate. In these terms the United States occupies first place on the economic and military planes, second place in regard to territorial extent, and fourth place in size of population.

Mexico, like the other developing countries, confronts great economic deficiencies and grave social problems. It is a so-called intermediate nation and occupies a privileged place within the spectrum of world nations. It is located in eleventh place in terms of population, thirteenth in terms of economic output, and ranks high in per capita income compared to other developing countries. By its own decision it occupies a modest place from a military standpoint.

The third structural element affecting relations is Mexico's economic and technological dependence on the United States. Mexico is very vulnerable to the policies and decisions of Washington or of U.S. transnational corporations to the extent that they have negative, extraterritorial effects on its economy.

The United States is Mexico's primary trading partner, as both buyer and supplier, while Mexico is the fourth most important outlet, and fifth-ranking provider, for the United States. The United States absorbs 68 percent of all Mexican exports and supplies 63 percent of Mexican imports. In contrast, in 1975 for instance, Mexico absorbed only 4.7 percent of U.S. exports and contributed a modest 3.1 percent of that country's imports. In 1979 its participation in the foreign commerce of the United States totalled only 5 percent.

Another important indicator is tourism. Even if the balance of exchange is favorable to Mexico, the relative importance for each country of income from this source shows the inequality of the relationship. For Mexico, the United States is the most important buyer of its services (approximately 85 percent), while for the United States Mexico is the second most important buyer after Canada. In Mexico income from tourism has until recently compensated for the country's trade deficit. For the United

States, by contrast, tourism from Mexico has been of minor importance, except in regions such as Texas and southern California, and in cities close to the border.

Another important indicator of Mexican dependence is direct U.S. investment. The book value of this investment rose to $3.7 billion in 1978, or 75 percent of total foreign investment, which is concentrated in two of the most dynamic and strategic sectors of the economy—tourism and heavy industry—as well as in those sectors characterized by the most sophisticated technology. By contrast, Mexican investment in the United States is marginal.

Finally, another important indicator of Mexico's dependence is her public and private foreign debt. The United States, which carries 70 percent of the total Mexican debt, public and private, is Mexico's most important creditor.[1]

MEXICAN CAPACITY TO NEGOTIATE IN RECENT PRACTICE

In the last forty years, despite the asymmetrical structure of the Mexico–United States relationship and Mexico's strong dependence, the Mexican state has maintained a broader margin for negotiation with the United States than have a majority of Latin American countries. The following factors gave Mexico a greater margin for negotiation compared to other Latin American countries: (1) solid political stability; (2) a high and sustained rate of growth; (3) a low rate of inflation; (4) self-sufficiency, defined in economic terms of real demand, in the areas of basic foodstuffs and petroleum; (5) extra sources for obtaining foreign exchange in addition to the export of goods, specifically the remittances of migrant workers and of tourism; (6) ample solvency in international financial markets; (7) an escape valve for unemployment and underemployment through temporary or permanent migration of workers. For a long time these factors permitted Mexico to confront development problems with greater security and with less urgency stemming from the scarcity of resources for financing. At the same time these factors assured Mexico a firmer negotiating position externally. However, in time many of these elements disappeared so that by 1976, when a triple crisis—economic, social, and political—emerged, Mexico's capacity for international negotiation declined drastically.

The administration that came to power in 1976 inherited a country in crisis. Its principal task, apart from solving the great economic prob-

---

[1]The public foreign debt of Mexico, as of December 31, 1979, reached the sum of $29,757 million. See José López Portillo, *Cuarto informe de gobierno*, Anexo Programático II-A 1979 (Mexico, September 1980), p. 757.

lems, was to restore the confidence of Mexicans in their own government. This was a very difficult task when the gap in the government's credibility had widened, when the national coffers were empty and international credit exhausted, and while the flight of capital persisted and a "dollarization" of bank accounts and of a large number of domestic commercial transactions occurred. Inflation had overtaken the country, groups with political power had become accustomed to pressing for constant revisions of wages and prices, and the economy in general had stagnated— all this in a country already afflicted by chronic unemployment and underemployment.

The weakening of Mexico's capacity for international negotiation was due not so much to the loans contracted by the Mexican government before and after the first devaluation, or to the limitations imposed by the IMF, but to the fact that the general crisis of the Mexican economy and the lack of confidence in political institutions on the part of foreign and national investors, and even of the average citizen, obliged Mexico to bargain from a position of weakness and urgency. At this juncture petroleum emerged as Mexico's salvation. To solve the economic crisis of 1976, the government decided to exploit the new oil and gas resources at an accelerated pace in order to make the country into a major exporter. Without this crisis it is unlikely that Mexico would have decided to exploit petroleum resources to such a high degree and at such an accelerated rate.[2]

The first task was to persuade public opinion, both national and international, of the magnitude of the nation's oil reserves. The exploration of different geologic strata was intensified, and specialized firms with ample reputation in the oil world were hired to certify the size of the new finds. Notwithstanding this effort and the fact that the production of crude rose from 293 million barrels in 1976 to 358 million in 1977, the international climate of doubt concerning the true size of the reserves persisted. The increase in value of exports, from 436 million to 1,019 million pesos between 1976 and 1977,[3] alleviated pressures on the balance of payments and allowed national and international investors, as well as the public at large, to recover lost confidence in the national economy. The value of oil

[2] Additional incentives that made an increase in production for export to international markets attractive were (1) the high prices at which the fuel was quoted in the international market, and (2) the new techniques for estimating reserves, which permitted the inventory of gigantic volumes, placed Mexico alongside the world's biggest oil producers, and also permitted the forecasting of generous surpluses. See Samuel del Villar, "Estado y petroleo en México: experiencias y perspectivas," *Foro Internacional*, 20, no.1 (Mexico, July–September 1979), 133–34.

[3] PEMEX, *Memoria de labores*, 1977.

exports went on increasing and, by the end of 1978, reached $1,725 million.[4]

By the time of his second State of the Union message to Congress, in September 1978, President Portillo could already declare,

We have programmed successive targets which define the global plan of national development in three biennial stages: the first two years, overcoming the crisis; the following two, consolidation of the economy; and in the last two, accelerated growth.

The first stage, the overcoming of the crisis, is nearing its conclusion. . . . In this first phase we removed the threat to our financial sovereignty; the flight of capital ceased and some returned. Our external debt and balance of payments position improved. In the last semester industrial production grew more rapidly and agricultural production recovered; the process of "dollarization" has ended and even reversed itself, a sign that we have assimilated the system of flotation of the peso with respect to the dollar, which is also floating, at times with difficulty, among other strong currencies.[5]

The president meant that the worst of the crisis—inflation with recession—had been left behind. Inflation would continue, but in the midst of rapid economic growth. In fact, by 1979 the country's economy had attained a rate of growth of 7.5 percent, four times greater than that in 1976.[6]

The oil surpluses served also to increase the financial capacity of the government, previously limited by ceilings imposed by the agreement with the IMF over foreign indebtedness and by the weakness of the Mexican system of tax collection. This financial self-determination, as the president called it, widened the margin of negotiation for Mexico, both externally and internally. Above all, the petroleum surpluses gave her the ability to increase and self-finance public expenditures, a basic instrument for reactivating and orienting economic development. By 1979 President Portillo informed the nation: "Oil is our potential for self-determination, because it will make us less dependent on external financing and will improve our international economic relations."[7]

With oil, the Mexican government recovered its earlier ability to negotiate with private entrepreneurs. As was plainly manifested during con-

[4]Dirección General de Estadística, *Annuario estadístico del comercio exterior,* 1970–1978. By the end of 1979 the value of exports reached the figure of $3,986 million; $9,429 million in 1980, and $13,305 million in 1981. See Banco de México, *Informes anuales,* 1979, 1980, and 1981.
[5]José López Portillo, *Segundo informe de gobierno* (Mexico, September 1978).
[6]Ibid., and Portillo, *Tercer informe de gobierno* (Mexico, September 1979). In his fourth governmental report (September 1980), the president corrected his own figure in announcing that the rate of growth had been 8 percent for the second consecutive year (*Cuarto informe de gobierno* [Mexico, September 1980], p. 13).
[7]José López Portillo, *Tercer informe.*

frontation with the Echeverría government in 1975 and 1976, that ability had become very weak as a result of the economic crisis. Petroleum widened the state's room for maneuver vis-à-vis business in an indirect fashion by permitting public spending to be increased and by reducing the dependence of economic recovery on private investment. The government of Portillo combined with businessmen to form an Alliance for Production, so that the business community would increase its investment. It was based on the supposed goodwill of each partner, but somehow left much to be desired during the regime's initial two years.

Hydrocarbons too gave the government a direct and concrete negotiating weapon, an incentive to invest through the provision of cheap energy. The case of the gas pipeline to Cadereyta illustrates this point, for the pipeline permitted the Monterrey industrialists, avid for gas, to obtain greater volumes and to replace fuel oil with gas, which is a cleaner and more powerful fuel.

Once the financial side of the crisis was under control, the government could confront the problem of its relations with the United States in a more relaxed atmosphere. The final meeting held by Presidents Portillo and Carter, in Mexico City in 1979, contrasted notably with the first meeting in Washington in February 1977. At the first meeting, Portillo had still employed the thesis of the moral responsibility that should exist between neighboring countries: "The United States has to face up to a great responsibility in regard to Mexico, not only as a geographic neighbor, but also as a neighbor which finds itself in a process of development."[8] By 1979, in a more confident atmosphere, and obviously disappointed by the final outcome of the gas negotiations, President Portillo went on to say:

Our peoples desire agreements in depth and not circumstantial concessions. Between permanent and not merely occasional neighbors, sudden deception and abuse are poisonous fruits which sooner or later turn back upon one. It is within this perspective that the complex phenomenon of our interrelationship must be situated, an interrelationship which must not under any circumstances be confused with dependence, integration, or dilution of frontiers. The two countries complement and need one another reciprocally, but neither would desire to depend on the other to the point where its international actions were annulled or where the space for its international action was reduced, or where it lost its self-respect.[9]

In this way petroleum gave Mexico a breathing spell to order its economy more rationally. For the future, however, petroleum may be either a lever supporting a more dynamic and equilibrated development, or a dis-

[8]Speech at the White House, February 14, 1977 (*Tiempo*, February 21, 1977, p. 8).
[9]*Comercio Exterior*, 29, no. 2 (February 1979), 160.

ruptive element generating chaos in the economy. As an instrument of international power, it has also definite limitations and involves potential dangers that, if not anticipated, may turn its benefits into negative consequences.

THE FUTURE OF RELATIONS BETWEEN MEXICO AND THE UNITED STATES

In the present decade and in the immediate term Mexico's relations with the United States will depend on various and complex factors: the perceptions that different American political sectors have of U.S. priority interests in relation to Mexico; Mexico's capacity to initiate internal policies that serve the interest of the majority of the nation; Mexico's ability to resist external pressures; and, finally, the type and magnitude of future international events.

A number of observers of Mexico–United States relations from both sides of the border distinguish between U.S. short- and long-run interests. They assert that both the government in Washington and interested private sectors suffer from a myopia, derived from short-term considerations, which impels them to force situations in relations with Mexico that, if realized, would work to the detriment of the true long-run U.S. interest in Mexico: balanced development and political stability.

Wayne Cornelius argues, for example, that those who advocate the closing of the border to Mexican workers as a short-run solution to the problem of the undocumented do not take into account the implications such a move would have for Mexico's stability, nor do they consider the possible negative effects on the U.S. economy, such as intensification of inflation in some sectors. To those who suggest closing the border to force the Mexican government and the country's elites to take drastic measures in matters of population policy, rural development, employment generation, and the distribution of income, Cornelius warns that such action, far from advancing these objectives, might have the opposite effect.[10]

To those who believe that Mexico should be forced to raise its oil production in order to generate more employment with its oil resources, he responds: "As Mexico's oil boom develops, the massive influx of public and private investment capital into the hydrocarbons sector may have a *negative* impact on the total job creation, by diverting capital from some of the more labor-intensive sectors of the economy."[11] Citing the rural

---

[10] Cf. Wayne Cornelius, *Immigration, Mexican Development Policy, and the Future of United States–Mexico Relations*, Working Paper in United States–Mexican Studies, no. 8 (San Diego, September 1981), p. 21.

[11] Ibid., p. 22.

development projects presently being implemented, Cornelius warns that, to the extent they are successful, their impact on the retention of labor in the countryside may be negative, for many peasants will develop expectations about emigration at the same time that they are now able to finance their own migration.[12]

David Ronfeldt and his fellow authors arrive at conclusions similar to those of Cornelius. According to them the three assumptions that prevail are: (1) that Mexican oil is vital to meet the energy needs of the United States; (2) that the United States can influence petroleum policy in Mexico in a significant way; (3) that oil must be the key point in relations between the two countries. They also observe that, on the basis of these assumptions, other political analysts now conclude that the United States must either exert special pressures or make concessions that will induce Mexico to produce and export as much petroleum as possible.[13]

The authors question the wisdom of this conclusion and feel that promoting Mexican oil as a cheap and convenient solution to the problems of U.S. energy security may be costly in other areas; that even if the United States were to realize this objective, the solution would be temporary and not a long-term solution to U.S. energy problems. Further, attempting to reach such an objective might lead Mexico into serious economic and political difficulties that in turn could have disastrous effects on relations between the two countries. The interests of the United States with respect to Mexico are too complex and multidimensional to be dominated by oil matters.

Ronfeldt and his colleagues doubt that Mexico has a significant potential to achieve such an increase. They also stress the importance of an understanding in the United States of the significance that oil possesses as a symbol of Mexican nationalism and for Mexico's political stability. They believe that only a few Americans realize that an exaggerated emphasis on immediate energy problems of the United States could lead to the adoption of policies that conflict with, or at least deviate from, traditional U.S. goals with regard to Mexico, namely, that it be a productive, stable, and cooperative neighbor.

All these arguments are logically consistent and politically rational. Nevertheless, they do not acknowledge that politicians and businessmen are moved by short-run considerations, that their horizons are limited by day-to-day pressures. The authors reason that the public interest must

[12] David Ronfeldt, Richard Nehring, and Arturo Gándara, *Mexico's Petroleum and U.S. Policy: Implications for the 1980s* (Santa Monica, Calif., June 1980); see also Michael Redclift and Nanneke Redclift, "Unholy Alliance," *Foreign Policy*, 41 (winter, 1980–81), 111–33.
[13] Ronfeldt et al., *Mexico's Petroleum*, pp. 70–73.

prevail over private factional interests, something that has not occurred in the United States except in cases of great crisis such as the Depression and the Second World War. Nevertheless, they are realistic insofar as they highlight the importance of basing Mexico–United States relations on the points of convergence between the interests of the two countries. Moreover, they illustrate examples of the importance that U.S. perceptions with respect to Mexico will have for future relations.

The future of Mexico–United States relations will also depend in great part on Mexico's capacity to resist external pressures as well as on its capacity to meet its internal needs. Although oil has permitted Mexico to enlarge its margin for international bargaining, it is still vulnerable to external pressures. Petroleum has indeed given Mexico a concrete and effective instrument of international negotiation that, apart from its commercial value, has an aggregate political value of even greater force.[14] Nevertheless, the negotiating power of oil has clear objective limits.

In great part the country is vulnerable because of the weakness of its balance of payments and its foreign trade. Petroleum has become Mexico's principal export and has come to compensate for the trade deficit, which would otherwise be greater. Viewed from another perspective, petroleum permits Mexico to maintain an import capacity to meet the needs of rapid development. On the other hand, and since the level of oil exports has been considered as a potential motive for discord on the United States–Mexico agenda, it follows that the United States will not have to exert any pressure in that regard, for Mexico's own internal needs will lead its government to raise oil production.

PEMEX, the national oil company, by itself generates a large part of the imports that must be paid for out of its own exports. Also, Mexico runs a large deficit in foodstuffs, which also have to be imported in good part with funds earned from oil.[15] For exports, the picture is also quite negative. Mexico's traditional exports have been losing their competitiveness in international markets or have disappeared entirely, as witness sugar, for example, which from being a prime article for export is now imported, to compensate for the deficit in domestic production. Tourism, whose surplus for many years played the strategic role of traditional balancer of the trade deficit—or, rather, permitted Mexico to import above and beyond its export capabilities—today also is much reduced and even in danger of becoming a deficit item. As a consequence, and for the first

---

[14] Richard R. Fagen, "El petroleo mexicano y la seguridad nacional de los Estados Unidos," in *Las perspectivas del petroleo mexicano* (Mexico, 1979), p. 341.

[15] Unofficial sources estimate that by 1980 9.5 million tons of food will be imported, or twice what was acquired abroad in 1979 (Banco Nacional de México, *Examen de la situación económica de México*, no. 656 [Mexico, July 1980], p. 359).

time in twenty years, the joint surplus from tourism and border transactions will decline.[16] In the face of this situation, the most probable outcome in the short run is that the country will once again have to raise the ceiling on its oil production. If that occurs, the interested U.S. sectors will have achieved their objective without lifting a finger.

In the short run, clearly, there is another alternative for restoring Mexico's competitiveness in international markets, both in goods and in tourism: to devalue. But this is a dangerous course that may stir up other economic problems and a lack of public confidence. The peso has been in "flotation" since August 31, 1976, but this is true only technically. Its fluctuations with respect to the dollar have been minimal and do not reflect the overvaluation to which the peso has become subject, nor do they require proof by complex mathematical arguments. It suffices to subtract the cumulative rate of inflation in the United States, Mexico's principal trading partner, from that in Mexico to demonstrate the point. There are numerous other external signs indicating the overvaluation. In reality the Mexican Central Bank has been supporting the peso out of the nation's oil reserves. Nevertheless, the word *devaluation* has been proscribed from Mexico's official vocabulary, so it is difficult for the government now to act. The resulting evils might be greater than the benefits obtained. Perhaps the only recourse would be to let the peso really float, in gradual fashion, until true parity is reached.*

Another alternative would be a system of exchange control, but in Mexico this is considered taboo. Such a system would be almost impossible to implement because of Mexico's long border with the United States, which is open to the massive transit of people, and also because Mexico generates and receives tourists on such a massive scale. A black market would be created by practically every traveler, making a shambles of any official exchange regime. But it is this impossibility of installing an exchange system that makes it all the more necessary to float the peso, especially if the disparity continues in rates of inflation between Mexico and the United States. Otherwise the trade deficit (petroleum aside) will go on

---

[16] Ibid., p. 394.

* Editors' note: A major devaluation to permit the peso exchange rate to "equilibrate" did not occur until February 1982, and then only after a major conversion of pesos into dollars as the public became aware of deteriorating balance of payments conditions exacerbated by lower oil prices, enormous increases in debt service requirements, and the inflationary consequences of public-sector deficits to meet rapid growth targets. The public response to devaluation was predictable and led to government-sponsored wage increases that have in turn added to expectations of inflation and further devaluation. Most recently (July 1982) price ceilings on a number of basic commodities, including sugar, bread, tortillas, and gasoline, were raised. As a result, corrective inflation is placing further pressures on prices and exchange rate expectations as well as on the basic cost of living. All of these circumstances enhance the timeliness and relevance of the author's comments today.

increasing, as well as the travel deficit, and the incentives for Mexicans to continue to invest in the United States will be maintained. If there is no gradual devaluation, a broad segment of investors will continue to fear the possibility of an abrupt devaluation, and the flight of capital will continue.

The Mexican government is aware of the external and internal vulnerability of the economy and has drawn up concrete plans for attacking these problems. One of them is the Mexican Food System (SAM), designed to attain self-sufficiency in basic foodstuffs. This program is very important, for if it is successful, not only will it make Mexico less vulnerable by reducing pressures on the balance of payments and by reducing the need to increase oil production, but it will also avoid the possibility that the country would ever be exposed to blackmail through food. If successful, the positive effects of the SAM will be felt only gradually. Thus in the short run there will be continued pressures to increase the production of petroleum. SAM, like other similar programs and measures that the government may adopt, requires not only political decisiveness and the overcoming of the technical, financial, and administrative problems that the system confronts, but also a national willingness to accept necessary sacrifices in order to reduce external vulnerability.

If the national will expressed the action of political parties, this would present no problems. In their platforms the parties of the right and the left, and the PRI in the center, all support a nationalist and independent foreign policy, particularly with respect to the United States. However, action is still very weak and consequently counts for little in Mexico's political life.

To reduce Mexico's external vulnerability would require great internal mobilization, especially of those sectors with the greatest political force and economic power, which are currently the beneficiaries of the status quo. It would require, in turn, a broad base of social solidarity and political consensus around a national project that would put greater emphasis on political autonomy and socio-economic development than on simple growth. In a society exposed for decades to a systematic depoliticization and to the exaltation of materialistic values, leading to a system that rewards individualistic survival through corruption, solidarity and consensus are sadly wanting.

Specifically, a number of concrete measures would be required. The upper and middle classes must accept certain sacrifices of their interests, especially where their pattern of luxury consumption puts pressures on the balance of payments through unnecessary importation, personal contraband, and frequent trips abroad. The residents of the border strip, where the population continues to grow rapidly and is accustomed to living under a regime of customs exceptions with free zones and perimeters, would also have to accept sacrifices. Their situation generates a massive outflow of foreign exchange with its daily purchases on the United States' side. The majority of citizens must determine that petroleum will not "overheat" the economy and destabilize the country or be utilized to postpone the economic and social reforms that the nation urgently needs.

The development of Mexico–United States relations will also depend, to an important degree, on the shape of future international crises. In the event of a worldwide international conflagration, the most probable outcome is that Mexico, as in the Second World War, would be forced to line up on the United States' side for obvious reasons of geography and economic dependence. In that case the question is, what degree of enthusiasm and cooperation would Mexico bring to its alignment with the United States? But such a crisis is unlikely. Rather, one must consider the revolution in Iran or the Iran-Iraq war that, by affecting the world petroleum supply, generates greater pressures on Mexico to augment its own production. These emergencies, which might be difficult to visualize in a period of a world oil glut, can lend new and stronger arguments to those who assert that the United States must rely on Mexico as a more secure source for a strategic reserve of oil.

On the other hand, the behavior of the U.S. and world economies will also affect the relations between the two countries. If the recession of the U.S. economy persists, Mexico will be affected in two important respects: in the volume of trade and tourism, and in the restriction of migration, which greater unemployment in the United States may induce. If inflation persists in the economy north of the border, it will be transmitted to Mexico in the higher costs for equipment imports and intermediate inputs into production, increasing the prices of the final products. Exports like Mexican beef, which aided in stabilizing prices in the U.S. market by raising supply, had the opposite effect in Mexico, where market prices rose owing to the reduction in supply.

As new and graver crises emerge in the Latin American region, particularly in the Caribbean and in Central America, the Mexican and U.S. perceptions toward them will tend to differ, and this might affect relations between the two countries, depending on the magnitude of the crises. Because of a common language and culture, political events in Latin America have different connotations in Mexico—and greater importance in both emotional and political terms—than they do in the United States. On the other hand, a foreign policy independent of Washington is a fact not equally accepted in U.S. political circles, no matter if this enhances political stability in Mexico.

Especially from the U.S. perspective, the agenda for Mexico–United

States relations in the near future will surely retain migration and hydro-carbons as the two priority matters. Removing obstacles to trade and tourism, limiting smuggling, and developing and integrating the border into the national economy will be important from a Mexican perspective. The drug traffic will cease to occupy a priority spot as third countries continue to be the principal suppliers of the U.S. market. In multilateral matters, the North/South differences and the ferment in Central America will continue to divide the United States and Mexican positions.

CONCLUSIONS

The future of Mexico–United States relations will depend in great measure on Mexico's capacity to reduce its vulnerability to numerous pressures, which in turn will depend on the determination of the domestic majority to carry out the necessary, implemental reforms. The future of those relations will depend also on the perceptions of U.S. sectors involved in defining the national interest in relation to Mexico, since on this in turn will depend whether or not the United States exerts pressures on Mexico. In the event that very short-run perceptions prevail—perceptions that accord priority to matters such as oil and migration—there will certainly be diverse pressures that will muddy the relations between the two countries. The outcome will be different if long-term perceptions prevail, based on what some call the U.S. traditional objectives in regard to Mexico, i.e., assisting with the balanced development and political stability of the country. Finally, U.S. perceptions may be affected by future events occurring in the international political arena. Such perceptions will depend ultimately on the magnitude of such events and on whether priority is given to immediate objectives or to long-term ones.

The Politics of the United States–Mexico Relationship

Richard R. Fagen

WHAT FOLLOWS is a preliminary analysis of some features of the United States–Mexico relationship, with special emphasis on its longer-run political aspects. Except for illustrative examples, the analysis does not deal with substantive matters and issues (petroleum, trade, agriculture, migration, security, etc.) that other conference participants have discussed, or with the multitude of on-going and future problems that both binds and divides. The basic question to be answered is this: What are the structural characteristics of the relevant political landscape that, if clarified, might help to order our understanding of "United States–Mexico events" during the next decade or so? I have not sought—nor do I think it possible at this stage—to construct a mapping sufficiently detailed to predict specific outcomes. Rather, I have attempted a preliminary sketch of the political space—and some of the rules of the game—in which bargaining will take place, alliances will be forged, and conflict will erupt and perhaps be adjudicated. Furthermore, as will become evident, the analytical framework is U.S.-centric. Since I know more about the United States than about Mexico, and because my intent was to move as quickly as possible to the politics of the relationship, I have slighted and even ignored the Mexican side of the equation.[1] It is my expectation that the work and comments of others will help to redress this imbalance.

THE POLITICS OF ASYMMETRY

Use what language you will, there is no way to escape the fact that Mexico will never be as continuously important to the United States as the United States is to Mexico. There is a double meaning to this observa-

---

[1] "The Politics of Race and Ethnicity" section of this essay is, in fact, wholly U.S.-centric. In other sections, the analysis of how Mexico functions politically is central to the questions raised.

tion. The first points to the realm of high politics, attentive publics, and diplomacy—broadly understood. While "the Mexican question," in its multiple forms, must always vie for space on the U.S. political agenda, the "North American question" simply cannot and will not disappear from center stage in Mexico.[2] At the more everyday societal level there is a related pattern. Despite the "Mexicanization" of the border states and some other areas, despite Chicano power, despite oil and gas imports, despite migration, and despite Spanish language radio, TV, and ballots, the overall impact of the United States as an economy and society/culture on Mexico is many times greater than the impact of Mexico on the United States.

In a broad sense, this is what power is all about, and in general no conspiracy theories are needed to explain why power is and will continue to be used, whether intentionally or unintentionally, to the advantage of the more powerful (although at times conspiracies, of course, do exist). But in the 1980s and beyond, as we have also seen in the 1960s and 1970s, power conceptualized in crude materialist terms (dollars, tanks, barrels of oil, etc.) is a poor predictor of international outcomes. This is particularly the case when domestic and international politics are as inextricably intertwined as they are in the United States–Mexico case. Thus, we are left with the challenging task of understanding a politics of asymmetry in which changing circumstances and the correlation of forces nationally and internationally make the power equation in bilateral relations between the United States and Mexico less unbalanced than a simple, quantitative (and historical) evaluation might suggest.

Speculating loosely on what bilateral United States–Mexico relations might look like in this context, the following hypotheses seem reasonable.[3]

1. U.S. perceptions of and reactions to Mexico will be profoundly shaped by global and regional factors. In the case of energy and economic relations this is so obvious that it needs no elaboration. In no less important fashion this is also the case for ideological and security issues. Thus, it is to be expected that after the Sandinist victory in Nicaragua (and while El Salvador is in the process of exploding and especially while Guatemala is heating up), we will hear much talk about Central American dominoes and even the "threat to oil-rich Mexico." If one needs an historical example with implications for the future, imagine the return of *Echeverrismo* in Mexican foreign policy—this time championed by an

[2] This reality is judiciously but forcefully expressed by Jorge Castañeda in his "En busca de una posición frente a Estados Unidos," in El Colegio de México, *Visión del México Contemporáneo* (Mexico, 1979), pp. 101–16.

[3] Two observations about the hypotheses: first, they are U.S.-centric to a significant degree, i.e., they concentrate on factors shaping U.S. behavior; second, they are in part extensions of currently observable realities rather than "new" speculations about the future.

oil-rich Mexican state. Needless to say, this would not be perceived in Washington in a strictly local or bilateral context.

2. U.S. actions relevant to Mexico will constantly be energized by a stop-and-go politics of crisis or semi-crisis. This is in part the direct consequence of a Mexico that must compete for attention with other international actors and problems. Thus the gas drama, the tomato and winter vegetable case, and 1979's cut-them-to-shreds border fence are the kinds of issues that propel Mexico to the center of policy attention. Further intensifying this tendency are the almost infinite webs of economic and social interests and contacts between the two societies. So deeply is the United States "into" Mexico—and to a lesser extent Mexico "into" the United States—that there are trip-wires everywhere. A serious incident involving tourists? A shooting at the border? The gas being shut off now that it is flowing? An ambassadorial (or presidential) gaffe? There are innumerable more complex and dynamic possibilities. This is not a prediction of catastrophe, just a reminder that a deep relationship coupled with long-standing national sensitivities constantly generates incidents that perturb, vulgarize, and even displace the long-term agenda.

3. Related to a politics of sporadic semi-crisis is what might be called a politics of many tongues. As has been pointed out *ad nauseam*, the multi-interest, multi-access, multi-bureaucracy U.S. political system confounds policy toward Mexico. Tomato growers want one policy, and they find their bureaucratic allies. Meanwhile, the State Department—with bigger fish to fry—takes a different position, and so on. In another domain, the gas negotiations illuminate an even more complex set of conflicts, between the Congress, the Energy Department, gas transmission companies, and many others. To escape total paralysis, most such conflicts get resolved. But meanwhile the tendencies toward sporadic, crisis-ridden, and—one might even say—irresponsible bilateral policies are reinforced.[4]

4. If U.S. policies toward Mexico will in general continue to have the characteristics just enumerated, what are the implications for Mexican politics toward the United States? At first glance it is tempting to fasten on Mexico's new bargaining resources and how they might be used. Although Mexico now has its petroleum cards to play, it is increasingly recognized that oil poker is not a simple, always-win game. What may in

[4]The case should not be overstated. The primary purpose of the executive branch review process which resulted in PRM-41 and the subsequent appointment of Robert Krueger as Coordinator for Mexican Affairs was to soften if not silence the many tongues, or to encourage them to speak—at least on important occasions—the same language. During 1979 and 1980 modest success was registered in this area. See the well-argued paper by Richard A. Nuccio, "The Redefinition of U.S.-Mexican Relations, 1977–1980," mimeo (July 1980). The Reagan administration, however, has abolished the position of coordinator for Mexican affairs.

fact prove more to Mexico's advantage in the long run is the essential coherence—or possibilities for coherence—in Mexican foreign policy. There is more consensus in Mexican society (deeply unequal though it may be), and in the Mexican state, on relevant bilateral issues than in the United States. The problem of many tongues is less vexing in Mexico, and Mexican elites are able to keep their eyes on the ball and on the bilateral game to a much greater extent than is the case in the United States. This is one important aspect of the politics of asymmetry that crude assessments of "power" fail to take into account. In the 1980s I would expect the Mexican political system to perform better than its U.S. counterpart in terms of consistency, tenacity, mind, and even audacity when bilateral exchanges are taking place.

In sum, as we have learned elsewhere, conflicts are not necessarily won by those who have the biggest bombers and the loudest voices. Some may object that the military metaphor is not the most appropriate to use in discussing United States–Mexico relations. But simple ideas like power and winning—and losing—are very much a part of peaceful exchanges as well, and the realities of past, present, and future contacts between the United States and Mexico suggest that just such simple ideas will remain central to the politics of asymmetry.

THE POLITICS OF ALLIANCES

All this is in several ways quite conventional. In emphasizing state-to-state relationships, seasoned with the spice of conflict, the approach fits well with the traditional body of international relations ideas (I hesitate to call that body of ideas a theory). By suggesting that the state, or at least the institutions and processes of government, is profoundly influenced by interests and dynamics generated in the larger society, the approach also acknowledges central concerns of the pluralist paradigm as well as the Marxist focus on the state/society nexus.

A cursory familiarity with the realities of U.S.-Mexican relations, however, suggests that this nation-centric optic, while useful, is insufficient to capture the full range of what is actually taking place. "We/they" approaches, in which the "we" is defined as the United States or United States interests, and the "they" as Mexico or Mexican interests (or vice versa), quickly lose their power when state-to-state negotiations are not the sole, or at least the primary, object of study. In fact, even when a first glance suggests that we might be dealing with an episode of state-to-state relations, more detailed study (at least in the case of U.S.-Mexican relations) often suggests that the world is more complicated.

Take the now much-discussed gas case of 1977–78. From a foreshortened historical viewpoint, the case began when PEMEX signed a letter of intent with six U.S. private corporations—gas transmission companies. The initial alliance was thus between one arm of the Mexican government and U.S. private capital. U.S. banks, construction companies, and capital goods suppliers were soon excited about the deal, joining the alliance to push the *gasoducto* through. In the context of the energy debate, deep splits in the U.S. Congress, and to a lesser extent in the Executive, soon arose. For quite different reasons, opposition also arose in Mexico, linking together left political groups and critical members of the PRI, the governing party, as well as deeply nationalistic "public opinion."

Throughout, the main axis of the "pro-alliance" was transnational, composed of certain sectors of the Mexican government and private capital on the one hand, and of multinational corporations, banks, and certain political actors in the United States on the other hand. No such firm "anti-alliance" of a transnational sort was forged, although certainly U.S. critics of the proposed pricing structure drew aid and comfort from Mexican nationalists protesting the deal on other grounds.[5]

Phase two of the gas imbroglio involved a somewhat different cast of characters and a substantially different setting.[6] On April 3, 1979, government-to-government negotiations on gas pricing began in the wake of President Carter's visit to Mexico. Powerful international forces entered into the equation. With OPEC-led price rises, the original "high" price for Mexican gas now became cheap. The impending arrival of expensive deregulated domestic gas in the United States further undercut the U.S. advocates of a tough (low) pricing line on Mexican gas. By January 1980, a new U.S.-Mexican pricing arrangement had been negotiated. A few days later, the Canadians announced large increases in the price of gas shipped to the United States, leapfrogging their prices over the recently negotiated Mexican deal. Needless to say, the Mexican price then had to be brought up to the Canadian level. By 1980 it was generally clear to almost all concerned that hemispheric energy questions were too important to be left entirely to the kinds of ad hoc transnational alliances that had characterized and confounded the first stage of the gas deal.

The second phase of the gas deal, involving as it did the direct intervention of high-level state representatives on both sides in order to resolve what had become an intolerable and embarrassing situation, is the exception that proves the rule. Only infrequently does the state have both the capacity and the will to "solve" a bilateral issue in this fashion. More typical is a *problemática* such as migration. Despite the existence of offi-

---

[5] This phase of the gas case is discussed in detail in Richard R. Fagen and Henry R. Nau, "Mexican Gas: The Northern Connection," in Richard R. Fagen, ed., *Capitalism and the State in U.S.–Latin American Relations* (Stanford, 1979), pp. 382–427.

[6] In this paragraph I follow Nuccio, "Redefinition," pp. 25–31.

cial policies on both sides of the border, no simple we/they dichotomy would be very useful for mapping the geography of support and opposition to either present policies or possible alternatives. In this area, transnational alliances are usually not as overt as was the case with phase one of the gas deal. They do exist, however, as witness the way in which users of undocumented labor cooperate across the border with *coyotes* to ensure a continuous supply of workers. This, of course, is only a mini-alliance, a mafia trafficking in human beings, which has its counterparts in drugs, consumer products, and the like. The potential for larger, less clandestine alliances still exists, as was amply demonstrated during the *bracero* program. And certainly, given the complexity of the interests and the social realities of migration, it is difficult to imagine the state stepping in to "solve" the migration problem in the same way that state-to-state negotiations solved the gas pricing issue, at least temporarily.

The purpose of these examples is not just to suggest that state-centric analytical frameworks both miss and mystify many important aspects of the United States–Mexico relationship. It is also necessary to speculate on the way in which alliances will form and cluster in the future. Being bold, I would make the following general prediction: In the 1980s, alliances between the Mexican state and private foreign capital (the extent to which this is U.S. capital depends on a number of factors) will increase. Also on the increase will be alliances between foreign private capital and Mexican private capital. Such alliances will, in many instances, be

	Mexican state	Mexican private capital
Industrialized foreign states	Mexican negotiating card is essentially petroleum. Foreign state often serves as broker for local private interests.	This is almost an empty cell, i.e., foreign industrialized states are not interested in Mexican private capital. The partial exception is Mexican capital that flees to foreign private markets, a transaction not usually mediated by the state.
Foreign private capital	A rapidly increasing web of alliances; rate of increase depends in part on domestic and international perceptions of "stability" of Mexican state. Mexican state often helps link domestic and international capital.	A rapidly increasing web of alliances; the main modalities are the joint venture, the service contract, and cooperation to open foreign markets that might otherwise be difficult to crack. See cell on left, as well.

Alliance Patterns for the 1980s

brokeraged by the Mexican state; in others the state will be a central participant, not just a broker. Somewhat ironically, the "pro-alliance" put together in phase one of the gas deal, although it ultimately failed, foreshadows the future. These predictions, somewhat elaborated, are roughly summarized in the figure on p. 336.

The summary is, of course, highly schematic, taking no account of intra-national alliance structures, transnational alliances that do not involve private capital, or a host of other factors. But it does suggest the limited reach of an analytical scheme that fails to recognize the increasing importance of alliances that are struck across national boundaries and that do not fall strictly within the modalities of state-to-state relations.

THE POLITICS OF THE NATIONAL INTEREST

At least in the United States the idea of the national interest is the last, and often the first, refuge of scoundrels. Thus we were told that the carpet bombing of Cambodia was "in the national interest," that the failed rescue attempt in Iran was "in the national interest," and so forth. In addition, almost every lobby, from the Chrysler Corporation to Florida tomato growers, attempts to wrap itself in the language and symbolism of the national interest as it seeks new benefits or struggles to retain those that it has. At first glance, political practice seems to have destroyed the conceptuality of the idea of the national interest, as an endless parade of persons and groups seeks legitimacy, justification, and advantage by stretching ever wider those already elastic words.

Yet precisely because the idea of the national interest looms so large in political discourse, and because its irreducible meaning is that there are, or ought to be, interests of the collectivity that are superordinate to particular and private interests, it must be taken into account by those who seek to understand United States–Mexico relations. In short, the continuing struggle to define, redefine, and appropriate the valuable symbolism of the national interest illuminates the interplay of private and public purposes in the political system. Where might one begin to examine this interplay? A useful point of departure is to analyze the evolution of quite concrete specifications of "the national interest," since the most general formulations are either tautological, banal, or both. Once again, Mexican oil and gas offer a good example.

Concentrating on the United States, a mini-history of conceptualizations of the U.S. national interest in Mexican oil and gas—particularly oil—would look something like this: First reactions were narrowly centered on volumes (production), particularly export volumes, and—even more particularly—export volumes to the United States. This might be called the "more the merrier" view of the U.S. national interest in Mexican oil. Second reactions, recognizing that world volumes, not destinations, are the crucial concern, put less emphasis on the importance of the United States as a direct buyer of Mexican oil. Later—as the debate about levels of production, inflation, disequilibria, and associated questions about sowing the oil spilled over from Mexico—a third reaction began to intercut with the others. This most recent conceptualization of the U.S. national interest emphasizes that the consequences for Mexico of the patterns of oil exploitation and resource utilization are also very important for the United States. This view might be called the "as long as reasonable amounts of oil are exported (about one million barrels a day in the short run?), then what's good for Mexico is good for the United States" view. Put more cynically, the view says, "If an extra barrel of oil means an extra bushel of unrest in Mexico, who needs it?"[7]

This sketch implies a hugely complex political-ideological process. Obviously these several positions have all been present in the U.S. debate on Mexican oil from the outset, and all are present today. But the mix and emphases have changed, and it is not happenstance that by 1979 conservative magazines like *Business Week* were closer to the "what's good for Mexico" position than one might have expected even a year earlier. Granted that this movement had been occasioned by the specter of a possibly destabilized Mexico and concomitant threats to U.S. investments and other interests. No altruism here. But then, discussions of the national interest have never been distinguished for their altruism or internationalism.

An additional perspective on the politics of the national interest is generated by the tomato and winter vegetable controversy.[8] As in almost all such cases, local interests damaged or merely threatened by foreign competition attempt to suggest that not only they but also "the American people" will be hurt if their particular claims are not supported. This is not, however, an easy position to sustain, for inexpensive, high quality Mexican imports clearly benefit hundreds of thousands if not millions of U.S. consumers. Furthermore, at least in theory, such cases turn on the technical determination of "unfair" competition (dumping), not on a simple determination of whether or not some or all U.S. producers are hurt financially by imports.

[7] For a clear, semi-official articulation of this view, see David Ronfeldt, Richard Nehring, and Arturo Gándara, *Mexico's Petroleum and U.S. Policy: Implications for the 1980s* (Santa Monica, Calif., June 1980). This report, prepared for the Department of Energy, carries Rand number R-2510-DOE. See also Comptroller General, *Prospects for a Stronger United States–Mexico Energy Relationship* (Washington, D.C., May 1, 1980).

[8] In the tomato case, I have depended heavily on Steven E. Sanderson, "Florida Tomatoes, U.S.-Mexican Relations, and the International Division of Labor," *Inter-American Economic Affairs*, 35, no. 3 (1981), 23–52.

What makes the tomato case of 1978–80 particularly interesting is that it took place in the context of long-standing and conflictual negotiations between the United States and Mexico on a whole host of issues, most particularly natural gas. What was, at one level, a complex but limited determination of fact—whether or not Mexican tomatoes were entering the United States at "less than fair value"—was, at another level, a test of the U.S. government's capacity to generate and enforce a version of the national interest that was other than the simple result of the pull and haul of special interests (growers, importers, consumers, etc.). The drama was heightened because at the very highest levels of the Mexican government, including the presidency, it had been made clear that a decision against the Mexican growers and exporters would not be seen as simply the inexorable working-out of an impartial process of administrative law.[9] To the contrary, had the various decisions gone against Mexico, it is entirely possible that the gas deal might also have been scuttled and relations in general taken a sharp turn for the worse.

There is no evidence—nor, in the nature of the case, is there likely to be—that the Treasury and Commerce Departments acted other than "professionally" in making their several determinations. Nevertheless, it stretches the imagination to believe that the larger political context in which the determinations were set was irrelevant to the decisions that were made. When the president of the United States has let it be known that better relations with Mexico have been placed fairly high on the national agenda, it would be a rare federal agency indeed that would subsequently close its bureaucratic eyes to that reality.

Do these cases or others suggest tendencies or trends? That is, can we predict with any confidence the substantive directions in which national interest debates will move in the United States when United States–Mexico relations are at the center of attention? Certainly as process, these debates will continue at least in part to reflect the fragmentary, "many tongues" character of U.S. politics. In terms of content, however, one can hazard a guess that the debates will increasingly be concerned with the question of "stability" in Mexico. This concern was overtly manifest in the gas case, implicit in the tomato case, and is very much in evidence when migration issues are discussed. For example, even advocates of a tighter border show increasing sensitivity to the domestic (Mexican) consequences of a less permeable frontier. A favorite metaphor invokes the danger of "screwing down the lid on the pressure cooker."

[9] The stakes on the Mexican side are significant. The winter vegetable trade amounts to approximately $500 million, generates employment for tens of thousands of workers, and has important, although not necessarily positive, implications for Mexican domestic consumption of foodstuffs.

A moment's reflection suggests how multi-motivated and ambiguous an evolving U.S. concern with stability in Mexico is and will continue to be. Were Mexico not petroleum-rich, the stability question would not be so prominently on the agenda.[10] Yet it would certainly be there to some substantial extent even without the hydrocarbon connection. After all, stability has historically been a prime, Mexico-related concern of U.S. policy elites. Even a superficial reading of U.S. reactions to the Mexican Revolution suggests how profound and long-standing that concern is.

Stability is subject to almost as many infusions of meaning as the concept of the national interest itself. For some if not most U.S. elites it means the continuance of Mexican capitalism, whatever the social and cultural costs. Thus defined, it implies structural continuity, particularly in the economic realm. For others it has a more overtly political meaning, referring to the capacity of the Mexican political system to handle the wide range of challenges that are being generated in a deeply stressed society. This view of stability is more "liberal," allowing for significant (and by definition "necessary") changes in economic arrangements so that "the system" in its more global sense can survive. These and other views of what constitutes stability are, of course, neither mutually exclusive nor inevitably contradictory.

In sum, to predict that the national interest debate in the United States will increasingly fixate on the issue of stability in Mexico is not to predict either rationality or benevolence. To the contrary, it is in part a prediction of increased tensions, as various publics in the United States move toward a vision of Mexican affairs that sees departures from the main lines of the status quo as decidedly less desirable than a continuation of business-as-usual. On the other hand, if the notion of stability is given general developmental and social content, the results of a "stability-of-our-southern-neighbor" theme in U.S. discussions of the national interest are not necessarily pernicious. For example, the shift away from a "more the merrier" toward a "what's good for Mexico" posture in the oil and U.S. national interest debate is probably positive for both societies. Or, if that is too general a statement, it can at a minimum be said that there is substantial complementarity of interests and perceptions between certain elites in the United States, their counterparts in Mexico, and at least some of those who "only stand and wait" on both sides of the border.

[10] Posed most baldly, the stability question translates directly into a national security question when Mexico is seen as a key supplier of hydrocarbons. I have elaborated on this theme in "Mexican Petroleum and U.S. National Security," *International Security*, 4, no. 1 (summer 1979), 39–53. With the triumph of the Sandinists in Nicaragua and growing unrest in Central America, particularly in Guatemala, more extreme formulations view the Mexican oil, security, and stability triangle in regional and even global rather than national terms.

THE POLITICS OF THE BORDERLANDS

Like two tectonic plates, Mexico (earlier New Spain) and the United States (earlier French and English colonies) have ground against each other for more than three centuries in the shifting terrain that we call the borderlands. The imagery is tempting: the steady pulverizing and mixing of cultures, the cataclysmic upwelling of the Mexican-American War (with the resultant changes in geography), the now-maturing strata of structures and boundaries within which changes occur more subtly, but not less relentlessly. Yet ultimately the imagery disappoints, just as surely as it tempts, for we have no really satisfactory conceptualization of past, present, and future meanings of the oft-noted fact that the United States and Mexico are "neighbors."

One reason for the conceptual shortfall is that this particular kind of "neighborliness" has no precedent. It is truly a *caso único*—by virtue of the length of the border (largely undefended), the different cultures in contact and conflict, and the widely divergent levels of wealth of the two nations. Since there cannot be a theory of a single case, it is hardly surprising that almost all discussions of the region move quickly toward straight description of the way things are—or are thought to be—or the direction in which they are headed. In thinking about the borderlands one is thus constantly pulled toward the specific, the unique—sometimes folkloric—and the problematic.

Can a virtue be made of this inevitability? More modestly, are there more general frameworks in which one can think about this *caso único*? Two perspectives seem appropriate. The first, already making headway in the literature about the borderlands, views the north of Mexico and the southwest of the United States as a complex and extremely dynamic economic system. It is a system that has a juridical line running through it (the border), which in turn affects exchanges in important ways. The overriding characteristic of the region, however, is not that it is made up of parts of two countries, but rather that it functions as a system both in spite of and because of its two-partness.

This approach to the borderlands does not claim or even imply that the system functions without conflicts and tensions. To the contrary, as in all complex economic systems, there are contradictions, conflicting interests, and a spillover into arenas that are not, strictly speaking, economic. For example, the park system of the city of El Paso receives heavy usage from residents of Ciudad Juárez, just across the border. With some justification, authorities in El Paso argue that this is an unfair burden on their tax base, but for political, cultural, and other economic reasons they have no desire, and even less capacity, to institute an exclusionist policy. Seeing this local issue as part and parcel of a regional and international reality, their preferred solution would be state and/or federal contributions to their local park system since they are, in effect, running an international facility.

The second, and complementary, perspective focuses less on the economics of the borderlands and more on the emerging politics. Here primary emphasis is given to the ties that divide rather than the ties that bind. The borderlands are a place where politically upsetting things happen, things that reinforce "we/they" identifications; where immigrants get beaten and occasionally shot; where fences get built; where a currency devaluation hits merchants and consumers immediately and dramatically minutes after it is announced in Mexico City; where the shutdown of a *maquila* (for "perfectly sound economic reasons," of course) throws hundreds of workers back into the ranks of the unemployed; where Mexican oil washes up on Texas beaches. Furthermore, the borderlands are also geographically and politically distant from their respective capitals, creating the partial paradox that immediate and vexing problems crop up in areas that are not otherwise at the center of elite political attention.[11]

Viewed politically, the borderlands are thus a zone where problems are spawned, not a zone where they are resolved. Multitudes of politically critical events—critical for United States–Mexico relations—either originate in the borderlands or are manifested there in particularly acute form. Yet few such events really get settled, mediated, or given their full national and international meanings in the localities and regions in which they originate or resonate most immediately. Inevitably, local, state, and regional politics tend to become enmeshed intermittently in national and international policy; and just as inevitably issues tend to get handled or mishandled in ways that reflect non-local perspectives and interests. In the borderlands the contradictory tangle of domestic and foreign affairs comes home to roost with a vengeance.

Is there discernible movement in this tangle, some emerging resolution of a situation in which much of the action (and reaction) is in the borderlands but most of the rules and judgments are made elsewhere? At least in the United States, one can hazard a prediction: There will be mounting pressure to make local rules of the game in response to local pressures and interests. In part this stems from an expectation that Hispanics will increasingly make their weight felt in local and national politics. In part it reflects new regional political clout deriving from the congressional reapportionment to take place in 1982. In an even more basic sense, increased

[11] This generalization holds more firmly for the United States than for Mexico.

borderlands autonomy will be fueled by mounting pressures toward decentralization in U.S. politics, moves to return to localities some substantial control over decisions that affect their lives most directly. There is a borderlands component of the larger revolt against big government, big bureaucracy, and "the Eastern Establishment."

There is also a darker side to the pressures to make local rules of the game in response to local pressures. At worst this implies vigilantism, taking the law into one's own hands, a return to the worst of the nineteenth- and early twentieth-century borderlands' history. This is easiest to imagine in the immigration field—armed bands doing what they feel the Immigration and Naturalization Service is not doing. In fact, this sort of politics, sometimes with the implicit blessing of the local authorities, has always been practiced to a greater or lesser degree on the border. There is also a more "respectable" face to actual and prospective political revolt in the borderlands. Planned or semi-planned noncompliance with national laws and rules of the game is already widespread in the borderlands and is likely to increase and gain legitimacy if national solutions continue to be imposed on what are felt to be predominantly local problems and issues. It is precisely in this many-sided tension between the local, the national, and the international that the key dynamic of the politics of the borderlands will be found for years to come.[12]

THE POLITICS OF RACE AND ETHNICITY

According to the 1980 census, Hispanics numbered more than 21 million at the beginning of the decade, the fastest growing ethnic/racial minority in the United States. And among Hispanics, Chicanos and Mexican-Americans are and will continue to be the largest subgroup. This is a trend with a very long history, rooted in the northward explorations of the Spanish *conquistadores* in the sixteenth and seventeenth centuries, colonial attempts in the eighteenth and nineteenth centuries to settle what are today the borderlands, and the dramatic territorial acquisitions by the United States before, during, and immediately after the war with Mexico. But it is immigration—once the territorial question was "settled" by war and conquest—which has contributed most dramatically to the Mexicanization of the United States. In the 1880s, when the railroads were hungry for cheap labor, trainloads of Mexican workers were imported. Perhaps as much as 10 percent of Mexico's total population moved north at that time. With ebbs and flows dictated by economic

---

[12] Because the subject is being treated at length by other authors, I have not attempted to illustrate this claim with the multiple examples that can be found in the migration field. It is in this area, however, that the politics of noncompliance, vigilantism, and local-national-international tensions are most immediately evident.

and political circumstances, the movement has continued ever since. Although it may be slowed in the future by fences, guns, and economics, it will not stop.[13]

If the trends are clear, the political implications are not, either nationally or internationally. Not only have Hispanics in the United States historically been fragmented into local and "country-of-origin" groups and organizations, but they have also paid relatively little attention to foreign policy questions. This is as true of specifically Mexican-American and Chicano groups as of the Hispanic community in general. In fact, it is not at all clear what a more organized national political presence of Mexican-American and Chicano groups might mean for United States–Mexico relations.* Speculations range from predictions of a new "Jewish lobby"—tightly knit, well financed, and with access to top decision makers—to predictions that Chicanos and Mexican-Americans will be so internally divided, of so many minds about Mexico, that collectively they will have almost no impact on U.S. policy.[14] Mexican elites obviously have their own hypotheses about these issues as well. Thus both the Echeverría and López Portillo administrations made efforts to establish relations with what are still fragmented Chicano and Mexican-American groups in the United States.

The long-run foreign policy implications of the Hispanicization of the United States will not, however, stem exclusively from the politics of lobbying. Of greater importance will be the dynamics generated by the politics of race and ethnicity as practiced within the confines of the larger U.S. social order. Despite some still-lingering mythology to the contrary, the melting pot melts poorly at present, particularly when stigmata of skin-color and language exist, and the tougher the economic times in the United States, the more poorly it seems to melt.

What immediately links these problems to United States–Mexico relations is, of course, the immigration issue. Anyone who has followed this problem in the United States can cite multiple examples of outright racist

---

[13] See Wayne A. Cornelius, "Mexican Migration to the United States," in Susan Kaufman Purcell, ed., *Mexico–United States Relations* (New York, 1981).

* Editors' note: So important are these questions to the grand issues of United States–Mexico relations over the next twenty years that a Chicano advisory board has been formed to work in coordination with this project on future aspects of its program with particular attention to the evolving role of Chicanos in U.S. economic and social change and in United States–Mexico relations.

[14] The "Jewish lobby" analogy is substantially misleading in any case. Jews in the United States are concerned with using their already existing economic and political power to influence U.S. policy toward Israel and the Middle East. Chicanos and Mexican-Americans are basically concerned with using newly awakened U.S. interest in Mexico to enhance their political and economic clout at home. The latter is substantially more difficult to achieve than the former.

opposition to the entry of dark-skinned, Spanish-speaking persons, whether legally or illegally.[15] Ex-CIA Director William Colby spoke for many when he said that Mexico is "a bigger threat to the United States than the Soviet Union" because the overflow of Mexicans into the United States will overload our schools, break down the social peace of our cities, and in general prove to be unmanageable socially, culturally, and politically.[16] Others, less constrained, act out their hostilities toward Hispanics in daily episodes of racism and violence along the border and in hundreds of towns and cities across the United States.

It is scant comfort that these are old ideas and issues in the United States. In 1845, when the question of annexing Mexico, or parts thereof, was high on the national political agenda, editorialist John L. O'Sullivan (the man who popularized the expression "manifest destiny") wrote, "how should we estimate the fitness of the Mexican people to enter into the enjoyment of our political institutions? Taking that people as they are, and are likely to continue . . . will they become a valuable acquisition to us in any respect? Beyond a question, the entire Mexican vote would be substantially below our national average both in purity and intelligence."[17] The historic rootedness of anti-Mexican and anti-Hispanic feeling in the United States suggests that it will be a feature of U.S. life for the foreseeable future.

There is, unfortunately, yet another dimension to the immigration/racism issue. When sufficiently inflamed, nativist and xenophobic U.S. opinion is inordinately undiscriminating. When anti-Iranian violence erupted in the spring of 1980 in a number of U.S. college towns, white thugs beat up Chicano and Latin American students at Fresno State University in California because they "looked Iranian." At the same time, feelings about Cuban refugees who rioted or simply protested in the United States spilled over into antagonism toward non-Cuban Hispanics in nearby areas. Coming tensions related to the status of Puerto Rico will

[15] Chilling examples may be found in Wayne A. Cornelius, "America in the 'Era of Limits': The 'Nation of Immigrants' Turns Nativist—Again," Working Paper no. 3 (Center for United States–Mexican Studies, San Diego, June 1979).

[16] From Colby's interview with the *Los Angeles Times*, June 6, 1978. Bitter state and local opposition to bilingual education and the bilingual ballot are only two manifestations of the resentment that is felt in many quarters. The surface argument against bilingualism in any form is what might be called hard-core melting pot. The central rallying cry of the opponents of bilingualism is, "Why can't they learn English like previous immigrants [my grandparents] did?"

[17] Quoted in Norman Graebner, ed., *Manifest Destiny* (Indianapolis, 1968), pp. 139–40. O'Sullivan's position is particularly interesting because, although he was an expansionist, he did not believe in taking "too much" Mexican territory because its inhabitants (if you get the land, you get the people!) were so inferior to the bulk of U.S. citizens. Thus, they would be difficult to assimilate and in the long run would weaken the Republic. Subsequently, O'Sullivan opposed the move to annex all of Mexico, essentially for these reasons.

undoubtedly affect the lives and safety of non-Puerto Rican (or just "Latin-looking") residents of the United States if the debate on the island's future is as acerbic, and the politics as confrontational, as many expect. It is true that generalized anti-foreign sentiment, although always cyclical in the United States, has undoubtedly diminished in depth and intensity since the days of Sacco and Vanzetti. But to imagine that the United States has ended its sorry history of anti-foreign and racist sentiments and actions is to engage in wishful thinking.

The point is important because the manner in which Hispanics, and particularly persons of Mexican descent, are treated in the United States (in such areas as civil rights, bilingual education, etc.) cannot help but increasingly affect U.S. relations with its southern neighbor. The oft-expressed Mexican concern for its nationals who are residents in or visiting the United States is legally and ethically legitimate, even when somewhat cynically used south of the border for political and other purposes. Increasingly, that concern will find its place on the bilateral negotiating agenda. This development, in turn, will prove extremely vexing for the United States. Whether referring to Fresno thugs or problems in the Texas public school system, national authorities will claim, with some justification, that while they deplore the incidents and the conditions there is little they can do. This plea of impotence will not quiet Mexican concerns, however, and continued evidence of anti-Mexican incidents and biases in U.S. society will only intensify the dynamic of charges, pleas of innocence, denials, and mistrust. Thus, one more element of the tangle of domestic and international factors affecting United States–Mexico relations comes into focus: A nation that cannot treat persons of Mexican origin or Mexican citizenship decently within its own borders will have increasing difficulty winning the degree of cooperation from other Mexicans that will be required if relations are to improve during the 1980s and beyond.

CONCLUSION

Despite the impossibility of understanding U.S.-Mexican relations in a purely national framework, the fact remains that the grip of "we/they" thinking is still very strong. The entanglement of the United States and Mexico is of long historical standing, the two cultural legacies are at least partially in conflict, and the feelings generated are deep and sometimes bitter. For many Mexicans, the United States is still the country that robbed half the territory of their nation in the middle of the last century, that invaded and schemed during the Revolution, that opposed the Cárdenas reforms and the oil nationalization in the late 1930s, and that still continues to covet, penetrate, and pillage the Republic. For many U.S. citizens, although the historical memory is shorter and probably less accurate, there is an equally rich set of images: Mexico as barbarous and corrupt, overbreeding and impoverished, opulent but not modern, and now arrogant and aggressive.

In more enlightened U.S. policy circles it has now become commonplace to argue that we must understand the anti-Yankee component of Mexican nationalism, apply a discount factor, and then exercise due prudence in both predictions and policies. What is less well understood, at least north of the Rio Bravo, is that the 1980s' version of U.S. nationalism itself also needs careful monitoring if the United States–Mexico relationship is to be capably managed. Although extremely painful to admit, and even more difficult to weave into the policy-making process, it is an historic fact that the United States is a declining imperial power. From Nicaragua to Iran, to the automobile factories of Detroit and the banks of London and Zurich, the evidence is everywhere around us.[18] It is only against this backdrop of eroding imperial power, and the frustrations and uncertainties attendant on it, that U.S. nationalism vis-à-vis Mexico can be more fully understood. At the same time, of course, newly oil-rich Mexico seeks ways to assert its independence and explore its new status and power, while keeping at least one eye on its shaken but still immensely powerful northern neighbor.

Thus, a model in which Mexico is seen as merely "closing gaps" with the United States (in terms of wealth, negotiating cards, etc.) is at best only partially true if not at times actually misleading. Such a model underplays the independent dynamics and contemporary histories of the two nations. Mexico and the United States are societies on different trajectories in a world system being rapidly restructured. The "we/they" feelings that each brings to its bilateral relations with the other reflect not only historical baggage—the deep impress of remembered and imagined events—but also the images that each has of itself in the 1980s and beyond. For the United States, at least, these are by no means predominantly positive images. Interwoven in substantial measure with frustration, bewilderment, and even rage, they are not the most solid platform from which to rework what has always been a complex and often a conflictual relationship. Once again, we are reminded that in United States–Mexico relations there is no escape from the larger forces that shape the two societies.

[18] A useful, short presentation of the global context in which U.S. hegemony is declining—and some of the consequences and dangers which inhere in the process—can be found in Immanuel Wallerstein, "Friends as Foes," *Foreign Policy*, no. 40 (fall 1980), pp. 119–31.

Mexico–United States Economic Relations and the World Cycle: A European View

E. V. K. FitzGerald

A "European view" of the development of economic relations between Mexico and the United States might not seem very interesting at first sight; Western Europe [1] still has relatively little economic or political stake in the process, and it is unlikely that direct lessons can be drawn from the European experience. It is the European view of its own economic problems—of reviving the rate of accumulation and reducing unemployment while finding a new place in the international division of labor through deliberate restructuring in the context of a world recession—which is relevant. These themes have not been given as much attention as they merit in discussions of Mexico–United States relations, largely because economic debates in the two countries tend to concentrate on sectoral issues and domestic "trends" rather than on overall restructuring. In both cases there is also a tendency to ignore world conditions as a whole in internal or mutual economic policy debates. Other chapters in this volume (particularly those by Reynolds and by Cordera and Tello) contribute to the rectification of the one imbalance. This chapter attempts no more than a schematic outline of how the other might be approached. It is, therefore, an agenda rather than a complete argument or an empirical study.

The economic relationship between Mexico and the United States should not be seen either as the interaction of two monotonic trends or as marginal mutual adjustment. On the contrary, both the nature of economic growth in general and the present situation of the world economy in particular indicate that future expansion will involve structural change

I am indebted to the late Oscar Braun for his help with an earlier draft of this essay. The reader should bear in mind that the viewpoint and bibliography are those of end-1980.

[1] The word *Europe* is used to refer empirically to Western Europe; intellectually, however, the "European view" is somewhat broader, encompassing as it does both orthodox and Marxian thought.

and considerable trend alterations. Above all, the renewal of capital accumulation will require considerable alterations for income distribution both within and between Mexico and the United States because it will be related to the restoration of profit levels and higher labor productivity. These changes will not necessarily be to the advantage of Mexico, even though the degree of her dependence on the United States does mean that growth in the two economies is strongly correlated. To contemplate the economic relationship between the two countries without taking into account the world cycle, which will continue largely without reference to that relationship, would be unrealistic and possibly dangerously misleading.

Ideally, this could be done by examining the relationship within an appropriate model of the world economy. Unfortunately, those models do not usually specify Mexico as such, nor do they handle structural change in inter-economy relations at all well, being based on broadly Keynesian assumptions about the effect of First-World growth on that of the Third. More seriously, they do not really confront the world cycle in theoretically satisfactory terms, seeing it as a matter of policy ("global management") rather than as an economic phenomenon. There is some truth in this view, of course, and it is interesting to note that, in world forums established to discuss such matters, Mexico is gradually emerging as a minor power. However, it is necessary to work out the logic of the present recession. If we are to speculate sensibly as to the form the recovery will probably take (no revival would involve shifts in geopolitical relationships beyond the scope of this paper), we must examine alternative analyses of the depression itself and the attempts of other regions to renew accumulation.

A European view, therefore, involves a particular experience of restructuring North-South relationships, now well under way, and a perspective on international relations that necessarily takes into account the world cycle as a whole. In this chapter we shall be making three points. First, that the European restructuring debate is concerned with themes similar to those of the Mexico–United States debate, but with a different perspective, particularly on the relevance of secular changes in the world economy. Second, that the way in which the present world recession is now interpreted implies substantially different prospects for world economic development during the rest of the century. Third, that economic relations between Mexico and the United States can be seen to depend to a great extent upon the form the eventual recovery takes. Both the declining hegemony of the United States over the world capitalist economy and the expansion of Mexico into the international economic arena make our theme increasingly relevant.

THE EUROPEAN RESTRUCTURING DEBATE

During the second half of the 1970s, a major debate took place in Europe on "economic restructuring"; it was one of the few occasions on which academics, politicians, bureaucrats, businessmen, and unionists found a common theme for positive discussion. At their most immediate, the issues arose from three apparently local problems: the declining competitive position of traditional European industries such as clothing and consumer durables, faced with cheap imports from the Third World; the need to create a specifically European policy for the EEC in relation to the ex-colonies; and the absorption of the new "southern accession" members (Portugal, Spain, and Greece) to the Community itself. Nonetheless, the parallel with the United States–Mexico relationship is clear, even without introducing the concept of the North American Common Market (NACM): the existing degree of economic integration to the United States is no less than in the EEC, but the social, labor, and fiscal integration of Community members is much greater; but this is presumably not what U.S. supporters of the NACM propose.[2]

Meanwhile, the debate was increasingly overshadowed by the realization that stagnation in trade and growing unemployment was not just a European problem—in other words, that this was part of a world recession and that the postwar boom had in fact come to an end. However, the European tradition of economic policy making, particularly on the Continent itself, has always involved a greater degree of explicit state intervention than in the Anglo-Saxon world, the tradition of government-led industrialization in Germany and France being reinforced by the more recent experience of postwar reconstruction.

The literature is enormous, but curiously the more interesting studies have come from official or semi-official sources—among them, the OECD (Organization for Economic Cooperation and Development), the Brandt Commission, the United Nations, and even the British Foreign Office.[3]

---

[2] See the discussion of "full exchange" in Reynolds's essay in this volume.

[3] For two recent, policy-oriented discussions, with bibliographies, see Institute of Social Studies, *Conference on Adjustment Policies: Final Report* (The Hague, 1977); I. Levenson and N. Wheeler, *Western Economies in Transition: Structural Change and Adjustment Policies in Industrial Countries* (Boulder, Colo., 1980). For views that correspond broadly to the "classical" approach as defined below, see OECD, *Interfutures: Facing the Future* (Paris, 1979), and *Economic Outlook* (Paris, July 1980); Independent Commission on International Development Issues (ICIDI, the "Brandt Commission"), *North-South: A Programme for Survival* (London, 1980); United Nations Industrial Development Organization (UNIDO), *Industry and Development* (New York, 1979); Foreign and Commonwealth Office (FCO), *The Newly Industrialising Countries and the Adjustment Problem*, Government Economic Service Working Paper no. 18 (London, 1976).

These documents reflect a general agreement on the need to restructure industry at the center of the world economy (particularly United States, West Germany, Britain, France, and Italy, but also the other member of the OECD "big six," Japan) toward more competitive branches, defined in terms of the use of new higher technologies, and away from labor-intensive, and toward capital-intensive, branches. This reduction of labor intensity refers to semiskilled labor because the new branches are in fact intensive in highly skilled labor (or "human capital"); in other words, there is a reduction in labor time per unit of output but not necessarily any reduction in wage content of production costs. Moreover, this does not correspond to the traditional distinction between light and heavy industry—steel and shipbuilding are becoming increasingly uncompetitive in Europe and subject to displacement by cheaper imports from the Third World. This is brought about not only by low wage levels on the periphery, but also by the fact that in semiskilled labor-intensive sectors at the center of the world economy the unit labor costs are continually pressed upward by the transmission of wage levels from more capital-intensive sectors, so that profits are reduced from both the price and the cost sides. This occurs also in tertiary sectors; although they are protected by their non-traded status, the phenomenon is a considerable contributor to the so-called fiscal crisis of the state in Europe because bureaucratic wages rise with industrial earnings without corresponding productivity increases.[4]

Apart from the vexed question of which branches to choose (the current favorites being product lines using microprocessors and biological engineering), the main problems have to do with implementation. The central policy issue is whether market forces or government subsidy are to be used to encourage the decline of some branches and the rise of others—in other words, whether the cost of restructuring should be borne by the declining branches (through bankruptcy and unemployment) exposed to the full rigors of international competition, or by the new branches that would be the ultimate source of any subsidies to the old ones. A secondary but still crucial issue is the degree of explicit involvement of the Third World suppliers in the process.

In essence, then, the problem concerns the income-distribution implications of a necessary renewal of the process of capital accumulation. The matter of distribution between wages and profits as a whole and between different industrial branches, often located in different areas of the country, adds a regional dimension to the debate. Naturally enough, divisions in the debate reflect the impact of restructuring on different interest

---

[4]See B. Rowthorn, *Capitalism, Conflicts, and Inflation* (London, 1980).

groups. Trade unions want the restructuring to be financed not out of wages (i.e., by unemployment) but out of profits (i.e., by taxation). The EEC Commission wants mutual planning of world trade in order to ease the restructuring, while individual member countries take a more mercantilist view of "preventive" restructuring and selective tariffs. Large business seems to be more enthusiastic about international competition than does small business. The fiscal crisis of the state and the effects of organized labor pressure on business are also adduced as contributory if not central problems that prevent the maintenance of full employment during this restructuring (i.e., creating new jobs as fast as the old ones disappear) because of the negative effects on inflation and the balance of payments. The division between Keynesians and monetarists in Europe is to a great extent concerned with this issue and not with demand management as such.

The contribution of the Third World (or more precisely the "newly industrializing countries" (NICs), of which Mexico is a prominent member) to this crisis may not, therefore, be the central element. Reliable sources argue that mechanization in threatened industries causes more unemployment than do cheap imports[5] and that the Third World (especially the NICs) is growing faster than the First in any case,[6] despite the fact that trade within the OECD grows quicker than that between North and South.[7] There are also interesting crosscurrents. For example, the application of defensive tariffs is supported by organized labor and small business, and opposed by consumer groups and large (i.e., transnational) enterprise; this in turn leaves both social-democratic and conservative governments without an obvious policy line. Even the mutual benefit to be gained from international trade is challenged by the revival of mercantilism among both the *dependista* left and the new nationalist right.

Finally, the rise of transnational corporations (TNCs) with a Europewide base and operations elsewhere in the OECD (particularly the United States) and the Third World has challenged the concept of the nation-state as an economic unit trading with other such units. This transnationalization is distinct from the interdependence brought about by trade and financial flows; rather, it is suggested that the transnational corporations themselves (with Europe in the lead) are organizing the restructuring of industry on a worldwide scale,[8] seeking not only independence from the imposts and restrictions of any one nation but also supplies of

[5] FCO (as in n. 3, above).
[6] International Bank for Reconstruction and Development (IBRD), *1980 Annual Report* (Washington, D.C., 1980).
[7] OECD, *Economic Outlook* (1980), as in n. 3, above.
[8] F. Fröbel, J. Heinrichs, and O. Kreye, *The New International Division of Labour:*

cheap and docile labor in the developing countries to produce goods for the corporations' metropolitan markets. The transnationalization involves not only the assembly of electronics in the Philippines (equivalent to Mexican *maquiladoras*) but also the relocation of car production in Spain, for example. It has also led to attempts to organize trade unions on a transnational level, although still not on a scale at all comparable to that of their employers.

During the debate itself, as the international recession has deepened and the similarity of the predicaments of the various OECD countries has become clearer, the terms of reference have changed not only from adjustment to restructuring, but also from technological unemployment due to a changing economic structure to a more serious problem of declining investment and mass unemployment reminiscent of the 1930s. The term *crisis* has properly remained the province of those optimistic Marxists who see these as the last days of monopoly çapitalism, but the new relationship with China, the difficulties of negotiating with Russia over security, the changing balance of economic power within the OECD, and the success of OPEC have contributed to the view that the changes required were not just ones of economic accommodation but rather of geopolitical restructuring. This restructuring was no longer a matter of retaining Europe's place in world trade, still less about uncompetitive shoe factories in Lancashire and Bangladeshi jute exports. It had become the key to the restoration of the dynamic of accumulation on a world scale.

THE WORLD RECESSION: THREE APPROACHES

It has now become clear that the recession is more than temporary and represents a turning point in the expansion of the postwar world economy. Projection of aggregate trends of any national strategy for the future must therefore contain some assumptions about the form that eventual recovery will take. The United States and Mexico, involved as they are in their own and shared problems, have tended until recently to pay little attention to the future of the world economy. It may well be that the European debate, coming somewhat earlier, can throw some light on the way in which logical alternatives for the future can be analyzed. Before we look at alternatives, we must first identify some widely agreed-upon elements of debate.

The long postwar boom, it is now agreed, came to an end by the 1970s, when the rate of productivity growth and of capital accumulation began

---

Structural Unemployment in Industrial Countries and Industrialisation in Developing Countries (Cambridge, England, 1980).

to decline, first of all in the United States.[9] This, in turn, is to be seen within the context of what is evidently a changing international division of labor associated with the emergence of a number of previously under-developed countries into world manufactured trade and the increasing transnationalization of capital itself.[10] No serious economic commentator would now deny this. It is also now clear that a number of contemporary phenomena are not themselves the cause of the recession.

First, this economic stagnation is not a problem of resource scarcity on a global scale, as was popularly believed ten years ago. Declining real commodity prices and the steady increase of production capacity (under the impulse of foreign investment in many cases) belies this, a fact not disproved by selective supply shortfalls from time to time.[11]

Second, despite the relevance for Mexico–United States relations, it is not caused by higher energy prices. They are a posterior phenomenon, even if they did exacerbate the recession, and in any case the effect on the growth of central economies has not been excessive. The OECD estimates that the long-run "shock" of the 1973–74 and 1978–80 oil price rises was about 2 percent of OECD GNP on each occasion—a large amount in absolute terms, but hardly in relative ones.[12] Authoritative assessments of the future clearly indicate that there is no dearth of energy sources either.

Third, the recession is mainly in the First World; the impact on the so-cialist bloc (Second World) has been relatively small,[13] and generally not as great on the Third World as had been anticipated. While in the 1963–74 period GDP growth averaged 5.3 percent per annum in the indus-trialized countries, as opposed to 5.6 percent in the non-oil developing countries (and there were, of course, variations between and within these countries), in the 1975–80 period the rates were 2.9 percent and 4.9 per-cent respectively.[14] There is, moreover, some evidence that Latin America at least has increased its capacity to resist the passing of the cycle out from center to periphery.[15] Indeed, it might be argued that this incapacity

[9] D. M. Leipziger, "Productivity in the United States and Its International Implications," *The World Economy*, 3, no. 1 (1980), 119–34; International Monetary Fund, *Annual Report, 1980* (Washington, D.C., 1980); J. Kendrick and E. Grossman, *Recent Trends and Cycles in Productivity* (Baltimore, Md., 1979).

[10] OECD, *Economic Outlook* (1980), as in n. 3, above; E. Mandel, *The Second Slump: A Marxist Analysis of the Recession of the Seventies* (London, 1978); Fröbel et al., *New International Division*.

[11] OECD, *Interfutures* (1979).

[12] OECD, *Economic Outlook* (1980); H. H. Landsberger, *Energy: the Next Twenty Years* (Cambridge, Mass., 1979).

[13] R. Portes, "Effects of the World Economic Crisis on the East European Economies," *The World Economy*, 3, no. 1, pp. 13–52.

[14] IBRD, *1980 Annual Report*.

[15] R. Thorp and L. Whitehead, *Inflation and Stabilisation in Latin America* (London,

to use the periphery as a buffer is exacerbating the central recession—a neat but consistent inversion of the views of the "unequal exchange" school.[16]

Fourth, persistent worldwide inflation is a symptom rather than a cause of the problem; although, once instituted, it does act as a depressive reinforcement mechanism through uncertainty, it is itself essentially a matter of conflict over the distribution of income.

The immediate reaction has been a frantic attempt by individual economies to implement stabilization policies, aided and abetted by the IMF, thus deepening the recession on the demand side. This result was hardly what the founders intended at Bretton Woods; Block points out that "The struggle of the United States to increase its freedom of action in international monetary affairs destroyed the old Bretton Woods system. Step by step the United States either broke the rules of the old order or forced other countries to break them."[17]

It is generally recognized that longer-term structural changes are required, but what these changes are to be depends upon the explanation of the declining rates of accumulation and profitability. We shall classify those views as "classical," "Keynesian," and "neo-Ricardian" diagnoses.

Starting with "orthodox" non-Marxist viewpoints, the classical interpretation of recession—as having to do with investment itself, with the adequacy of the capital stock, and with productivity—is clearly expressed in the authorities quoted here in the context of the European restructuring debate and in those American establishment sources cited by Leipziger.[18] The mechanism is not well specified at the theoretical level, but presumably corresponds to the traditional trade-cycle analysis established by Schumpeter: prominence is given to the process of investment rather than to demand or income distribution. In the specific context of the United States, reference is also made to the alleged cost of environmental controls.

The Keynesian viewpoint is easily identified, for it corresponds to the tradition of postwar policy making in the West, although the center of attention has moved from the national to the international scene. The difficulty with utilizing existing excess capacity arises from the high propensity to import (or "suck back" exports) when demand is stimulated, causing balance of payments difficulties, unless other economies also expand in order to maintain export demand. The weakening of the U.S. external

---

1977), ch. 2; M. Kuczinski, "Semi-Developed Countries and the International Business Cycle," *Bank of London and South America Review* (June 1976).

[16] S. Amin, *Accumulation on a World Scale* (New York, 1974).

[17] F. L. Block, *The Origins of International Economic Disorder: A Study of United States International Monetary Policy from World War II to the Present* (Berkeley, 1977), p. 203.

[18] Leipziger, "Productivity," p. 122.

account has naturally increased acceptance for this approach, which in the postwar period had tended to be a purely British view, and concern with the recycling of OPEC surpluses reinforces it. This argument is presented in an expanded form in *Economic Outlook* (1980); it can be developed further in a somewhat "structuralist" way in order to allow formally for the import propensities, as in Cripps and Godley. Finally, it can be argued, as ICIDI does,[19] that the true problem lies with the Third World, where only a lack of liquidity prevents the expansion of demand for the products of excess capacity in the First.

The term *neo-Ricardian* is used here in the sense in which, at the theoretical level, it is applied to Sraffa: that is, an analysis in which the complementary level of profits and wages is determined by the struggle between capital and labor rather than by the economic process. This in turn affects the level of investment (through both finance and expectations), technical change, and growth itself. Under this heading, surprisingly enough, can be found financial institutions such as IMF and BIS.[20] The argument is clear enough: that wage pressure ("unit labor costs") is a major cause of inflation and declining profitability, which lead in turn to low levels of investment and curtailed technological progress. Curiously, it is this wage pressure, rather than purely monetary arguments, that forms the longer-term view of these institutions, doubtless because monetarism (like neoclassical economics) has little of substance to offer by way of an explanation of either accumulation or the world recession.

A similar division is to be found among Marxist economists. Weisskopf identifies the rate of profit as the central theme, but classifies three ways of looking at "the crisis of capitalism" as being "rising organic composition of capital" (ROC), "rising strength of labor" (RSL), and "realization failure" (RF).[21] This debate makes reference not only to the data but also to the work of Marx himself. The ROC view is the orthodox Marxist one, of course (based in particular on vol. III, pt. 3, chaps. 13–15, of *Capital*), and relating the declining rate of profit to overinvestment in the past and an inappropriate stock at present. It fits, therefore, into our category of classical viewpoints as defined above, referring as it does to the quality of capital. Writers such as Mandel come under this heading.

In contrast, the RSL view explains falling profits by reference to the rising strength of organized labor as an autonomous force (relying on vol. I,

[19] OECD, *Economic Outlook* (1980); F. Cripps and W. Godley, "Control of Imports as a Means to Full Employment and the Expansion of World Trade: the UK Case," *Cambridge Journal of Economics*, 2, no. 3 (1978), 327–34; ICIDI, *North-South*.

[20] IMF, *Annual Report, 1980*; Bank of International Settlements (BIS), *Fiftieth Annual Report 1980* (Basel, 1980).

[21] T. E. Weisskopf, "Marxian Crisis Theory and the Rate of Profit in the Postwar U.S. Economy," *Cambridge Journal of Economics*, 3, no. 4 (1979), 341–78.

particularly chap. 25, of *Capital* for theoretical support). The term *neo-Ricardian* is thus reasonably applied to proponents of this view, who include Glynn, Sutcliff, and Rowthorn. Finally, there is the interpretation of "underconsumptionist" writers such as Sweezy, who refer to scattered citations in Marx and the historical experience of the United States in the past fifty years. This is the RF view, according to which the product cannot be sold owing to the inadequate level of effective demand derived from an unequal income distribution, which necessitates state intervention (by either military or more peaceful expenditure). As such it can reasonably be said to fall within our Keynesian classification.

As in the case of non-Marxist economists, any one author will take a mixed view; nonetheless, the logic differs. For example, the ROC writers would admit the "assault on labor" stressed by the RSL group, but attribute it to the exhaustion of the labor supply ("reserve army") and the need to make labor more mobile. Again, state intervention is noted by the ROC group, but as a creator of technology rather than of demand as in the RF view. In terms of political theory it is worth noting that the ROC view does not really include the concept of either state or class, but just capital; the RF view does have a state as distinct from capital, but still no classes; the RSL view, however, includes both state and class.

Once again, it should be remembered that coincidence between right and left on a viewpoint does not correspond to an identity of analysis; still less do prognoses agree. The parallels are none the less striking.

We can now return to the empirical question of the recession itself. The classical viewpoint locates the problem in an excessive and inadequate capital stock; the key phenomenon is seen as the deceleration of productivity growth, particularly in the United States. The initiation of a new wave of accumulation would thus require a technological revolution, particularly in the service sector. There is also the implication that a tight labor supply has been a problem, not in terms of wage cost (as in the neo-Ricardian view) but rather in terms of its flexibility in response to changes in production techniques, location, and so on. The low rates of profit derive from this "over-accumulation" in the past, and the current lack of investment from low profitability and expectations thereof. To some extent, then, this is a "supply" analysis, with the specific detail that new energy prices have rendered the existing capital stock even more inadequate. Logically enough, much of the argument for restructuring derives from this form of classical analysis of the depression.

The Keynesian viewpoint sees the problem on a world scale, as being essentially one of the management of aggregate demand, in both volume and composition; the lack of effective demand at a world level prevents the expansion of production into the existing capacity and the stimulation of further investment. The traditional remedy of domestic demand reflation in any one country is of no effect because it leads to balance of payments deficits or (with flexible exchange rates) to devaluation and inflation—unless, that is, all countries do this in a coordinated fashion. More realistic alternatives proposed are that the "locomotive" surplus economies (e.g., Germany, Japan) start the process or that the Third World economies be allocated funds (in a nice combination of altruism with long-term self-interest) to do much the same job, in a way similar to that proposed by Keynes (as opposed to Harry Dexter White) at Bretton Woods. In other words, the problem is a lack of global demand management. In this analysis oil prices are not a problem as long as the funds can be recycled in an appropriate manner; indeed, it can be argued that the net effect is to stimulate OECD investment through the demand for capital goods and arms from OPEC while reducing consumption expenditure. The low rate of profit is seen to be the result of a low level of effective demand combined with a stable markup ("normal profits"), while the lack of technological progress (and low productivity growth) is the consequence and not the cause of low investment because of the embodiment of the former in the latter. In other words, technological progress and labor productivity would pick up with investment.

The neo-Ricardian viewpoint sees the main problem as the rate of profit itself, which has been put under pressure from two directions: on the one hand, rising wages (or, more precisely, real unit labor costs) in the First World, due to stronger union organization and secular labor shortages caused by growth itself; on the other, the turning of the terms of trade between manufactures and primary commodities against the manufacturers by the resource producers. Lower rates of profit depress investment, and thus technical progress as well. The restoration of the previous growth model would require the cutting of real wages (both directly and by reducing government expenditures on welfare) and the reversal of the trend in the terms of trade—in the former case, monetarism as applied in practice rather than in theory, and in the latter the "liberalization" of world trade. In this analysis, energy prices are related to the problem as an increase in rent that reduces profits. In essence, then, this is an "income distribution" approach.

These are, in fact, the alternative permutations on the problem of profitability,[22] and thus of accumulation in a capitalist world economy. As such, they are stylized models, and any empirical explanation will contain aspects of all three; moreover, the interpretations are not the province of one or another ideology, although naturally the prognoses do dif-

---

[22] Because profitability by definition depends upon the product of the profit margin (distribution) and the volume of output (demand) divided by the capital stock (technology).

fer sharply. It is the object of this essay to explore the consequences for Mexico and the United States—and for relationships between them—of these viewpoints in terms of the shifts that might take place as the world economy moves out of the depression. This assumes, of· course, that it will do so with a recognizable degree of institutional continuity and that the trade cycle is not quite as mysterious as Kondratieff implied.[23]

RESTRUCTURING THE MEXICAN AND U.S. ECONOMIES: THE EFFECT OF THE WORLD CYCLE

The next step in the argument should be to examine our two economies in detail, establish the link between them, and assess the effect of the world cycle on this link. This paper can hardly begin on such a task, however; here we will merely draw out the logical implications of the foregoing analysis as the basis for discussion. As we shall see, stepping beyond the implicit Keynesian framework in which much of this linkage is usually cast produces somewhat different results. We shall concentrate here on industrialization and the labor force, the center of any definition of economic development.

It is conventional wisdom that the transmission of the U.S. business cycle into the Mexican economy through the volume of trade is one of the major links between the two economies, along with the more structural factors such as the penetration of manufacturing by U.S. multinationals. Reynolds observes the statistical correlation between national product in the two countries between 1940 and 1963, but seems to feel it needs no detailed explanation.[24] Indeed, the two links that he mentions—between Mexican exports to the United States and U.S. GDP on the one hand, and Mexican manufacturing output and Mexican GDP on the other—do not seem to fit together very logically. Nor, for that matter, does the study of Fajnzylber and Martinez, a key source on this subject, indicate just how the articulation works, or whether the impact of TNCs is different from that of large firms generally, or even that U.S. firms act in any particular way.[25] Nonetheless, it is usually assumed that the link is based mainly on demand pressures on both sides, with an increasingly joint technology transferred southward.

There is, however, some cause to believe that this linkage may have changed during the past decade, for a number of reasons. First, the trans-

[23] J. A. Schumpeter, *Business Cycles* (New York, 1939); there are also Kondratieff influences in Mandel, *Second Slump*. In a recent popularization, J. B. Shuman and D. Rosenau locate the trough in the mid-eighties (*The Kondratieff Wave* [New York, 1972]).

[24] C. R. Reynolds, *The Mexican Economy: Twentieth Century Structure and Growth* (New Haven, Conn., 1970).

[25] F. Fajnzylber and T. Martinez, *Las empresas transnacionales: expansión a nivel mundial y proyecciones en la industria mexicana* (Mexico, 1976).

mission mechanism may well operate through price levels rather than through volume, both because the demand for Mexican exports is highly elastic in any case and because there is a very strong "demonstration effect" across the border.[26] Second, there is some evidence that Mexico is now able to operate a more independent monetary (and thus price) policy than previously,[27] although this may be constrained by increased official indebtedness. Third, there is reason to believe that the traditional capacity of the United States to determine within its own economy the world terms of trade between the primary and secondary sectors has been eroded if not lost.[28] Mexican oil, silver, and coffee prices, for instance, are now determined internationally rather than in the United States as before 1973. Fourth, the evidence is that the oligopolistic nature, rather than the "foreignness," of the transnationals is their defining characteristic;[29] indeed, large Mexican firms are investing in the United States and are borrowing directly on international capital markets. Fifth, the Mexican state itself has become more closely involved in the economic (as opposed to the political) link, thanks to its involvement in technology transfer to its own industries, its negotiation of energy and other exports, and its dominance of capital flows themselves. Finally, the decline of the United States' dominance over the world economy and the strengthening of Mexico's trade links with Latin America, Europe, and the Pacific imply an increasing capacity of Mexico to adopt an independent cycle of accumulation and thus a gradual reduction in the dependency relationship between the two. The link remains a strong one nonetheless.

The most complete model that analyzes formally the United States–Mexico link within the world economy is the modification of the World Bank's SIMLINK model used in the *Global 2000* study (see Table 1).[30] This model projects a relatively high income growth rate for the United States relative to the rest of the developed world but considerably lower than the OECD *Interfutures* forecast; this is then linked into LDC growth through foreign trade earnings, giving higher growth rates in the Third World than in the First. Nevertheless, the world growth rate is forecast to slow down in the rest of the century, and this applies to both the United States and Mexico; the income per capita growth rates actually imply a

[26] For a preliminary discussion of this, see FitzGerald, "Stabilization Policy in Mexico: The Fiscal Deficit and Macroeconomic Equilibrium 1960–77," in Thorp and Whitehead, *Inflation*, ch. 2.

[27] M. I. Blejer (who is, incidentally a monetarist), "The Short-Run Dynamics of Prices and the Balance of Payments," *American Economic Review*, 64, no. 3 (1977), 419–28.

[28] BIS, *Fiftieth Annual Report*.

[29] R. Jenkins, "Transnational Corporations and Their Impact on the Mexican Economy," in J. Carriere, ed., *Industrialization and the State in Latin America* (Amsterdam, 1979).

[30] U.S. Government, *Global 2000 Technical Report* (Washington, D.C., 1980).

TABLE I

Global 2000 Projections for the United States and Mexico

Category	More developed regions	Less developed regions	World total	U.S.	Mexico
GNP (billions of dollars)					
1975	4,892	1,133	6,025	1,509	71
1985	7,150	1,841	8,991	2,233	122
2000	11,224	3,452	14,677	3,530	233
Growth rate per annum					
1975–85	3.9%	5.0%	4.1%	4.0%	5.6%
1985–2000	3.1%	4.3%	3.3%	3.1%	4.4%
Population (millions)					
1975	1,131	2,959	4,090	214	60
2000	1,323	5,028	6,351	248	131
Population percentages					
Increase, 1975–2000	17%	70%	55%	16%	119%
Increase per annum	0.6%	2.1%	1.8%	0.6%	3.1%
Percent of world total in 2000	21%	79%	100%	4%	2%
GNP per capita					
1975	4,325	382	1,473	7,066	1,188
1985	5,901	501	1,841	9,756	1,454
2000	8,485	587	2,311	14,212	1,775
Per capita GNP growth rate per annum					
1975–85	3.2%	2.8%	2.3%	3.3%	2.0%
1985–2000	2.5%	2.1%	1.5%	2.5%	1.3%

SOURCE: *The Global 2000 Report to the President*, II, "The Technical Report," from tables 3-3; 3-4; 2-10.

continued deceleration in productivity growth. The reason for this pessimistic picture is the *Global 2000* assumption, reflecting concerns of the mid-seventies, when the study was commissioned, that resource constraints for energy, food, and pollution would prevent a recovery of the world cycle. Indeed, the outlook for the nations out on the periphery of the world economy (Mexico being on the semi-periphery) is of declining income per head and widespread famine unless concerted international action to directly redistribute income is undertaken.

The *Global 2000* model generates a strong linkage between GNP growth in the United States and Mexico, but interestingly this appears to weaken over time, with the "elasticity" between the two declining from 1.3 in 1970–85 to 1.0 in 1985–2000.[31] Unfortunately, neither SIMLINK nor *Global 2000* includes explicit modeling of industrial structure. Leontief's work for the UN does handle the input-output matrices of fifteen regions of the world (unfortunately without identifying Mexico explicitly) but, although technological progress and changing industrial structure are included, the linkage mechanism is still that of the volume of effective demand for imports and exports.[32] Moreover, the UN model is aimed at the calculation of "aid" requirements, so that, although it does underline the continued resource availability until the end of the century, it does not suggest what the net effect of the world cycle will be. Nonetheless, this model does generate much higher growth rates in heavy industry in the semi-periphery in support of its output growth than in the past.

In sum, however, these models are fundamentally Keynesian in our sense, so that if a gradually accelerating growth rate for the United States were built in, then Mexico would grow in step—presumably rather faster—because of increased demand for Mexican exports, expressed in higher volumes and prices. Employment levels in the United States would rise again, followed by new investment as capacity constraints are approached, and this in turn would generate expanding demand for Mexican exports of manufactured goods and natural gas, while oil prices would strengthen again on world markets. In essence, then, this would be equivalent to a return to the pattern of 1945–65 in both countries, but there are difficulties with the viability of this projection. On the U.S. side, it is difficult to see how this sort of "Democratic" reflation of the economy within an unchanged industrial structure could be achieved without very strong protective tariff measures and a weakened dollar, both of

---

[31] From the range of forecasts reported in *Global 2000*, we can derive the linear relationships for the annual growth rates (R):

$$1975-1985: R_{mex} = 0.5 + 1.3\ R_{usa}$$
$$1985-2000: R_{mex} = 1.5 + 1.0\ R_{usa}$$

[32] W. Leontief, *The Future of the World Economy* (New York, 1977).

which would seriously depress the rate of real export growth from Mexico and thus, according to the type of models discussed above, GNP growth and development. In other words, the "open" relationship between the two economies would have to be sacrificed as the U.S. economy closed in upon itself. The only exception would be labor, for the homogeneous expansion of the U.S. economy would require large infusions of unskilled labor to keep output, especially in agriculture and services, expanding with aggregate demand.[33]

This sort of recovery is in fact also assumed in the "neoliberal project" supported by financial groups, including the central banking authorities, in Mexico.[34] In leaving the sectoral development of the Mexican economy to market forces, so that *desarrollo estabilizador* can be reestablished, however, the unrealistic assumption has to be made that the U.S. economy is not changing. This sort of growth, moreover, would not lead to development of the Mexican economy, because Mexico too would have to keep real exchange rates and real manufacturing wages down to retain not only a light manufactured export market—thus leading to a deteriorating income distribution and stagnation of heavy industry—but also an agriculture biased toward exports rather than basic needs, once oil resources approach exhaustion. Far more realistic, within this Keynesian approach, would be the *Global 2000* forecasts of slow growth until the end of the century. The implications for unemployment, and thus for social stress in both countries, are alarming. The likelihood that the collective wisdom of advanced capitalist states could arrange global demand management along Brandt lines is low. In sum, a Keynesian recovery would be not only unlikely but also undesirable, to the extent that a continuation of the past United States–Mexico relationship would only exacerbate existing problems.

The combination of monetarism and supply-side economics, when applied in practice (a practice more familiar to Latin Americans than to their northern cousins), amounts to a strategy for a neo-Ricardian recovery derived from the restoration of profit levels at the center of the world economy on the basis of real wage reductions. The investment that would follow would not be such as to restore full employment, and other aspects of income distribution (e.g., welfare services) would also deteriorate. Indeed, a higher "natural" rate of unemployment is central to this strategy, which in U.S. terms might well be called "Republican." There would also be a permanent reduction in world trade growth and less de-

[33] This seems to be the implication of Reynolds's chapter in this volume.

[34] For this label, see the Cordera and Tello chapter in this volume. A good example of what they call the "neoliberal model" is "Special Study of the Mexican Economy: Major Policy Issues and Prospects," in IBRD (as in n. 6 above).

mand for consumer goods in particular, forcing a deliberately increased competition between newly industrializing Third World suppliers. Finally, the terms of trade between raw materials and energy on the one hand and equipment and technology on the other would be restored in favor of the center, while restrictive world monetary policies would maintain significant real interest rates.

Overall, the effect upon the Mexican economy, in terms of the prospects for the real value of energy supplies, manufactured exports, and the cost of borrowing, would be poor. Continued unemployment and depressed wage levels in the United States would reduce the demand for immigrant labor and would make social conditions more difficult for Mexican-Americans already there. Ironically, this model of recovery, while clearly bad for the Mexican economy in terms of expansion, might well force it back in on itself and thus be the most propitious economically (although probably not politically) for a nationalist development strategy. The most immediate parallel is the Great Depression itself, when the sharp deterioration of the terms of trade and the redistribution of income within the United States forced Mexico onto a path of independent financial control, import-substituting industrialization, and considerable social progress.[35] The irony was that Mexico could recover more rapidly than the United States in the 1930s because of the strength of her agriculture and her pre-Keynesian demand management policies. This time, however, forced industrialization would find no natural domestic market unless there were a massive redistribution of income within Mexico and some contemporary equivalent of land reform.[36]

The classical recovery, in contrast, would imply a substantial rise in productivity at the center of the world economy, centered on the United States but with Japan and the EEC increasingly acting as pivot. This would obviously concentrate on manufacturing but would also rely on increased efficiency in the use of energy and raw materials (despite pollution) and the rationalization of services. Old industries would be run down, and new high-technology ones would come in.[37] The projection in turn implies that labor requirements would grow slowly or would fall, particularly for unskilled labor; as far as Mexico is concerned this would imply less U.S. demand for immigrants. The restructuring of U.S. industry might mean, however, the phasing out of traditional heavy industrial lines such as steel and cement, where Mexico would be well placed for

[35] E. V. K. FitzGerald and E. Rovzar, "Restructuring in a Crisis: The Mexican Economy in the Great Depression 1925–40" (paper presented to the 1982 Congress of Americanists), forthcoming.

[36] Cordera and Tello, "Prospects and Options for Mexican Society," in this volume.

[37] See Nichols's chapter in this volume.

secure and low-transport-cost supply and could continue the recent trend toward exporting on the basis of industrial integration instead of prices based on cheap labor. Relatively high wages would continue to shift consumer goods manufacturing out of the United States toward the periphery, but probably away from Mexico too (with an overvalued exchange rate for industry due to oil). Moreover, this restructuring would presumably involve greater energy-efficiency and reliance on domestic sources of fuel in the United States, so that the oil terms of trade might be expected to turn against Mexico.

The net effect is difficult to judge, but it would probably be consistent with the national industrialization project for state-led investment financed from oil in heavy industry, capital equipment, and wage-goods as laid out in the Industrial Plan;[38] it would not support a strategy based on primary exports or on the alleviation of poverty through immigrant remittances. The irony is that the strategy implicit in the Industrial Plan (implicit, because the need for a heavy industrial export market is not brought out properly) is a highly nationalist one, which might not fit well with the industrial integration with the United States on a political plane.

SUMMARY

We shall not attempt to draw definite conclusions from a paper that is itself little more than an agenda; the most logical conclusion would be an outline for a future research program. The central point is that both the nature of economic growth in general and the present situation of the world economy in particular indicate that future expansion of both the United States and Mexico will involve structural change and considerable trend alterations. We have separated three explanations of the present recession. In reality a well-founded interpretation would include elements of each—technological advance, expansionary world demand management, and control of unit production costs. But above all, the renewal of capital accumulation will require considerable alterations for income distribution because it will be related to the restoration of profit levels and higher labor productivity. These changes will not necessarily be to the advantage of Mexico.

We must also take into account political considerations, and not just the support for one or another policy: the European debate does indicate that the inevitable restructuring of the central economies (especially the United States) and the complementary planning of the inner periphery (including Mexico) does imply a certain degree of relative autonomy of

---

[38] Secretaría de Patrimonio y Fomento Industrial (SPFI), *Plan nacional de desarrollo industrial* (Mexico City, 1979). The point is emphasized here because it is the most coherent and concrete statement of long-term economic strategy in Mexico.

the state in the sense that at such critical periods in history a power over and above the different economic groups must be available to undertake the necessary long-run decisions. In other words, the state must have the ability to identify options, choose sectors for investment, and carry out its policies. This is implicit in the three approaches we have analyzed above: a technological revolution, the management of the world economy, the control of wage pressure and raw materials prices, all require a strong and independent state at the center, and strong, independent states at the periphery to gain a place in the sun in such circumstances.

It seems, however, that current political trends in the OECD in general, and in the United States in particular, are toward a less interventionist and less relatively autonomous state, which would be conducive only to the neo-Ricardian recovery, although it could be argued that the renewal of military expenditure would accelerate technological change. The increasing concentration of corporate ownership and the internationalization of production and finance, both exacerbated by the recession itself, make independent state action more difficult. At the international level it is also difficult to see the emergence of a hegemonic power capable of managing aggregate demand on a world scale. In Mexico the situation is not quite so clear. There are good reasons for suggesting that the capacity for reform of the Mexican state has been declining over the past quarter-century because of the contradictions of industrialization itself, but these external pressures and the opportunity provided by oil may serve to reverse this trend.

Overall, then, the best prospect for traditional U.S.-Mexican economic relations would be the Keynesian recovery; the national industrialization project, in contrast, would be most favored by a classical recovery, although the consequences for external dependency and income distribution in manufacturing (a point logically implicit in the Industrial Plan but unsurprisingly not made explicit) would be serious. However, if it is felt that *desarrollo hacia adentro* under strong state direction is in any case the best course, it may well be that the neo-Ricardian recovery, by forcing the periphery to defend itself, would be more helpful in the long run. Historically, it would appear that a classical recovery is what usually takes place.

Index

"Absent workers," 307–11 *passim*
Advanced industrialized countries (AICs), 170ff
AFL (American Federation of Labor), 275, 301
Africa, 254
Agrarian reform, 12, 211f, 223, 234f
Agriculture: crisis in, 12; trade policy for, 14; labor intensity in, 27; exports and employment generated in, 28, 30; and neoliberal project, 56f; production policies for, 206f; prices of exports in, 218; public investment in, 219f; strategies for development of, 225f; factors affecting progress of, 231–44; international aspects of, 255ff
AICs (advanced industrialized countries), 170ff
Alien Address Program (1979), 311f
Allende, Salvador, 185
Alliance for Production, 323
Alliances, politics of, 4, 335ff
American Federation of Labor, 275, 301
Andean Pact, 173
Anderson-Clayton & Co., 238
ASEAN (Association of Southeast Asian Nations), 173
Asia, 254, 260–63 *passim*
Asymmetry, politics of, 321–34
Australia, 254
Autonomy, state, 366f

Balance of payments, 10, 321, 326
Balance of power, 195, 198
Beans, 209f
Bell, Daniel, 100
"Benign neglect," 198
Berney, Robert, 134

Berry, R. Albert, 231
Beverages, 27f
Bilateral relationship, 12, 17f, 162–65
Blejer, Mario, 32f
Block, F. L., 356
Bogotá, 190
Borders, 19, 274f, 310, 322, 341ff
Bracero agreements, 261ff, 267–74 *passim*, 293, 302f, 317. *See also* Migrant labor
Brandt Commission, 351
Braun, Oscar, 349n
Brazil, 140, 174
Bretton Woods, 356, 359
Brewster, John M., 242f
British Foreign Office, 351
Brzezinski, Zbigniew, 103f
Business, U.S., 49f, 360f
Businessmen's Coordinating Council, 48f
Bustamante, Jorge A., 16, 299f, 306

Camacho, Avila, 266
Campesinos, 211, 214, 220, 232
Canada, 140
Capital: as percentage of GNP, 116f; accumulation of, 121f, 352; private, 336f; rising organic composition (ROC) of, 357f
Capitalism, 77f, 357; and neoliberal project, 53; and nationalist project, 62
Caracas, 190
Cárdenas, Lazaro, 211, 265f
Caribbean Basin Initiative, 202
Caribbean countries, 140
Carreras de Velazco, Mercedes, 265
Carter, Jimmy, 186, 274, 323; immigration policies of, 276, 289
Castañeda, Jorge, 274

Castro, Fidel, 185, 199
Cattle raising, 211f
CENIET (Centro Nacional de Información
  y Estadisticas del Trabajo), 35n, 307–13
  passim
Central America, 131, 140, 184, 200, 203,
  340n; Mexico's role in, 185ff
Centro de Investigación de Desarrollo
  Rural, *see* CIDER
Centro Nacional de Información y Esta-
  disticas del Trabajo, *see* CENIET
Chemical fertilizers, 208
Chemicals fabrication, 27f
Chevalier, François, 248
Chicanos, 19, 343f
Christainsen, Gregory, 125
CIDER (Centro de Investigación de Desa-
  rrollo Rural), 250
Clark, William, 246ff
Class sectors, 189, 358
Cline, William R., 231
Clothing, 27f
Coahuila, 235n
Colby, William, 345
Commercial producers, 209–15 *passim*,
  220f
Commission on the Californias, 139n
Communism, fear of, 186, 190, 192, 199f
Concentration, agrarian, 211n, 217
Confederación de Trabajadores de México,
  51
Congress, U.S., erosion of, 90f
Congress of Labor, 50f
Conservatism, 99f
Constitution, U.S., amendments to, 91f
Consumption, 63
Cooperation: industrial, 163; between U.S.
  and Mexico, 317
Cordera, Rolando, 3ff
Corn, 206f, 214, 257
Cornelius, Wayne, 294f, 302n, 322f
Corredor, Jaime, 8ff
Costa Rica, 140, 186
Cotton, 237f
Crop and Livestock Promotion Law, 13,
  221
Crop-and-livestock sector, 57, 212ff, 220
Crops, output of, 236f. *See also*
  Productivity
Crude oil, 140, 150, 177. *See also* Oil;
  Petroleum
Cuba, 185, 199

Deagle, Edwin A., Jr., 11
Defense, U.S., Mexico's importance to, 318

Demand, 358f, 366
Demographic factors, 240ff
Denison, Edward, 126, 134
Dependence, economic, 138–43 *passim*,
  318ff
Deportation, 266, 273, 294, 307n, 312f
Détente, 104f
Deutsch, Karl, 83
Devaluation, 10, 31–35 *passim*, 327f
Developing countries, 168f. *See also* LDCs;
  Third World countries
"Development approach," 20
Díaz Ordaz, G., 270
Dillingham Commission (1911), 262f
Dominican Republic, 190, 199
Durango, 235n

Echeverría, Luis, 268, 272f
Eckstein, Shlomo, 237
"Economic restructuring," 351
Economy, Mexican, 21, 71, 149–55, 178f,
  267, 321f, 360f
Economy, U.S., 5–8 *passim*, 14, 24–42,
  108–12, 113f; projections for, 114ff,
  129–32
Education, 59, 69, 309n
EEC (European Economic Community),
  19, 169, 173f
Ejidal Bank, 230, 236
Ejidatarios, 67, 213, 235f, 240, 248
Ejido farms, 227–37 *passim*, 248
El Chamizal, 317
El Salvador, 185ff
Elections, U.S., 90, 93
Emigration, 265, 269ff. *See also* Immi-
  grants; Migration
Employers, U.S., 71f, 275, 305
Employment, 27–30 *passim*, 34f, 58; pro-
  jections for, 38, 129
ENEFNEU (National Household Survey for
  Emigration), 306–14
Energy: policies for, 8, 112, 125ff, 130,
  256; supply of, 143–48; U.S. crisis in,
  182, 184
Energy Program, Mexican, 9f, 145, 158
Enzler, Jared, 113n
Ethnicity, politics of, 19, 343–46
European Economic Community (EEC),
  19, 169, 173f
European restructuring debate, 351–54
Excess capacity, 356f. *See also* Surplus
Exchange, 29f, 327f; full, 2f, 22n, 23ff;
  prospects for, 10, 174ff; free, 42–45
Exports, Mexican, 28, 139ff, 160, 218,
  321f, 325f; projections for, 29–35

Factor price equalization theories, 22, 25f
Fagen, Richard R., 18ff
Fajnzylber, F., 360
Falcon, Walter P., 11–15 *passim*
Family planning, 248
Fertilizer, 252
Fishing, 27f
FitzGerald, E. V. K., 18ff
Flores, Edmundo, 232
Flores de la Peña, 236
Flotation, *see* Devaluation
Foodstuffs: prices for, 14, 242n; production of, 57, 206–10; state policy for, 64, 326, 328; self-sufficiency in, 158, 257, 328; imports of, 216–19, 326
Ford, Gerald R., 268, 272
Foreign capital, 39–42, 66, 139, 161f; impact of oil earnings on, 156ff
Foreign debt, 161f, 320, 326
Foreign policy, proposals for, 11, 328f
Forestry, 27f
France, 140
Frederickson, Craig, 303n
Free exchange, 42–45
Free trade, *see* Exchange
Full exchange, *see* Exchange

Galarza, Ernesto, 269, 272, 303
Galvan, Felix, 187f
Gamio, Manuel, 265
Gandara, Arturo, 155n, 338n
García y Griego, Manuel, 16f, 293f
Gas, pricing of, 335
"Gasoducto" (1977–78), 334f
Gasohol, 256
GATT (General Agreement on Tariffs and Trade), 138, 141, 167f, 173
GDP, Mexican, 149, 151, 157n, 354, 360
General Agreement on Tariffs and Trade, *see* GATT
General American Common Market, 173
General Law of Population (1936), 266
Glazer, Nathan, 100
Global Development Plan, 154n
Global system, 9, 52f, 102, 196ff, 200; and neoliberal strategy, 54; management of, 359
Global 2000, projections of, 361–64
GNP, 10f, 96, 116ff, 123, 362f
Gollop, Frank, 125
Good Neighbor policy, 197f
Gordon, R. J., 113n
Grain: prices of, 14, 218, 255ff; pattern of trade in, 254; SAM support for, 220f
Gramlich, E. M., 113n

Gross Domestic Product, *see* GDP
Gross National Product, *see* GNP
Growth rates, estimates for, 158, 361f
Guest-worker program, 273, 279, 281–87, 301f

H-2 visa program, 273
Haciendas, 231f
Hansen, Roger D., 231f, 234
Harrigan brothers, 273
Haveman, Robert, 125
Hay-Paunceforte Treaty (1917), 197
Health, 69f, 248
Heckscher, Eli F., 22
Heer, D. M., 294
Hispanics, treatment of, 346
Hogg Foundation, 21n
Housing, 70
Huntington, Samuel P., 94, 100, 102
Hybrids, 238f
Hydrocarbons, 159, 163f. *See also* Crude oil; Natural gas; Oil; Petroleum

ICRISAT (International Crop Research Institute for the Semi-Arid Tropics), 239f, 245
Identity cards, 281
Illegal aliens, 281; amnesty for, 273, 280. *See also* Undocumented migration
Immigrants, 17, 36f, 263ff, 269, 273, 289; policy on, 279–82, 289; history of, 343f. *See also* Migration
Immigration and Naturalization Service, *see* INS
Imports, 26, 64, 131, 141; GATT restrictions on, 168f; of foodstuffs, 216–19, 326
Income, 361f, 366
India, 140
Industrial Plan, 266f, 366
Industry: national promotion of, 68f, 75f, 111f; cooperation in, 163; structure of, 176ff, 352. *See also* Internationalization
Inflation, 53ff, 63, 322, 329, 356
Infrastructure, 218–29
INIA (Instituto Nacional de Investigaciones Agrícolas), 245
Innovations, 242
INS (U.S. Immigration and Naturalization Service), 268f, 298, 307n, 311f, 343
Instituto Nacional de Investigaciones Agrícolas (INIA), 245
Insurgency, rise of, 199f
Integration, in industry, 75f
Interamerican Defense Board, 190

Inter-American Development Bank, 13
Interchange, free, 55
Interdependence, 2, 11, 20, 142, 174ff
Interest groups, *see* Commercial producers; EEC; Unions
International Crop Research Institute for the Semi-Arid Tropics, *see* ICRISAT
Internationalism, defined, 3
Internationalization: economic, 56, 143f, 154f, 159, 255, 367; of trade and industry, 167–78 *passim*, 353; of issues, 329, 333
Intervention, by state, 55, 358
Investment, 123, 152, 154; public, 73, 152, 211ff, 219f, 234–39 *passim*, 244, 252; nonresidential, 118–22 *passim*, 133f; by U.S., in Mexico, 120, 164f, 320
Irrigation, public investment in, 211ff, 234–39 *passim*, 252
Isolationism, 197
Israel, 140

Jamaica, 140
Japan, 140, 200, 231, 233
"Jewish lobby," 344
Johnson, D. Gale, 256
Johnston, Bruce F., 11–15 *passim*

Keesing, Donald B., 37n
Kennedy, John F., 199
Kerr Foundation, 21n
Keynesian economy, 356, 358f, 364
Kissinger, Henry, 186
Kristol, Irving, 100

Labor, 15f, 25, 50, 267, 358; productivity of, 27–33 *passim*; Mexican contribution to U.S., 36f; projections for, in U.S., 115f, 129, 290; costs of, 226f; rising strength of (RSL), 357f. *See also* AFL; Migration; Nationalist project; Unions
Laguna region, 235n, 240
Land reform, 12f, 67, 210ff, 232f, 244
Landowners, *see* Commercial producers
Landowning, Mexican pattern of, 233f
Latifundios, 212
Latin America, 198ff, 329f
LDCs, 173–76 *passim*, 362
Leftist movements, 97
Leontief, W., 365
Lerdo Law (1856), 231
Lerner, A. P., 22
Less developed countries (LDCs), 173–76 *passim*, 362
Liberalization of trade, 170–73
Linkages, U.S.-Mexican, 360–65

Lipset, Seymour Martin, 100
Literacy, 248
Lobbying, 91
López Portillo, José, 274, 322f
Los Mochis, 235n
Luiselli, Cassio, 12

Machinery, 27f
Macroeconomic policy, 255
Maira, Luis, 6f, 133
Maize, 230, 238f
Mandel, Ernst, 357
Manufacturing sector, 30, 160
Maquiladoras, 33–34
Margáin, Hugo, 274
Market forces, 352
Martin, P. L., 282, 284f
Martinez, T., 360
Marxism, 235, 357
Mass participation, 3, 70, 81
Massey, D. S., 294
McCarran-Walter Act (1952), 262
Mechanization, 221f, 252
Metal industries, 27f
Mexican Food System, *see* SAM
"Mexicans," defined, 37n
Mexico: U.S. relations with, 9, 14, 137f, 193–203, 315–324 *passim*, 360–65; and U.S. defense, 57; impact of petroleum in, 148–55, 182ff; and Brazil, 174; internal structure and political system of, 175, 178ff; and Central America, 185ff, 202f; stability of, 270f, 339f; GNP of, 362. *See also* Economy, Mexican; Exports; GDP
Mexico–United States Border Research Program, 21n
Mexico City, 288
Middle classes, 72
Middle-income countries, grain imports to, 254
Migrant labor, 16f, 36f, 254, 261ff, 295–98 *passim*, 305, 306–14
Migration, 34–39, 59, 288f, 300, 313; planning for, 278f; policy paralysis on, 279–92; history of, 292f; program for, 296ff; estimates of, 311ff. *See also* Undocumented migration
Military power: U.S. attitudes toward, 195f; U.S. superiority in, 199
Military sector, 187–91 *passim*
Minerals, non-metallic, 27f
Minifundistas, 67, 211, 213
Mining sector, exports in, 27–30 *passim*
Ministry of Agriculture, 238
Modernization, 68f, 222f

Monroe Doctrine (1823), 194ff
Mortgages, 131
Most-favored-nation status, 170
Moynihan, Daniel P., 100, 102
MTN (multinational trade negotiations), 169
Multinational enterprises, 176ff. *See also* Transnational enterprise
Musgrave, Richard A., 130

NACM (North American Common Market), 351
Nalven, Joseph, 303n
National Center for Labor Information and Statistics, *see* CENIET
National Corn Commission, 238
National Family Planning Program, 249
National Household Survey for Emigration (ENEFNEU), 306–14
National Industrial Development Plan, 3f, 145, 218, 366
National interest, U.S., 337–40
National security, 182ff, 186–203
Nationalism, 3f, 67f
Nationalist project, 51, 61–74
Natural gas, 27f, 150. *See also* Petroleum
Nehring, Richard, 155n, 338n
Neoclassical synthesis, 6f, 112ff, 130
Neoconservative project, 99–104
Neoliberal project, 51, 52–61, 364
"Neo-Ricardian" view, 356–59 *passim*, 364, 367
New Zealand, 254
Newly industrializing countries (NICs), 169–73
Nicaragua, 140, 184f
Nichols, Donald A., 6ff
Nonintervention, 185f
Non-oil products, 10, 164f, 174f
Nonresidential investment, 118–22 *passim*, 133f
Nontradable goods, 27
North America, grain movements in, 254
North American Common Market (NACM), 351
Nutrition, 210

OECD (Organization for Economic Cooperation and Development), 351, 361
Ohlin, Bertil, 22
Oil: policy for, 57f, 67f; price of, 113f, 145–48; significance of, 141–58 *passim*, 201, 316, 321–36 *passim*, 337f; supply of, 149, 156, 178f, 324f; international trade in, 168, 321–25 *passim*. *See also* Petroleum

Ojeda, Mario, 18f, 190
OPEC, 200
Open agricultural policy, U.S., 256
Open markets, U.S. preference for, 171
Operation Wetback (1954), 268, 270
Organization for Economic Cooperation and Development (OECD), 351, 361
Organizational issues, 49ff, 245–50
Organized labor, 50f. *See also* Unions
O'Sullivan, John O., 345
Output, 129, 228f, 236f, 360; U.S., 253. *See also* Productivity

Panama Canal, 196f
Paper fabrication, 27f
Partido Revolucionario Institucional (PRI), 234f
Party system, U.S., 92
Passel, Jeffrey S., 311n
Peasants: organizational goals of, 49; policies concerning, 66f, 71; productivity of, 207f, 215f; and agrarian reform, 211f, 223
Pellicer de Brody, Olga, 11
PEMEX (Petroleos Mexicanos), 149n, 151, 153, 326, 334ff; savings of, 155f; overseas investments of, 177f
Pension savings, 119
Peso, *see* Devaluation
Petrochemicals, 150
Petroleos Mexicanos, *see* PEMEX
Petroleum, 27–30 *passim*, 182–84; effects of growth in, 148–62. *See also* Oil
Phelps, E. S., 113n
PIDER (Programa de Inversiones Públicas para el Desarrollo Rural), 13, 213, 226, 243, 260
Pierce, James L., 113n
Plastics fabrication, 27f
Polarization, 210, 216, 270
Political system, 321–24; U.S., 83–88, 106; Mexican, 178ff
Pollution abatement, 118–21
Popular Movement, 76–81. *See also* Workers' Project
Population growth, 123f, 227, 240–43, 362
Poverty, 15, 59, 227, 244–50, 280
Power asymmetry, 318f
Preferential trade agreement, 174
Pressure groups, 91
PRI (Partido Revolucionario Institucional), 234f
Prices, 6, 14, 218, 335; policy on, 209, 221, 242n, 361

Primary sector, 160
Private sector, 228f, 306
Production: development of, 61ff; resources for, 212–16
Productivity, 13; of labor, 27–33 *passim*; and neoliberal project, 57; and nationalist project, 62f; fluctuations in, 121f, 124–29 *passim*, 230f; of peasants, 207f, 215f; U.S., 253; and wages, 352
Profits, 21, 357ff
Programa de Inversiones Públicas para el Desarrollo Rural, *see* PIDER
Project ENEFNEU, 306–14
Project on United States–Mexico Relations, 4, 11, 20
Protectionism, 9, 55, 172f
Public administration, 73
Public sector, 65f, 152, 156

Quarrying, 27f

Rabasa, Emilio, 272f
Racism, 343–46 *passim*
Rainfed Agricultural Development Project, 250
Rainfed areas, 14, 211, 214, 237, 239, 245
Reagan administration, 102f, 203ff; and guest-worker program, 281f, 287; immigration policies of, 289
Realization failure (RF), 357f
Recession, 20, 94ff, 322, 329, 351f, 354–60
Recovery, economic, 48, 365f
Refined products, *see* Petroleum
Reforms, 4f, 61, 70. *See also* Land reform
Regulation, 134–35
Reichert, J., 294
Repatriation, 266
Research Center for Rural Development (CIDER), 250
Restructuring, in Europe, 351–54
"Returned workers," 307
Revolution, Mexican sympathy for, 11, 185f
Revolutionary Coalition, 234f
Reynolds, Clark W., 2ff, 232f, 360
Robinson, J. Gregory, 294, 311n
Robles, García, 273
Rockefeller Foundation, 238
Rodino, Peter, 268
Ronfeldt, David, 155n, 325, 338n
Roosevelt, Franklin Delano, 85f
Roosevelt, Theodore, 196
Ross, Stanley, 21n
Rubber fabrication, 27f
Ruddle, K., 37n

SAM (Sistema Alimentario Mexicano), 13, 38, 141, 205n, 213n, 226, 242n; strategies and goals of, 219–24, 243ff, 328
Samuelson, Paul, 22, 112
Sanderson, Steven E., 338n
Sanderson, Warren C., 16f, 299–306 *passim*
Sandinista Revolution, 184f
Savings: personal, 117–23 *passim*; PEMEX, 155f
Scitovsky, Tibor, 8, 120–23 *passim*
Sectors, defined, 27
Security, 11, 182ff, 186–91, 193–203
Seed technology, 252
Sehgal, E. F., 282, 284f
Select Commission on Immigration and Refugee Policy, 279ff, 306
Self-determination, 322f
Self-sufficiency, 158, 257, 328
Siegel, Jacob S., 311n
"Silent integration," 9, 17
SIMLINK, 361, 363
Simpson-Mazzoli bill, 17, 279n
Sistema Alimentario Mexicano, *see* SAM
Small landowners, 14f, 232. See also *Ejidatarios*
Smith, T. C., 233
Social welfare, 33f, 80. *See also* Education; Health; Housing
Socialist bloc (Second World), 355
Socio-economic reform, 70
Sorghum, 215f
Sovereignty, Mexico's policy of, 190
Soviet Union, 200, 203, 205, 254
Spain, 140
Sraffa, 357
Stabilization policies, 109f, 356
Stagnation, 355
Stanford University, 21n
State, 244; in neoliberal project, 53f; intervention of, 55, 358; in nationalist project, 61–64 *passim*; policy of, for foodstuffs, 64, 326, 328; autonomy of, 366ff
Status quo, 280f, 289, 304
Subsidies, 9, 209, 220f, 352. *See also* Investment
Sunbelt, U.S., 43f
Surplus, 9, 158–61
Sweden, 22f, 140
Sweezy, Paul, 358
Synfuels Bills, 256

Taiwan, 231, 233
Tariffs, 168f, 353

Technology, 39–42, 72f, 208, 221f, 271, 283f, 354, 366. *See also* Exchange
Tello, Carlos, 3ff
"Texas proviso," 270
Textiles, 27f
Third World countries, 97f, 257, 353, 357; power of, 200f; capital accumulation in, 353; growth rates in, 361. *See also* LDCs
Tillage, 239f, 245
TNCs (transnational corporations), *see* Transnational enterprise
Tobacco, 27f
Tobin, James, 113n
Tomato controversy, 338f
"Tortilla curtain," 276
Tourism, 318f, 326f
Trade, 10, 14, 21, 353; liberalization of, 8f, 170–76; as dimension of exchange, 25–29
Transnational enterprise, 40f, 52, 103–6, 139, 335ff, 353f
Transportation, 252
Trilateral Commission, 7, 103ff

Underconsumption, 358
Undocumented migration, 259–62 *passim*, 268–72 *passim*, 286; problems of, 273–78; estimates of, 293ff; proposals on, 304f
Unemployment, 259f, 353f, 364
Unimodal strategies, 225f
Unions, 53, 58ff, 173
Unit labor costs, 357, 366
United Nations, 351
United States: economic crisis in, 7f, 94ff; Mexican relations with, 9, 14, 137f, 193–203, 315–24 *passim*, 360–65; decline in power of, 18; Mexican contribution to labor in, 36f; political system of, 83–88; political crisis in, 89–94, 333;

loss of hegemony by, 96ff, 200; petroleum exports to, 140; energy crisis in, 180, 184; security of, 197f; grain exports of, 254; GNP of, 362. *See also* Economy, U.S.; Labor
United States–Mexico Project, 20
Urban population, 240ff

Venezuela, 154n, 183, 186
Vernon, Raymond, 8ff
Vietnam, 200
Vigilantism, 343
Visa program, 273

Wages, 6, 64; and trade, 21; stabilization of, 109f; and productivity, 352; and profits, 357
Wanniski, Jude, 101f
Warman, Arturo, 11ff
Water management, 213ff. *See also* Irrigation
Wealth, concentration of, 270
Weisskopf, T. E., 357
Wellhausen, E. J., 243
Wheat, 206f, 214f, 222, 238
Whetten, N. L., 235n
White, Harry Dexter, 359
Wilkie, J. W., 37n
Winter vegetable controversy, 338f
Wood-related industries, 27f
Workers' Project, 50f, 76ff
World Bank, 13, 361
World cycle, 350, 360–66
World War II, 197f, 267, 316f

Yaqui Valley, 235n
Yugoslavia, 140

Zero exchange, 23